SIR HALLEY STEWART TRUST PUBLICATIONS

ELIZABETHAN
NONCONFORMIST TEXTS
Volume IV

THE WRITINGS OF
JOHN GREENWOOD
1587-1590

Together with the Joint Writings of
HENRY BARROW AND JOHN GREENWOOD
1587 - 1590

THE WRITINGS OF
JOHN GREENWOOD
1587-1590

TOGETHER WITH THE JOINT WRITINGS OF
HENRY BARROW AND JOHN GREENWOOD
1587-1590

Edited by

LELAND H. CARLSON
PH. D.

Published for
THE SIR HALLEY STEWART TRUST

GEORGE ALLEN AND UNWIN LTD
RUSKIN HOUSE
MUSEUM STREET LONDON

FIRST PUBLISHED IN 1962

PRINTED IN GREAT BRITAIN
by
EAST MIDLAND PRINTING CO LTD
BURY ST EDMUNDS, PETERBOROUGH
AND ELSEWHERE

THIS VOLUME IS DEDICATED TO
THE STAFF OF
THE FOLGER SHAKESPEARE LIBRARY
WITH GRATITUDE AND RESPECT

CONTENTS

A*

THE WRITINGS OF
JOHN   GREENWOOD
1587-1590

1587

I

FRAGMENT OF A LETTER

This treatise, *Fragment of a Letter*, is a part of the Giles Wiggenton manuscript in the Congregational Library at Memorial Hall, London (I. e. 14). It is the fourth of seven treatises in all, and occupies folios 27-40. It was printed by T. G. Crippen in the *Transactions of the Congregational Historical Society*, II, no. 5 (May, 1906), 346-352, and reprinted by the same editor in his pamphlet, *Relics of the Puritan Martyrs*, 1593 ([London], 1906), pp. 24-30.

The author is probably John Greenwood. It is clear that the writer is a Separatist who defends his poor persecuted church. The references in the letter to suffering, and to " ministring to a poor distressed lambe of Christ's fold," seem to point to one who is a prisoner. On the last folio the initials I. G. are given twice. Since John Greenwood is the only Separatist with these initials, the clues certainly lead one to this attribution of authorship. Furthermore, the subjects of read prayers versus spontaneous prayers of the spirit, of stinted liturgies versus true worship of God, of the *Book of Common Prayer* and the popish Latin portas as the origin of the deadly collects and patched prayers, are favourite topics in the writings of Greenwood.

In the conclusion of the letter the date of 1587 is given with the initials. Since the letter seems to refer to sufferings and distress, presumably in prison, we may date the letter after October 8, 1587, when Greenwood was first arrested. It was not until six weeks later, on November 19, that Henry Barrow visited Greenwood in prison and was also arrested. Since there is no reference in the letter to Barrow, it is possible that this letter was written between October 8 and November 19, 1587. The argument from silence is not conclusive, since

1

twenty-one persons were arrested on October 8, of whom at
least eleven were still in prison in May, 1589. Greenwood
makes no specific reference to these eleven or twenty-one,
although he does refer generally to " our herts," and to " us."
It is possible that the letter was written in December, 1587,
but a date between October 8 and November 19 is more likely.

To whom is the letter addressed ? We do not know the
person's name, but we can ascertain a few facts. Greenwood
had sent him a previous letter, which others had also read.
He had replied to Greenwood, had sent him money to aid him,
and had disagreed with Greenwood on several points. He
had suggested that the Separatists were wrong in establishing
a church before the queen had permitted it. He had criti-
cized Greenwood for his attitude toward those who had made
possible the *Book of Common Prayer*, especially Archbishop
Cranmer. He had even intimated that Greenwood was a liar
because he had asserted that those who used read prayers
were actually quenching the spirit. In his own circle of
friends he had known those whose hearts had been quickened
to pray after reading or hearing set prayers. He had re-
proached the small struggling Separatist church by asking
what it was in comparison with the Church of Geneva, which
was older, stronger, and of larger membership. This latter
comparison may point toward a Presbyterian or Reformist,
one who knew of Greenwood's Separatism, who liked Greenwood personally, but who disagreed with his views.

* * * * * *

FRAGMENT OF A LETTER

The peace of God which passeth all understanding keeps your and our herts to Christ Jesus; and I praye God we maye make straight steppes, least that which is halting turne us out of the waye; and God's grace make us able through the suffering and victorie of Jesus Christ to strive to enter in at the straight gate. Soe be it. Soe be it.

I have receaved your letters, and the mony therin conteyned, with my four letters, and likwise your loving tokens (sent by my deare brother that brought you my letters). For all this your love, not onlye nowe, but of long tyme heretofore alsoe, I give God herty thankes throughe Christ Jesus, and noe doubt of it, thoughe there be some controversies betwixt you and me, in wrighting, yet this your grace in ministring to a poore distressed lambe of Christ's fold, cannot be without great recompense, for his sake; for God is not unrighteous (as sayeth the apostle) that he should forget your worke and labor of love, which you shewed towarde his name, in that you have ministred to his saincts, and yet minister:[1] and it maye be you chide me in folye for my follye in that I sent those letters, and your letter especiallye, soe openlye; but it shalbe soe noe more, soe long as you and I continewe in freindshipp together. But surelye my purpose was not that any shold have seene them but our brethren at W.H.[2] with you and whome you should thincke it good. For inde[e]d we had need be as wise as serpentes and as harmles as doves.

I have considered your letter thoroughe, and therby I perceive that you and I are at some controversye; but I praye God for his sonne's sake that it breake not out into froward contention, and soe by that meanes breake that bound of love and peace which is nowe, and soe to continewe betweene you and me. For thoughe my povertye be very great, and you and my brethren with you the cheife suppliers therof that I have in this world concerning man's ayde, yet all this may not make me a dombe dogg, to hold my peace. But in many poyncts of your letter I am urged in conscience to speake against, yet not in any reveng of my owne parte, and that

[1] Hebrewes 6: 10.
[2] W. H. may be William Hutton, who is one of the Barrowist prisoners in 1590.

my God knoweth; but I wishe from the bottome of my hearte, bothe that I and you and all God's children to prease [press] hard to wards the marke for the price of the hye callinge of God in Christ Jesus. Philippians 3: 14.

First you saye that you did not crosse me in alleadging that David was forbidden to build; then I saye you must prove that God hath forbidden the queene to command the rearing up of his apparant church here in England;[1] or else your applicacion is not good; besides that the rearing up of the churche is appertayning to the godlye pastors and ministers of God's worde, nowe in theise last dayes, onlye with the whole; and the queene, yf she hath not denyed the fayth, have noe more to doe in the rearing upp of the same than an other faythfull Christian hath, as she is a member of the same churche. But I confes and allwayes have said, as she is civill and cheife magistrate, she hath to give forthe her letters to maynteyne the builders therof, and to be their defence, from the enemye; and, as you have well sayd in your letter, she hath to punishe the faltings of the churche, and to have a good eye that all things maye be done agreeing with the word of God. But all this shee must do civillye, as you have very well proved. Therefore the churche maye not tarye the rearing upp therof untill God send a Salomon to doe it, for God hathe commanded it to be done and not left undone; and the charge to reare it upp is committed to those whome God givethe graces to preache his worde; and God must be obeyed before man.

And nowe you saye further in your letter, that you are sorrye and sore mislike my rashe judgment of them, that first made the booke, to be antichristes; but you saye surelye I sclaunder them, for they were good men, *etc.* You doe not well, to saye that I condemne for antichrists those good men that made the *Booke of Common Prayer*, as namely Cranmer; for I never did thincke that Cranmer, Ridley, or Latymer,[2] to be antychrists, but I reverence those good men as muche as I maye by the word of God. Not withstanding, I saye this, their great sin of ignorance hath beene our great and deadlye plague, in that they translated out of the Latin portues [portas] of the pope in to Englishe theyre deadlye collects and prayers, and soe made a booke of them. Not that they made the

---

[1] There is a manuscript treatise probably by Barrow, called *Profes of Aparant Churche*, which is published in volume III. Also, the phrase, " visible church," is used frequently.
[2] Archbishop Thomas Cranmer, Bishop Nicholas Ridley, and Bishop Hugh Latimer all died as martyrs in the reign of Queen Mary.

4

prayers and collects them selves, but antichriste, as I said, made them; and theise good men their ignorance was suche, that they translated those his prayers and collects into Englishe, and mended here and there places which were to to vitious, and put in some of their owne words in the romes [places] of that vile stuffe: soe then you cannot well denye but theise prayers were first coyned in that Latin shop of antichrist, and after were drawne out of the Latin shopp into Englishe by Cranmer, and patched up together by some of his owne coyning, and theirs with his; soe by this your common prayers are but patched prayers. But alas, let us consider that these men were in the time of great darknes over [beyond which] we are nowe, and by the reason thereof they were greatlye blynded by the mist of antichrist. But I say in that they knew, they shewed themselves faithfull unto the death; therfore they [were] gatherers with Christ and not with antichrists. Soe by this meanes I may judge better of the men than I can judge of that their wicked worke, in making and calling that vilde [vile] booke together, which hath bene sence that tyme a deadlye poyson to manye thousands, as you knowe. Then take my judgment is this of those men: I saye we must not condemne those whom God hath justified, but he did never justifie their wicked fact, but pardoned it. He hath done therfore, what can we saye? Thoughe God did pardon the drunckennes of Noah, and imputed unto Cham [Shem] the skorning of his father's nakednes,[1] though God did pardon that wicked dissembling and mistrust of Isacke in consulting with Rebecca, to bid her say thou art my sister,[2] and that his untoward love to Esau to give to him the blessing, thoughe it was proper to Jacod [sic] by God's appoyntment; and yet imputed to Ishmael his mocking; and though God did pardon Jacob's having of two wives and of two whores, and his lyeing to his father; yet he ymputed to Esau the selling of his birthright:[3] thoughe God did pardon the wickednes of the patriarkes in despising poore Joseph, and afterward their posterityze, thoughe they were murmurers and rayled uppon Moyses, delivered throughe the Red Sea; yet he ymputed to Pharoo and his host the persecuting of them:[4] though God pardoned the wickedness of Aaron in making a false god, yet he imputed to his two sons, Nadab and Abihu, the taking of straung fire:[5]

1 Genesis 9: 20-27.
2 Genesis 26: 7-12.
3 Genesis 27: 18-38.
4 Exodus 13: 7-22 ; 14: 1-31.
5 Numbers 3: 4.

though God did pardon Miriam against Moses, yet he ymputed to Corah, Dathan, and Abiram, with their companye, their rebellion, pride and disobedience:[1] and to be short, thoughe God did pardon all the falts of all the good princes unto David, yet he did ympute to the wicked their obscure darknes; though God did pardon David's sin, murther, whoredom, and the having of manye wifes, yet he ymputed to Saule the saving of one kinge and fat cattell, alive, contrarye to God's commandmente:[2] thoughe God did pardon Peter's denyall and blasphemye, yet he ymputed unto Judas his traiterous kisse;[3] and even soe thoughe God did pardon Cranmer for making that vile book, and his being metropolitaine, yet he condemned Francis Spira[4] for denieng his master Christe and sinning agaynst the Holye Ghost. Thus you may see God doth what it pleaseth his majestie to doe; yet it is he that condemneth, and it is he that saveth, soe that it is not for me to judge Cranmer to be an antichrist, because the true good and Christ in his members but was persecuted for them even to the death. And yet I saye, his calling to be metropolitan was antichristian.

---

[1] Numbers 16: 1-35.
[2] I Samuel 15: 9. Saul spared Agag, king of the Amalekites, and also the best of the sheep, oxen, fatlings, and lambs, contrary to the commandment of the Lord as spoken by Samuel.
[3] Matthew 26: 47-50; Mark 14: 45; Luke 22: 47, 48; John 18: 2-5.
[4] Francis Spira was born about 1502 in Cittadella, near Padua, Italy. He was a successful civil lawyer, unscrupulous, clever, and unprincipled. Converted by Lutheran doctrines and writings, he refused to heed his own conscience, yielded to the pressures from the Catholic legate, and made a public recantation. Then his real problems began as he became mentally ill, tormented, and burdened. He was obsessed with the conviction that some sins were so enormous and filthy that Christ's blood could not wash them away. Many persons had feared that they had committed the unpardonable sin, but Spira limited the power and the love of Christ, as well as the mercy of God, in saying that they did not and could not extend to him, despite true repentance. He suffered untold mental and spiritual agony, and died a miserable death about 1549. See Nicholas Bacon, *A Relation of the Fearefull Estate of Francis Spira, in the Yeare*, 1548 (London, 1638). See also Mathew Gribaldus, *A Notable and Marveilous Epistle of the Famous Doctour, Matthewe Gribalde, Professor of the Lawe, in the Universitie of Padua, concernyng the Terrible Judgemente of God, upon Hym That for Feare of Men, Denieth Christ and the Knowne Veritie*; with a Preface of Doctor Calvine (London, [1570 ?]). See further Nathaniell Woodes, *An Excellent New Commedie, Intituled*: THE CONFLICT OF CONSCIENCE (London, 1581). There are materials in Italian, Latin, and German by Emilio Comba, C. S. Curio, Matthaeus Gribaldus, and Karl Roenneke, and there are two articles by Celesta Wine in *Review of English Studies*, XV, 458-463 (1939), and in *Publications of the Modern Language Association of America*, L, 661-668.

Fragment of a Letter

And for your part, you thincke me a lyer, because I sayd reading prayers is a quenching of the spirit in them that have the gifte of prayeng. But I saye it is not soe, for if we would narrowlie examine our selves, we should find a great untowardnes in our selves or in our fleshe, which striveth against the spirit, for our fleshe telleth like a white devill,[1] it is dangerous going to God by our conceived manner of prayer; for, saith it, thou mayest set downe thy words undiscretlye, and soe thy prayer [may?] be will tourne to be a curse unto the[e]; therfore make sure work, and take the[e] to a book prayer. But the spirit that striveth against the flesh saith unto us, why [,] yield not unto the fleshlye and mistrusting motion, for I will helpe the[e]: goe unto prayer, and I will guide they [thy] words, and tell the[e] how to praye, and what to saye, and to whome, and in whose name: I will make the[e] to be full of great sighes and grones, with care not to be expressed; but he that sent me to the[e] to make the[e] crye, abba father, he knoweth the meaning of the spirit in the[e]. Yet for all this yf the fleshe over commeth the working of the spirit, and make us take a reading prayer, yt is conceived to our handes, which is both undangerous and without payne as saith our fleshe. Now yf I shall take a reading prayer in hand, shall I quench the former motion of the spirit, judge ye? And [by?] lacke of exercise in conceiving prayers my giftes decrease, but the often exercise therof doth make my gift encrease; then that which maketh it increase is best, and that which maketh it decrease is a quenching of the spirit. Al this have I said unto you by onlye feeling in my selfe; for true it is, my fleshe is more willing to take a booke prayer to

---

[1] " The White Divil " is a play by John Webster, first published in 1612. The title character is an alluring, scheming, murderous woman. The general meaning is that of a devil with a pleasing external appearance. The phrase is used by Thomas Adams in a sermon preached on March 7, 1613, at St. Paul's Cross — *The White Devil, or the Hypocrite Uncased* (London, 1613), pp. A 2 *recto*, A 4 *recto*, and 1, 2. It was evidently used by Martin Luther and by the Church Fathers. See *The Complete Works of John Webster*, ed. F. L. Lucas, I, 194. See also Matthew 23: 27, where Jesus denounces the Scribes and Pharisees as hypocrites because they were like " whited sepulchres, which indeed appeare beautiful outward, but are within full of dead men's bones, and of all uncleannesse." See also 2 Corinthians 11: 14. See further Morris Palmer Tilley, *A Dictionary of the Proverbs in England in the Sixteenth and Seventeenth Centuries*, pp. 151, 155.

It is interesting to find this phrase in 1587, about twenty or twenty-five years earlier than its use by Webster. In his sermon, Thomas Adams defends his " so strange a title," and speaks of Judas as a devil, " blacke within and full of ranckour, but white without, and skinned over with hypocrisie."

goe before my God with all, five tymes rather than I should goe once by conceiving prayer. Then yf it were but this one thing, that reading prayers are most pleasing to the fleshe, ye may conjecture they are the lesse pleasing to God. Besides, yf prayer be nothing but a powring our greife unto God in asking the thing that we knowe needfull, with a hungrye desire to obteyene them, whether for ourselves or for our brethren, or for common wealthe, or especiallye for the glorye of God and halowing of his name, howe can we with peace of conscience take a booke of prayer of an other man's greife to God to God [*sic*] with all, and not rather laye all things aside and fall downe at Christ's feete, and poure forth that our greife unto him?

For surelye, yf the poor publican had taken a book in his hand when he was striken with a feeling of his miserye, and cried out, God be mercifull unto me a sinner, he could not have powred out his owne greife so aptlye, nor yet with the like feelinge;[1] and likwise the holye women, falling often downe at Christ's feete.[2] But the Scriptures are full of such examples in the Newe Testament; but their [there] is not any example to prove that they used booke prayers. But yf some weake brother for want of knowledge and good instruction doe take a booke prayer, we will not saye soe much to it, especiallye not that vile *Booke of Common Prayer*, for you knowe that booke by authoritye hath set it selfe against all that is called God, and therfore an accursed enymye to God. And seing that it is an accursed thing, whoe dare bring an accursed thing into the preasence of the Lorde to serve him with all. For let us carye an accursed or vile thing before [the queen?] which is her enemye, and she will hate it, and will she not reject us and that our message; and shall we then be soe bolde to carye an accursed thing before a righteous God? But here, it maye be, you will replye, and save you, take the best of those prayers. I annswer the best of them are accursed and blinde and lame prayers, and even like sacrifices a [as?] rehersed, Malachi 1, 6, 7, 8, 9 verses:[3] thoughe I grant this place is ceremoniall, with a reproof of their prayers; yet it affordeth that doctryne which reprooveth al false worshipping, and all false bringinge of cursed thinges before the Lord. As the whole booke, the best in the same is accursed as well as the worst therof. Therfore, saith the Lord, cursed be the

[1] Luke 18: 13.
[2] Matthew 28: 9.
[3] Sacrifices as rehearsed or recounted or described in Malachi 1: 1, 6, 7, 8, 9.

8

deceiver that hath in his flocke and voweth and sacrificeth unto the Lord a corrupt thing.[1] This doctryne wilbe afforded out of this place; they be accursed that wilbe content to offer any of those uncleane or cursed prayers to God in sacrifice, especiallye when God hath given them the gifte to praye, [that] wilbe content to use those vile prayers which are accursed with the whole booke; and [we?] have better prayers than any of them, both of master Calvine's and of other good men,[2] that yet were never urged, but left free to men to use them: thus you se that I utterlye deny not but some man maye read a prayer and prayers; but yet I had rather he should read them as he doth other good bookes, for his meditacion and education in marking howe well it is framed, and the words therof placed in due order; and in beholding what abundance of feeling hath beene in other men more than I have, and therby condemne my blockishnes and drousynes, and soe stirre up my selfe to be the more earnest, and to goe the oftener to praye, and sighe and grone inwardly to God that I might more and more feele my miserye and dangerous estate that I stand in, and of him looke to have a remedye throughe Christe, and for his sake.

Thus we ought to doe either in reading prayers or other good bookes. But I saye this is rather the true use of reading prayers, than to make reading prayers to be as sacrifices and service unto God, to goe before him. But let us goe before him with a broken and contryte hearte and troubled spirit, for that God will never despise. And I for my part carye such an hatred to that vilde [vile] booke that as neare as I can I leave the phrase and wordes therof out of my prayers (Jude 1: 23). And in that you saye other [persons] have told you that their harts have beene quickned to praye when they have read or heard reade with inwarde desier the godly prayers that others have made and soe will set in order, this is noe more, as I take it, than I have said before, that reading of good prayers is rather a teacher as al other good books are, than the prayeng it selfe, for you saye that their harts hath beene but quickned to praye, that is, as I take it, hath given them [the desire] to praye, *ergo*, then he hath not prayed, but nowe is redye to goe and talk with God in reverence and in feare, to poure out his greife to him, and ask those [things] which he seeth and feeleth the want therof. And agayne you say you are sorye to heare me saye there ought noe reading prayers to be used for publique service; you

[1] Malachi 1: 14.
[2] John Calvin, Martin Luther, Theodore Beza, Martin Bucer.

saye it is agaynst the Scriptures. Yf it be soe, I praye you, tell it me for my learninge, yf I maye take profit therby. You bring in those churches and men to prove the matter; althoughe I reverence [them] soe farr as they hold Scripture, yet I appeale to the Scripture, for that they are not Scripture, but had and have their errours, and that foule ones, and yf you list to knowe them, send me worde yf you doe not knowe.

And you saye what is our church in comparyson of the church of Geneva. You seeme to reproch, as you saye, our church, but I saye not our church but Christ's church, and Christ the head, lord, and king therof. Thus you put the poore persecuted churche to great dishonnor in sayeng what is our church in respecte of that. I praye you, let us see what difference is betweene them, that the churche of Jeneva hath, that this which you call our churche hath not. They have one head to their lord and king together and one faith and baptisme, one spirit, on[e] God and Father above all, which is over all and in them all, leaving out hipocrits. Yf that church hath separated her selfe from knowne hipocrits, soe hathe this churche. Yf that have the word sincerely preached, soe hath this churche; yf that [church] have the sacraments sincerelye ministred by faithfull pastours, soe hath this. Yf that have ecclesiasticall discipline trulye practised, soe hath this. Yf that hath a free place for prophecye, soe hathe this. Yf that hath her doctours, pastours, elders, deacons, and widowes, soe hath this. But yf that church hath knowne hypocrits, so hath not this. Yf that minister the Lord's Supper, soe doth not this. Yf that observe their superstitious feasts in the years as Eastor, Whitsontyde, soe doe not this. Yf the pastor of that can persuade our Englishe preachers, rather than to dispeare [disappear, despair ?] to be put out of the ministery, soe doe not this churche. Yf that church is at ease, soe is not this. Yf that have the name and prayse of all, soe hath not this. But herein I agree with you, they are of longer continuance and mo[r]e in number than this church is. O poore churche, how thou art hated! The lord and king take thy parte, and keepe the[e] from evel, soe be it, soe be it.

And nowe you deal but somwhat unkindly with me, in sayeng I begin to come somwhat neare unto the opinion of those that hath denied all publique places and soe all publique prayers. But this is not so, for my letters doth give you noe suche matter agaynst me; for I hold it to be certeyne that the godlye pastor ought to praye in the bodye of the godlye churche, publiquelye: with suche prayers and service as God hath in his churche, and for his churche, even as the ould churche of the Jewes used their prayers and manner of service, wherof David and Salomon were good fore-runners. Even soe would I we did use these sacrifices and service which Christ and his apostles hath appoynted. And that reading prayers you would beare me in hand is one parte of our publique worship nowe in the churche, and for your proofe you bring in the institucion [instruction?] of Paule to the Corinthians.[1] 1 Thisellonians [*sic*] 14.[2] Therfore let us searche that chapter: yf there be any suche matter, I will yeild, yf not, [then] yeild you, and give glorye to God. First, therefore, in this chapter he willeth them to follow after love,[3] without the which all their gifts were to noe profit.

[*Here the letter breaks off abruptly, at about one-third from the bottom of the page. There is a pen sketch resembling the opening of a flower. Included with the design is a double set of initials, I. G., presumably for John Greenwood. The date of 1587 is also given.*]

[1] I Corinthians 14: 12-17.
[2] Evidently I Thessalonians is a misprint or a mistaken reference for I Corinthians 14.
[3] This is a reference to I Corinthians 14: 1, which begins: " Follow after charity."

1588

II

REASONS AGAINST READ PRAYER

About the latter part of 1587, or in the early months of 1588, a schoolmaster in Essex brought to George Gifford in Maldon two writings of the Separatists. One was called "A Breefe Sum of Our Profession," and the other consisted of divers arguments which we may term "Reasons against Read Prayer." Gifford was asked to refute these articles, and when he refused to do so, the schoolmaster reported that many people were troubled and "did hang in suspense." Thereupon, Gifford agreed to reply in writing to the arguments of the Separatists. Thus began the long controversy between Gifford and Barrow, originating from "A Breefe Sum of Our Profession," and between Gifford and Greenwood, stemming from "Reasons against Read Prayer."

In all the writings of Barrow and Greenwood, Barrow assumes the main task of denouncing the Church of England, defending separation, explaining the ideas and practices of the primitive church, and justifying the purposes of the Separatists. Greenwood's main role is twofold: to explain the attitude of the Separatists regarding true worship versus read prayers, and to defend his friends from the accusation that the new separation was but the old Donatism writ large. His views on true worship are expressed in his brief article, "Reasons against Read Prayer," in his "Reply to George Gifford," in his book, *An Answere to George Gifford's Pretended Defence of Read Praiers, and Devised Litourgies*, and in his long article, "A Fewe Observations of Mr. Gifford's Last Cavills about Stinted Read Prayers and Devised Leitourgies." His denial of the charge of Donatism is presented in his work "A Breife Refutation of Mr. George Gifford His

Supposed Consimilitude betwene the Donatists and Us."

" Reasons against Read Prayer" may be the earliest writing of Greenwood that we possess. It may have preceded the " Fragment of a Letter " of 1587, but we cannot be sure. Gifford replied to it in 1588, and printed it in 1590 (*A Short Treatise against the Donatists of England, Whome We Call Brownists*, pp. 17-21). From his reply we may date it early in 1588, with the proviso that it may have been written in 1587, and it may have been circulated in London before a schoolmaster brought it to Gifford in Maldon, Essex.

The first nine points constitute the " Reasons against Read Prayer." To these Gifford replied in manuscript, but we do not possess Gifford's manuscript. Greenwood issued his " Reply to George Gifford," also in manuscript, in 1588, but Gifford did not reply until two years later, in 1590, when he issued his printed book, *A Short Treatise against the Donatists of England, Whome We Call Brownists*. In this work Gifford reproduced the " Reasons against Read Prayer." He also summarized some of his own manuscript reply, as well as some of Greenwood's manuscript " Reply to George Gifford." We are indebted to Gifford for reproducing material from manuscripts which have disappeared.

*   *   *   *   *   *

[REASONS AGAINST READ PRAYER]

[17]

John 4: 23, 24. God is a spirit, and must be worshipped in spirit and truth.

The reasons why wee disalow of read prayer, in stead of
spiritual prayers, that though they may be read for meditation, The
as any other men's writs, yet is it idolatry to offer up to God Brownists
such manner of sacrifices eyther privately, or in publique assem-
blyes.

1. No apocripha must be brought into the publique assemblyes, for there only the lively voyce of God's owne graces, of the word, and the spirit, must be heard in the publique assemblyes. And more lawfull is it to use homelyes, than reade prayers unto God.
2. To do any thing in the worship of God without the testimonie of his word, is sinne; but there is no ground in the Scripture for such manner of praying, as having no witnesse of the word, whether God be pleased with them, or no.
3. Admitte that it were a thing indifferent, as we call it, for the forme of prayer, which is but a mockery, to call reading in stead of spirituall calling on God, to be but altering the forme, or chaunging the manner, whereas in deede it is [18] changing the worke of the Spirit into an image, or idoll. Yet it is a bondage, and breaking of that libertie, which Christ hath purchased for us, and therefore most detestable.
4. Because true prayer must be of faith and knowledge uttered with the h[e]art, and lively voyce unto God, I am persuaded it is presumptuous ignorance to bring a booke to speake for us such things, as we could not otherwise utter in God's sight.
5. To worship the true God after another manner than he hath taught, is idolatry; but he hath commaunded us to come unto him being heavy loden [ladened], with contrite hearts, yea, to cry out unto him in the griefe of our soule, yea, and as St. Paule sayeth, " The Spirit helpeth our infirmities with groning and sighing that can not be expressed," [Romans 8: 26] and how dare we then being a dead tree unto God, to stand reading of the same in stead of faithfull petitions, quenching the Spirit.
6. We must strive in prayer with continuing, with fervency, without wavering, which we cannot doo uppon a booke.

14

7. We must call uppon God in prayer at all times, as the necessities of the time requireth, not making a babling of many things, whereof we have not any present necessitie; but stinted service cannot be so applyed, so it is but a babling of vaine repetitions.

8. All the devises of antichrist, though it were otherwise lawfull, not being necessary, ought to be abhorred of true Christians, especially such reliques as maintaine superstition, but to reade other men's bookes to God in stead of true prayers, and stinted service, were devised by antichrist, and maintaine superstition, and an idoll ministerie: therefore ought to be disallowed. [But it is intolerable to reade other men's bookes to God instead of true prayers; it is intolerable to use a stinted service. Such practices were devised by antichrist, perpetuate superstition, and maintain an idol ministry.]

9. The prayers and worship of such ministers and people as stand under a false government, are not acceptable, nor have any promise in God's sight, not only because they aske amisse, but because they keepe not his commaundements. [19]

III

REPLY TO GEORGE GIFFORD

Greenwood's brief writing, " Reasons against Read Prayer," was answered in manuscript by Gifford. We do not possess this manuscript, and have only a brief recapitulation of it in Gifford's printed book, *A Short Treatise against the Donatists of England, Whome We Call Brownists.* Greenwood replied in manuscript to Gifford, sometime in 1588, perhaps in the early months of the year. Although this manuscript seems to have disappeared, we have Gifford's summary of it, and this summary is printed with the caption, " Reply to George Gifford." It may be found in Gifford, *A Short Treatise,* pp. 17-21.

Gifford's main arguments, which Greenwood seeks to refute, are as follows:

1. A man may pray in spirit and truth, with true faith, when he uses set prayers from a book.

2. Prayers conceived without faith, with or without a book, are not acceptable to God.

3. Read prayers are useful not only for meditation, as is true of books for edification, but also for praying in the spirit.

4. Prayers which are devoid of faith are but vain babbling.

5. It is an error to designate the use of read prayer as false worship and idolatry.

* * * * * *

REPLY TO GEORGE GIFFORD

" God is a Spirit, and must be worshipped in spirit and in truth."

The Scripture doth most briefely and pithily sever The Brow[nists] all fantasticall devises of man, from the pure and sincere worship of God, prescribed in his word. For seeing all flesh is grasse,[1] and the wisedome thereof foolishnes with God, it must needes follow, that men earthly minded should please themselves in such pretended religion, as agreeth nothing with the divine nature of God. It is needfull, then, in the worship of God, that we thus always consider with our selves, we have to do with God himselfe, and not with men, who is so farre differing from us, that those things which are most easy, and pleasing unto us, is a wearisomnes and abhominable sacrifice in his sight; and although God dwelleth in the heavens in his divinitie incomprehensible, yet have we a perfect rule, whereby we know what is agreeing to his will, namely, his written word, for that we may be heere taught: 1. That all hipocrisy in such things as hee hath commaunded, be carefully avoyded. 2. That wee attempt not to do any thing in his worship, whereof we have not speciall warrant from his word, of which sort we take all manner of stinted prayers offered up as a worshipping of God, disagreeing from the nature of God (which seeth in secret) and so agreeth with our fleshly nature, that we can not pray as we ought, and so we seeke to help our selves with such a broken staffe, wearying our selves with our owne devises, without any promise to receyve blessing thereby.

And therefore where you [George Gifford] affirme, that a man may pray in spirit and truth, with sighes, and grones, proceeding from faith, when prayer is read, that is not true, for if their sighes came from faith, it would minister matter and prayer without a booke, yea, no doubt, a troubled mind is the penne of a readie

[1] I Peter 1: 24. Isaiah 40: 6.

17

writer;[1] and to worship God in spirit, is, when the inward faith of the heart bringeth forth true invocation, and it is [20] then in truth, when simply it agreeth with God's word. But you would teach men in stead of powring forth their harts, to help themselves upon a booke, yea, to fetch their cause of sorrowing and sighing from an other man's writing, even in the time of their begging at God's hand. We graunt, that prayers conceaved without faith, ar not acceptable, yet may the same be called spirituall, because it is the gift of the Spirit, though not sanctified in him that so hipocritically mocketh with God. But what maketh this to our question of stinted read prayers in God's worship? But say you, to make read prayers only to serve for meditation, is false doctrine, wherein, me thinke you offer great injurie, for we affyrmed that it had such use as other of men's writings have. But it seemeth you make little conscience to slander us, and heere you fall into an error your selfe, affirming, and going about to prove, that reading of prayers is not for meditation at all; the proofe you bring, is, that Christ said not to his disciples, "when ye meditate, say thus, *Our Father*, but when you pray, say thus, *etc.*" Where, beside that you make no difference between your owne liturgies, and the holy word of God, which is not of any private interpretation; besides this, I say, you seeme to prove, that the Lord's Prayer, and all other prayers in the canonicall Scripture serve not at all for meditation. Well, you have hereby made the matter apparant, that read prayers upon a booke are as acceptable, as faithfull prayers conceived by the spirit, and uttered with understanding. You say that prayers read or conceived, being void of faith, is but vaine babling; we say the same, but what of this forsooth?

You cannot see by what censure it can be called idolatry. If false worship cannot be called idolatry, let the first and second commaundements be witnesses, so that it is not our pennes, but the penne of God's own finger that hath judged all devises of man, and hipocriticall worship of idolatry. And although all the

[1] Psalm 45: 1 — " My tongue is the pen of a ready writer."

Reply to George Gifford

breaches of the first table were not idolatry, yet you
know that to worship our own devises, is idolatry.   Is
not prayer a speciall part of the first commaundement,
and our saviour Christ comprehendeth all the foure
first commandements in this, that we love God above
all; [21] the transferring of any part whereof from God,
must needs be idolatry.   But say you, if we do thus and
hold withall, that no idolator can be saved, then surely
are all lost, *etc*.   This is countrey divinity,[1] if the salt have
have lost his savour, what should be seasoned therwith,
we hold that no idolator can be saved without true repentance, and renouncing their sinne so far as God
shall shew it them, yea, and crave with David for
pardon for their hidden and secret sins.   And doo you
thinke any man living is void of idolatry, either inwardly or outwardly, so long as we live, or that we can
keep any one commandement in perfection ?   The Lord
therfore give us repentance; for in some things we sin
all.   Me thinks this should not be, Mr. Gifford's language to be so ignorant in the principles of religion, and
if you have waighed our arguments no better than your
preface,[2] it shall be greevous to me to make any aunswer.

---

[1] This phrase " countrey divinitie " implies rustic, naive and false ideas.
It is an application to Gifford of his own phrase, because he published
in 1581 a book entitled, *A Briefe Discourse of Certaine Points of the Religion, Which Is among the Common Sort of Christians, Which May Bee
Termed the Countrie Divinitie.   With a Manifest Confutation of the Same,
after the Order of a Dialogue* (London, 1581).   The running title throughout the book is " The Countrie Divinitie."

[2] Probably the preface to Gifford's first manuscript reply.   Compare
Gifford, *A Short Treatise*, signature A 1 — A 4.   See especially A 2 *verso*.

19

1589

IV

GREENWOOD'S EXAMINATION,

[MARCH 24, 1588/9]

Greenwood may have been examined in October, 1587, shortly after he had been arrested, and again about April-May, 1588, but no record of either examination has survived. The Bishop of Winchester, in March, 1589, asked Greenwood if he had not referred a year ago to the *Book of Common Prayer* as "popish, superstitious, and idolatrous," and Greenwood admitted as much. These words may have been used at an examination in the spring of 1588, perhaps when Barrow and Greenwood were indicted upon the statute for recusants, but we cannot be certain. In his "Reasons against Read Prayer," Greenwood makes the charge of superstition and idolatry, but there is no mention of "popish."

The present examination is not dated, but undoubtedly it was conducted the same week, if not the same day, as Barrow's fifth examination. The same judges, the same ecclesiastical dignitaries, and the same civilians seem to be present at both examinations. The same basic questions are used for Greenwood and Barrow. A further bit of corroborating evidence is found in Greenwood's reference to his child, Abel, who has remained unbaptized for a year and a half because of his father's imprisonment. Since Greenwood was arrested on October 8, 1587, we arrive at a date of April 8, 1589, if we take the age of the boy to be exactly a year and a half. If we assume the age to be approximately seventeen and a half months, or if we assume that the boy was born about the last week of September, 1587, we arrive very close to March 24, 1588/9, as the correct date for Greenwood's examination.

Furthermore, the date of Greenwood's examination helps to confirm the year which has been attributed to Barrow's fifth examination.

This examination is printed in the rare tract, *The Examinations of Henry Barrowe, John Grenewood, and John Penrie before the High Commissioners, and Lordes of the Counsel. Penned by the Prisoners Themselves before Their Deaths*, signature C *verso* — C iii *recto*.

*   *   *   *   *   *

B

[C i *verso*]

THE ANSWERS OF JOHN GRENEWOOD AT LONDON PALLACE[1] BEFORE THE TWO LORD CHEIF JUSTICES OF ENGLAND, THE MASTER OF THE ROLLES, THE LORD CHEIF BARON, TOGITHER WITH THE ARCH BISHOP OF CANTERBURY, THE BISHOP OF LONDON, THE BISHOP OF WINCHESTER, WITH OTHERS:[2] TO CERTAINE INTERROGATORIES AS FOLOWETH:

Question: What is your name?

Answer: John Grenewood.

Question: Lay yowr hand upon the book. Yow must take an oath.

Answer: I wil sweare by the name of God if ther be any need, but not by or upon a book.

Question: We wil then examine yow without an oath. Are yow a minister?

Answer: No, I was one after your orders.[3]

Question: Who disgraded yow?

Answer: I disgraded my self through God's mercy by repentance.[4] (Then, after many wordes, they brought forth a paper conteyning certaine articles in manner of questions as foloweth.)

[1] London Palace, or the seat of the Bishop of London. Benjamin Hanbury, in his *Historical Memorials*, I, 62, says that the commissioners sat at the Bishop of London's palace, called London House, Aldersgate street.

[2] The two Lord Chief Justices were Sir Christopher Wray, Chief Justice of the Queen's Bench, and Sir Edmund Anderson, Chief Justice of the Common Pleas. Gilbert Gerard was Master of the Rolls, and Sir Roger Manwood was the Lord Chief Baron of the Exchequer. The three ecclesiastical officials are John Whitgift, John Aylmer, and Thomas Cooper. Among the " others " mentioned, Dr. Edward Stanhope is present, and it is highly probable that Baron Thomas Gent, Richard Young, Richard Cosin, Robert Some, and William Hutchinson were also included. William Hutchinson, who was chaplain to Bishop Aylmer and archdeacon of St. Albans, says that he was present at Barrow's examination at this time. In all likelihood, he is present at Greenwood's examination also.

[3] This reply indicates that a prelate is the interrogator. In the third following question, the phrase " I will heare no pratling " is reminiscent of Archbishop Whitgift's " choler " and his peremptory conduct in examining Barrow on November 27, 1587.

[4] Greenwood was ordained deacon about 1581 by the Bishop of London, and was ordained priest by the Bishop of Lincoln. In 1585 he resigned his position as a priest in the Church of England and proceeded to London.

Greenwood's Examination

Question: Is it lawful to use the Lorde's Prayer publickly or privatly as a prayer, or no ?[1]

Answer: It is a doctrine to direct al our prayers by: but seing it conteyneth the doctrine of the holy Scripture, no man can use the same as a private or publick prayer, because he hath not present need to aske al the peticions therin conteyned at one time: neither can comprehend them with feeling and faith.

Question: Is it lawful or no ? I wil heare no pratling.

Answer: It is not lawful, for any thing I can see by the Scripture, for ther is no commaundement to say the very wordes over: and Christ and his apostles prayed in other wordes according to their present necessitie.

Question: Is it lawful to use any stinted prayers either publickly or privatly in prayer ?[2]

Answer: They are Apocrypha and may not be used in the publick assemblie: the word and the graces of God's spirit are onely to be used there.

Question: Answer directly, is it lawful to use them publickly or privatly ?
[C ii recto]

Answer: Paul saith in Romans 8: [verse 26]: the spirit of God maketh request for us, and that we know not what to aske, but the spirit helpeth our infirmities.

Question: Answer directly.

Answer: It is not lawful to use stinted prayers invented by man, either publickly or privatly, for any thing I can see by the Scriptures.

Question: What say yow then to the *Book of Common Prayer*, is it superstitious, popish, and idolatrous, yea or no ?[3]

Answer: I beseech yow that I may not be urged by your law: I have thus long bene close prisoner, and

---

[1] This is the same as Barrow's first question. See his fifth examination on March 24, 1588/9, both his own account and that of the register.
[2] Also Barrow's second question.
[3] Also Barrow's third question. The Separatists regarded the form of worship in the Church of England as " false, superstitious, and popish." See " A Briefe of the Positions Holden by the Newe Sectorie of Recusants " in *A Collection of Certain Sclaunderous Articles,* in volume IV.

John Greenwood

therfore desire yow to shew me wherfore, and not now to entangle me by your law.

Question: Is it not yowr law now as wel as ours: it is the queene's law; yow are a good subject.

Answer: I am obedient as a true subject. But I took it we had reasoned of your popish canons.

Question: Is not the *Common Prayer Booke* established by the queene's law?

Lord Cheif Justice [Wray]: Tel us what yow thinke of the *Book of Common Prayer*. Yow shal have libertie to cal back what yow wil againe.

Answer: If it were in free conference, as it hath bene often desired by us, I would so doe.

Winchester: Have yow not used these wordes a yeare a goe, that it was popish, superstitious, and idolatrous?[1]

Answer: Yes, I thinck I have: for it was taken out of the pope's portuis [portas].

Question: Why should yow not answer so before?

Answer: Because I see yow goe about to bring me within the compasse of the law.

Judge Anderson: What say yow now to it?

Answer: That ther ar many errors in it, and the forme therof is disagreeable to the Scriptures.

Arch Bishop: Is it contrary to the Scriptures?

Answer: It must needs be contrary if it be disagreable.

Winchester: Whither hold yow it idolatrous, superstitious, and popish?

Answer: I have answered what I thinke of it: I hold it ful of errors, and the form therof disagreable to the Scriptures.

Question: What say yow for mariage: did not yow marie

---

[1] This may refer to the Barrow and Greenwood controversy with Gifford about January—February, 1587/8 (Gifford, *A Short Treatise*, pp. 17-21), or possibly to oral statements made about May, 1588, when Barrow and Greenwood were found guilty of violating the law against recusants (23 Elizabeth, *Caput* I).

one Boman and his wife in the Fleet ?[1]

Answer: No, neither is mariage a part of the minister's office.

Question: Who did use prayer ?

Answer: I thinke I did at that time use prayer.

Question: Who joyned their handes togither ?

Answer: I know no such thing. They did publickly acknowledge their consent before the assemblie.

Stanup:[2] I wil make them doe penance for it.

Answer: Ther be some had more need shew open repentance than they.

B[ishop[3] ?]: They may make such mariages under a hedge, and it hath bene a long received order to be maried by the minister.

Answer: No, ther were many faithful witnesses of their consentes: and if it were not lawful, we have many examples of the ancient fathers, who by your judgement did amisse.

Question: What say yow to the Church of England ? Is it a true established church of God ?[4]

Answer: The whole common wealth is not a church.

Judge Anderson: But doe yow know any true established church in the land ?

Answer: If I did, I would not accuse them unto yow.

Question: But what say yow ? Is not the whole land as it standeth now ordered a true established church ?

Answer: No, not as the assemblies are generally ordered; if it please yow, I [C ii *verso*] wil shew yow the reasons.

Lord Cheif Justice [Wray]: No, yow shal have ynough hereafter to shew the reasons. It is not now to be stood upon.

---

1 Christopher Bowman was married in the Fleet prison, in defiance of Church of England regulations, and in accordance with simple Barrowist rites, sometime between May, 1588, and March, 1588/9. He was one of those who presented an offensive petition to the queen on March 13, 1588/9, was imprisoned March 17, probably examined the next day, and kept in prison for this offence. In September, 1592, he was elected a deacon of the newly organized church in London, and after his exile served in the same office in the Amsterdam church of Francis Johnson. Bowman was married to his second wife at the home of John Penry, probably in the autumn of 1592.

2 Dr. Edward Stanhope, Chancellor of the Diocese of London, and member of the Court of High Commission.

3 Probably Bishop Aylmer.

4 Similar to Barrow's fifth and seventh questions.

John Greenwood

Question: What doe yow say to the Church of England as it is now guided by bishops; is it antichristian?

Answer: By such bishops and lawes as it is now guided, it is not according to the Scriptures.

Winchester: Thow hast Scriptures often in thy mouth: is it then antichristian?

Answer: Yea, I hold it contrarie to Christe's word.

Question: What say yow to the sacramentes then, are they true sacramentes?[1]

Answer: No, they are neither rightly administred according to Christe's institution, neither have promise of grace, because yow keep not the covenant.

Question: Speak plainly, are they true sacramentes or no?

Answer: No, if yow have no true church, yow can have no true sacramentes.

Question: How say you, are we baptised?[2]

Answer: Yea, yow have the outward signe, which is the washing, but no true sacrament.

Question: How can that be?

Answer: Very wel. (Then I thought to have shewed reasons, but I could not be suffred.)

Question: Is it lawful baptisme?

Answer: Yea.

Question: Need we then to be baptised againe if we had that ministrie and government yow speak of?

Answer: No.

Question: Should we be baptised at al?

Answer: Yea, or els if we contemne it, we deny the profession of grace.

Question: Doe yow hold it lawful to baptise children?

Answer: Yea, I am no Anabaptist, I thanke God.

Question: How far differ yow?

Answer: So far as truth from errors.

Question: Yow have a boy unbaptised, how old is he?

Answer: A yeare and a halfe.

Question: What is his name?

Answer: Abel.

Question: Who gave him that name?

Answer: My self, being father.

[1] Also Barrow's fourth question.
[2] Also Barrow's sixth question.

Greenwood's Examination

Question: Why hath he not bene baptised?

Answer: Because that I have bene in prison, and cannot tel where to goe to a reformed church, wher I might have him baptised according to God's ordinance.[1]

Question: Wil yow goe to church to St. Brides?[2]

Answer: I know no such church.

Question: Wil yow goe to Paul's?

Answer: No.

Question: Doe yow not hold a parish the church?

Answer: If al the people were faithful, having God's law and ordinances practised amongst them, I doe.

Question: Then yow hold that the parish doe not make it a church?

Answer: No, but the profession which the people make.

Question: Doe yow hold that the church ought to be governed by a presbyterie?[3]

Answer: Yea, every congregation of Christ ought to be governed by that presbyterie which Christ hath appointed.

Question: What are those officers?

Answer: Pastor, teacher, elder, etc.

Question: And by no other?

Answer: No, by no other than Christ hath appointed.

Question: May this people and presbyterie reforme such thinges as be amisse, without the prince?[4]

Answer: They ought to practise God's lawes, and correct vice by the censure of the word.

Question: What if the prince forbid them?

Answer: They must doe that which God commaundeth, neverthelesse.

---

[1] This confirms the date of examination as March, 1588/9. The period from October 8, 1587, when Greenwood was imprisoned, to March 8, 1588/9, closely approximated one and a half years.

[2] The parish church of St. Bride's stood on the south side of Fleet Street between Bride Lane and Salisbury Court. The vicar from 1573/4 to 1591/2 was Roger Foster. In 1586 Mr. Goodman was the rector or parson. See Wilberforce Jenkinson, *London Churches before the Great Fire*, p. 235. See also John Stow, *A Survey of London*, ed. C. L. Kingsford, I, 69, 70; II, 22, 43, 44, 45, 64, 117, 145, 363, 364. See further, Edward Geoffrey O'Donoghue, *Bridewell Hospital, Palace, Prison, Schools from the Earliest Times to the End of the Reign of Elizabeth.*

[3] Barrow's eleventh question.

[4] Barrow's eighth question.

John Greenwood

Question: If the prince doe offende, whither may the presbyterie excommunicate the prince or no ?

Answer: The w[h]ole church may excommunicate any
member of that congregation, if the partie continue obstinate in open transgression.

Question: [C iii *recto*] Whither may the prince be excommunicate ?

Answer: Ther is no exception of person: and I doubt not
but her majestie would be ruled by the word,
for it is not the men, but the word of God, which
bindeth and looseth sinne.

Question: Whither may the prince make lawes in the
government of the church, or no ?[1]

Answer: The Scripture hath set downe sufficient lawes
for the worship of God and government of the
church, to which no man may adde or diminish.

Question: What say yow to the prince's supremacie ?   Is
her majestie supreme head of the church: over
al causes, as wel ecclesiastical as temporal ?[2]

Answer: A supreme magistrate over al persons to punish
the evil and defend the good.[3]

Question: Over al causes ? etc.

Answer: No, Christ is onely [solely] head of his church,
and his lawes may no man alter.

Question: The pope giveth thus much to the prince.

Answer: No, that he doth not, he setteth himself above
princes, and exempteth his preisthod from the
magestrate's sword.

Question: What say yow to the oath of the queene's
supremacie, wil yow answer to it ?[4]

Answer: If these ecclesiastical orders be meant such as

---

[1] Barrow's ninth question.
[2] Barrow's ninth question.
[3] The Act of Supremacy of 1559 designated Elizabeth as "the only supreme
governor of this realm and of all other her Highness' dominions and
countries, as well in all spiritual or ecclesiastical things or causes as
temporal." The questioner, probably Archbishop Whitgift, uses the
phrase "supreme head of the church," which was given to Henry VIII
in the Supremacy Act of 1534. Greenwood is careful to reply —
"a supreme magistrate."
[4] The oath is included in the Act of Supremacy, 1559, I Elizabeth, *Caput*
I, Section 9.

be agreeable unto the Scriptures, I wil, for I deny al forreigne power.[1]

Question: It is meant, the order and government with al the lawes in the church as it is now established.

Answer: Then I will not answer to approve therof.

[Here follows an account of John Penry's examination on April 10, 1593. (This will be printed in the forthcoming edition of Penry's works.) Then follows the " Faultes escaped."]

---

[1] The oath included a renunciation of foreign jurisdictions, powers, superiorities, and authorities. What Greenwood, Barrow, the Separatists, and many Puritans did not like in the oath was to swear faith and true allegiance to the Queen's Highness (which they would do), her heirs and lawful successors (which they would not do if a papist succeeded). Also, to swear that the queen was supreme governor in all spiritual or ecclesiastical things or causes, including Articles of Religion, the *Book of Common Prayer*, interrogatories, subscriptions, canon law and regulations stipulated by the Anglican hierarchy, was a strain on the conscience of conscientious Separatists.

B*

1590

V

AN ANSWERE TO GEORGE GIFFORD'S PRETENDED DEFENCE OF READ PRAIERS AND DEVISED LITOURGIES

Gifford's *A Short Treatise against the Donatists of England* was published about May, 1590. Greenwood's *An Answere to George Gifford's Pretended Defence of Read Praiers and Devised Litourgies* was published about August, 1590. It was printed at Dort by one Hanse or Hause (Hans Stell ?), who had also printed *A True Description out of the Worde of God, of the Visible Church* (1589), *A Collection of Certaine Sclaunderous Articles Gyven out by the Bisshops* (1590), and *A Collection of Certain Letters and Conferences Lately Passed betwixt Certaine Preachers and Two Prisoners in the Fleet* (1590).

The edition ran to about 500 copies, of which about one-half were given to Barrow and Greenwood for distribution. Since both men were in prison, it is likely that the Separatists out of jail were mainly responsible for distributing and selling the books. Robert Stokes, who saw the volumes through the press, and who conveyed them to England, may also have aided in dispersing the books.

There are first editions in the Bodleian Library, Lambeth Palace Library, and Folger Shakespeare Library, each with forty-two pages. In the two copies at the Bodleian Library (Tanner 270 and Crynes 744), there is a slight difference on the title page. The Tanner 270 copy has on line 4 " praiers," but the Crynes 744 copy has " Praiers." On line 11 Tanner 270 has " Prisoner," but Crynes 744 has " prisoner." The Folger copy is identical with Crynes 744.

This book was reprinted in 1603, with a statement, " To the Christian Reader," probably by Francis Johnson. Added to the work is another treatise by Greenwood, " A Fewe

Observations of Mr. Giffard's Last Cavills about Stinted Read Prayers and Devised Leitourgies," pages 45-66. This latter treatise was written about the spring of 1591, too late for inclusion in Greenwood's *An Answere* of 1590, but it was included in Barrow's *A Plaine Refutation* of 1591. Inasmuch as all but two copies of *A Plaine Refutation* were confiscated by the authorities, before the printed stock ever reached the public, it is understandable why the editor included it in the 1603 edition. It is highly probable that this editor was Francis Johnson. He had collaborated with the authorities in Holland, had been responsible for the confiscation of the entire edition of *A Plaine Refutation* in 1591, and had kept two copies for himself and a friend. After reading the confiscated volume, he returned to England, conferred with the Separatists, became pastor of the Separatist church organized formally in September, 1592, suffered imprisonment, went to the New World in 1597, returned to England and escaped to Amsterdam. In making available Greenwood's work in 1603, and Barrow's work in 1605/6, Johnson was giving to the world what he had destroyed in 1591.

There is a copy of the 1603 edition of Greenwood's *An Aunswer to George Gifford's Pretended Defence*, plus his *A Fewe Observations of Mr. Gifford's Last Cavills about Stinted Read Prayers and Devised Leitourgies*, in the British Museum (3475 b. 20). On the title page is the date 1590, which has misled some librarians, but there is an intrusive black letter section, Ai *recto* — A iv *verso*, " To the Christian Reader Grace and Peace from God Our Father and Jesus Christ Our Lord," with the correct date, 1603.

Greenwood's book was printed again in 1640, with the title, MORE WORKE FOR PRIESTS, or, *An Answere to George Gifford's Pretended Defence of Read Prayers and Devised Leitourgies, Comprised in the First Part of His Booke*: Intitaled, A SHORT TREATISE AGAINST THE DONATISTS OF ENGLAND.

*   *   *   *   *   *

31

AN ANSWERE TO GEORGE GIFFORD'S PRETENDED DEFENCE OF READ PRAIERS AND DEVISED LITOURGIES WITH HIS UNGODLIE CAVILS AND WICKED SCLANDERS COMPRISED IN THE FIRST PARTE OF HIS LAST UNCHRISTIAN AND REPROCHFULL BOOKE ENTITULED

A Short Treatise Against the Donatists of England

By JOHN GREENWOOD

CHRIST'S POORE AFFLICTED PRISONER IN THE FLEET FOR THE TRUTH OF THE GOSPELL

1590
[Dort]

[A i *verso* — blank]
[A ii *recto*]

THE PREFACE TO THE READER

I Cor. 2: 11. *What man knoweth the thinges of a man if not the spirit of man which [is] in himself.   Even so the thinges of God knoweth no man if not the Spirit of God.*

I Cor. 2: 12. *Now we have received not the spirit of the world, but the spirit which [is] of God, that we might knowe the thinges of God given unto us.*

I Cor. 2: 13. *Which thinges we also speake, not in the wordes taught of man's wisdome, but in wordes taught of the Holy Ghost, we compare spirituall thinges to spirituall thinges.*

My first writing[1] being about that spiritual exercise of praier and true invocation of God's reverend name, wherby the distressed soule of man, loaden with the burden of sinne, compassed also about with so many deceitful enimies, contynual assaults of Satan, rebellion of the flesh, entisements of the world, *etc.*, seeketh daylie help of God the Father, giver of all good giftes, having thorough Jesus Christ free accesse by the direction of his Holy Spirit, for all

---

[1] Greenwood's manuscript treatise on read prayer. It came into the possession of Gifford, and stopped there, and never was retrieved. Very likely this was similar to " Reasons against Read Prayer," printed in this volume. Some idea of the contents can be obtained from Greenwood's brief summary in this first paragraph.

occasions to unburden it self of whatsoever grief, or occasion of thankes it is moved with. I ought still, and by God's assistance shall keepe me in the meeknes of the spirit, not withstanding his[1] unchristian railinges, sclanders, and reproches against me and the truth. I then shewed that no other prayer could utter and ease the severall occasions and distresses of this conscience, and that no other man's writing could speake for this soule unto God, but the heart and mouth of him that prayeth for himself, or is chosen the mouth of manie, uttering to God his or their mindes for their present wantes or occasions of thankes giving, according to the will of God, as neede and occasion urgeth, and the spirit giveth utterance. And I furder proved that onlie this prayer pleaseth God, and is grounded of faith; to this effect I brought many reasons out of God's worde, admiring the ignorance of this age, wherin (having had the gospell of Christ thus manie yeares in our owne language to search and try all things by) whole congregations do make no other prayer to God, than reading over certeine numbers of wordes upon a booke from yeare to yeare, moneth to moneth, day to day, *etc.*, the same matter and wordes as they were stinted,[2] even out of that portuis, Englished out of antichrist's masse-booke; besides private reading of men's writings instead of prayer. And seing this counterfeit shew of worshipp and pretended prayers was made common mar-[A ii *verso*]chandize in everye assemblie by this antichristian priesthood, and that all men every where were compelled to bowe downe hereunto, and to offer up such counterfeit sacrifices; I perceaved the first principle of religion (which is to invocate the name of the true God, through the mediation of Christ in spirit and truth, with heart and voyce, for our present wantes according to the wil of God) was never yet sincearly taught by these time-serving priests. But as an agreeable service to the humors of earthlie minded men which have not the spirit of God, this ware was thrust upon all people, they well knowing, that such a ministerie and such a church of wordlinges [*sic*] could never have stood, without such a Samaritan worshipp, and Egiptian calf; and like earthlie devises to counterfeit a religion, al men inclyned to some. And long have I heard this pretended worship inveyed against by many (sometymes zealous) for the errours and confused order therof. Yet could I not heare anie to sett downe or teach,

---

[1] George Gifford's *A Short Treatise against the Donatists of England, Whome We Call Brownists*.

[2] The *Pater Noster*, or Lord's Prayer, portions of the *Book of Common Prayer*, and collects.

which was the true prayer that only pleased God, manie contriving divers formes of wordes, as though they had knowen the heart of man, counselled them to reade them, day unto day, yeare unto yeare, at evening, morning, dinner, supper, *etc.*, by portion, measure, and stint, as an offring to God, what state soever the soule were in; not teaching the difference betweene reading upon a booke, and prayer unto God, all this tyme. So that true and only prayer hath not beene taught all this tyme, and those that knewe how to pray aright neglect it, this reading being most easie as they thinke, and they aptest therunto, compelled in the publique assemblies thus to mocke with God, after the maner of the papists' mattins, true zeale no where founde, but in the persequuted [*sic*] remnant.

These my first writings, carried abroade by such as desired true instruction, and willing to make others partakers of such benefites as God imparted unto them, it fell into Mr. Gifford's hand;[1] who (as it seemeth, being a marchaunt of such ware, fynding the gayne of the priesthood to depend hereupon, or, as he saith ("the peace and uniformitie of the church") made head unto it; and that not with purpose (as the fruite of his labour sheweth) to edifie others, but standing himself a minister to this liturgie, having made shipwrack of that conscience he sometimes was thought to have;[2] with all bitternes of spirit, and carnall wisdome, having no more savour of grace in his writings, than there is taste in the white of an egge, fleeth upon me with uncharitable raylings, sclanders, *etc.* And loadeth not only me, but all the faithfull that walke by the rule of God's worde, with oppro-[A iii *recto*]brious titles, of Donatists, Brownists, Anabaptists,

---

[1] Probably Gifford received this manuscript about December, 1587, or January, 1587/8, at the same time that a school master in Essex brought him Barrow's *A Breefe Sum of Our Profession.*

[2] Gifford was a reformer of Presbyterian convictions in the 1580's. He was a part of the classis movement. In 1584 Gifford was presented to Bishop Aylmer for his failure to subscribe, deprived of his position, but permitted to continue in a lectureship. There were letters from the parishioners of the church in Maldon, Essex, written in 1584, requesting that Gifford be restored to his position. Gifford was suspended by the Bishop of London, defended by Lord Burghley, examined by the Court of High Commission, and found not guilty. Therefore he was restored to his preaching, but again was accused, again suspended, and again supported, this time by a lengthy petition, signed by two bailiffs, two justices of the peace, four aldermen, fifteen leading burgesses, the vicar, and twenty-eight others from Maldon. Once more he was restored by Bishop Aylmer. See John Strype, *Historical Collections of the Life and Acts of the Right Reverend Father in God, John Aylmer* (1821), pp. 71-73. See Lansdowne MSS. 68, item 48.

heretiques, schismatiques, seditious, folish, frantick, *etc.*, to bring not only us, but the truth of God into contempt with our sovereigne prynce, and all that feare God; for he ceaseth not with laying all reproches he can devise upon our persons; as one of those locustes, Revelation 9: [3-8], whose similitudes are like unto horses prepared to battell, whose faces like men, but their teeth as the teeth of lyons; but also perverteth, blaspheameth, and by all meanes defaceth the truth offred him.   Well, seing the naturall man perceaveth not the thinges of the spirit of God (I speake not heare of the giftes of the spirit but of the grace of God, which sanctifieth the same, many having charismata that have not charin),[1] and seing I am alreadie thus rent, God's truth delivered by me, troden under his feete, I will followe the councell of Salomon who forewarneth me that " he which reproveth a skorner receaveth to himself shame, and he that rebuketh the wicked himself a blott;"[2] and so tourne me from him, leaving him to the consideration of his owne wordes: where he saith in his Epistle to the reader: " He that seemeth most zealous in religion and refrayneth not his tongue, hath but bitternes in his hearte in stead of heavenly zeale."[3]   And though nothing els can be looked for at their handes that are apostate from that light they have sometymes themselves published[4] (of which sorte the world was never more full), yet for the good of God's chosen scattered abroad, and for the defence of God's truth, I cannot hold my tongue.   And for the more playnenes, I will answeare as to him, though I minde not to have anie more to do with him, till God give him repentance, wishing grace by the direction of God's Holy Spirit to him that readeth, to weigh both sides uprightly, and to follow the truth to his owne salvation.

John Greenwood.

---

[1] Charismata — the gifts, favors, or benefits of God's grace.
Charis — grace, the unmerited favor of God.
[2] Proverbs 9: 7.
[3] *A Short Treatise*, signature A 3 *recto*.
[4] In 1581 Gifford published *A Briefe Discourse of Certaine Points of the Religion Which Is among the Common Sort of Christians*. He also published *A Dialogue betweene a Papist and a Protestant*, in 1582 ; *A Catechisme*, in 1583 ; *A Discourse of the Subtill Practices of Devilles*, in 1587 ; and several sermons.   In 1590 and 1591 he published three books against the Barrowists.

John Greenwood

[A iii *verso* — blank]
[A iv *recto* — page 1]

G.G.   *To condemne and overthrow read praier, ye bring as the
ground or foundation of all your matter, this sentence. God is
a spirit and to be worshipped in spirit.* John 4: [24]. *This
Scripture in deede is cleare and strong to cut downe all carnall
worship, as disagreing from the nature of God. And if anie
[doo] mayntaine that the verie bodily action of reading [prayer]
is the worship of God, it may fitly be alleadged against them,
etc.*[1]

J. G.   *Wisdome is justified of her children.*[2]
It is agreed upon and consented unto on both sides,
that seing God is a spirit, and only requireth such to
worship him, as worship him in spirit and truth, all
carnall worship is cut downe hereby, of what sort soever, as disagreing from the nature of God.   And that
all fantasticall devises of men; namely, whatsoever is
not warranted in his worde, is carnall worship, a weary-
somnes unto him, and lothsome in his sight.   So that
no man ought to intermedle, attempt, or practize anie
thing in shew of worship, wherof they have not sure
grounde of his worde.   For even our God is a consuming fire.

Now to put away all your (bodily) distinctions and
earthly cavils, I still affirme (as I have proved) the
stinting, imposing men's writings upon publique assemblies, to have them read over by number and stint, or
anie other way, as a worship of God in steade of true
invocation, is a meere devise of man, and so carnall
worship; as also all other reading of men's writinges
publiquely or privatly in this abuse, for praying to God.
Yet say you to apply this Scripture, John 4: 22, 23, in
this manner against read prayer, is frivolous.   Where
I appeale to all men's consciences, for the weight therof.   It is frivolous, you say, except I can prove that a
man cannot pray by the spirit of God with sighes and

---

[1] *A Short Treatise*, p. 21.   From Gifford's replies it is sometimes possible
to recover some of Greenwood's points — his " first writing," which was
never published.
[2] Matthew 11: 19.   Luke 7: 35.

36

groanes upon a booke, or when praier is uttered after a
prescript forme, *etc.* At the first step you go about to
alter the question. All our prayers ought to be uttered
after a prescript forme, even that perfect rule and forme
our saviour gave to his disciples and all posterities. But
this is nothing to the [2] matter. For the other which
is nothing but a begging of the question, I alleadged
certaine reasons to this effect. First, that those sighes
and groanes in reading instead of praying, were not of
faith, seing in praying the sighes and groanes that pro-
ceade of faith, minister matter to pray without a booke.
Secondly, that you did but barely assume the question
in calling it praier by the spirit when one doth reade,
seing reading is not praying at all; for as I then alleadged,
to invocate the name of God in spirit, is by the worke of
the spirit to bring fourth of our hearts praier to God,
which is then in truth, when it agreeth to God's worde.[1]
But reading is another matter, namely, a receaving of
instruction into the heart from the booke. Out of the
first Mr. Gifford maketh men beleeve he hath fetched
two heresies; the one a perfection of faith, the other that
faith cannot be joyned unto, or stand with anie outward helpes for the encrease therof. Litle marveile he
found so manie heresies in our whole writinges, that
could find two or three in my first reason; but that you
may remember your self better (though you had two
yeares to consider),[2] I will bring the wordes before you
againe, if peradventure you may have grace to call
backe your self. I said if the sighes and groanes (in
that kinde of praying) were of faith, it would minister
matter without a booke:[3] this sentence I may confirme
by manie testimonies of Scripture, that no perverted
spirit can gainesay or resist; the Scripture teacheth us
every where, that in praying the spirit onlie helpeth
our infirmities, no other helpes mentioned or can be
collected in the present action of prayer through the
Scripture. He hath sent into our hearts the spirit of
his sonne, crying: Abba Father. We beleeve, ther-

---

[1] " Reply to George Gifford."
[2] Gifford replied in 1590 with his *A Short Treatise*. Therefore Greenwood's
" Reply to George Gifford " may be dated 1588.
[3] " Reply to George Gifford."

fore we speake. Yet here is not anie shew of perfection of faith, but of the contrary, praying for our wantes.
But this may be gathered, that God only accepteth the
fruits of his owne spirit in prayer, and requireth no
more of anie, but that everie one according to the
proportion of faith pray unto him, as occasion in them
requireth. Now to conclude that because in praying
we neede not a booke to speake for us, when the heart
it self and booke of our conscience speaketh with God,
that therfore faith never needeth instruction, but is
perfect, were sclanderous, false, and senselesse. The
cause then of these heresies proceed hereof, that your
self, Mr. Gifford, would needs frame two syllogismes,
and in the moodes of your malice, constraine the proposition of the present action in praying, to a generall
sentence of all times and actions, though both our
question here was of the verie action of praying, and
in the conclusion of that verie pointe within six lynes
after this, you had [3] these wordes: " Even in the time
of their begging at God's handes."[1] So that these
heresies must be Mr. Giffard's and not myne, seing they
are founde to be coyned of his idle brayne, and godles
heart, onlie to defame the truth. But (say you) the
most part are ignorant, weake, short of memorie, *etc.*,
therfore need all helpes to stirr them up to pray, *etc.*,
where, by your owne confession, reading is not praying, but a help to stirr up to pray. And even hereupon
all your errors arise, that you cannot discerne the difference of spirituall giftes, with the distinct use of them.
We doubt not but before prayer, and all the dayes of
our life, we have need of helpes of instruction to pray
aright, and for the fitnes of the minde and bodie often
fasting, reading, meditating, *etc.*, are great helpes to goe
before to humble our selves in praying; but in the
present action of prayer, when the heart is talking with
God, the eyes, handes, *etc.*, with attention lift up to
heaven, al the powers of our soules and bodies conversant with God, to take a booke and reade cannot be
called in this action a help, but a confounding of the
minde, of God's ordinances, and a doing we knowe not

[1] *A Short Treatise*, pp. 23, 24.

what, though before and after, it be an excellent meanes
ordeyned of God, to instruct us to pray and all other
dueties.

As for the confirmation you talke of, where I alleadged
that a troubled minde is the penne of a readie writer,[1]
therfore needeth not a booke to speake for it in the
action of praying; by troubled minde I understood such
a minde, as is presently moved with the sight of some
sinne, or urged by other occasion: a broken spirit, a Psal. 51: 17
broken and contrite heart, and not such a minde as in
dispayre or doubt is perplexed; and that the heart which
is moved in faith with present occasion to call upon
God is the penne of a readie writer (that is), hath matter
and wordes enough without a booke to utter yt [its]
owne wantes, we may reade throughout the Psalmes.
" My throte is dry " (saith David) " I am wearie with
crying, *etc.*"[2] But here againe instead of answere, you
tell me, I runne upon the rocke of an hereticall opinion
of perfection: wherin I wonder (but that I perceave
your right eye is blinded) you should be so carelesse
what you say, nay, what after two yeares' studie you
put in prynt.[3] Doth it follow, that because the heart,
moved with occasion through the worke of faith, hath
wordes and matter enough in praying without a booke
to speake for it, that therfore faith is perfect ? Let
equal judges consider.

Here you say manie are so troubled and perplexed
in minde, that they cannot pray till they have some
consolation by the direction of others; which when
they cannot have, reading upon a booke is a notable
help.[4] I allowe al this and agree, if you would make
reading one thing, and prayer an other, divers exercises of the [4] spirit, *etc.* But in the verie action of
praying to have an other speake unto us never so good
wordes of exhortation, were but a confounding of the
minde and action, and an abuse of both those holie

---

1 " Reply to George Gifford." See also Psalms 45: 1
2 Psalms 69: 3.
3 This observation agrees with Gifford's statement that " for more than
two yeares past, there were brought unto me certaine articles which the
Brownists doo call, ' A breefe sum of their profession, with divers arguments against read prayer ' " (*A Short Treatise*, signature a 2 *recto*).
4 *A Short Treatise*, p. 22.

exercises. Even so, by your owne comparison, reading upon a booke in the action of praying, seing we cannot do both at once. It is the spirit of God in the verie action of prayer that helpeth our infirmities. David in praying finding his soule heavie, stirreth up himself thus. " My soule, whie art thou cast downe, whie are thou disquieted within me, waite on God; for I will yet give him thankes, my present help and my God."[1] He had a troubled minde, his mouth wanted no wordes to provoke the Lorde to heare his complaint, and his heart to waite upon the Lorde; and so through all the psalmes you shall finde the conversing of the soule with God to be such, as it were a mockery to think reading upon a booke could have anie place in that action, or that anie man's writing could lay out the present estate of the soule, with the passions therof. The priest may say, my booke, whie art thou so evill prynted, for when they reade, the heart cannot reason and talke with God.

To the second poynt, which was but your bare assuming of the question, to say a man may pray by the spirit upon a booke, *etc.*, I alleadged that to worship God in spirit, is, when the inward faith of the heart bringeth fourth true invocation, *etc.*;[2] this you graunt to be most true, and that none other is accepted of God, than that which proceedeth from the inward faith of our owne heart. But you think that reading upon a booke is to bring fourth of the heart true invocation. This cannot be if we consider the difference betweene *proseuche* and *anagnosis*, prayer and reading;[3] the one being a powring fourth of vowes, petitions, supplications, the other a receaving into the soule of such thinges as we reade. This therfore I leave to all men's consciences to be considered, whether the matter we reade can be said a powring fourth of the heart; the whole use of those divers actions through the whole Bible shew it cannot. Now where I said that you teach men insteade of powring fourth their hearts, to help them-selves with matter and wordes out of a

[1] Psalms 42: 5, 11 ; 43: 5.
[2] " Reply to George Gifford."
[3] Proseuchē, prayer; anagnosis, reading.

booke,[1] you say I speake fondlie and foolishlie, *etc.*
Mine answeare now is, it is well I lyed not; if I had
said you compell men to reade upon a booke, in all
your publique assemblies, certaine wordes of your owne
writings by number and stint, from yeare to yeare, and
day to day, the same, instead of powring out their
hearts before the Lorde for their present wants, I had
not lyed. Now let all men by that which hath bene
said consider the grossnes of it, and so the follie re-
mayneth to your self. But to help this matter, and to
deliver your self conningly in such a strayte, you say
you wish all men to use the help of the booke, [5] that
they might the better powre fourth their hearts unto
God, being such as are not throughly able. First you
graunt here, the prayers read upon the booke, is not
the powring fourth of the heart, but ought to be used
only as an help; wherbie you graunt the whole question;
and furder all your assemblies have had no other invocation of God's name this many yeares, but a help to
teach them to powre fourth their hearts. But whether
men's writings may be read in the publique assemblies
to this use, we shall after make manifest; here it is
graunted but an help, and not the powring fourth of
the heart. And to whom is it an help? To such as
are not able to pray. Here either you must confesse
your whole ministrie is unable to pray, or that they
transgresse in this high worship of God, for in an other
place you graunt in all your assemblies this reading is
used of men's writings for prayer;[2] thus you may behold your best worship to be nothing but a help to
teach you to pray.

Where I said that you teach men to fetch the cause
of their sorrowing from the booke, even in their tyme
of begging at God's hand,[3] you say I speake fondly
[foolishly] to call that the cause, which is the mani-
festacion of the cause, *etc.* You here forget your artes;
is ther no more causes than one? If it be the in-
strumentall cause, it is sufficient to prove, that if your
ministers had not their booke, they had nothing to

[1] " Reply to George Gifford."
[2] *A Short Treatise*, pp. 16, 17, 21, 22.
[3] " Reply to George Gifford."

aske, or els asking that which is in the booke, they aske
Luke 11: 11, 12 not that which before was in their owne heartes; so
not comming heavie loaden, they goe emptie away,
and leave the matter in the booke as they founde it,
till the next day, and then sing the same songe. But
true prayer is, when the heart is first prepared, and
moved with the sight of their wants, as the child that
asketh breade. So we should not pray of custome,
but aske the verie thing wherof our heart feeleth the
want, *etc*. Your comparison againe betwixt the being
stirred up by a sermon, and stirred up by reading,
sheweth, that your self will not make the reading the
powring fourth of the heart.

Ther is no question but the exercise of reading is
chieflie for instruction and encrease of knowledge, and
meditating is not the same, nether can be said to be
all the use of reading, though we denie reading to be
praying: but because we are forbidden contention about
wordes, and I have offred you as much wrong in saying
you denyed reading to be for meditation at all, I will
proceede to the more necessarie doctrines. Also for the
controversie of canonicall and apocryphall, we shall
speake in due place.

Thus (say you) *you have answered nothing at all unto
this commandement given by our saviour Christ to use that
prescript forme of prayer, say, Our Father, etc., but by shift
and cavill, etc.*[1] Here you thinke you have put me to
a plunge, your self [6] needed nothing doubt, but that
I allowed the commaundement holie and good, and to
extend to all Christians, as well as to the apostles;
namely, to use that prescript forme of prayer as the
perfect patterne and direction to all men's true prayers.
But you, I trust, will make difference betwixt a forme
to all prayers, and praying, or prayer. And here you
vehemently urge me to answeare you, before I see you
conclude any thing from the place, and so I should runne
into follie, to answeare a matter before I heare it. In
your first entrance of this discourse, you were rounde
in your syllogismes, by two at once to wrast my wordes,
and can find none for your self. It seemes your con-

[1] *A Short Treatise*, p. 25.

science is witnes the matter would not hang togeather. And me thinkes you had never more neede to have shewed what you would drawe from this place, Luke 11, seing I either mistooke you last time, or els you made a simple collection: which was this. *Christ said to his disciples, when you pray, say, Our Father, etc., and not when you meditate, say, Our Father.* Now what would you conclude of this, except as I said that Christ would not have them meditate that Scripture. But this I perceave was not your meaninge; now I partlie thinke your argument should be (if the sworde were not broken in the sheath) thus. Christ commaunded his disciples when they prayde to say, *Our Father, etc.* Therfore to be tyed to reade over or say by roate certeine wordes, is lawfull praying. For the first, that our saviour Christ tyed no man nor commaunded none to say over those verie wordes when they prayde, but to pray according to that forme, after that maner, as Matthew 6, I manifested in my first writing: 1. that our saviour did not commaunde us to use those wordes; 2. that Matthew 6 doth not keepe the same wordes, nor that number of wordes which Luke 11 doth;[1] 3. that he did not say, read these wordes when you pray, or say these wordes by roate. After all which reasons slilye passed away in both your answeres, you come with your bare affirmation, that he commaunded those wordes to be said over by roate or reading; yea, a litle after you say, it is false to say that he commaunded not the verie wordes to be said over when we pray. And you furder conclude, that because Christ commaunded his disciples to say over those wordes, therfore all men's writings in the forme of praier may be brought into the publique assemblies to be read for praier, being agreable to the worde.

---

[1] In the Revised Standard Version, the two versions of the Lord's Prayer in Matthew 6: 9-13 and Luke 11: 2-4 vary. Matthew has " debts " and Luke has " sins." Luke omits " who art in heaven " and also the line — " thy will be done, on earth as it is in heaven." Matthew has " but deliver us from evil," but it is missing in Luke. In the earlier versions of the Bible, the variants are less significant. Matthew has " debts " and Luke has " sins." Matthew concludes with " for thine is the kingdom and the power, and the glory, for ever. Amen." Luke omits this, but in the Revised Standard Version Matthew also omits it.

John Greenwood

To which I answere that seing no man's writings are without error, it is pernitious and blaspheamous doctrine you collect. First, because you make men's writings of equall authority with the forme of prayer Christ hath prescribed; 2. for that you gyve men as mich [much] liberty and authority to frame and impose their liturgies as Christ had to set downe a forme of prayer, he being Lord of the house. The wickednesse of which [7] collections you shall never be able to answeare. And because you here urge me therunto, I will make answeare to your two places of Scripture, wherwith by false interpretation you deceave the simple; which taken from you, your matter is nothing but cavilling; the places are these: Luke 11, Nombers 6, and because the one explanes the other, and your collections the same from both, I will beginne with Nombers 6: 32, 33, 34, *etc.* [Numbers 6: 22-27.] *Thus shall you bless the children of Israell, saying, the Lorde bless thee and keep the[e], etc.* Here you say they were commaunded to use the verie wordes prescribed, in all their blessings. This I say is not true, for the Hebrew worde is [verse 23] *Coh Teborcou.*[1] *Thus shall you bless*: wher the worde *Coh* is an adverb of similitude, as we say, *after this maner*; which cannot be to say the same, but according to the same instructions. This worde *Coh* is used throughout the Bible in this maner, in all the prophets when they say, thus saith the Lorde: where the same [sum ?] of their prophesies are onlie recorded to us by the Holy Ghost, and not all the wordes. Againe this blessing is used in the Psalmes and Cronicles[2] in prayer for the people in manie other wordes. Ely blessed Hanna in other wordes, *etc.*[3] And where by Luke 11: 2, it is recorded, that our saviour Christ commaunded his disciples, *when you pray, say, Our Father, etc.*, it is playne by the doctrines following, 4, 5, 6, 8, 11 verses that Christ tyed no man to the verie wordes saying over, for he teacheth them to aske their particular wants, as a childe asketh breade or an egg of his father; also to importune the Lorde for our par-

[1] The Hebrew word literally means thus, like this [koh].
[2] 1 Chronicles 29: 10, 11. Psalms 67: 1, 80: 3.
[3] I Samuel 2: 20.

ticular wants. But to make this place more playne, the same Holy Ghost in the 6. of Mathew, 9. verse, saith, " when you pray, say thus, Our Father, *etc.*", where the Greeke word *houtos* hath the same signification that the Hebrew worde *Coh* had, which is, " after this maner "; and cannot be referred to the verie wordes saying over; wherupon Mr. Calvin upon those wordes saith. *Noluit filius dei prescribere quibus verbis utendum sit. The sonne of God would not prescribe what wordes we must use.*[1] Now consider how falslie Mr. Gifford hath interpreted these Scriptures, to say the priests wer commaunded to use the verie wordes, and that Christ commaunded us to use the verie wordes. As for his collections, that therfore men's writings may be imposed upon publique assemblies by stint and number to be prayde, it is intollerable error, and bringeth in all popery.

Here I must call all men that reade this fruictlesse discourse to be witnes of Mr. Gifford's abuse of his tongue, to the defacing of God's truth. In his Epistle he proclaymed, that I called all men idolaters;[2] which you shall perceave to be his owne wordes, and to that end I will breifly repeat it. In my first writing I affirmed the reading imposed liturgies by stint and limitation instead of true [8] invocation, as also all reading men's writings for praying, to be idolatrye.[3] In his answeare he sayd, he could not see by what collour it could be called idolatrye, or maintayned out of God's worde so to be; but it seemes the penners of these things take every sinne against the first table of the lawe, to be idolatry; if they do so, (saith he), and with all do hold that no idolater shalbe saved, then doubtlesse all are lost, *etc.* To this ignorant excursorie[4] I answered, that all false and devised worship by man's invention was idolatrye, as the first and second commandements

---

[1] John Calvin, *Commentary on a Harmony of the Evangelists, Matthew, Mark, and Luke,* translated by William Pringle (Edinburgh: Calvin Translation Society, 1845), I, 316.
[2] *A Short Treatise,* p. 26 and also in Gifford's first manuscript reply.
[3] " Reasons against Read Prayer." See especially reasons 1, 3, 5, 8.
[4] Rambling speech.

John Greenwood

did testifie.[1] And so admit all the breaches of the first table were not idolatrye, yet reading of men's writinges instead of praying must needes be idolatry, seing it is a transgression of the second commandement. Furder (though I needed not have followed his emptye head, even a cloude without water), yet I proceeded to prove, that no idolater could be saved but by repentance for their knowne sinne, and craving pardon with David for their hidden sinnes and secreat faults.[2] Moreover (said I), do you thinke anie man is free from all inward and outward idolatrye, seing we cannot keep one commaundement, and in some things we sinne all.[3] In which wordes I plainelie reproved his grossnes, that concluded all men idolaters which committed any idolatrye, and that no idolater could be saved; and distinguished betweene the sinne of ignorance, weaknes, and imperfection, *etc.*, in God's children, and open professed obstinate idolatrye. Yet this godles man would lay to my chardg, that I should call all men idolaters, wheras I never used such a worde in all my writings; but only answered his folly in this running out from the question; they were his owne wordes that brought this upon his owne heade, by concluding, that if every sinne against the first table were idolatrie, and no idolater could be saved, then all are lost; let the grosnes then be his and not mine. And I leave it to the consideration of all men, whether I may not say, that they which transgresse the first or second commaundements, do commit idolatrie, without absurdity. But, saith he, though it be so, yet the Scripture calleth not the godly, murtherers, idolaters, *etc.*, for the reliques of sinne remayning. I answere that therfore your former absurd cavilling, where you said, if we hold it idolatrie, *etc.*, is by your owne mouth fully answered.

But to avoide this foyle, he hath an other evasion. I thought (saith he) we had reasoned about such grosse idolatrie as a church is to be condemned and forsaken, which is defiled therwith. Here againe you misreport

[1] " Reply to George Gifford."
[2] " Reply to George Gifford."
[3] " Reply to George Gifford."

me; I never reasoned to that end in this whole discourse, but only laboured to shew all men this error of reading men's writinges instead of praying, that they might learne [9] how to converse with God and their owne conscience, in prayer. And what mendes will you make for this sclandering and defacing of the truth, to all the world? All that I desire is your repentance and amendement, which God graunt unto you if you be his.

It followeth in your booke thus. *But seeing you confess that all men be idolaters, that is, touching the remanents of sinne, it must needs follow there is no church free from spots, etc.*[1] This worde " idolaters " must still be yours, and then I willinglie graunt, that no man living is free from idolatrie, concerning the reliques of sinne; also that no church upon earth can be without spot upon earth, so that now by your owne confession I pleade not for persecution in this life, though the more we want, the more we ought to endevour. With what face then could you publish me an Anabaptist in your Epistle, and out of one mouth give contrarie sentence? Doth your Ordinary teach you to cast out such bitter waters of untruthes? Was it possible I should hold al men idolaters, and some men without committing of sinne after regeneration, especially to mainetaine both such heresies as you gyve out? Well consider your self, before the Lord call you to accompt for defacing his truth, and pleading for Baal. I grant, yea, I were not of God if I should speake otherwise, that the deare servants of God fall into most lothsome sinnes after regeneration, that the riches of God's mercy might appeare in their repentance, through the worke of his grace. Then you reason thus: if ther be allwaies spottes and imperfectnes in the true church upon earth, then all your arguments you bring against the Church of England, are of no force, except you will mainetaine a perfection. Myne answeare is, I will not meddle with your church to prove it a false church in this treatise, but refer you to him that handleth that

---

[1] *A Short Treatise*, p. 26.

part of your booke.[1] Yet I must tell you your argument is verie simple. For after the same maner you might reason thus. If ther be no true church without spottes upon earth, then the church of Rome is the true church, for it hath manie spottes, and you all schismatiques. Againe you assume the matter you should prove. It wilbe proved against you, that you have not ecclesia, a people called fourth of the world to the obedience of Christ. Then that the spottes of your church are Egiptian ulcers, incurable running botches. But I purposed not to deale with your church, only my mind is to shew the unlawfullnes of this reading and imposing men's writings upon men's consciences in stead of true praying. Of which sinne the Lord give you and this whole land grace to repent, that so men may learne more fervently to cal upon God.

[10]

Argument 1

J. G. *No apocrypha must be brought into the publique assemblies: for there onlie God's worde and lively voyce of his owne graces must be hearde in the publique assemblies.[2] But men's writings and the reading them over for praier are apocripha; therfore may not be brought into the publique assemblies.*

G. G. *First touching the proposition; no apocrypha is to be brought into the publique assemblies. What can be more false? Apocrypha is opposed against canonicall. If nothing may be brought into the publique assemblies but canonicall Scripture, then the sermons and praiers of pastors are to be banished, etc.[3]*

J. G. In the answere of this, you will needes oppose against both propositions, and yet have nothing to say, if not to royle [muddy, disturb] the doctrines delivered with your feete, least others should drinke therof. The part of a wise man had beene to lay his hand on his mouth. In the first proposition you would oppose the word *apocrypha* against the lively voyce of God's graces, when you see I said onlie, that no apocrypha might be brought into the publique assemblies. And furder to

---

[1] Barrow deals with this in *A Plaine Refutation*.
[2] " Reasons against Read Prayer," no. 1.
[3] *A Short Treatise*, p. 27.

explane my minde, least you should willingly finde such a cavill, I added this reason, *for there only God's worde and the lively voyces of his graces are to be heard;*[1] where I acknowledged those livelie voyces to be God's ordinance, yet nether to be called apocrypha nor canonicall. How can you say then that I would have these, or that these are banished, if all apocripha writings be banished the publique assemblies? Yet as I told you, I take apocrypha to be all writings, but the canonicall [to be] authentique Scriptures.[2] But (say you), then I will exclude the *Paraphrases*[3] upon the Scriptures and the psalmes in metre, *etc.* Affirme you them to be apocrypha as you do, and can do none other, and I will through God's grace prove they ought not to be brought into the publique assemblies. First, no man's writings are given to the church by testimonie of God's spirit, and we are onlie commaunded to heare what the spirit saith; therfore though men's writings be permitted to be read privatlie of them that will, and therupon called apocrypha (that is, hidden), they may not be brought into the publique assemblies. Secondly, no man's writings are without errour and imperfections; therfore not to be brought into the publique assemblies; the church is the [11] pillar of truth. Thirdlie, the church is builded upon the foundation of the prophetts and the apostles, other foundation can no man laye, etc.[4] Christ Jesus being the cheif corner stone, and not upon men's writinges; therfore men's writings may not be brought into the publique assemblies. Ephesians 2: 20 and I Corinthians 3. Fourthlie, if we might bring in anie men's writings into the publique assemblies, then all men's writings which we judg agreable to the Scriptures. But this is forbidden, Ecclesiastes 12: 11, 12. My proof of the first proposition is this: if anie men's writings are to be brought into the publique assemblies by God's commaundement, because they are agreable to the Scriptures, as you in an other place

---

[1] " Reasons against Read Prayer," no. 1.
[2] Another possible reading or meaning could be: " I take *apocrypha* to be all writings but [except] the canonicall authentique Scriptures."
[3] The Paraphrases of Erasmus were widely used as commentaries on the Scripture.
[4] I Corinthians 3:11.

alleadge, then all that are thought agreable to the Scriptures ought of necessitie by the same commandement; and if ther be no commaundement, then none are to be made authentique which God hath not made authentique; for that were to set man in the place of God. No man's writings cary that majestie, that the penne of the Holy Ghost [possesseth]. No man's writings are *Cecuromenai*.[1] *Authentique*, confirmed by signes and wonders from heaven, sealed by Christe's blood, that one worde or title shalbe unfulfilled. The Scriptures are all sufficient. All men must walk by that one rule. To thinke ther were not rules ynough prescribed by the Lord for his house, were blasphemous and papisticall. Now for the explication, interpretation, *etc.*, and speach unto God in prayer: God hath given giftes unto men to pray and prophecye, and ordeyned his ministerye of pastors, teachers, whose lively voyce is appointed to be the mouth of God unto the people, and of his people unto himself, in the publique assemblies. And these graces are not apocriphall; for no prophecie of the Scripture is of private interpretation, *idias epiluseōs*.[2] "To every one is given the manifestation of the Spirit to profit withall."[3] Most excellent men serve but their tyme in the publique assemblies.[4] Now I may conclude as I beganne. *That only God's holy word and the lively graces of his Holy Spirit are to be heard and offred up unto him in the publique assemblies.*

Where then in the way of answere to the minor proposition, you say you see not how our speach unto God should be apocrypha. It answeareth not me, who deny an other man's writing to be our speach in prayer unto

---

[1] *Cecuromenai*. Perfect middle of Kureō, to be right, hit the mark, proved to be right.

[2] II Peter 1: 20 — of private explanation or interpretation.

[3] I Corinthians 12: 7.

[4] Possibly the meaning is that many excellent men, who are compelled to use the liturgy and give obedience to the ordinances of the Church of England, give their time reluctantly. Another possible meaning is that excellent men serve as lecturers in public assemblies but have no other pastoral responsibility. Perhaps the best interpretation is that the best of men, pastors and teachers, are the channels of God's spirit, the recipients of his grace and gifts, and therefore they give not private interpretations but God's message. They are the mouthpiece of God, and give only or merely their time.

God. But convinceth your self by your owne mouth, thus: true prayer is not apocrypha, but all men's writings are apocrypha; therfore men's writings is not true prayer. Here when you have nothing to say for your self, you woulde make me believe that I accompt the psalmes and the other formes of prayer in the Scripture to be apocrypha when they be read, though a litle before you confessed, you had in your last writing donne me wrong therin. I do accompt the reading of them for praying, to be a grosse and superstitious abuse of them, yet [I consider] them to be holie and canonicall Scripture. [12] And here you have flatly overthrowen your self: saying the worde *apocrypha* is used with us for that which is not God's undoubted worde unto us. And in your last writing, which should have beene your answeare, you said: God speaketh to us only by the canonicall Scriptures.[1] Now seing you would make your liturgies and devised formes of prayer, helpes and instruction, and yet cannot make them canonicall, or God's undoubted truth; they must not be brought into the publique assemblie, much lesse imposed by lawe upon the consciences of all men. And here remember all your liturgies are cast out of the doore; besides that, you have not made in both writinges[2] one direct answere to this most firme proposition, which I will still leave upon you, thus.

> *Only the canonicall Scriptures and lively voice of God's owne graces are to be brought into the publique assemblies for doctrine and prayer.*
>
> *But men's writings are nether canonicall Scripture nor the lively voice of God's graces in such as he hath appointed to speake in the publique assemblies.*
>
> *Therfore no man's writings may be brought into, nor imposed upon, the publique assemblies.*

Thus might I make an ende with this vayne man, considering the whole matter is proved against him, all that followe being but repetitions of these former cavills, but that I must cleare my self of his unconscionable sclanders.

[1] *A Short Treatise*, pp. 26, 27, 32, 34.
[2] Gifford's manuscript reply of 1588 and his printed reply, *A Short Treatise*, of 1590.

John Greenwood

J. G. *We must do nothing in the worship of God without warrant of his worde.*[1] *But read praiers have no warrant in his worde.*

Therfore read praiers are not to be used in the worship of God.

G. G. *To this I answere at the first, that it is a greate audacitie to affirme that there is no warrant in the worde for read prayers, when ther be sundry testimonies to warrant the same; unless you will make difference betweene that which a man readeth upon a booke, and that which he hath learned out of the booke. Furder I said, I do not remember that ever I have read that God commaunded in the Scriptures the prayer shalbe read upon a booke, etc.*[2]

J. G. Seing you have indeed not answered one reason or proof I alleadged in my last writing, but with much evill conscience (as [13] the handling sheweth) perverted them, I will leave them to be judged of them that shall see my writing. And here, seing you would not prynt it, I will answere your cheif objections. First then you graunt, that if I put difference betweene reading upon the booke, and that which he hath learned out of the booke, mine argument is sounde; for by your owne confession, God hath not given anie commandement to read prayer, and so it hath no warrant. Wherupon I gayne thus much: first, that they which impose read prayer upon the church, do that wherof they have no warrant in the worde, and that in the high service of God. Then that they which reade upon a booke for praying, do that, wherof they have no warrant in God's worde: wherupon all your ministers must leave reading their stinted prayers upon the booke, or els stand under God's wrath, and all that so pray with them; which wilbe a fearefull reckoning if they repent not their sinne shewed them. And although our question be cheiflie concerning the reading of men's writings instead of praying, yet I am content the other abuse of the Scriptures be included also, though I make not both in the same height of sinne, as shall appeare in my severall

[1] " Reasons against Read Prayer," no. 2.
[2] *A Short Treatise*, p. 27.

reasons. As an unconstant man, then, you in the latter end of the answere to this argument would call backe agayne that, which you here have granted; namely, that there is no commandement to reade prayer upon a booke for praying,

Of the contrary thus you reason. The people of God did reade the psalmes upon a booke when they did singe; therfore men may reade upon a booke when they pray. I deny your argument; besides that all men may see your unstablenes in denying and affirming with one breath; you now go about to make reading of prayer a commandement: thus you prove it. *Singing* (say you) *is a part of praier: singing may be read upon a booke: therfore praier may be read upon a booke.* Admit that singing were a part of prayer, yet doth it not followe that all prayer may be read upon a booke.[1] But you speake like an ignorant man to say that singing is praier, seing they are two divers actions and exercises of our faith: the one never read for the other, nor said to be a part of the other through the Scriptures, but are plainely distinguished, I Corinthians 14: 15. " What is it then ? I will pray with the spirit, but I will pray with understanding, I will sing with the spirit, *etc.*" Agayne " if you be sad, pray, and if you be merye, sing psalmes."[2] proseuksomai and psalō.[3] I will pray, and I will singe, are divers exercises of the faith; if a man should say reading a chapter of the Scripture and prophecying were all one, were he not wide ? Even so every part of God's service is not prayer. I graunt we are every where commaunded to singe psalmes unto God. And alleadged that place of the apostle to the Ephesians 5: 19. " Speaking to your selves in psalmes and himmes and spirituall songes, *etc.*" [14] and that of the Collossians onlie [3: 16] to this end, that in psalmes singing we do not alwaies speake unto God, as in those psalmes which are only instructions and prophecies; in the first and second psalmes you have not one worde spoken unto God. Againe, as all reading of the prayers in the

---

[1] The syllogism is not valid, as Greenwood observes. What is true of a part is not necessarily true of the whole (*ibid.*, p. 32).
[2] I Corinthians 14: 15. James 5: 13.
[3] I will pray, and I will sing. From proseuchomai and psallō.

C

Scriptures is not praying or speaking unto God, so the reading or singing of psalmes I took to have beene a speaking to our selves, a stirring up of God's graces in us, *etc.* But I do not now, nor did not then, hold it so, in al psalmes singing. And where you say I purposely left out the latter part in both places,[1] which was this, *sing unto God with a grace in your heartes,*[2] the Lorde knowes I had no purpose to inurie [*sic*] the Scriptures, nor mantayne an untruth; but thought we might do those thinges with a grace to God in our heartes, which were not properly and directly a conversing by thought and worde with him alone; but one thing might have kept you from crying out, heresie, in that I added this, that I would not stand upon that reason, but desired to knowe it furder. But how unjustly could you number this for an heresie maynteyned of us al in your Epistle, that we should denie that psalmes should be songe unto God. The Lorde keepe me from such errour. And a wofull phisition you are, if I had bene in such errour. For the 102 psalme I never denied: but that it was a most excellent psalme penned by Daniell or some other prophet,[3] and gyven to the whole church to be songe or read as other psalmes, in the forme of prayer; but you must prove that the church did use it as you say, to reade it over for praying, or were commaunded so to do. This is proof ynough they did not, because it is a psalme. Now though the church speake manie tymes in the singular number, yet it is expressed in some other verse that it is so. But now admit that you could prove that the psalmes were read insteade of, or for, invocation, which you shall never be able to do, it doth not followe that men's writinges should be brought into the assemblies and read for prayer. The 6. of Nombers I have answered before. From the 92. psalme you reason thus. *If the psalmes and other formes of prayer in the Scriptures were read or said by rote the verie forme of wordes for praying; then reading instead of or for*

---

1 *A Short Treatise,* p. 31.
2 Colossians 3: 16.
3 The author of the 102 Psalm is unknown, but it seems to be an exilic one. This psalm is a prayer of one afflicted, and the speaker may be the nation.

praying.[1] Here you durst not set your assumption, it was so false; which should be thus. *But the psalmes and other formes of prayer were read for praying, etc.* This I shewed you was verie untrue, they were never commaunded so to be used, nor never so used. My proof was this; they are given by the Holy Ghost for other uses, as singing, reading, *etc.*, and not commaunded anie where so to be used; so that you do but cavill, not having one proof for all your shameles assertions. Now where I demaunded what this made for your liturgies, and reading men's writinges for praying, except you would make your owne writinges of equall authoritie with the Scrip-[15]tures; you answere, that if I denie the consequence, *it was lawfull to use the psalmes, therfore men's writings*, then I will shut out all prayers, even the prayer of the pastor. See your carnall handling, shuffling, and confounding God's ordinances; doth it followe that because men's writinges may not be brought into the publique assemblies, or there read for praying, therfore the prayers uttered by the lively voyce of the pastor, should herebie be excluded? This your shift was answered in the first argument; your cavills are stale, you are againe convinced. Touching the other matter of conning phrases and formes of prayer by roate, to say over certeine number of wordes, it is popish and a meere evasion, and bewrayeth your ignorance in prayer. In this you have granted me, that he which prayeth not with a feeling of his present wants of his soule, but saith over certeine number of wordes of custome or affectation, he is an hipocrite; which is true[,] proved. Mathew 6: 7. Now by this examine your daylie, monethlie, annuall, *etc.*, saying over, nay, reading over certeine wordes, every tyme the same, as you are stinted. It is playne the sacrifice of fooles. Ecclesiastes 4[: 5]. The two poyntes wherin you protest so willinglie to agree with me, were these. First, whether only such prayers as were made without the booke, were accepted of God's children. Secondly, whether the same spirit teacheth us to pray, that taught the holie men of God before tyme. You grant both

---

[1] *A Short Treatise*, pp. 30, 31.

these, but that you would seeme to alter the first question: well then, God's owne spirit that taught them to pray without a booke, or stinting of wordes, teacheth us so to pray nowe, and in the action of praying giveth the mouth to utter what the heart desireth, moved with the same spirit. Still then after your long shifting to and fro, I trust you will stand to your first wordes; that you never read in the Scriptures anie commaundement for reading of prayers. Secondlie, to say over certeine numbers of words or phrases of the Scripture of custome or affectation, without feeling of, or asking for our present wantes, is hipocrisie. Therfore I will conclude as I beganne, myne argument standing good, that, *to do any thing in the worship of God wherof we have no warrant of God's worde, is synne. But read praiers have no warrant in God's word. Ergo, etc.*[1]

Argument 3

J. G. *We may not in the worship of God receave anie tradition which bringeth our libertie into bondage.*[2]

Read praier upon commandement brought into the publique assemblies is a tradition that bringeth our libertie into bondage.

Therfore read praier, etc. [16]

The minor is thus proved; that God hath left it in all men's freedome to pray as the present occasion requireth and the spirit giveth utterance, according to his will. Againe, no man hath power to commaunde anie thing in the worship of God, which God hath not commaunded, *etc.* Marke 7: 7, 8, 9. Mathew 15. Galatians 5: 1, *etc.*

G. G. *I say it is ungodlie and neere unto blasphemie to affirme that prescript forme of praier is a tradition bringing our libertie into bondage, etc. My reason was and is that the Lord by Moses prescribed a forme of blessing, etc.* Nom-

---

[1] This attitude of Greenwood is reminiscent of the view that one may do only that which the Scripture allows or enjoins. Gifford's attitude seems closer to the belief that one may do whatever is not expressly forbidden by Scripture. Between this Calvinist and Lutheran point of view is a vast middle area where disagreement ensues. According to Greenwood's argument, the use in the worship service of wireless or movies or electric organs or reading of poetry would be without warrant in the Bible and therefore sin.

[2] " Reasons against Read Prayer," no. 3.

bers 6. *The prophets in the psalmes have prescribed manie formes of praier. Our saviour Christ prescribed a forme of praier, etc.*[1]

J. G. Here is a great storme, and yet nothing but wynde. If you were in Caiaphas his place, you would ether have rent your clothes for zeale, or els condemne me before you understand what I say. Is it simple dealinge, do you thinke, to say, *I* [Greenwood] *hold it a bondage breaking our libertie for the Lord by Moses, the prophets, our saviour Christ also, to set downe a forme of praier, or to prescribe a forme of praier*? Did you not see that the minor proposition speaketh of the reading, for praying, and not of the forme of prayer? Agayne of the commandement wherby men are compelled to reade instead of praying? Did you not see that the worde brought into the publique assemblies did specifye the matter to be men's writings to be read in the assemblies as a worship, yea, invocation of God's name, which is a grosse mockery, not that ther is any commandement to reade over those formes of praier mentioned by you, for praying, and so the commandement so to reade them for praying is an abuse of them, and a commandement of men and not of God, *etc.* But that much more odious it is to bring in men's writings into the publique assemblies, proved unlawfull in the first argument; and then to commit idolatrie with them by reading them instead of praying, and that to compell men by commandement wher God had set no commandement so to use them, was a bringing all men into bondage of popish traditions. So that your common recitall of these places of Scripture is abuse of them, and you do but palinodian canere[2] [*sic*]. I thinke if you geate St. Jhon's gospell about your necke as the papists, you will thinke you have religion ynough. The more fearful is your apostacy: you proceede from evill to worse.

G. G. *About the commaunding a prescript forme of praier to be* [17] *used, our church doth agree with all godly churches,*

---

[1] *A Short Treatise*, pp. 32, 33.
[2] To repeat yourself, to go back again over the road. Literally, to sing the road or journey again. Palinodia, a retracing of one's path.

yea, the reformed churches have and do practize the same. Here therfore I wish thee [the] reader to observe, that you Browinsts [Brownists] do not only condemne the Church of England but all the reformed churches whatsoever, and can be no other but Donatistes.[1]

J. G.   I trust your madnes will appeare to all men, the poyson of aspes is under your tongue;[2] he that cannot rule his tongue, his religion is in vayne.[3] Shall I in your heate be pressed with multitude of churches? Then heare what the Lorde saith. " Thou shalt not followe a multitude to do evill."[4] We have the worde amongst us; we shall by that worde be ether justified or condemned. Then ether prove your matter from the Scriptures, or els give eare to the Scripture. If those churches you speake of, bring men's writinges into the publique assemblies, and inforce them to be read for praying, I would see their warrant; we believe not because men say so, or do so, but because God speaketh; and where he speaketh, all men must be silent. You may accuse other countries as you will, I knowe not their estate, but your drudgery insteade of true worship, is loathsome; the priest with his masse-booke, and beggar with his clapdish,[5] canuize[6] over the *Pater Noster* for their bellie, which is your common worship, with other trinkets. We shall speake of a liturgie in due place. Here you breath out your accustomed lyes, sclanders, and railings. First you terme us Brownists and Donatists, wher as I never conversed with the men nor their writings. I detest Donatus his heresies. And if they had beene instruments to teach us anie truth, we were not therfore to be named with their name, we

---

1 *A Short Treatise*, p. 33.
2 Romans 3: 13.
3 James 1: 26.
4 Exodus 23: 2.
5 The dish, generally wooden, which was carried by lepers and beggars to give warning of their approach, and to collect alms.
6 Not given in this form in the *New English Dictionary*. Canter means to chant, to intone. Cant means to beg, to speak in the whining tone used by beggars ; to affect pietistic phraseology ; to use professional jargon insincerely. Perhaps the word is " canvas," one form of which is canvize. This carries the meaning — to beat, knock about, to bargain, deal with, discuss, debate.

were baptized into Christ's. Browne is a member of
your church, your brother, and all Brownists do fre-
quent your assemblies.[1]   And here you wish the reader
to consider, that I condemne all reformed churches.   Do
I condemne all churches for reproving a sinne by God's
worde ?   May not the true churches (if they were such)
err ?   Did I affirme at anie tyme that they were no
true church that used read prayers ?   Remember your
self, you knowe who is the father of such untruthes.   But
because your conscience bare you witnesse [that] you
had wrongfully chardged me, and for me, all true
Christians; you bring it in by necessary consequence,
thus.   *You* [Greenwood] *affirme* (say you) *prescript formes
of prayer brought into the publique assemblies to be the changing
the worke of the spirit into an idoll, a tradition breaking Christian
libertie, a deade letter quenching the spirit, etc., and therfore
most detestable.*[2]   *But all reformed churches receive and use
it, etc., therfore.*[3]   You can reason well to bring [18] the
truth into contempt, your mouth is open and tongue
whet as a sworde therunto.   If the proposition be true,
drawe what consequence you will, it is yours and not
myne; if the doctrine be true, it is God's worde that
giveth sentence against the sinne.   And if you have
anie sparke of grace, procure that we may decide the
truth with other churches.   Doth it follow that because
imposing of men's writings to be read for praying is an
heynous synne, therfore they that use it are no church ?
If I should say so, I should justlie be called an Anabaptist.
And here you accuse me to pleade for such a freedome
in the church, that nothing be receaved which is imposed by commaundement.   Abaddon[4] is the father of
such prophets.   Doth it follow that because we would
have the church free from all traditions of men, which
have no warrant in God's worde, that therfore we
would not receave God's ordinances by commaundement ?   That we ought to receave nothing by com-

---

[1] Robert Browne made his peace with the Archbishop on October 7, 1585,
and for the next forty-eight years remained with the Church of England,
outwardly conforming in part, but inwardly unconvinced.

[2] " Reasons against Read Prayer," no. 3, no. 5.

[3] *A Short Treatise*, pp. 33, 34, 36.

[4] Abaddon, " the angel of the bottomless pit ; his name in Hebrew is
Abaddon, and in Greek he is called Apollyon."   Revelation 9: 11.

maundement in the worship of God, which God hath not commaunded, the second commaundement with the Scriptures I have rehearsed, are evident. Deuteronomy 5: 32, 33. Matthew 15: 2, 3. Gallatians 4: 9. Collossians 2: 20. But seing your self graveled, considering all the world cannot lay a commandement to bring their owne inventions into the assemblies, wher God hath laide none, but forbidden it: you ranne to your former places of Scripture to wrast them as before, where your collections are but vayne repetitions of that which hath beene convinced before. *Moses, the prophets, etc., prescribed formes of prayers, therfore men now may thrust their writings into the publique assemblies*: Your argument is denied, and it here is no warrant for the reading them over for prayer.

G. G. *The church hath power to expounde those prayers mentioned in the Scriptures, and to apply them to their severall necessities, etc.*[1]

J. G. If you meane by expounding, the breaking up of them by doctrine, and by doctrine and prayer to aplye them to the severall uses of the church by lively voyce, far be it from me to think otherwise. But if you meane by expounding, to make homilies upon them, or liturgies by writing to be t[h]rust upon the publique assemblies, you are wide, and now justifie homilies instead of preaching, and written prayers instead of praying: shew your warrant; the churches' power is limited by the word.

G. G. *When the prayers be framed and composed of nothing but the doctrine of the Scriptures, and after the rules of* [19] *true prayer, nothing is brought in which God hath not commaunded.*[2]

[J. G.] This might have comen in before your raylings, but you sawe it was too silly; where is that commandement of God, that all men's writings in forme of prayer

[1] *A Short Treatise*, p. 35.
[2] *Ibid.*, p. 35.

agreable to the Scriptures should be brought into the publique assemblies? Your bare worde is not enough to put me to silence. And when you have gott them into the church, you must prove that God hath commaunded they should be read for prayer.

Where I said our saviour Christ never used the wordes when he praied, of that forme of prayer he gave to his disciples, nether commaunded his disciples to say over these wordes, nether do we reade that ever his apostles did use them, or enforced others to use anie certeine number of wordes; you say I speake untruelie. For, say you, the disciples desired him to teach them to pray, as John taught his disciples, and he commaunded them, when you pray, say, *Our Father, etc.*, Luke 11, and St. Mathew, an apostle, hath delivered the same to the whole church. I answer I have never heard that Jhon Baptist taught his disciples to say over certeyne wordes, nether can it be gathered by our saviour Christe's answere: for he answeared not alwaies their verie demaunde according to their wordes, but therupon tooke occasion to instruct them as he sawe neede. And I have proved by the 6. of Mathew that our saviour did not commaunde them to say over the very wordes when they prayd: for the word *houtos* in Mathew signifieth *after this maner*; againe that Mathew redcordeth [*sic*] not the very number, or the very same wordes that Luke doth. And now I reason thus: if Christ had commaunded those very wordes to be said over in praying, then we must alwaies when we pray, say over those wordes: for in Mathew 6. he sayth, when you pray, pray thus. *Our Father, etc.* The word *when* sheweth, that this commaundement is to be observed at all tymes; and then the apostles sinned in praying other wordes, Acts 4: 24, 25. Furder it being the most summary forme of prayer, most ample, most perfect, *etc.*, if those wordes were commaunded to be said over, then we ought not to use any others; for he is accursed that bringeth not the best offrings he hath. Malachi 1: 14. By all these it is evident that our saviour nor his evangelists tyed no man to the very wordes saying over; but according to that forme and those instructions; and now I leave of your popish dreames. Yet you would make men believe I reasoned thus, that the apostles did not, nether our saviour himself, nor anie that we reade of, use these wordes in prayer, therfore they did not use it. Nay, I said they did not use those verie wordes in their prayers, but used other wordes [20] according to their particular wants, as our saviour in the 17. of John is said to do; therfore he nether used nor commaunded others to say over those wordes. And so I may well conclude, that to impose certaine wordes to be read or said by roate for praying, upon the church, espeaciallie men's writings, is an intollerable pride, even a setting of men in the place of God; also to use them or bowe downe unto them in that order, is sinne, and breach of God's lawe.

Argument 4   J. G. *Because true prayer must be of faith, uttered with heart and lively voice. It is presumptious ignorance to bring a booke to speake for us unto God, etc.*[1]

Argument 5   *To worship the true God after an other maner than he hath taught, is idolatrie. But he commaundeth us to come unto him, heavie loaden with contrite heartes, to cry unto him for our wantes, etc.*[2] *Therfore we may not stand reading a dead letter, instead of powring fourth our petitions.*

Argument 6   *We must strive in praier with continuance, etc.*[3] *But we cannot strive in praier and be importunate with continuance, reading upon a booke. Therfore we must not reade when we should pray.*

G. G. *These three I joyned togeather as having no weight. You say I answeare by plaine contradiction without Scripture, etc. And afterwardes, is not my bare deniall as good as your bare affirmation? etc.*[4]

J. G. Stay your selves and wonder, they are blind and make blind. Is ther anie doctrine more spirituall, anie

[1] " Reasons against Read Prayer," no. 4.
[2] " Reasons against Read Prayer," no. 5.
[3] " Reasons against Read Prayer," no. 6.
[4] *A Short Treatise*, p. 36.

more inculcated by the Holy Ghost, than this accesse unto God in the mediation of Christ, by his owne spirit, to make our mindes knowne unto God, to offer up the fruits of his owne spirit in us, and fetch encrease from him by this secreat worke of true invocation with the heart and voice? This colloquie with the highe majestie of God, is it a matter of no weight to learne to discerne betweene diverse exercises [21] of the spirit, and to exercise his graces aright according to his will? Rightly is it said, the wisedome of God is foolishnes to the naturall man.[1] But Mr. Gifford will say he graunteth the propositions true and weightie matters, it is the assumptions that be so frivolous, and as he saith a litle after, ridiculous: well, let them be wayed. 1. That reading instead of praying is not a powring fourth of the heart by lively voice. 2. That it is a quenching of the spirit, to reade an other man's wordes upon a booke, in the very action of powring fourth our heart as we pretend. 3. That it is not an unburdening of a contrite heart by faith, but an ignorant action to reade for praying. 4. That we cannot strive in prayer, continue in prayer, be importunate, *etc.*, by reading upon a kooke [*sic*, booke]. These are the matters he thinketh of so litle weight: the bare deniall and contradiction wherof he holdeth of such credit, that it must suffice for answere, seing he saith he hath before proved the use of reading. See here he calleth it the use of reading: he could not say that reading is praying, nether that these two exercises of our faith can be used both in one instant, as one action. I have shewed that *proseuche* and *anagnosis*, praying and reading, are divers actions both of the minde and body; let the reader consider what weight then this matter is of, to talk with the lyving God.

But for the benefit of such as have grace to savour the things that are of God, I will a litle illustrate these assumptions, at least some of them. 1. That it is a quenching of the spirit to reade an other man's wordes upon a booke when I should powre fourth mine owne heart, the word it self must be considered; the apostle

---

[1] I Corinthians 2: 14. See also I Corinthians 1: 20, 21, 25.

commaundeth, saying, I Thessalonians 5: 19, " extinguish ye not the spirit." Now to suppresse and leave unuttered the passions of our owne heart by the worke of the spirit, giving us cause of prayer, and instead therof to reade an other man's writing, I doubt not wilbe founde and judged of all that have spirituall eyes to see, a quenching of that grace: yea, in that action, the reading hindreth us from pleading our cause with God, according to the occasions we see in our owne hearts. And by not teaching men to drawe out the graces of God in them, to offer up the sweete incense of his owne spirit in prayer, but an other course devised by fleshly pollicye, the people growe in such atheisme, that they learne not all the dayes of their life to lay open their owne soule before the Lord in prayer. How much more then, by imposing stinted wordes to be read in the whole assemblies insteade of the lively graces, making it a sufficient ministerie to reade over such beggarlie ware, do you abandon God's spirituall giftes, and make an assemblie of atheists in most places of this land; yea, in the best assemblies you compell such ware to be read, when and where the lively voyces of God's present graces should only be [22] drawen fourth, as an holie odour unto the Lorde. Yea, I appeale to the consciences of all that feare God, if this have not brought the land generally into atheisme, that not one amongst an hundred can call upon God. 2. That it is an ignorance to presume to come into so neere a conversing with God, and to do one action for an other, so offring the sacrifice of fooles, let it be sufficient proof that reading is not praying. That it is presumptious, to bring such lame sacrifices when you know to do better, let it be considered whether you would so uncircumspectly, and carelesly, approache to the presence of the prince or any noble personage. Then if he be our Lorde, where is his honour, his feare, *etc.*, when we will teach men and compell men to do they knowe not what in his sight, and to offer such lame sacrifice? The priests themselves care not what offring they bring him. Malachi 1. [3.] Thirdly, the reading praier can be at no hand a striving in praier: for the worde *agoniso*[1] which is read, Romans 15: 30, signifieth to contend in fervency both in minde and worde, to prevaile with God as Jaakob wrestled with the angell, and said, " I will not let thee go except thou blesse me." Genesis 32: 24, 25, 26. Such strift you shall see through out the psalmes in the prayers of David and the prophets; alas, howe this should be performed eyther in fervencie or contynuance, let the wise consider. 4. For importunacy and contynuance in prayer, wherof we have many precepts, let the worde be looked upon, which is *proscartereo*,[2] to insist by perseverance, *etc.*, as we see our saviour Christ make plaine unto us by a parable Luke 11: 5, 6, 7, 8 and Luke 18: 1, 2, 3, 5, 7. Now shall not God avendge his elect which crye night and day? Experience we see in Moses, who when he lifted up his handes to heaven, the Israelites so long pervayled. You can not make your read prayers serve in this use with all your devises. For how would you effect this, except to make the priest reade till he sweat againe, with vaine repetition, and the people that use such stinted prayers to say them often over, as the papists their fifteene *Ave Marias* and five *Pater Nosters* as a cure of all their grives [griefs]. By this litle I have spoken, it may appeare (though the Lorde knowes I am a man of uncircumcised lippes, nether able to utter that God giveth me by faith to see in these high thinges, nether yet comprehending anie title [tittle] of the excellency of them), yet I hope it shall appeare to God's children, how odious your marchandize is in God's eyes, and howe you make the ordinances of God of true praier, of none effect, by your traditions; he only approving the lively graces of his owne ministerie, and such as have giftes and are caled therunto, to be his mouth unto the people and the people's mouth unto him in the publique assemblies: you invent a newe worship and extinguish his, which maketh men fall into dissolutenes and bloudye tyrannie against his sainctes. And [23] where I alleadged that Paul would pray with

---

[1] Agonizō and agonizomai, strive, agonize.
[2] Proskartereō, persist obstinately in, adhere firmly.

the spirit and understanding, and therfore not upon a booke; you answere that Paul had no such neede of a booke as other men have. But if you had looked upon the text better, you should see, that the apostle in his owne person teacheth what ought to be donne in all churches and of all men; and that he there taketh away the abuse of spirituall giftes, 1 Corinthians 14: 15, and in the same chapter sheweth that this and all other his doctrines are commaundements of God, verse 37. Nowe ether God prescribeth two wayes to pray, or els your reading for praying is a devise of man. But your self have confessed there is no commaundement to reade praier for praying. Yet here you cavill with your stale shift, that Paul taught others to singe psalmes upon a booke, which is a meere evasion, seing singing is not praying. The same apostle saith to all that are borne of God. " Because we are sonnes, God hath sent fourth into our heartes the spirit of his sonne, which cryeth, Abba Father."[1] So that although we have not like measure of grace, yet if we cannot pray we have not the spirit of God. Galatians 4: 6.

I alleadged as you say a reason here why prayer read cannot be true prayer. In reading we fetch the matter from the booke which moveth the heart; in true prayer we fetch the matter from the heart which causeth the mouth to speake. Your answere is, that this is a most ridiculous vanitie; for tell me (say you) this, when we bring fourth in true prayer matter from the heart which causeth the mouth to speake, hath not the heart bene first moved with the worde of faith, *etc.* ?

Let men here witnesse with me, what cause I had to esteeme you as a skorner; againe, how emptie you are of anie spiritual souour [*sic*].[2] And here you have no answere to give, but aske me certaine questions. First, whether when we bring fourth in true prayer, *etc.*, the heart hath not beene first instructed. To this I answere, that againe you confesse the reading praier upon a booke is not praying, but an instruction of the heart to praye. If you would stand to this we should not

---

[1] Galatians 4: 6 and Romans 8: 15, 16.
[2] Probably " savour," but " favour " and " **honour** " are possibilities.

neede have so much labour, and all the places of Scripture which you have alleadged for to prove reading
praying, have beene meerly wrasted by you to deceave
the simple. Wel (say you), but if the heart be first
instructed before it can utter matter in praier, whie may
not the heart againe be moved with hearing or reading
the worde, and so utter praier. Yes, I graunt, and
still you graunt me, that reading is not praying but
moveth to prayer. Then all your assemblies that have
no prayer but reading prayers, have no prayer at all,
and all that use read prayer for praying do not praye
but mocke with God. See if your Ordinarie will [24]
here be pleased with you. Yet you would denie all
this with the same breath by a shifte, saying: the heart
is moved when one heareth the prayer of the minister,
and presently sendeth fourth prayers togeather with
him. I trust you will not say that the heart of the
hearer prayeth one thing, and the minister an other;
againe the praier of the minister is the praier of the
people, by God's ordinance: whiles they thinck one
thinge, and are mett to one end, for avoyding confusion one speaketh, yet al pray togeather one thing.
But the minister may as well preach and pray, or reade
anie chapter and praye, as reade praiers, and pray,
both in one action of the minde, and voyce, which
were strange. Your cavill, then, whether the heart
may be moved, and pray, both at once, is taken awaye,
seing you graunt reading and praying two severall
exercises of the heart and voyce, which cannot be performed at once with lively voyce. The conclusion is,
then, that ether ye must fetch the matter out of your
booke when you reade prayer, and so do not pray for
the particular wants wherwith the heart is moved and
pressed before you come, or els you pray not with lively
voyce at al, when you read. The Lorde then having
taught us to breake up our owne hearts, and powre
fourth our owne petitions with heart and voyce, gyve
grace to all his people so to worship him.

J.G. *We must pray as necessitie requireth.*[1] *But stinted*

---

[1] " Reasons against Read Prayer," no. 7.

John Greenwood

prayers cannot be as necessity requireth.   Therfore stinted praier is unlawfull.

G. G.   *To this I answered, approving the proposition.   And in the assumption I did distinguish of matters to be prayed for: as that there be thinges necessarie to be praied for at all tymes, and of all men: of these a prescript forme may be used at all meetings of the church.   There be matters not at all tymes needfull to be praied for, for such there can be no prescript forme to be used contynually, etc.*[1]

J. G.   I have proved in the first argument, that no men's writings are to be brought into the publique assemblies, for there the lively graces of God's owne spirit and canonicall Scriptures only must be heard.   In the seconde, the unlawfullnes of reading for praying; in the third, the unlawfullnes to impose any thing by com-maunde-[25]ment, that God hath not commaunded. And here we shall handle in few wordes the end of your stinted prayers.   Your distinction is far differing from the wisedome of the spirit, for though many thinges be at all tymes needfull to the publique assemblies, yet stand not the assemblies, ether all at any tyme, or anie at all tymes, in the same neede and feeling of them, or fitnes to receave them; so that except you can make all assemblies in the same want of such thinges as are al-waies needfull, or any at al tymes, in the same pre-parednes to aske, and use them that be needfull, you can make no stinted prayers for them.   Give eare then to the Scripture in this pointe 1. Corinthians 2: 11: " For what man knoweth the thinges of a man, if not the spirit of man which in himself, *etc.*"   Agayne, who knoweth what (shalbe) to morow[2] whiles you then thought to have founde out more than the only wise governour of his house sawe needfull for his worship in his church, and of evrie soule, you have lifted up your self into his seate, and taken the office of his spirite upon you, who searcheth the heartes and knoweth the reynes, and teacheth his people how and when to aske,

[1] *A Short Treatise*, p. 37.
[2] James 4: 13, 14.   Matthew 6: 34.

68

according to his will and their needs. Romans 8: 26, 27: " Also the spirit helpeth our infirmities, for what we should pray as we ought we know not. But the spirit if self maketh request for us with sighes and groanes which cannot be expressed." Yet searching the heartes knoweth the meaning of the spirit, because he maketh request for the saincts, according to the wil of God. And wher you say then, that if we marck the prescript forme of prayers of all churches, we shall see this regard, that nothing be left out which is necessarie, *etc.*[1] This bewrayeth your shallownes; the wisedome of the flesh is foolishnes with God: who hath searched the depth of God's spirit, or knowne the minde of man ? Who can prescribe the estate of all churches, and what every moment is needfull to be praied for ? Odious then is such drosse of a fleshly man's heart.

Your second provision, that nothing be prayed for in your liturgy that falleth seldom out, but they are limited to the time.[2] Your church hath not this provision; you compel men to pray against thunder and lightning at midd winter, and in your most solemne feastes against sodeine death: but the truth is, till you amend your wayes, God will accept no sacrifice of you, much lesse requireth this at your handes, to do more in his worship than he hath commaunded. And where you say in the Church of England the preachers are not limyted touching the matter of their praiers, it is not true; you are all sworne to your portuis,[3] howsoever you may omitt some of it for your sermons, and under pretext therof, what part you will. And why is ther not a forme for prayer prescribed, to be used after and before your sermons ? Is it because the text is not allwaies the same, or that the speaker is not in like fit-[26]nes, or the auditorie in the same preparednes ? I assure you these thinges might be sufficyent cause why you cannot use alwaies the same wordes, and pray according to your necessities; and even so standeth the case for all other affayres in the church. The dispo-

---

[1] *A Short Treatise*, p. 37.
[2] *Ibid.*
[3] The *Book of Common Prayer*.

John Greenwood

sition of the soule and the distresses therof, continue not
in one state one howre. But let me tell you whie you
have no forme of prayer for your preachings. In manie
of your parishes, or (as you would have them) churches,
sermons are of those rare thinges, wherof you saye ther
can be no prescript forme of prayer; yea, your liturgie
approveth a ministerie and sufficyent administration
without anie doctrine; which sheweth it came out of
the divell's fordge, and not out of Christe's Testament.

But seing you would take uppon you to set so manie
prescript formes of prayer, as ther is thinges necessarye
for everie assemblie to pray for, wher Christ hath set
none; and if it were a thing so necessarie to have prescript wordes at the administration of the sacraments, I
asked you whether our saviour Christ had not forgott
himself as you thought, that when he commaunded his
ministers to go preach and baptise, and shewed them
the wordes of institution, and the elementes to be used
with all things therunto needfull, he did not prescribe
some forme of wordes for prayer in particular. In the
tabernacle everie pinne was prescribed, so that ether
such formes of prayer are not necessarie, or Christe's
Testament hath some wants. To this you answere,
that it is not of necessitie ther should be a sett forme of
prayer prescribed for the administration of the sacraments. The minister may conteine [sic] prayer, etc.[1]
Hold you to this that it is not of necessitie: you will denie
it againe the next argument. Well, here you graunt,
it is not of necessitie; but you have not answered me,
till you tell me whether you hold it necessarie or no:
if it be at all times necessarie, the Testament is not
perfect. Againe, you do not hold it of necessitie, when
you excommunicate men, and depose your ministery
for not observing it. But you saye it is for conveni-
encye. If it be a part of God's worship, and all tymes
convenient, then is it necessarie, and if it be not necessarie, put such conveniency in your cornerd capp, or
surplus [surplice].

Nowe if it be necessarie at all times, [then] you must

[1] This is a misquoting or misprinting. Gifford wrote: " for the minister
may conceive the prayers at the administration of the sacraments "
(*A Short Treatise*, p. 38).

prove it is commaunded in God's worde, or els say that all thinges necessarie in God's worship be not conteyned in God's worde, which were blasphemous and papisticall to affirme. To this you graunt all things necessarie and convenient are conteyned, and aske if I be ignorant that ther be manie thinges conteyned in the Scriptures, that are not expressed in particulars, but be gathered from the generall rules. No, I am not ignorant of this: but if it may be gathered ether by expresse wordes, or by generall rule, that ther should be pre-[27]script formes of prayer for the administration of the sacraments, or anie other particular action of the church, then must it be so of necessitie, because God hath commaunded it, though not in particular, yet in generall rules: but you graunt it is not of necessitie, therfore it is not commaunded in particular, nor conteyned in anie generall rule. Yet you demaunde of me, if one should object that ther were not commaundement in the Scriptures, nor example for anie prayers to be made at all before preaching, *etc.* I would say he should lye against God, we have both. For the apostle sheweth it was the chief part of their office, to perdure [continue] in the worde and prayer. Acts 6: 14. 1 Corinthians 14 and 1. Timothy 2: 1. Acts 2: 42. Besides, all things are sanctified unto us by the word and praier. And because they never used doctrine in church, but prayer went before, their meetings is said to be unto prayer. Some things ther are, I graunt, that are not prescribed in particular, and yet are commaunded by generall doctrine, as baptisme of infants. But whatsoever is commaunded ether in particular or necessarie collections from generall rules, are of necessitie to be obeyed, as the commaundements of God, and may not be altered; but your particular formes of prescript wordes have no such warrant. Nowe seing you would have no prescript wordes of prayer for the minister to use before his preaching, nor of necessitie for the sacraments, and have none for excommunication, *etc.*, I wondred wherof your portuis is made, and wherto it should serve, except for churchings and burialls and such popery, wherby you leave the commaundements of God, to sett up your owne traditions. And herupon I demaunded wherupon you would make your stinted and sett prayers. You marveile I should be so babling and make such questions: you meane about your babling worship. You saye of the particulars of the Lorde's prayer. I demaunde nowe againe whether you can number the starres of heaven, or the sandes of the sea; if not, much lesse the particulars of the Lorde's prayer; there is medecine, and direction of praier for everie soule, and everie disease therof to be drawen fourth by doctrine and prayer as the need requireth: you would sett a liturgie upon some thinges, and compell men therunto everie meeting, which were nothing els but to seale up the fountaine, and send men to the drye pitts of your execrable devises, from the whole fountaine, to a pitcher of water, from the lively graces of doctrine and prayer, to your owne writinges. Paul commaunded to pray for kings and princes, yet bounde no man what wordes to use.[1] The Lord gyve you repentance of such presumptious sinne, as to alter his worship. If you cannot knowe the estate of the soule before hand, you can make no formes of wordes for it. [28]

J. G. *Read praiers were devised by antichrist, and maintaine superstition and an idoll ministery;[2] therfore read praiers and such stinted service are intollerable, etc.*

G. G. *Antichrist devised manie blasphemous wicked praiers. But to say that the reading or following a prescript forme of praier was his, is most false. For there were liturgies in the church of olde, before antichrist was set in his throne, etc.[3]*

J. G. The Scripture never inforced to reade praiers for praying, nether stinted us what, or howe manie wordes to use, nether is the formes of prayer prescribed in the Scripture, anie devise of man. Let us then hold these two to be the matters in hand; the one, reading insteade of praying, the other, stinting and limiting by

---

[1] I Timothy 2: 1, 2.
[2] " Reasons against Read Prayer," no. 8.
[3] *A Short Treatise*, p. 39.

a written liturgie, what and howe manie wordes to pray, with all other such prescriptions as your liturgie conteyneth. All may be affirmed antichristian, which is not warranted by Christe's worde. Yet your liturgie is even from that antichrist lifted up into the throne you speake of, as may of all men be seene that will compare it with the portuis. And (as I have heard) the pope would have approved of your liturgie, if it might have bene receaved in his name. Nowe we have proved in the discourse before,[1] that reading for praying hath no warrant from God's worde, which maketh them two severall and divers actions every where. Here then we must consider something for an other liturgie than Christe's Testament, which we shall find to be nothing els, than an other gospell. And because Mr. Gifford saith ther were liturgies in the church before antichrist was lifted up into his throne (which I will not denye), I would have all men understand that I do not go about to prove the church no church that hath a liturgie (as mine arguments are falselie wrested to that purpose) but to prove the unlawfullnes of such liturgies thrust upon men's consciences, is onlie my determination through God's assistance. The worde *leitourgia* signifieth *publicum munus, ergon laon,*[2] the worck of, or for the people: that is the very execution of the ministeriall actions in the church, according to the worde of all the officers therof, that is the practise of those ministeriall duties prescribed by Christ, we may every where reade. In the first of the gospell of Luke the 23. verse, it is said. "And it came to passe that when the daies of his ministration were past he went home to his house," meaning Zacharias; where we see the worde *leitourgias* for his execution of his ministeriall function. Now this *leitourgia* of the Newe Testament, [29] is even the rules and function prescribed by Christ, for the publique actions to be donne in his church: which leiturgie of Christ is perfect, and he pronounced accursed that

---

[1] See "Reasons against Read Prayer" and especially the "Reply to George Gifford."

[2] *Publicum munus,* a public office or duty; "ergon laon" is the Greek equivalent. Liturgus, or o leitourgos, one that fills a public office; a servant of the state.

addeth any thing therto, or taketh & [&c.][1] any there-from: yea, all men are bounde to keepe the true patterne therof, without alteration or innovating anie part of the same; it is called a commaundement to be kept without spott, till the appearing of our Lorde Jesus Christ. Nowe, to make other leiturgie, is to lay an other foundation, and to make an other gospell, not that ther is an other gospell, but that ther are some willing to pervert the gospell of Christ. Then your leiturgies to which you are sworne, and by which you administer, being (as you cannot denie) an other liturgie than Christe's Testament, is plaine an other gospell; for the canons and rules you prescribe and impose are such, as he hath not prescribed or commaunded; or at the best, a trans-forming of his ordinances. Now if you should say, you do nothing but make lawes of particular thinges collected from the Scriptures, and with that collour impose your liturgies, we have shewed the unlawfullnes of bringing anie man's writinges, as rules into the church. For the explaning of the whole will of Christ, so far as is meet for us, he hath given us his officers to administer, according to his lyturgie by lively voyce, and due execution of all things by one rule. Making then a newe *litourgia*, you must also make a newe ministerie, for Christe's ministerie cannot administer after a counterfeit liturgie. And that antichrist was the cheif innovator of this liturgie (howsoever the thing might be long a working by litle and litle), it is plaine when he is called antikeimenos, that opposite man, or layer of an other foundation.[2] Now we must not make all liturgies beside the Testament, of like wickednes or blasphemie; but how neere the most heynousest yours approach, let him that answereth the other part of your booke witnesse unto me.[3] Nowe where I said you had confessed that you never read in the Scriptures any warrant to reade prayers unto God, you say now, I knowe I have falsified your wordes. Surely it would

[1] Revelation 22: 19. Deuteronomy 4: 2. Proverbs 30: 6.
[2] See Exodus 23: 22 ; Isaiah 66: 6. Enemy or adversary.
[3] Barrow replied to pp. 1-17 and 47-110 of *A Short Treatise* ; Greenwood confined himself to the first part of Gifford's book, which pertained to prayer, pp. 17-46.

be knowen, for I would not willinglie so do, your wordes you say were these, to your remembrance: *God never commaunded a man to reade praier upon the booke*.[1] Is not this the same that I saye: *you confess ther is no warrant for reading praier*, is ther anie thing warranted in his worship, that he hath not commaunded? Then you aske me if I wil gather thus, it is not expreslie commaunded, therfore it is not warranted. No, you forgot the worde *expreslie*, to help your self to saye and unsaye. I gathered, that because you said absolutely it was not commaunded, therfore it was not warranted. Here you come againe to shewe your ignorance in the Scriptures, to say ther is not anie expresse commaundement to use praier before or after doctrine. [30] And remember you here will have it a commaundement, and said before you hold it not of necessitie.

G. G.   *There would sundry inconveniences growe for want of a lyturgie, or prescript formes of publique praiers.*[2]

J. G.   Still I must put you in minde of the wisedome of that governour of his house, the builder, beginner, and finisher of our faith, Christ Jesus: he foresawe what inconvenience would have growne if either men or angells should make newe liturgies, or other formes of prayer, than he hath prescribed, for the publique assemblies. Here therfore you deeply chardge him, not to have donne all thinges that were needfull, in not prescribing you more formes than he hath donne, or not suffred learned divines to impose their owne writinges upon publique assemblies, as rules for the church, and worship unto God. But see what the Scripture saith; "who hath knowen the mynde of the Lord, that he might instruct him." Againe, "wher is the wise, where the scribe, where the disputer of this worlde?"[3] Hath not God made the wisedome of this world foolishnes? To put you out of doubt, then, that we neede not any newe liturgie, nor anie men's writings to be brought into the publique assemblies, the Holie Ghost saith,

[1] *A Short Treatise*, p. 40.
[2] *Ibid.*
[3] Romans 11: 34.   I Corinthians 1: 20.

2. Timothy 3: 16. " The whole Scripture is *theopneustos,* inspired of God, and profitable unto doctrine, unto improof,[1] unto correction, unto erudition which [is] in righteousnes; that the man of God may be perfect, absolute, perfect unto everie good worke." Nowe if onlye the Scriptures be *theopneustos,* and sufficient to make God's children absolutely perfect, what blasphemie is it to say, sundrie inconveniences would growe, if men's writinges wer not imposed upon the publique assemblies. And in this your wisedome, let us see what is the chiefest inconveniency that would growe. You say everie franticke spirit (of which sorte ther be manie in the ministerie) would not only be unlike themselves, but varye from others. I answered, and still do, that the papists have not so weake a reason for their idolatrous liturgies, rubricks, and canons. You say it appeareth by all my arguments, how meete a man I am to judge the weight of reasons alleadged by the papists, and others; well, I am weake, and you strong, [I am] foolish, and you wise; yet might you have shewed me a weaker reason, which they alleadge for their constitutions ecclesiasticall, as they call them. But my chief answer was (wherby you might have beene satisfied) that if it were but in phrases the ministerie should differ, it is no sufficient cause to ordeine liturgies. And if they offend in matter of doctrine or conversation, the censure of the church should help that. The first you graunt, the second also you confesse, that the church should censure such thinges. But you say ther are sundrie other differences [31] in administration of publique praiers and sacraments, as in order and ceremonies, which the church is to have regard of, and not to leave arbitrarie. All other ceremonies in God's worship than [except those which] Christ and his apostles have prescribed us, are diabolicall, and not apostolical. Then, for all thinges donne in the church in those publique actions, the offenders must be admonished, if they transgresse the rules of the word. And for the orders you speake of, you meane circumstances of time, place, kneeling, sitting, standing, *etc.*, of them ther can be no

---

[1] Obsolete form. Rebuke, reproof, censure.

furder lawes, than Christ hath prescribed, that all things
be donne to edifying, in comelynes and decency, *etc.*,
of these to set particular lawes, were to breake the lawe
of God, which leaveth them in the churche's liberty,
as neede requireth, to the glorie of God.   In these
thinges to do anie thing contrarie to the generall rules
of order, edifying, decencye, *etc.*, the transgressour is
by those rules to be instructed, admonished, and censured.   Well, here you have made a faire hand, to
make read prayers but a matter of order, which is all
the worship you have; to bring in men's writings into
the publique assemblies, to make them ether rules to
bind the conscience, and so put them in the place of
God's booke, or to reade them over for praying, is but
a matter of order; well, then, put them in your cornerd
capp, we have enough rules for the ordering of Christ's
spouse, without such Babilonish ware.   Here you say
mine experience is not so great as my boldnes.[1]   I passe
not to be judged of you, it is not like that the enchaunters
of Egipt should knowe the beautye of Sion; ther is a
cloude betweene you and us; we have (blessed be our
God) a pillar of fire before us.   An other fault you say
in my former reason, is, that because the censure of the
church should redresse defaultes, therfore ther needeth
no liturgie.[2]   Naye, take all with you; *no fault can be
censured that is not a transgression against the rules of God's
worde, and those to be censured by the doctrine and admonitions
of the church, therfore we neede no leiturgies.*   To the worde
of God only, ought all men to be bounde by covenant,
and for the transgressions therof only, to be censured.

G. G.   *The church hath this power, to ordeine according to
God's worde, and to appointe such orders in matters of circumstance, etc., as shall most fitly serve to edification.   And then
these orders being established, the church is to drive men to the
observation of them.*[3]

J. G.   First, in this your papisticall mudde, I must tell

[1] *A Short Treatise*, p. 40.
[2] *Ibid.*
[3] *Ibid.*, p. 41.

you, your reading of men's writinges for prayer, is a false worshipp of God, and not a matter of circumstance. And for matters of order and circumstance, which are no part of the worship, ther can be no [32] other lawes made of them, them [*sic*, than] Christ hath made. And for ordeyning of lawes in the church, is to plead for unwritten verities, and to make the lawe of God unsufficient; nether can it be according to the worde, to make anie lawe, that God hath not made, but an adding to his worde, which is execrable pride; these your wordes then (*according to God's worde*) was but a cloake to cover the grossnes of your position: for the worde, ordeyne, or create lawes, is to make some, that are not made before; let us then se your cleane sentence to be this. *The church hath aucthority in matters of order and circumstance to make and ordeine lawes in his church, for his worship*:[1] nowe see how you contradict these Scriptures: Revelation 22: 18, 19; Proverbs 30: 5, 6, " everie worde of God is pure, *etc.*," " put nothing to his worde least he reproove thee and thou be founde a liar." Likewise Deuteronomy 4: 2 and 12: 32 and Galatians 3: 15: " though it be but a man's conuenant [covenant], when it is confirmed, no man doth abrogate it, or superordeine anie thing to it." And the second commaundement forbiddeth anie such humane tradition in the worship of God; all the pope's trinckets might be brought in by the same grounde. We would willingly have seene your warrant for this doctrine, your bare worde is not sufficient to impose other lawes than God hath made, upon his church. This is the foundation of poperie and Anabaptistrie, to give libertie to make lawes in the worship of God; yet you will go furder, that such lawes being ordeyned and established by publique auctoritye, the discipline and censures of the church are to drive men to the obseruation of the same. By your judgment our saviour Christ was an Anabaptisticall schismatique, that would not himself, nor his disciples, obey and oberve the traditions of the elders. And what saith he unto pleaders for traditions? It is thus written, Marke 7: 5

[1] *Ibid.*

[7: 5-7]: " then asked him the Pharises and the Scribes, whie walk not thy disciples according to the tradition of the elders, but eate meate with unwashed hands. Then he answeared, surely Isay hath prophesied well of you hipocrites, as it is written, this people honoreth me with their lippes but their heartes are far from me. But they worship me in vayne, teaching [for] doctrines men's precepts. For you lay the commaundement of God aside and observe the tradition of men." And to helpe fourth your evill matter, instead of proof from the Scripture, you fall out into furious exclamation against them that desire only to have the worde practized: saying, who is able to imagine the innumerable divisions and offences in the practize of your Anabaptisticall freedome, in which you deny the church to have power to ordeine and impose any orders?[1] Let all men judge the venemousenes of this tongue; Christ pronounceth them accursed that add or superordeyne any thing to his worde, and you pronounce judgment of them, that only obey his worde. Shall it be said that Mr. Gifford holdeth, that the only practize of God's worde, would be the cause of innumerable divisions and offences? This hath bene Satan's old accusation in the mouth of the most enimies of Christ's gospell; [33] nowe yt must be Mr. Gifford's accusation of God's ordinances, to be insufficient, unperfect, *etc.*, fearfull in his apostacy from that truth he hath knowen. I take it, it is more like to be Anabaptistry, to practize any thing without warrant of the word, to make their owne devises, lawes, in God's worship, than to do nothing but what God hath commaunded, within the limites of our callings. For the franticke ministery, it came of your owne wordes, that therfore you must needes have a liturgie, because ther are manie frantick spirits in the ministerie; then I say, is it like [probable] you have a frantick ministerie, that cannot be governed without an other liturgie than Christ's Testament. For their great giftes you speake of, I will not compare with them, I am content to knowe nothing, if not Christ crucified. My reason [is taken]

1 *Ibid.*

from the Colossians, that as the church there is commaunded to admonish their pastor Archippus, if he
transgressed, and to stirr him up to his busines,[1] so all
ministers that caused divisions, contrary to the doctrine
of Christ, were to be admonished, and avoyded, if they
repent not; so that the worde of God, and admonition
by the same, if they transgressed, is the waye to keepe
all men in due order, and not imposing liturgies upon
the church, besides Christ's Testament. And where
you collected thus, that if read praiers and imposed
liturgies be idolatrous, then wher will you finde a visible
church, say you. I answered that the true church
might erre, even in this poynte, though not in like
heigh[t] of sinne. Then you desire, that the churches
of England may find like favour at our hand; to which
I answeare, that let him[2] that handleth that question
with you, shew you, how your sinnes herein exceede
other countries, and persequut [*sic*] such as reprove you.
Your church (as you call it) cannot pleade ignorance.
Your rayling speaches, of blind schismatiques, Donatists, *etc.*, bewray what sweet water is in the heart: if
you cannot prove your church to be the established
church of Christ, they light all upon your self. Ther
are none schismatiques, but such as departe from the
faith; shew wherin we have transgressed, and will not
be reformed. In the meane tyme you are schismatiques
from Christ, in that you practize the statutes of Omry.[3]
You chardge us with pride, for that (you saye) we
imagine to knowe more than all the churches uppon
earth.[4] This also hath bene Satan's old weapon to
deface the truth, Jeremiah 18: 18. Why maye not a
simple babe in Christ see that, which whole nations have
not seene? We cannot but speake the things God's
worde teacheth us; if we speake trueth, you need not
oppose that we judge anie man, it is the worde of God
shall judge us all; and I saye, it is an old popish argument to reason thus (*all churches do such a thing, therfore
it is lawfull*), except you hold with the pope, that the

---

[1] Colossians 4: 17.
[2] Henry Barrow, in *A Plaine Refutation*.
[3] I Kings 16: 16-28. Micah 6: 16.
[4] See the preface of *A Short Treatise*.

church cannot erre, which were blasphemous. You are not well [34] pleased that I will not say it is no church that hath a liturgie imposed upon it; and because you have so often sclandered me, that I hold it so, you take great paynes to conclude it. I have said that to impose men's writings, to be read in stead insteade [*sic*] of praying, is to worship God after a false maner, that it is a devise of antichrist, a deade letter, quenching the spirit, stinting the spirit, not of faith, idolatrous, a changing the worke of the spirit into an idoll, breaking our christian libertye, and so most detestable. By these speaches I condemne all churches, say you: this is not true, I condemne but the sinne. But you have sayd I deny that to be the church, that hath any thing ymposed. I say you speake an open untrueth and remember the judgment of him that inventeth and maketh lyes. And God give you grace to repent, if you belong to him. The consideration of this our discourse, I hartelie commende to be dulie and uprightly wayed, of all that feare God, who graunt us his grace to forsake any sinne, where it shalbe shewed us, by how weake instruments soever it be reproved, and pardon me all my defaults, in this my hastie answere. Thus have we seene the unlawfullnes of thrusting men's writings upon publique assemblies, and reading, instead of praying.

J. G.   *The praiers of such ministers and people, as stand under a false government, are not acceptable, not only because they aske amisse, but because they keepe not his commaundements.*[1]

The praiers of such ministers and people as be subject to antichrist are abhominable.

Those ministers and people which stand subject to the bishops and their courts, are subject to antichrist, etc.   Therfore their praiers, etc.

I. G.   *These do concerne the third and fourth accusation, and* [G. G.]   *therfore the answere is included in the answere to them.   Yet I take exception against the first; that the church may be holden by force from executing God's commaundemen[t]s*

1 " Reasons against Read Prayer," no. 9.

touching externall government, and yet be the true church of
God. And for example, I alleadged the church that was
holden captive in Babilon, etc.

[35] Here, after your acustomed maner, you offer me
great wronge: first, insteade of answere, you alter the
question very subtilye; then you dismember my former
answere; and not only so, but you have nether let my
former answere be answered, nor prynted. Thus you
alter the question, and answere not; where the proposition speaketh of a ministerie and people standing
under a false government, you say the church may be
holden by force, from executing God's commandements
in externall governement, wherof I never doubted: what
is this then, but to deceave your reader, both to judge
sinisterlie of me, and be drawen from the truth himself.
But indeed you meane not this (*holden by force*) of civile
bondage or persequution, for then ther were no difference betweene us, and myne argument should stand
untouched. You affirme then that the church may stand
under a false government, inforced therunto by the
tyranny of the ennemie, and yet in that estate be the
true apparant church, by open profession; which is
nothing els, than that the church may professe Christ-
ianisme and Antichristianisme, both at a tyme; subject
in minde to Christ, and subject to antichrist in outwarde
obedience. That you holde this doctrine in this place,
the processe of your matter proveth; and to make
all plaine, your wordes in the last writing (which here
you summe up) were these. *But if the church at any tyme*
be by mayne force restrayned from some priviledges, or have
some governement set over it, which agreeth not with God's
worde, which is [it] cannot avoide, etc.[1] See nowe howe
smoothly this man hath put awaye the crosse of Christ,
by teaching men to stand under a government, contrarye to Christe's. I thought the ordinances of the
Newe Testament had beene a kingdome that could not
be shaken, Hebrews 12: [28], that none could have beene
a member of Christ, that receaveth the marcke of the

---

[1] *A Short Treatise*, p. 44. These words are summarized from Gifford's
previous manuscript reply, written about December, 1587.

beast, though it be but in his hand, or could be holden a member of Christ, by outward profession; that here had beene the patience of the saincts, to suffer unto death, rather than to bowe downe, either in minde or bodie to an other government, than Christ's. How is he a Lorde to them that are not governed by him? Well, I needed not have stand upon this doctrine, but that he nether prynted my former answere, nor answered in these poyntes, and myne owne copie taken from me by the bishops: so that this man may retract what he will, and accuse as please him: if he have anie common honestie, let my former answere be seene.[1] But to prove the church may be subject to an other governement than Christ's, which is even to say, that a man may gyve all allegeance by outward practize to the kinge of Spaigne, and yet be her majestie's true subject; he saith, *the church was holden captive in Babilon,* where he as conningly hideth himself as before; though in my last writing I urdged him to answere, [36] whether the church in Babilon was subject to their idolatrie, or no. To the civile power I doubt not they were: but if the priestes and Levites stood priests to the idolatrous worship in Babilon, whether the people of Israell bowed downe to the outward practise and obedience of their idolatrie, or no; then, if they did so, whether they stoode by profession the children of God, or apostatate in that estate. None of these thinges have you answeared me. Let the examples of Hanania, Michaell, and Azaria testifie, Daniel 3: [1-30].[2] The people that retourned repented their transgressions, wher they had any of them sinned, and made a new covenant with the Lorde, before they were receaved, Ezra 9: 14, 15; and 10 *caput,* 2, 3, 8. Yea, the voyce of God was this, " come out of

---

[1] Greenwood's first manuscript fell into Gifford's possession, perhaps about November, 1587. See " Reasons against Read Prayer." But Greenwood's " Reply to George Gifford," which we have only in Gifford's summarized form, is referred to here. Greenwood's own copy was confiscated by the bishops, either at one of his examinations or in his prison cell by a warden. Barrow and Greenwood suffered periodic riflings of their prison possessions.

[2] Hananiah was renamed Shadrach, Mishael was called Meshach, and Azariah became Abed-nego, after the Babylonion king, Nebuchadnezzar, had defeated Jehoiakim, king of Judah, in the year 605 B.C. See Daniel 1: 1-7. See also Edwin Thiele, *The Mysterious Numbers of the Hebrew Kings,* pp. 159 f.

her, my people, and touche no uncleane thing and
I wilbe your God." " We are before thee " (saith
Ezra) " in our trespass, and we cannot stand before
thee because of it."[1] You never renounced your antichristian ministerie, you never made newe covenant
since the deepe defection of poperye, but still minister
in that kingdome, and wil not repent, yet boast your
selves to be the church of God, cryinge out, the temple,
the temple. I answeare then directlie, that whiles you
stand subject unto, and practize and communicate with
other orders and governments, than Christe's, you are
not by outwarde profession the churches of Christ. I
may not with you omitt the worde (willfull) because
you persequute the light, and so much higher is your
sinne.

Here I must forwarne the reader, with diligence to
consider Mr. Gifford's disagreement and mine; he
having accused me of a fundamentall heresie (as he
calleth it), wheras he himself still maintayneth most
grosse errors; wherof I reproved him, yet he persisteth;
namely, that the regenerate man may be said to stand
in bondage to sinne, by reason of the corruption of the
fleshe that is in us, and of our unperfectnes in this life.
Then that one standing in outwarde bondage to open
knowen sinne, may in that estate be accompted and
communicated with, as the servant of Christ, by outward profession, both at one instant: which is asmuch
to say, we may be to man's sight, the servaunt of the
devill, and the servaunt of Christ, both at one tyme, by
outward profession; so none should be excommunicate,
none be without, the world and the church, light and
darcknes, Christ and Belial, should be mingled togeather.

The heresie wherof, he most unjustly and untruly
proclaymeth to be mainteyned by us, is, that the regenerate man consenteth not to sinne, after regeneration, although in the last writinge I testified the contrary;[2] namely, that the whole church might erre,

---

[1] Isaiah 52: 11, 12. II Corinthians 6: 17. Ezra 9: 15.
[2] Eternal security is a doctrine that a truly regenerate person cannot sin
and fall from grace. Gifford charged the Barrowists with the heresy of
perfectionism.

might committ some kinde of idolatrie, that no man
was free from committing sinne, *etc*. And now I testifie
to all the world, that I was never infected with anie
such Anabaptistry, but have everie where resisted such
damnable heresie. I have learned and taught manie
degrees of sinne, [37] and differences of transgressions,
which the deare children of God fall into, after regeneration, in thought, word, and deed, of ignorance, of
knowledge, of presumption, slippes, transgressions, and
obstinate sinne; yea, that ther is no sinne, except the
sinne against the Holy Ghost, but God's children, may
committ it after regeneration, and be renued by repentance, which we ought to pray for in all sinners, but
that one sinne except. Not that men should hereupon
take boldnes to sinne, because God giveth repentance
to his elect, wherin the riches of his mercy appeareth;
but rather serve him in trembling and feare, as a jealous
God, least with Esaw we find no place to repentance,
though we seeke it with teares. Againe, though in
God's sight, his elected are never forsaken utterlie, nor
the Holy Ghost utterly extinguished in the regenerate,
yet to man's judgment he that committeth open knowen
sinne, and persisteth obstinatly in the same, cannot be
held the child of God to us, by outward profession, but
must be cutt off, Nombers 15, Mathew 18, and 1.
Corinthians 5, till they repent. Much more none that
stand open professed members of the false church,
subject by the least outward bowing downe to this
antichristian hierarchie, and so contynuing in bondage
to a false government, can be holden of us the true
professors of Christ's gospell. Now let us peruse the
severall doctrines. Mr. Gifford affirmeth, that the true
church might stand in bondage to a false government,
yet in that estate be holden, and communicated with,
as the true church, by outward profession: his wordes
in waye of proof, be these. They may with St. Paule
say, it is no longer I that do it, but sinne that dwelleth
in me: for if the yoake wherwith he was held captive in
part, could not take from him, but that he was the
Lorde's free servant, it is no reason that some outwarde
bondage should make the church not to be the spouse

D

of Christ.[1]   If a man commaund his wife (saith he) to do a thinge, and ther be violent force to withhold her, shee is not to be blamed. Romans 7. Mine answere to this he durst not print, but perverteth my wordes, so manie as pleaseth him; nether can I yet come by a copie of my former writing,[2] to shew, what I then replyed. Now consider what government is, and what bondage is, and then behold the wickednes of this man: spirituall government is that soevereigntie, dominion, and regiment that Christ Jesus, by his spirit, lawes, ordinances, and officers, exerciseth in, and over hys church, as it is written. " And thou Bethleem Juda art not the least among the princes of Juda, for out of thee shall come a governour that shall governe my people Israell." Agayne, " thy scepter is an everlasting scepter." " I have set my king upon Syon my holy mountaine." Mathew 2: 9.[3] Psalms 2. and Psalms 110. These lawes and ordinances wherby this kinge raigneth, are caled " a kingdome that cannot be shaken," Hebrews 12: [28]. They that have not him to reigne over them, are by outward profession none of his. " If I be your lord, where is my honor? "[4] [38] Againe, " those myne enimies which would not that I should reigne over them, bring hether [hither], and slay them before me." Luke 19: 27. Bondage or servitude is to be at commaundement, and to yeild obedience in subjection. Now to be in outward bondage to an other outward government, other lawes, officers, and ordinances than Christ's, is to be by outward subjection servantes of antichrist, which layeth an other foundation: for by outward profession we cannot stand (to man's judgment) professed subjects to two kings at enimitye, but we must be an enimie to the one, and so esteemed of all men, much lesse members unto two divers heades.

This then is mine answere here. 1. That it is an

---

[1] *A Short Treatise*, p. 46. Romans 7: 1-25.
[2] This seems to imply that there was one main copy circulating, which Gifford effectively stopped, but the statement is ambiguous.
[3] These Scripture references should be Matthew 2: 6, Psalms 45: 6 or Hebrews 1: 8, and Psalms 2: 6.
[4] Malachi 1: 6.

heresie to say, a man may stand in bondage to open
knowen sinne, and the free servaunt of Christ to us by
outward profession, both at one instant. 2. That it
is a falsifying of the Scripture, to say, that St. Paul (in
the 7. to the Romanes) was in bondage to sinne, when
he, in the inner man resisted sinne, and daylie prevailed
against the sinne, which his flesh would have led him
captive in, if there had beene a stronger power to overcome that enimie: for he ther reasoneth of the benefite
of the lawe, to manifest our sinne, and our conquest
over sinne by daylie repentance, and reproving of sinne
in our selves, fighting against sinne, victory over sinne,
thoughe it contynuallie rebell. 3. How blasphemous
were it to contynue in knowen sinne in bondage to it,
and to say it is sinne that dwelleth in us, and not we,
and so still to blesse our selves without amendement.
O horrible pervertinge of the Scriptures to men's
destruction. 2 Peter 3: 16. 4. That ther is no argument to be drawen, nor consequence to followe, from
the reliques of sinne, and corruption of the fleshe in
one man, or the whole church, and a professed bondage
to a false government, no, not betweene the open committing of sinne in the whole church, or some members
therof, and a professed homage and subjection unto a
false government; we cannot be partakers with the false
church and true, at no hand. 1 Corinthians 10: 21.
Lastlie, that the subjection to an other government, is
as a wife that committeth adulterie. Hosea 2. I then
reason thus on the contrary with you: any man that
after regeneration committeth open knowen sinne, and
contynueth obstinate, as a bond servaunt therunto,
standeth not the professed servaunt of Christ, but of
synne, Ezechiell 18, till he repent; so the whole church,
that persisteth in open knowen sinne, and persequuteth
the messengers that reprove the same. Then as everie
member of the false church standeth a professed servaunt of sinne, so the whole assemblies that stand professed subjects of false government; no censures of admonition belonging unto them, but calling of them to
repentance and seperation from the false church. Then,
as the wife that giveth herself to be one [39] with an

other man, is an adulteresse, Romans 7: 3, so that
church that subjecteth herself to an other government,
ordinances, and lawes than Christ's, is an harlot. Now
lett all men say, whether I had not just cause to say,
you spake like a carnall libertine, and an athiest; yea
nowe, as one having his conscience seared, to affirme,
that the church, remayninge in open knowne bondage
to a false government, may saye as Paul said, " it is not
I that sinne."[1]   And that contynuing in that adulterie,
she is the spouse of Christ by outward profession.   You
would saye it were a false argument, to say, the church
hath manie imperfections, ignorances, transgressions,
etc., therfore standeth in bondage to sinne, nay, standeth
in bondage to an other heade, and an other government
than Christ's; even so, to saye the church doth sinne,
therfore may contynue in bondage to sinne, is false
doctrine; nay, to say it may stand in open professed
subjection to antichrist, and be esteemed the church of
Christ by outward profession in that estate, as damnable doctrine.

It is the flat contradiction of all the rules of the
Scripture, to say, a man may stand in bondage to
sinne, and the free servaunt of Christ by outward profession, by man's judgment, at one tyme, seing the
obstinate offenders are to be cast out the assemblie;
but nowe, though the regenerate may fall into these
high sinnes, and contynue in their synne a long time,
yea, manie yeares deprived of God's grace, to man's
seeming, and to us is the servant of Satan for anie thing
wee see, yet the spirit of God is never utterlie extinguished or departed, after regeneration, but will recover
the man againe, and bring him to repentance, as David
after a whole yeare; for the stronge man once displaced
and cast out by a stronger than he, the spirit never
utterly departeth againe, for then it were impossible
that man should be renewed, Mathew 12: 31; Hebrews
10: 26 and 6: 4.   And hereupon I might say, Paul
never contynued captive in sinne, but was alwaies
renewed by repentance.   Furder, this spirit of God (the
sparkes wherof were never quenched utterlie) did not,

[1] Romans 7: 17.

nor could not consent or give place unto sinne; for here is the enimitye and battell betweene the spirite and the flesh, everie where spoken of, Galatians 5: 16, 17; Romans 7. May I not now say then, that Paul never contynued captive unto sinne, nor consented unto sinne concerninge inner man or gave place unto sinne in that place mentioned, without heresie; and still reprove you, that when Paul reasoneth of the old man, or corruption in him, you will conclude it of the new man, or inner man, and of the whole man, when you see evidently, he opposeth the one against the other? For whiles the spirit striveth against sinne and raigneth in us, thoughe the fleshe rebell, and cause us to sinne seaven times a daye, yet are we not overcome of sinne, so to remayne in bondage to sinne, that it should contynue to [40] reigne in us; as you may see in the same chapter, Romans 7: 5, 6, where you alleage then, that Paul saw a lawe in his members, which did lead him captive unto sinne, you do falsifie the text: for he saith, " leading me captive," and not " did leade," *etc.*, for ther was a stronger man, or a stronger than man, that suffered not the lawe of his members to reigne; for, saith he: " I my self in my minde serve the law of God, but in the flesh the law of sinne," so that the whole man could not be said to serve sinne. But (say you) afterward as concerning then the inner man we may [be] said to serve the lawe of God, and therupon be called the free servantes of Christ, notwithstanding this corruption of sinne in the fleshe: so the whole man by reason of our imperfectnes may be said to be the servants [*sic*] of sinne. No, it is not true, for the whole man is called after the part that hath greater rule in us; as if the fleshe rule in us, we are the servaunts of sinne, and ledd by Satan at his pleasure; but if the spirit rule in us, we are the servauntes of God, sonnes of God, sainctes of God, citizens of Jerusalem, holie and free people, kinges, and priests: not that we are perfect, or sinne not, but that sinne reygneth not in us, but the spirit, wherby we suppresse sinne, reprove sinne, strive against sinne, subdue sinne; and though we fall seven times, yet we rise againe by repentance, and serve not sinne. Rightly therfore did I saye, that no man can serve two masters, for his servantes we are to whom we gyve our selves as servants to obey, whether it be of sinne, unto death, or of obedience, unto righteousnes, Romans 6: 16, 18, being made free from sinne, we are made the servantes of righteousnes. So that the regenerat man, or he that is by outward profession the servant of Christ, cannot be called the servant of sinne, by reason of the corruption of the old man, and dregges of sinne, neither can he that standeth in bondage to anie sinne, and giveth himself over to it, be called in that estate the servant of Christ, till he repent, but the servant of sinne. 2 Peter 2: 19. Therfore you must recant your false interpretation of Paul in the 7. to the Romans and cease your blasphemous raylings, in calling the trueth of God, the rocke of Brownisme. And consider the height of your sinne, by concluding a bondage unto sinne of the whole man, for the corruptions of the fleshe, which through the worke of the spirit is daylie subdued, though never utterly rooted out of our earthlie members, and from the committing sinne through frayltie, an obstinate professed bondage to the false church, false government, false ministerie, *etc.*, which is plainly the marck of the beast, to whom with outward obedience they bowe downe, and stand servants in his kingdome, Revelation 14: 9, 11, 12. As for the 4. of the Galatians, 26, where the apostle saith, "Jerusalem which is above is free with her children," you durst not open it, nor expound it, but blaspheame, raile, and sclander, as though we should pleade for such a freedome, as should detract from magistrates' lawfull [41] aucthorities, from having God's ordinances established by commaundement upon the church, *etc.* Yea, that we should hold Anabaptisticall freedome, as though we had power not to committ, or consent unto sinne, wheras we have everie where by practize and protestation, by word and writing, testified to our sovereigne prince, and to all men, the contrarie. But Satan that old accuser and detracter of God's children, to deceave the world, sendeth out such lyinge spirites to deface the trueth. We, with all subjection and willinge obedience to our sovereigne prince, teach all men their obedience to the higher powers; subjectes to magistrates, flocke to overseers, children to parentes, wives to their husbands, servantes to their masters, *etc.*, in all things in the Lorde; and if they commaund us anie thing contrary to the lawe of God, we then patientlie suffer without resistance, or rebellious thoughtes. The freedome then we have to speake of here, which Christ hath purchased for us, is first, that tryumphe over hell, deathe, and damnation, through the merites of Christ apprehended by faith, wayted for in hope, Romans 8. Secondly, that because we were sonnes by election, he giveth us the spirit of adoption, and sanctification, wherebie we mortifie the fleshe, have reigne and dominion over sinne, that it shall never reigne in us more unto condemnation, repenting daylie our trespasses, and craving pardon for our hidden sinnes, and secreat faultes. Thirdly, we are throughe the same spirit and worde of trueth delivered from all subjection of antichrist, of the false church, false ministerie, false government, *etc*. And they that have not this freedome, are not by outward profession the servauntes of Christ. Furder, we have freedome from all traditions of men, that seing we are bought with a pryce, we are no longer servauntes of men, to be in bondage to anie beggerly rudimentes or devises of men, but in all peaceable maner, to worship and serve God within the limites of our callings, according to the word of God, as it is revealed unto us; we have freedome to speake the trueth with all boldnes, though all men should inhibite us; we would not have the doctrine limited, stinted, bought and sold, for Jewishe tythes or mercynarie stipendes.

We have freedome to seperate from such false prophetts as your self, to come out of Babell, *etc*. And in the true church to reprove and withstand anie sinne or traditions of men, in due order, only to be guided and governed by Christe's lawes and ordinances. In all this I trust you shall not find anie Anabaptistrie in the freedome we professe; this is the truth of the gospell, wherbie we are made free. Thus then we still affirme, that they which stand in [42] open knowen bondage to sinne, are the servants of sinne, and not of Christ, till they repent, by outward profession. Furder, that all which stand members of your parish assemblies, stand not members of Christ, by outward profession, but in bondage to a false and antichristian ministery, government, worship, *etc.*, and the bond woeman and her sonne must be ca[s]t out. Furder, for all liturgies, and other devises of men, besides the canonicall Scriptures and lively graces of his spirit, we hold they ought not to be brought into the publique assemblies, nor imposed upon men's consciences; but if anie will write such or reade such, let it be for their privat use, as all other men's writings; we despise not any directions by word or writing, that may furder us anie way to the practize of God's ordinances, yet may they nether be imposed upon men's consciences, nor be made a part of God's worship. The Lorde therfore that hath thus far fourth discovered the chaff and mist of antichrist's delusions, even to babes and sucklings, publish the glorious light of his blessed gospell, that the people may see the counterfeit juglinges of all such false prophetts, and come out from amongst them, that you may be ashamed of your execrable wares, and forsake your Romish priesthoode, and gyve glory to God, that yet offereth grace. Amen.

Christ's unworthie witnes for the truth of his gospell,

JOHN GREENWOOD.

FINIS

VI

AN INTERCEPTED LETTER

This letter is known to us only because Richard Bancroft printed it in his book, *A Survay of the Pretended Holy Discipline* (London, 1593), p. 430. John Greenwood is mentioned as the possible writer, and there is a hint by Bancroft that the letter was addressed to Thomas Cartwright. But Barrow is also the possible author, if we may so conclude from similar language used by him. (See *The Writings of Henry Barrow*, 1587-1593, p. 433.)

The date is approximately 1590 or 1591. The reference to the pamphlets of John Penry and Martin Marprelate enable us to date the letter after 1589, and the entry on March 5, 1592/3, of Bancroft's book in the *Stationers' Register* would indicate that Bancroft had possessed the letter for at least a few months prior to the entry. We may certainly date the letter, therefore, between 1589 and 1592, and *if* the letter is addressed to Thomas Cartwright, and *if* the letter was intercepted in prison, we may narrow the possibilities further, because Cartwright was sent to the Fleet prison in October, 1590, remanded in 1591, and released before May, 1592.

The letter is interesting because it reveals Greenwood's attitude toward the Martin Marprelate controversy and toward John Penry. Although Dr. Henry M. Dexter tried to prove that Barrow was really Martin Marprelate (*The Congregationalism of the Last Three Hundred Years, as Seen in Its Literature*, pp. 192-202), it seems clear that both Barrow and Greenwood were anti-Martin Marprelate. John Penry, who was commonly regarded by many of his contemporaries as Martin Marprelate, joined the Separatists in 1592.

*   *   *   *   *   *

D*

AN INTERCEPTED LETTER

[TO THOMAS CARTWRIGHT ?]

No date.   Probably seized in prison, about 1590—1591.

I like well of the arguments you have drawn against them from their own groundes. Againe, surely it were a not able [notable][1] worke, and no doubt might doe much good in these times, for some one that God hath indued with sound judgement and sharp sight, to gather the majors or antecedents, of all those scattered pamphlets of Penrie's or Martin's, *etc.*, and to put newe minors or conclusions unto them: and so in one little nosegay, but as bigg as an almanack, to turne them upon them-selves, and present them unto them, for an answeare.
Richard Bancroft, *A Survay of the Pretended Holy Discipline* (London, 1593), p. 430.

---

[1] Bancroft probably intended to mislead or entertain his readers by purposely allowing a slight space between the t and the a. Since the book is well printed by John Wolfe, I do not think the spacing is a printer's error. Even if we assume that it is, we may conjecture that Bancroft allowed it to stand.

THE JOINT WRITINGS
OF
HENRY BARROW AND JOHN GREENWOOD

1587 — 1590

1588

VII

THE TRUE CHURCH AND THE FALSE CHURCH

In the last four pages of *A Collection of Certain Letters and Conferences* are printed some criteria on the true and false churches. Although these had not been printed previously, they had been formulated and circulated in manuscript before November, 1588. These criteria were also refuted about three months later by Richard Alison, in "A Short Answere unto Certaine Arguments Which Are Used by the Brownists, to Prove the Church of England Not to Be the True Church of God," printed in *A Plaine Confutation*, pp. 121-129 [139].

This treatise includes a description of the true church, a denunciation of the false church, and a related series of eleven arguments why the Church of England is not the true church. The treatise concludes with a plea for separation as the best method of preserving purity of worship, and for a life of christian patience and godliness as the best way of refuting the penal laws of the ecclesiastical hierarchy. These arguments represent a challenge issued to the Presbyterian or Reformist leaders, Thomas Cartwright, Walter Travers, William Charke, and William Floyde (or Fludd). Since these arguments had remained unanswered for more than a year and a half, they were included for printing, perhaps in the hope of re-challenging the Presbyterian leaders to reply.

It is possible that this treatise was written by Henry Barrow alone, but we cannot be sure. Greenwood may have collaborated in the writing or in the suggesting of arguments.

*   *   *   *   *   *

John Greenwood

The righteous men they shall judge them after the maner of harlots and after the maner of murtherers, for they are harlots and blood is in thier hands: Ezekiel 23: 45.

Before we can judge the false church, it is expedient that we discerne the true church, which is thus described in the Scriptures. The true planted and rightlie established church of Christ is a companie of faithfull people; seperated from the unbelevers and heathen of the land; gathered in the name of Christ, whome they trulie worship, and redily obey as thier only king, priest, and prophet; joyned together as members of one bodie; ordered and governed by such officers and lawes as Christ in his last will and testament hath thereunto ordeyned; all and each one of them standing in and for thier christian libertie to practise whatsoever God hath commaunded and revealed unto them in his holie word within the limites of their callings, executing the Lorde's judgements against all transgression and disobedience which ariseth among them, and cutting it off accordinglie by the power which thier Lord and King, Christ Jesus, hath comitted unto them.

Now who so shall measure thies parish assemblies, as they generally stand in England, by this rule, shall evidently finde them in everie point so transgressing and defective, as he that hath eyes to see, or but a will to search, cannot be deceaved or mistake these parish churches for the true churches of Christ. Thies parishes consisting of a company of prophane and ignorant people; gathered by the sounde of a bell in the name of antichrist; worshipping God after a false and idolatrous maner; denying all obedience unto Christ in his three offices as thier only king, priest, and prophet; lyving in disorder among themselves; standing in confusion, being disordered and overruled by such lawes and officers as the pope left and not as Christ left; standing in bondage to the Romish courts and cannons; having no power to execute the Lorde's judgements or to redresse the least sinne or transgression amongst them-

The True Church and the False Church

selves, but are driven to the comissaries' courts, and so cast out Satan by the power of Satan.[1]

1. Thier churches consiste not of a company of faithfull people, but of a multitude of prophane people. Therefore they are not the true church. [p. 68 — K1 recto].

(1)
Jere. 31: 34
Acts 10: 43
Acts 15: 9
1 Cor. 1: 2

2. They have made no seperation from the heathen of the land, but all are received and reteyned in the bozome of thier churches: Therefore: etc.

(2)
Isay. 65: 11, 12
Lev. 20: 24
Jere. 15: 19
Ezek. 16: 25
Ezek. 23: 44
Joh. 15: 1, 9
2 Cor. 6: 14

3. They are not gathered in the name of Christ, but in the name of antichrist, whom they obey as shall afterward appeare. Therefore, etc.

(3)
Isay. 11: 10, 12
John 12: 32
Mat. 18: 20
1 Pet. 2: 4, 5

4. They worship not God truelie, but after a false and idolatrous maner, as witnesseth thier popish leiturgie, thier stinted booke of thier common prayer. Therefore, etc.

(4)
Deut. 5: 8
1 Cor. 10: 28
Revel. 21: 8

5. Thei receive not, nor obey not Christ as thier king, priest, and prophet. Therefore, etc.
Not as thier king; rejecting his government and receiving and standing under the antichristian yoake of thier popish government.
Not as thier priest; sacraligiously prophaning his name with thier idolatrie, prostituting his blood; and making him a priest and sacrifice to infidells and the most wicked offenders.
Not as thier prophet; giving no obedience to his worde, using it as a mantill to cover thier sinne, rather than as a rule whereby to direct thier lives, not seeking a true ministrie but mainteyning a false, of which sorte the wholl ministrie of the land is, which are permitted to teach in thier publicke places, to whome they give eare.

(5)
Deut. 18: 15
Isay. 42: 1
Mat. 17: 5
Acts 3: 22
1 John 4: 3
Mal. 1: 6
Luk. 19: 27
John 3: 36
Ezek. 16: 17, 19
and 44: 7
Lam. 1: 10
Deut. 13: 3
Mat. 7: 15
and 15: 14
Rom. 16: 17
2 Tim. 3: 5
2 John 10
Jere. 23: 29

6. Thier people are not kint [knit] togeather as members each of other in one congregation, but both rove and goe, assemble, and departe, at thier

(6)
1 Cor. 12: 12
1 Pet. 2: 4, 5
Rom. 12: 5

[1] This introduction and the following eleven arguments are answered by Richard Alison in September, 1590. See his book, A Plaine Confutation of a Treatise of Brownisme, pp. 121-129 [139].

pleasure when they will, whether they will, and as they will themselves; as also live in continuall disorder. [p. 69 — K1 *verso*].

(7)
Rom. 12: 8
Ephes. 4: 11
Psal. 2: 2, 3
Luke 19: 14

7. Thies parishes are not ordered and governed by such officers as Christ hath appointed to his church. They have no true pastors, teachers, elders, deacons, releevers. But insteade of thies they remaine most servilely subject to the antichristian government of thier popish arch-bishops, bishops, chaunchellors, archdeacons, deanes, commissaries, doctors, proctors, advocats, notaries, regesters, pursevants, cursetors, summers, *etc.*[1] And from the apostolicall seat of the bishops, they receve as antechristian and false a ministrie, as thier parsons, vicars, curates, hirelings, lecturers, mercenarie preachers, *etc.*, which togeither with this people stand bounde and subject to thies bishops and thier popish courts, of High Commission, of Faculties, of Arches, of Prerogative, of Delegats, of thier Commissaries, *etc.*[2] Therefore, *etc.*

(8)
1 Tim. 6: 13, 14
Ephes. 4: 11, 12
1 Cor. 14: 37
Heb. 12: 28

8. Thies assemblies are not ruled by the Olde and Newe Testament, but by the cannons, injunctions, and decrees of thies antichristian and popish courts. Therefore, *etc.*

(9)
John 8: 36
Gal. 4: 26
1 Pet. 2: 9

9. Thies people stand not in and for thier christian lybertie but all of them remaine in bondage to thies Aegyptian and Babilonish yoakes, yeilding obedience unto thies courts and thier cannons. Therefore, *etc.*

(10)
Psal. 149: 9
Isay. 45: 17

10. Thies assemblies have not the power which Christ hath given unto his church unto the world's end,

[1] Commissaries were deputies of bishops or archdeacons, exercising a somewhat limited and undefined jurisdiction within a diocese. Proctors were employed as agents for the collection of tithes ; also, they were lawyers practising in courts of ecclesiastical jurisdiction. Pursuivants were messengers or warrant-officers, who served and executed warrants. Cursitors were clerks of the Court of Chancery, who prepared original writs *de cursu, i.e.,* of official routine for a shire. Summoners were petty officers who served citations for court appearance.

[2] These courts were: the Court of High Commission ; the Court of Faculties ; the Court of Arches ; the Prerogative Court of Canterbury ; Court of Delegates ; Commissaries' Courts (agents of the bishop or archdeacon).

and all the powers in earth and hell cannot take Mat. 18: 17
from them; *viz.*, to binde and loose and to reforme Luke 10: 19
1 Cor. 5: 4
things that are amisse, but are driven to the com- 2 Cor. 10: 4, 5,
missary courts.   Therefore, *etc.* 6

11. Thies assemblies cast out Satan by the power of (11)
Satan, namely, by thies impes of antichrist, the Mat. 12: 25
bishop's commissaryes and priests.   Therefore
they are not, and for all thier [*sic*, thies ?] reasons
severall and joyned, cannot be held in anie
christian judgement, the true churches of Christ.

Infinite were the reasons which from thies severall heades, as
likewise from thier particuler transgressions and defaults, might
be drawne.   But the best argument to confute and cut downe all
this trumperie at once, is, according to the commandements of
God, to perserve [*sic*] our bodies and soules free from thies abhominations, by a speedie seperation and withdrawing our [p. 70 —
K2 *recto*] selves from amongst them; and to confute their last and
only argument whereby they upholde their ruinous kingdome,
namely, their penall lawe, by christian patience, and an upright
and godlie life.

> *Here is the patience of the saints: here are they that kepe the
> commaundements of God and the faith of Jesus.   Revelation
> 14: 12.*

> *He that overcometh shalbe clothed in white aray, and I will
> not put out his name out of the booke of life: but I will confesse
> his name before my Father and before his angells.   Revelations
> 3: 5.*

These arguments were more than a yeare and an halfe since de-

John Greenwood

livered to Mr. Cartwright, Mr. Travers, Mr. Charke, and Mr. Floyde, which will remaine upon them unanswered.[1]

FINIS

[Ornamental design]

---

[1] Four Presbyterian leaders: Thomas Cartwright, Walter Travers, William Charke, and William Floyde (or Fludd). This challenge did not go unanswered. About 1592-4 these men compiled a manuscript treatise, with the title, *The Church of England Is a True Church of Christ*. This is a refutation of Barrow's eleven arguments given above, as well as of his *A Brief Discoverie of the False Church* (1590) and of his *A Plaine Refutation* (1591). The *Short-Title Catalogue* (no. 10,398) and the British Museum Catalogue list this Presbyterian work as (1592 ?). The manuscript was not published until 1644, when William Rathband issued it with the title *A Most Grave, and Modest Confutation of the Errors of the Sect, Commonly Called Brownists, or Separatists* (Thomason tract E 31 (16). Another copy in the British Museum, listed as the 1592 work (117 f. 50), actually is a 1644 copy minus the title-page. There was no printed edition of 1592, the *Short-Title Catalogue* is in error, and understandably W. W. Bishop's *Checklist* reveals no American copies. In a letter of March 10, 1644, Robert Baillie said he had received Mr. Rathband's piece (*The Letters and Journals of Robert Baillie*, II, 144).

102

1590

VIII

A COLLECTION OF CERTAINE SCLAUNDEROUS ARTICLES GYVEN OUT BY THE BISSHOPS

Within two years of Robert Browne's submission to the terms of Archbishop Whitgift, on October 7, 1585, the Separatists were creating new problems for the Anglican hierarchy. Their ideas were circulating in manuscript copies ; they absented themselves from the church services and held their own meetings. On October 8, 1587, at least twenty-two of them were holding a private conventicle in the home of Henry Martin when they were arrested by the authorities. Six weeks later, on November 19, Henry Barrow was apprehended, and in the following months others were seized. During 1588 George Gifford and Robert Some wrote against the Separatists. These polemics and the petitions of the prisoners advertised their cause. In March, 1588/9, the Separatists finally secured a hearing before the Privy Council, the two Lord Chief Justices, and three of the leading bishops of the land. Widespread attention was given to the radical ideas of the Separatists, and their vehement attacks upon the Church of England were causing apprehension.

Upon the order of Archbishop Whitgift, and with the advice of the two Chief Justices, Sir Edmund Anderson and Sir Christopher Wray, the Bishop of London decided to utilize the services of forty-two clergymen and scholars to hold conferences with the fifty-two Separatists in six prisons. On February 25, 1589/90, he sent a letter, in the name of the queen and of the ecclesiastical commissioners, ordering these men to hold conferences with the prisoners twice weekly to convert them from their errors. It was not specified how many weeks the conferences should extend, but the conferences seem to have been terminated more quickly than expected because of their failure. The Separatists refused to be reduced from their errors. Regarding the visitors as inquisitors, they derided the meetings as " Spanish conferences." Although the prisoners were eager to justify themselves by the Word of God and prove the validity of their positions, they resented the false charges of error and heresy. Consequently, they decided to publish to the world the results of the prison conferences, repudiate the aspersions, and reply to the charges of disloyalty to the queen and the realm.

In 1587-1589 the Separatists had circulated their writings in a few manuscript copies. In the closing month of 1589, or in the early weeks of 1590, there had appeared in print a small eight-page pamphlet, *A True Description out of the Worde of God, of the Visible Church.*

The first substantial Separatist publication to appear in print, about May, 1590, was a 56 page tract, entitled, *A Collection of Certaine Sclaunderous Articles Gyven out by the Bisshops against Such Faithfull Christians as They Now Unjustly Deteyne in Their Prisons Togeather with the Answeare of the Saide Prisoners Therunto. Also the Some [Summary] of Certaine Conferences Had in the Fleete According to the Bisshops' Bloudie Mandate with Two Prisoners There.* This work is comprised not only of articles and conferences but also of other material. It is a collection which may be listed under seven divisions.

1. A statement to the reader. The language of this statement is similar to that of several Barrowist petitions, but it hardly seems possible that Barrow wrote it. There are several sentences that imply the hand of an editor, and there are references to the prisoners in the third person. One statement is: " the credit of these wrytings, I partly refer to the conscience of the men that wrote them, as they will answere to the contrarye before that great Judg[e]." Barrow is unlikely to have written this, and if an editor added this prefatory statement, he may have been Robert Stokes, or Arthur Billett.

2. Letter or commission of the Bishop of London to Archdeacon Mullins and forty-one other preachers in and about London. The letter is dated February 25, 1589/90, and is signed by John

Aylmer, Bishop of London; John Herbert, Master of Requests; Edward Stanhope, Chancellor to the Bishop of London; and Richard Cosin, Vicar-General of the Province of Canterbury. All are members of the Court of High Commission, and the commission is issued by virtue of the powers of this court, upon the order of Archbishop Whitgift, and with the advice of Sir Christopher Wray, Chief Justice of the Queen's Bench, and Sir Edmund Anderson, Chief Justice of the Court of Common Pleas. The task of carrying out the commission was entrusted to John Mullins, Archdeacon of London.

3. " A Briefe of the Positions Holden by the New Sectorie of Recusants." These positions constitute a list of twelve " errors " which were given to the preachers before they visited the prisoners. The list was intended to acquaint the visitors with the views of the Separatists, and to forearm them.

4. A list of forty-two preachers, fifty-two prisoners, and six prisons. In the original assignment, there is one preacher who is assigned to one prisoner in the Gatehouse; nine preachers are individually assigned to two prisoners each; one preacher is assigned to three prisoners in the Fleet; there are twelve teams of two preachers each assigned to visit two prisoners; one team of two is scheduled to visit one prisoner in the Counter Poultry; another team of two is scheduled for a visit to three prisoners in the Gatehouse. It is interesting to note that one team of three able persons — Archdeacon Mullins, Dr. Lancelot Andrewes, and Archdeacon William Hutchinson — is assigned to visit Barrow and Greenwood. Mr. Mullins never visited the prisoners, but Dr. Andrewes made two visits and Mr. Hutchinson made four.

5. " A Brief Answeare to Such Articles as the Bishopps Have Given out in Our Name, upon Which Articles Their Priests Were Sent and Injoyned to Confer with Us in the Severall Prisons wherein We Are by Them Detayned." The Separatists said that these articles were cunningly devised, represented forged positions, and misrepresented their true beliefs. These articles had been formulated without the knowledge or consent of the prisoners, who disliked the use of the phrase " newe sectorie " and who resented the application of the word " recusants " to themselves. Actually, the articles are fairly stated, and the replies are clarifications and explications rather than denials. Barrow disliked the term " sect "

and refused to be labeled a sectory. Nevertheless, he did belong to " the true church," to a unique group, or to a new denomination or congregation of believers, separate from the established *Anglicana Ecclesia*.

6. A summary of four conferences. These conferences were held on March 9, 17, 18 and April 13, 1590. Mr. Hutchinson participated in four of them, Greenwood in three, Barrow in two, and Dr. Andrewes in two. The first three conferences are reported in a natural way of questions and answers, challenges and responses, arguments and counter-arguments, but the fourth is summarized by twenty-two propositions or statements, with answers to less than half of them.

7. " A Breif Answeare to Certayne Sclaunderous Articles and Ungodlie Calumniations Sparsed Abrode by the Bishops and Theire Adherents against Diverse Faithfull and True Christians, Her Majestie's Loyall and Lovinge Subjects to Colour Theire Owne Ungodly and Tyrannicall Dealing with Them, and to Bring Them into Hatred both with Prince and People." These articles and the answers thereto are somewhat different from those in division 3 above. In the present set of articles, the fourth article on laymen, the eleventh article on the oath, and the twelfth on marriage, are not found in the first set of articles. Where the articles are substantially the same, the answers vary. The articles were prepared from material gathered by Dr. Robert Some, from depositions made by the prisoners, from testimony in the courts, and from material seized in prison from Barrow and perhaps from other prisoners.

A Collection of Certaine Sclaunderous Articles Gyven out by the Bisshops was published about May or June, 1590. The conference of April 13 is a *terminus a quo*, and the testimony of Robert Stokes reveals that *A Collection of Certain Letters and Conferences* was published in midsummer of 1590. Since this latter work was printed after the aforementioned book, the date would be some time between May and June at the earliest and approximately June or July at the latest.

It is probable that Greenwood's wife was the one who smuggled the manuscript out of prison. Robert Stokes caused the book to be printed in Dort, paid the costs, and conveyed

them from the Netherlands to England. Some 500 copies
were printed, of which about half were in the disposition of
Barrow and Greenwood. The other half were probably delivered to one Mychens, to be sold at eight pence each, or to
be distributed to the faithful brethren. Greenwood's maidservant, Cycely, brought copies to the prison.

*A Collection of Certaine Sclaunderous Articles Gyven out
by the Bisshops* appeared in the early summer of 1590, and
was refuted about three months later by Richard Alison,
who had been one of the preachers assigned in February to
visit the Separatists in prison. His book is entered in the
Stationers' Register to Thomas Scarlet on September 4, 1590.
It is entitled *A Plaine Confutation of a Treatise of Brownisme,
Published By Some of That Faction, Entituled*: A Description
of the Visible Church [*A True Description out of the Worde
of God, of the Visible Church*]. Pages 1 - 104 constitute a
refutation of *A True Description*, and pages 105 - 121 com-
prise a refutation of *A Collection of Certaine Sclaunderous
Articles*. Pages 106 - 113 deal with the first set of twelve
articles and pages 113 - 121 pertain to the second set of twelve
articles.

*　　*　　*　　*　　*　　*

[A i *recto*]
A COLLECTION OF CERTAINE SCLAUNDEROUS ARTICLES GYVEN OUT BY THE BISSHOPS AGAINST SUCH FAITHFULL CHRISTIANS AS THEY NOW UNJUSTLY DETEYNE IN THEIR PRISONS TOGEATHER WITH THE ANSWEARE OF THE SAIDE PRISONERS THERUNTO. ALSO THE SOME [SUMMARY] OF CERTAINE CONFERENCES HAD IN THE FLEETE ACCORDING TO THE BISSHOPS' BLOUDIE MANDATE WITH TWO PRISONERS THERE
1590
[DORT]

[A i *verso* blank]

[A ii *recto*]

Grace to the reader with wisdome
from above, to discerne the truth, and to walke in
the same aright.

These copies of the bishops' articles and the awnsweres therunto, as also of these late conferences had in the Fleet, being come unto my hands, I thought no lesse than my dutie to impart unto thee, and publish to the view of all men:

1. that: the true cawses of these controvercies;
2. the bishops' dealing with Christ's poore servants;
3. and cheifly [that] the truth it self might the sooner be brought to light and appeare.

The cawses of controversie thow maist [thou mayest] herby perceave to be no light or small matters concerning things indifferent or some fewe trifling ceremonies (as they have long labored to make the world beleeve, although even those least litle trifles being brought into and thrust by way of law upon the church having no warrant in the Testament of Christ ought not to be suffred for the space of an howre), but most high and waightie are these matters, concerning the whole building of the church; which is affirmed to be altogether out of order from the verie foundation to the top, and not according to the patterne of Christ's Testament either in the people, ministerie, ministration, worship, government, order, al things out of frame, such as can neither stand before the face of Christ, neither may anie of God's children joine unto with promise of salvation.

108

Now the course the bishops and their cleargie have taken, to approove themselves unto all men to be no such deceitfull work men, theire building to be no such wood, hay, stubble, hath not beene to bring their workes to the light, and to submit it and themselves, to be measured by the golden reed of God's word, therby justifying themselves, convincing and perswading others. But in stead of this, they first imprison all such as make anie scruple or question of theire doings: yea, all such as but speake against them, they shut up in close pryson, there to continewe without bayle or mainprice,[1] all the daies of theire life, except they submit and recant. Some they cast into most noisome and vile dungeons,[2] without ayre, foode, bedds, or so much as strawe to lye uppon, keeping them from their wyves, children, trades, labours, to the utter undoing and affamishment of them, their [A ii *verso*] wyves, and children; others they lade, with as manie yrons as they can beare;[3] som others they a while produced to the Sessions, there indicting them as recusants uppon the statute made for the papists;[4] publishing them by theire prynt with priviledg, Anabaptists, hereticks, schismaticks, sectories, Donatists, conventiclers, seditious, turbulent; sparsing abrode through all the land certeine articles of theire owne devising against them, to bring them into hatred with the whole land, wher unto also they have not spared theire toungs, in their pulpits, where every one of theire priests might forge what opinion he lyst against them, and confute it with the same mouth, in theire name: and all this, without once producing them, to anie christian triall where they might have place given them, to defend themselves, and produce theire reasons, or once endevoring to perswade or confute them by anie one place of Scripture; yet not content with all this, they can take no rest in themselves, or thincke theire kingdome safe, untill they have

1 Mainprice or mainprize. The right to obtain release by obtaining sureties.
2 The prisons in which the Barrowists were confined were the Clink, the Gatehouse, the Fleet, Newgate, the Counter Woodstreet, the Counter Poultry, Bridewell, and the White Lion.
3 John Purdy was ladened with irons, and Roger Waterer, about eighteen years old, was kept in irons for more than a year, in a dungeon. In his prison interview with Lancelot Andrewes, Barrow gloried in his bonds.
4 Barrow and Greenwood were brought before Newgate Sessions about May, 1588, and were found guilty of having violated the statute of 23 Elizabeth, *Caput* 1, entitled, "An Acte to Reteine the Queene's Majesties' Subjects in Their Due Obedience." See *Statutes of the Realm*, IV, Part I, 657-8. The Puritans maintained that this statute was intended for the papists. See Barrow's reply to Lord Burghley at his trial on March 18, 1588/9.

devoured the pray [prey] they have taken, and rydd them out of the way, which wil not bow downe, and worship the beast, and his image. And hereunto (having no hope to accomplish theire bloudy purpose, by the common law of the land, seing they can finde no occasion against these men, except it be in the law of theire God) they of late contrived this new Spanish conference, sending certeine of theire select souldiours unto them into theire prisons, there by way of conference to fish from them som matter, wheruppon they might accuse them to theire holy fathers the bishops, who theruppon might delyver them, as convicts of heresie unto the secular powers. But blessed be God, that in these points, hath hewed theire hornes shorter in the beginning of her majestie's reigne, not allowing that to be heresie, which they should so pronounce, but what they by the Scrip[ture] should so prove: againe, no heresie to be capitall or punished by death, but what by the first four councells, and by the Scriptures, was so adjudged;[1] els had they by this, shed more innocent and christian bloud, than ever theire predecessors did in this land before them. But now, as they will at no hand, be drawne unto this peaceable and christian triall, to have these matters decided and judged, by the word of God; so have they not gayned that [which] they sought by these theire messengers, who (through the power of God) were intangled in theire owne words, not being able to spurne against the pricks, or to get such matter at the hands of these prysoners as they sought; which, they espying, followed not the sute half so hotely as they were injoyned, comming but twice, whereas they ought to have

---

[1] The first four councils were Nicaea, in 325; Constantinople, in 381; Ephesus, in 431; and Chalcedon, in 451. The reference to heresy is based on the Supremacy Act of 1559, I Elizabeth, *Caput* I. Section 20 is a proviso that those who were given jurisdiction by Letters Patents to reform errors, heresies, or schisms did not possess the power to determine or adjudge any matter or cause to be heresy, "but only such as heretofore have been determined, ordered or adjudged to be heresy by the authority of the Canonical Scriptures, or by the first four General Councils or any of them, or by any other General Council wherein the same was declared heresy by the express and plain words of the said Canonical Scriptures, or such as hereafter shall be ordered, judged or determined to be heresy by the High Court of Parliament of this realm, with the assent of the clergy in their Convocation; any thing in this Act contained to the contrary notwithstanding." See Great Britain, *Statutes of the Realm*, IV, Part I, 354. See also G. W. Prothero, *Select Statutes and Other Documents Illustrative of the Reigns of Elizabeth and James I*, 4th ed., (London, 1949), p. 12.

com twice every weeke, at the least.[1] At which [A iii *recto*] tymes, how they behaved themselves, let such as were present report; and also such as read these conferences judge, what cause they have to exclaime, and accuse of heresie, *etc.*, such as call them to the Testament of Christ, and would have theire whole church, and all theire proceedings therin, buylt theruppon. Which course they are so far from receaving, as they open theire mouthes bouldly into a most high blasphemie, against God, and his tabernacle, and them that dwel in the heaven; theire handes they have armed to violence, theire feete are swift to shed bloud, seeking by all subtile and indirect meanes to suppresse the truth. Wherfore, so much the more is it the dutye of every true servant of Christ, even by all meanes to publish the same; which hath caused me at this tyme, to exhibit these things unto the reading and view of all men; not regarding the blame that I ame like to sustaine at all hands therfore, so som may reape anie good therby. Yet see I not whie anie should justly be offended with this my doing, seing therby no wrong is don to anie man. As for these prysoners that are named, and had to do in this busines, there is no cause they should be offended, seing they under theire owne handes have made relation therof unto the church, and have (for so doing) the practise of the apostle, Acts 4, verse 23, as also of owre late martyres in Queen Marie's dayes, in the lyke cases. The credit of these wrytings, I partly refer to the conscience of the men that wrote them, as they wil answere the contrarye before that great judg; but cheifly, to the testimonie of the witnesses present and to the indifferent consideration of anie man, that will compare the arguments and answeres, to the present subject of the discourse.

As for the other side, if nothing should be published, untill theire consent were had, theire should never anie of these things com to light. But if they thinke themselves injuryed, let them set downe the particulars wherin, or, for the further satisfying of all men, let them yet at length condiscend to som christian and free conference, where both sides may have lyberty to produce theire reasons, a true record of them be kept, by faithfull and indifferent notaries, ech side be allowed to have a copie therof, and time to consider of what is passed accordingly. Thus might the thruth, sone, and preceablye [truth, soon, and peaceably] be knowen,

---

[1] The instructions said that the preachers were to visit the prisoners " twise every weeke (at the least)," but no duration of time was specified. Barrow and Greenwood were interviewed on March 9, 14, 17, 18, 20, April 3, and 13, 1590.

where the word of God may be judg betwixt them: from which, who so departeth, and wil not be reduced, let him to his wne [owne] perill, undergoe such censures, and judgments as are due to his error and syn. Only this is sure; *Wisdome is justified of all her children.*[1]

Farewell in the Lord.[2]

[A iii *verso*]

To owre loving freinds, Mr. Archdeacon Mollins,[3] Mr. Doctor Andros,[4] Mr. Cotton,[5] Mr. Hutchinson,[6] and the rest of the preachers, in and about London with in named.

After owre harty commendations; I, the Bisshop of London,[7] have received order from my lord's grace of Canterburye with the advice of both the cheiffe justices,[8] that conference should presently be had with these sectories, whiche do forsake owr church, and be for the same commytted prysoners: for that it is intended, if by owr good and learned perswasions, they will not be reduced to conforme themselves to their dutifull obedyence, that they shalbe proceeded with all according to the course of the common lawe. Therfore, these are to will and requyre you, and every of you whose names are mencioned in the schedule hereunto anexed, in her

---

[1] Matthew 11: 19. Luke 7: 35. Greenwood used this verse in his *An Answere to George Gifford's Pretended Defence of Read Praiers*, A iv *recto* (page 1).

[2] There is no clue to the person who wrote this introduction. I believe that Barrow may have written at least a part of it, and that Greenwood may have contributed to it. There is also the possibility that Robert Stokes, who guided the book through the press, and smuggled the books into England, may have written this introduction. Arthur Billet, or Byllett, who served as a proof-reader for several volumes, may have written it.

[3] John Mollins, or Mullyns, archdeacon of London (1559-91) and prebendary of St. Paul's. In the British Museum, Additional MSS. 29,546, f. 55, the signature is given " per me Johannem Mullyns." In the *D.N.B.* he is listed as Molyns.

[4] Lancelot Andrewes (1555-1626), linguist, devotionalist, translator of the Bible, preacher, writer, apologist, Master of Pembroke Hall, Cambridge, and Bishop of Chichester, of Ely, and of Winchester.

[5] William Cotton, rector of St. Mary's, Finchley, archdeacon of Lewes, and later Bishop of Exeter (1598-1621).

[6] William Hutchinson, prebendary of St. Paul's, archdeacon of St. Albans, and rector of St. Botolph's, Bishopsgate.

[7] John Aylmer (1521-1594), friend of John Foxe the martyrologist, Marian exile, and archdeacon of Lincoln, became Bishop of London in 1577.

[8] Sir Christopher Wray (1524-1592), Chief Justice of the Queen's Bench, and Sir Edmund Anderson (1530-1605), Chief Justice of the Court of Common Pleas.

majestie's name, by vertue of her high commission, for causes ecclesiasticall, to us and others dyrected; that twise every weeke (at the least) you doe repayre to those persons, and prysoners, whose names are in this tycket set doune, and that you seeke by all learned and discrete demeanure you may to reduce them from their errors. And for that eyther their conformitye, or disobedyence, may be more manifest, when they shall com unto theire trial; therfore we requyre you to set downe in wryting the perticuler dayes, of your going to confer with them, and lykewise your censure what it is of them, as that if occasion doe serve to use it, you wilbe sworne unto; and for that Mr. Doctor [Edward] Stanhope, chancellor to me the Bisshop of London, is gon out of the citie, therfore we requyre Mr. Mollins, to send for all those severall preachers, and delyver them the names of the prysoners togeather with the prysons wherunto they are assigned to resort, and to requyre them as aforesaide, to take the chardg uppon them, according to the trust commytted unto them: and in case anie of them refuse, that then you require him or them, forthwith, to repayre to me to Fulham, and to certefie me of their aunswers, before theire comming. And so we byd you farewell: the 25 of Februarye 1589 [1589/90].

Your loving freinds
John [Aylmer, Bishop of] London, John Herbert,[1] Edward Stanhope,[2] Richard Cosen[3]

We have sent you herewithall a note of som part of their errors, wherby those preachers that are associat unto [A iv *recto*] you, may the better consider how to deale in conference with them.

---

[1] John Herbert, one of the Masters of Requests.
[2] Edward Stanhope, chancellor to the Bishop of London. In 1593, he was one of the Masters in Chancery and a Justice of the Peace for the County of Middlesex.
[3] Richard Cosin (1549 ?-1597), Dean of the Court of Arches, Vicar-General of the Province of Canterbury, Master in Chancery, and member of the Court of High Commission.

113

John Greenwood

A BRIEFE OF THE POSITIONS HOLDEN BY THE NEWE SECTORIE OF
RECUSANTS.[1]

1. That it is not lawfull to use the Lord's Prayer publiquely in the church, for a set forme of prayer.

2. Secondly, that all set and stinted prayers are meere babling in the sight of the Lord, not to be used in publique christian assemblies.

3. Thirdly, that the publique prayers and worship of God in England, as it is by lawe in the Church of England established, is false, superstitious, popish, and not to be used in anye christian congregation.

4. That the Church of England as it is now established is no entier member of the church of Christ.

5. That the government of the Church of England, as it is now established, is no lawfull government, nor christian, but antichristian and popish.

6. That the sacraments of babtisme and the Lord's Supper, as they are administred in the Church of England, be not true sacraments.

7. That infants ought not to be baptised, according to the forme of baptisme ministred now in the Church of England, but are rather to be kept unbaptised.

8. Manie of them make scruple to affirme, that the queen's majestie hath supreame aucthoritie to govern the Church of England in cases ecclesiasticall and to make lawes ecclesiasticall, not contrary to Christ's lawes.

---

[1] These positions are taken from the questions asked Henry Barrow at his examination on March 24, 1588/9. I believe Dr. Robert Some formulated the position of the Barrowists, and very likely aided Archbishop Whitgift, in compiling the questions. See Robert Some, *A Godly Treatise, wherein Are Examined and Confuted Many Execrable Fancies*. This treatise refutes fourteen points held by Barrow, Greenwood, and Penry. These positions are in Lansdowne MSS. 109, f. 1. They vary somewhat in wording and order, and items 11 and 12 have no parallel. Items 1 — 10 are substantially the same as those given here.
There are also " The Assertions of the Conventicles Lately Apprehended," printed separately in the Appendix. These are similar, but also have new material. They are included in the latter part of this section, with replies, in " A Breif Answeare to Certayne Sclaunderous Articles and Ungodlie Calumniations."

9. That the lawes ecclesiasticall already established, by the auctoritie of the queene and realme, be not lawfull.
10. That if the prince, or majestrate under her, doe refuse or defer to reforme, such faults as are aimsse [amisse] in the church, the people may take the reforminge of them into theire owne hands, before or without her auctoritie.
11. That the presbiterie, or eldership, may for som causes after admonition, if there ensue not reformation, excommunicat the queene.
12. That the Church of England, as it now standeth by lawe established, professeth not a true Christ, nor true religion, that it hath no ministers in deed, nor sacraments in deed.

[A LIST OF PREACHERS, PRISONERS, AND PRISONS]

[A iv *verso*]

[PREACHERS][1]	[PRISONERS][2]	[PRISONS]
Doctor Bancraft[1]	James Forester	prysoners in Newgate
	John Francys	
	Robert Batkine	in the Fleete
Doctor Grant[2]	Thomas Freeman	in the Gatehowse

1. Doctor Richard Bancroft, ardent advocate of episcopacy by divine right, arch-enemy of the Puritans, Presbyterians, and Martinists, Bishop of London (1597—1604), and Archbishop of Canterbury (1604—1610).
2. Doctor Edward Grant was a Latin and Greek Scholar, Master of Westminster School, 1572—February, 1592/3, prebendary of the twelfth stall, 1577—1601.

[1] There are forty-two or forty-three clergymen listed. I have identified all of them in the following brief descriptions, but two or three are uncertain. The identifications are based on Richard Newcourt, *Repertorium Ecclesiasticum Parochiale Londinense*; George Hennessy, *Novum Repertorium Ecclesiasticum Parochiale Londinense*; John Le Neve, *Fasti Ecclesiae Anglicanae*; C. H. Cooper and Thompson Cooper, *Athenae Cantabrigienses*; John Venn and J. A. Venn, *Alumni Cantabrigienses*; Joseph Foster, *Alumni Oxonienses*; " The Names of All the Parishes, Parsons, and Curates within and Near Adjoyning about London," (*ca.* 1586), *The Seconde Parte of a Register*, ed. Albert Peel, II, 180-184; R. F. Laurence, *A General Index to the Historical and Biographical Works of John Strype*; *Dictionary of National Biography*.

[2] For these prisoners, see Champlin Burrage, *Early English Dissenters*; see also Albert Peel, *The Noble Army of Congregational Martyrs*; see further F. J. Powicke, " Lists of the Early Separatists," *Transactions of the Congregational Historical Society*, No. 3 (July, 1902), pp. 141-158. See also the Appendix, where the prisoners are identified.

John Greenwood

Doctor Wood[3]	Thomas Settel	
	John Debenham	
Mr. Egerton[4]	George Collier	in the Clynke
	John Sparowe	
Doctor Sallard[5]	Edmond Nicolson	in the Clynke
Mr. Jackson[6]	Xpofer Raper	
Mr. Dunscombe[7]	Xpofer Browne	in the Clynke
	Quintan Smyth	
Mr. Smyth[8]	Androwe Smyth	in the Clynke
	William Blakborowe	
Mr. Phyllips[9]	Thomas Lemar	in the Clynke
	Thomas Michell	
Doctor White[10]	Anthonye Clakston	in Newgate
	William Forester	

3. Doctor Richard Wood, prebendary of Westminster, 1587—1609, and of Portpoole, vicar of All Hallows', Barking, 1584/5—1591, and rector of Stisted, Essex. He was appointed a licenser of copies of books, on June 3, 1588.
4. Doctor John Egerton was possibly the Mr. " Edgerton " who was pastor of Anne in the Blackfriars. He was appointed in 1594 to the *Domus Conversorum*, a church for converted Jews. In 1377 this church had been annexed, by patent, to the Keeper of the Rolls of Chancery. He held conference on March 20, 1589/90, with Barrow and Greenwood in prison, and also exchanged letters with them.
5. Doctor Sallard. Probably Thomas Staller or Stallard, rector of St. Mary-at-Hill, 1574—1605/6, of All Hallows', Lombard Street, 1573—1605/6. In one list of ministers for the year 1586, his name is given as Stollard, of the same parish. There is also listed a Mr. Stollard of Mary-At-Hill. Doctor Thomas Stallard was appointed on June 3, 1588, a licenser of books to be printed, on the recommendation of Archbishop Whitgift. See W. W. Greg and E. Boswell, *Records of the Court of the Stationers' Company, 1576 to 1602, from Register B*, p. 29. See also Albert Peel (ed.), *The Seconde Parte of a Register*, II, 180, 182.
6. William Jackson, rector of St. Swithin, 1587—1605 ; vicar of Bedfont, 1595—1597 ; archdeacon of Rochester.
7. Mr. Thomas Dunscombe was appointed to the church of St. Thomas the Apostle on September 7, 1587. In a list for 1586, " Duncom " is listed as curate, and Doffeild as parson and preacher.
8. Probably Andrew Smyth of the vicarage of Fulham in the patronage of the Bishop of London. There is a Thomas Smith, vicar of Ruislip, 1565—1614/15, and also a Henry Smythe, vicar of the St. Stephen, Coleman Street, 1580—1588. There is a Nicholas Smythe, of the vicarage of Fulham in the patronage of the Bishop of London, 1550—1589, who died in 1589. There is also a Robert Smith, perpetual curate, of St. Mary, Hampstead.
9. Thomas Philips, rector of St. Augustine, on Watling Street, 1572/3—1600.
10. Dr. William White, rector of St. Benet, Gracechurch Street, 1591—2. Mr. White is listed as preacher in Dunston in the West about 1586.

A Collection of Certaine Sclaunderous Articles

Mr. Sparke[11]	William Denford	in Newgate
	Roger Waterer	
Mr. Eryle[12]	Edeth Burrowghe	in Newgate
	William Burt	
Mr. Turnball[13]	George Smels	in the Counter Wood-
	Xpofer Bowman	street
Mr. Edmonds[14]	Robert Jackson	in Counter Woodstreet
Mr. Haughton[15]	Nycolas Lee	
Mr. Gylpenne[16]	Robert Andrewes	in Counter Woodstreet
Mr. Coper[17]	William Hutton	
Mr. Archpoole[18]	John Buser	in Counter Woodstreet
Doctor Hanmer[19]	John Fissher	
[B 1 recto]		
Doctor Crooke[20]	William Clarke	in Counter Woodstreet
Mr. Trypp[21]	Richard Maltusse	

11. Mr. [Thomas ?] Sparke. Christofer Simkins testified on April 5, 1593, that he had been influenced by the sermons of Mr. Sparkes, one of the " forward " preachers. Thomas Sparke (1548—1616), rector of Bletchley, archdeacon of Stow, prebendary of Lincoln, and chaplain to Thomas Cooper, Bishop of Lincoln. As a puritan, nonconformist, and scholar, he was invited to the Hampton Court Conference in 1604.
12. Mr. Thomas Early, rector of St. Mildred, Bread Street, 1564-6. Died 1604.
13. Richard Turnbull, curate of St. Mary, Colechurch, 1581—1593, and rector of St. Pancras, Soper Lane [Queen Street], 1582—1593. He is listed in 1586 as preacher at " Prancrase Cheapside."
14. Thomas Edmunds, rector of Laingdon Hills, Essex, and of All Hallows', Bread Street, 1585—1610/11.
15. Mr. Haughton — uncertain. There is a Hawton listed as the parson of Lawrence Pountney, and a Hawtonn listed as preacher at Alhallowes the Lesse.
16. Joshua Gilpin, rector of Saints Anne and Agnes ; rector of St. Vedast, 1578—1603 ; rector of St. Michael — le Querne, 1577—1603. A Mr. Gilpin is listed as preacher in 1586 at Foster's Parish and also at Michael Quearne.
17. Either Martin Cooper or Robert Cooper, both appointed on April 29, 1590, to the College of the Twelve Minor Canons of St. Paul's Cathedral. He engaged in a conference with Barrow and Greenwood in prison on April 3, 1590.
18. Mr. Archpoole was the rector of St. Peter in Cornhill.
19. Meredith Hanmer, vicar of St. Mary's, Islington, 1583—1590 ; also vicar of Shoreditch and treasurer of Christ Church, Dublin.
20. Dr. Thomas Crooke, rector of Great Waldingfield, Suffolk, preacher to the society of Gray's Inn.
21. Henry Tripp, rector of N. Ockendon, Essex ; rector of St. Stephen, Walbrook, 1572—1601 ; rector of St. Faith's, 1583—1612. He is listed in 1586 as " Trippes — Faiths under Paules."

Mr. Morrison[22]	William Fouller	in Counter Woodstreet
Mr. Crowe[23]	Richard Skarlet	
Mr. Browne[24]	Roger Rippine	in Counter Woodstreet
Mr. Hall[25]	John Clarke	
Mr. Moslee[26]	Rowland Skipworth	in the Counter Poultrye
Preacher at Bridewell	George Knifton	
Mr. Anderson[27]	Richard Hayward	in Counter Poultrye
Mr. Gardiner[28]	John Lankaster	
Mr. Cotton[29]	Thomas Endford	in Counter Poultrye
Mr. Cheyne[30]		
Mr. Mollins[31]	Henry Barrowe	in the Fleete

22. Mr. Morrison — uncertain. There is a Thomas Mortyboys, rector of St. Martin, Orgar, 1570/1—1593 ; rector of St. Alphage, 1567—1593. There is a curate, Mr. Morrison, serving at " Botolphe Aldersgate " where Mr. Goodman was the preacher.
23. Thomas Crowe, rector of St. James, Garlickhithe, 1579—1613 ; rector of St. Martin's Ludgate, 1585—1613.
24. Mr. Browne — uncertain. There is a Mr. Broune listed as preacher of " Benet Fincke " about 1586.
25. Possibly Thomas Hale, rector of St. Olave, Hart Street, 1583—1590, rector of Beaumont, Essex ; vicar of Tolleshunt Darcy, Essex. A Mr. Hailes is listed for Clements by Eastchepe and also for " Nicholas Achon." Mr. Haile is listed for " Oliffe in Hartstreete."
26. Mr. Moslee, preacher at Bridewell. There is a Roger Massye, appointed in 1588 as rector of St. Peter ad Vincula. This Chapel, under the jurisdiction of the Bishop of London, became a donative in Elizabeth's reign. There is also a Thurston Mosley, a Northampton Puritan ringleader, who was deprived in 1574 of his parish.
27. Mr. Anthony Anderson, vicar of the Church of Stepney, Middlesex, 1586/7—1593 ; rector of Dengy, Essex.
28. Richard Gardener, rector of St. Mary, Matfellon, Whitechapel, 1570—1617. There is also a Michael Gardener, rector of Great Greenford, 1584—1630, and rector of Littlebury, Essex. The former is the better choice, I believe, because of his age and experience in London. He is listed in 1586 as Mr. Gardner of Whitechapel Church.
29. William Cotton, rector of St. Mary's, Finchley, 1581—1599 ; rector of St. Margaret, New Fish Street, 1577/8—1599 ; rector of W. Tilbury, Essex ; archdeacon of Lewes ; bishop of Exeter, 1598—1621. Appointed a licenser of books on June 3, 1588.
30. Mr. Cheyne — uncertain. There is a W. Cheyney who matriculated from Clare College, Cambridge, in 1566, and a W. Cheyney who matriculated from Christ's College, Cambridge, in 1581. There is also a Henry Cheyney, graduate of St. Alban Hall, Oxford, and who served as rector in Ringwold, Kent, in 1569.
31. John Mullyns, archdeacon of London, 1559—1591 ; rector of St. Botolph's, Billingsgate ; prebendary of Kentish Town, St. Paul's, 1559—1591.

A Collection of Certaine Sclaunderous Articles

Mr. Androwes[32]	John Greenwood	
Mr. Hutchinson[33]		
Doctor Saravea[34]	Daniell Studley	in the Fleete
Mr. Gravet[35]	Walter Lane	
Mr. Fissher[36]	Edmond Tomson	in the Gatehouse
Mr. Judson[37]	John Nicolas	
Mr. Temple[38]	William Dodson	in the Gatehowse
Mr. Allison[39]	John Barrens	
Doctor Blague[40]	John Cranford	in the Gatehowse
Mr. Herd[41]	Richard Wheeler	

32. Lancelot Andrewes, prebendary of St. Pancras, St. Paul's, 1589—1609; vicar of St. Giles, Without Cripplegate, 1588—1605; dean of Westminster, 1601—1605; prebendary of Westminster, 1592/3—?; Bishop of Chichester, 1605—9; Bishop of Ely, 1609—1618/19; Bishop of Winchester, 1618/19—1626.
33. William Hutchinson, prebendary of Wildland, St. Paul's, 1588/9—1590, prebendary of Hotton, St. Paul's, 1591—1605/6; rector of St. Botolph's, Bishopsgate, 1584—1590; rector of St. Christopher-le-Stock, 1581/2—1587; rector of St. Michael, Bassishaw, 1589—?; archdeacon of St. Albans. On June 3, 1588, he was appointed a licenser of copies of books to be printed, by Archbishop Whitgift. He held a conference with Greenwood in prison, March 9 and 17, 1589/90, and with Barrow on March 18 and April 13, 1590.
34. Doctor Hadrian de Saravia, prebendary of Westminster, 1594—1601. Distinguished foreign scholar and author. See William M. Jones, " Foreign Teachers in Sixteenth Century England," *Historian*, February, 1959.
35. William Gravett, vicar of St. Sepulchre's, Holborn, 1566—1598/9; prebendary of Willesden, St. Paul's, 1567—1598/9. He was appointed June 3, 1588, as a licenser of books to be printed, on the recommendation of Archbishop Whitgift.
36. William Fisher, vicar of St. Martin-in-the-Fields, 1588—1591.
37. Richard Judson, rector of St. John the Evangelist, Watling Street, 1579/80—1585/6; rector of St. Peter-le-Poer, 1583—1615; rector of St. Peter's, Cheapside, 1585—1615.
38. Robert Temple, prebendary of Consumpta-per-Mare, St. Paul's, 1592—1598; prebendary of Harlesden, St. Paul's, 1593/4—1596/7; rector of St. Nicholas Acon, 1585/6—1592; rector of St. Michael, Queen-hithe, 1591—1595; chaplain to John Aylmer, Bishop of London.
39. Richard Alison, rector of St. Thomas the Apostle, 1591/2—1612; rector of St. Leonard, Shoreditch, 1596—1612. He was the author of a book entitled *A Plaine Confutation of a Treatise of Brownisme*, which was a refutation of Barrow's *A True Description out of the Worde of God, of the Visible Church.*
40. Dr. Thomas Blage, rector of St. Vedast, 1571—1578; rector of Great Braxted, Essex, 1570—1611; dean of Rochester, 1591/2—1611.
41. John Heard, rector of St. Leonard, Eastcheap, 1582/3—1609/10.

Mr. Harvye[42]   Thomas Canadine   in the Gatehowse

42. Robert Harvie, rector of St. Alban, Wood Street, 1588—1595 ; rector, St. Botolph's, Billingsgate, 1595—1597. A Mr. Harvey is listed for 1586 at Clements without Temple Bar. In John Udall's examination, he said that a cause for his being silenced by Archdeacon Hone may have been the secret suggestions of Mr. Harvie. See Cobbett, *State Trials* (London, 1809), I, 1274.

[43.] Thomas Sperin is not included in this list, but he held conference with Barrow in prison on March 14, 1589/90, and with Barrow and Greenwood on March 20, 1589/90. His congregation on Milk Street was the parish church, Mary Maudlin (or St. Mary Magdalen). In the 1586 list he appears as Mr. Speareing.

[B i *verso*]

A BRIEF ANSWEARE TO SUCH ARTICLES AS THE BISHOPPS HAVE GIVEN OUT IN OUR NAME, UPON WHICH ARTICLES THEIR PRIESTS WERE SENT AND INJOYNED TO CONFER WITH US IN THE SEVERALL PRISONS WHERIN WE ARE BY THEM DETAYNED.

How charitablie soever theis forged positions conningly contrived, may seme to be framed, in respect of the sclaunderous priveledged pamphletts, heretofore dispersed through the whole land, by the enemies of Christ and suppressors of all righteousnes, to bring us in contempt with all men; yet if we consider the end, and more seriously way [weigh] the present drift of theis bishops, theire preists, and new reconciled Reformists, set aworke in this busines, we shal finde they never went more craftely about the spilling of owre innocent bloud. For they in theire secret consultations having collected theis articles, have allso togeather with them constituted and commaunded certaine theire priests, twise every weeke, during this Lent, to offer us private conference in way of examination, or auriculer confession, to fish farther cause of accusation uppon theis poincts; whose testimonie and verdict of suborned witnesses, they think to frame to their bloudthirstie appetites; we in the meane tyme not suffred, eyther to set downe owre owne positions, neyther before equall wytnesses to answer or discover theire false allegations. Wherfore we thought it good (being all close prysoners) to relate unto all men that desire the truth, owre simple judgments in theis doctrines, wherat they thus snarrle: we resting still most desirous of anie christian or equall conference before indifferent witnesses set downe and recorded, if we might obteine the same uppon the dispence of owre lyves: yea, the God of heaven knoweth, how willing and ready we are to be instructed or corrected in anie thing wherin we err, when it shalbe shewed us by the booke of God.

First, then, understand, that theis accusers affirme theis to be owre positions, which they have framed of theire owne braine, without owre knowledg, much lesse consent. Secondly, they pronunce us newe sectories, although we hold no other thing in judgment or practize, more than Christ and his apostles have taught us in the Scriptures, and confirmed by theire examples and deathes; and whether Christ's Testament in [or] theis men's antichristian lawes and ordinances, fetched from Rome, or devised by themselves, be now to be holden newe doctrines, let all men consider. Thirdly, they call us Recusants, having neither forsaken the fellowship of the true church or least member of [B ii *recto*] Christ that walketh in the communion of the faith, submytting himself to be guyded by Christ's lawes and ordinances, nor refused anie truth approved unto us. Only we, according to the commandment of God, have forsaken all spirituall fellowship with theire false church, as also the inventions and popery, yea, all the execrable merchandize of that ministery and confused Babell, even that world of wickednes; out of which the Lord drawe fourth all his elected.

1. *That it is not lawful to use the Lord's Prayer publiquely in the church for a set forme of prayer.*

The Lord's Prayers we take to be those prayers which himself offred to his Father, in his owne person, as he was man uppon earth, according to his present occasions, and the will of his Father poured fourth. The forme of prayer gyven to his disciples and to all posterities by the record of the evangelists, we hold and acknowledg most holy canonicall Scripture, to be used of all churches in that use, and to that end for which owre savioure gave it: namely, to be the perfect patterne and rule of all owre prayers, whether deprecations, supplications, thanksgyving, *etc*. Not that we are bounde to the very words saying over, or asking all things therin conteined every tyme we pray, nether that the words re[a]d or sayd over by rote can be called a prayer, seing all prayer must proceede of God's spyrit from owr owne harts according to owre present necessities. So that where he calleth it the Lord's Prayer, he falsefieth the text, seing Christ never did or could use it as his

121

owne prayer:[1] for there is petition made for remission of synnes, he never trespassing. And where he saith we hold it unlawfull to be used publiquelye in the church for a set forme of prayer, he sclaundereth us; we graunt it to be the absolute, perfect, and only forme of all true prayers. If anie demaund further, whether we may use the words therof, eyther wholy as they are set downe, or anie sentence of them in prayers, we answer, by explication, or application, tending to edifying and expressing owre present estate, we may. The same questions may be demaunded of the prayers mentioned in the Psalmes[2] and dyverse other Scriptures, to which we aunswere, that we restraine no man of the use of anie parcell or sentence of Scripture, rightly applyed. Yet hereuppon is not justified eyther theire fyve tymes saying over of theire *Pater Noster* in theire English morrow masse [mattens],[3] nor yet theire superstitious repetition of theis words in the conclusions of theire prayers after or before theire sermons, when as they say they knowe not what to aske, and therfore pray as Christ hath [B ii *verso*] taught them (by repeting these words which thei call the Lord's Prayer), where in thei lye.

2. *That all sett and stinted prayers are meere babling in the sight of the Lord, and not to be used in publique christian assemblies.*

For such formes of prayer as are canonicall, such as be commended to us by God's spirit in his word, we have already in the former article set downe the true and holy use of them to be for instruction, *etc.* But, that anie man should thrust his devises into the worship of God and christian assemblies, we wonder at theire ignorant presumption, and much more that they dare be so bold as to set and stint the Holy Ghost, what, when, and how manie words to utter in prayer. So that your annuall, monthly, dayly, morning and evening prayers, wherin you bynde men's consciences to the prescript repetition of your owne words as an offring to God, we hold them by the evidence of God's booke not only a babling,

---

[1] Part of the difficulty here is a semantic one. The phrase, "Lord's Prayer," may mean the prayer used by Christ himself in praying, or it may mean the prayer taught by Christ to his followers. The former meaning Barrow denies.

[2] It is a rewarding experience to read through the Book of Psalms and note how the phraseology has become a part of the worship service. See especially Psalms 4, 5, 6, 7, 8, 16, 17, 25, 38, 43, 51, 54, 55, 56, 57, 61, 64, 67, 86, 96, 98, 103, 107, 139, 140, 143.

[3] Mattens, or matins. One of the canonical hours of the breviary. It was a midnight office, but could be anticipated by recitation in the afternoon or evening. Also, it sometimes was recited at daybreak, followed by lauds.

but apochriphall and idolatrous, contrary to the second commaundement, bringing the wrath of God uppon the imposers and
receavers; for by theis idolls you take away the whole lyberty,
fredome, and true use of spirituall prayer; yea, you stop the springs
of the lyving fountaine which Christ hath sealed in his church.

3. *That the publique prayers and worship of God in England as it is by
lawe in the Church of England established, is false, superstitious and
popish, and not to be used in anie christian congregation.*

If Christ Jesus, the author and finisher of owre faith, have
constituted and confirmed the ministration of the New Testament
perfect for all ages and persons how to serve him according to his
wyll, then your liturgye drawn out of the pope's portuis [breviary]
is not only idolatrous, superstitious, and a devised worship, the
inventions and precepts of men in stead of the livelye graces and
present guifts of his spirit wherby men call uppon his name, but
a bondle of infinite grosse and blasphemous errors, yea, even a
pseudēs diathesis or counterfeit gospell,[1] not only set above the
gospell of Christ but dyrectly instituting an other ministry and
ministracion than Christ hath commended and commaunded to
his church till his apearing in the clouds to judgment: unto which
idoll and huge chaos of long gathered and patched errors all your
ministery is sworne, wherby they renounce Christ's Testament and
must administer by this liturgye, babling over the severall parcells
therof as thei are lymited, prescribed, and stinted from yeare to
yeare, and day to day; by which liturgye or new gospell the priests
of that order are approved sufficient without preaching or the
guyft of [B iii *recto*] teaching, and the repeating of that massbooke
accompted sufficient for all men's salvation; and if anie do preache,
his doctrines must be conformed to the orders hereof. The errours
in this idolatrous booke conteyned, would not be easely repeated
in half a day; yet this we are able to prove, that it instituteth and
apointeth another ministery and ministration in all points, than
Christ's Testament hath confirmed; not only perverting, and making
of no effect the ordinances of God concerning the worship of his
people, but establishing another in the place therof, as in theire

---

[1] A false gospel. The printing is not clear. Perhaps the reading could
be read as " os " or " es," but one would expect the feminine, nominative
singular. The word "diathesis" is "diathēkē" in *The New Testament in
the Original Greek,* edited by B. F. Westcott and F. J. A. Hort. Its
meaning is that of disposition of property by will, a covenant, testament,
arrangement between two parties. The New Testament word for "gospel"
is "euaggelion."

prayers, sacraments, fasts, feasts, offrings, purifications, maryages, buryalls, *etc.*, manifestly apeareth.

4. *That the Church of England, as it is nowe established, is no entire member of the church of Christ.*

The common wealth of England, or parish assemblies, as they generally stand under and subject unto the aforesaide worship and ministery, consisting of all sorts of uncleane spirits, atheists, papists, heretickes, *etc.*, are not the true apparant established churches of Christ, or communion of saincts; and so by outward profession, they neither being gathered from the world to the obedyence of Christ, neither having power or freedom to practise Christ's Testament, as the truth is revealed, are no entire member of the body of Christe.

5. *That the government of the Church of England, as it is now established, is no lawfull government, nor christian, but antichristian, and popish.*

Having in the former articles sufficiently proved theire worship and ministerye to be idolatrous, forbidden in the second commaundment, as all apochripha and inventions of men; it is evident to all men, and confessed of owre enemies, that the ministers, lawes, and other ordinances, wherby the parish assemblies are governed, are not such as Christ apointed to his church, of pastor, teacher, elders, deacons, *etc.* But by such officers, courts and canons as are hatched from Rome, as archbishops, lord bishops, *etc.*, whose titles, office, or administracions, were never heard of in the Scriptures.

6. *That the sacraments of babtisme, and the Lord's Supper, as they are administred in the Church of England, be not true sacraments.*

There neither being lawfull ministery to administer, nor faithfull holye free people, orderly gathered unto the true [B iii *verso*] outward profession of Christ as we have before shewed, and consequently no covenant of grace, the sacraments in these assemblies of baptisme and the Lord's Supper, gyve unto atheists, papists, whoremasters, drunkerds and theire seede, delyvered also after a superstitious maner according to theire liturgye, and not according to the institution and rules of Christ's Testament, are no true sacraments, nor seales with promise.

7. *That infants ought not to be baptised according to the forme of baptisme ministred now in the Church of England, but are rather to be kept unbaptized.*

No godly Christians, seperat from the false church, ought to bring theire infants to theis parish assemblies to be baptised into that felowship or profession, by that ministery, or according to that order; but in the true church to seeke the seale of the covenant so sone as it may be had by the true ministerye in the congregation according to Christ's institution, we still affirme.

8. *Manie of them make scruple to affirme that the queen's majestie hath supreame aucthoritie to governe the Church of England in cases ecclesiasticall, and to make lawes ecclesiasticall not contrarye to Christ's lawes.*

All true Christians within her majestie's dominions acknowledg her majestie to be the supreame majestrate and governesse of all persons with in the church, and without the church, yea, over all causes ecclesiasticall and civill; yet allwayes with this caveat, that no flesh may presume to add anie thing to his word, or diminish anie thing from it. This we make no scruple to affirme.

9. *That the lawes ecclesiasticall alreadye established by the aucthoritie of the queene and realme, be not lawfull.*

Seing the ecclesiasticall lawes, canons, injunctions, articles, courts, ministery, *etc.*, wherby these parish assemblies be governed and guyded, are not deryved from the booke of God, or can be warranted therby or grounded theruppon, but are the inventions of men which tourne away the truth, abrogating Christ's lawes and ordinances, yea, seing they are culled out (if not whollie receaved) from that great antichrist his canons, orders, and divelish polecies, as most malignant oppositions against the will of God, confirmed and perfected with Christ's bloud and miracles from heaven; therfore these canons, injunctions, and articles how plawsible soever they agree to the world, yet are they the execrable wares of antichrist, statuts of Omry, and not to be receaved or obeyed of anie, that love the Lord Jesus Christ. [B iv *recto*]

10. *That if the prince or majestrate under her doe refuse or defer to reforme such faults as are amisse in the church, the people may take the reforming of them in theire owne hands, before or without her aucthoritie.*

Neyther do we looke for anie reformation of Babell, that is this world of confusion your false church, neither do we take uppon us to intermeddle with the magistrat's sword, but keepe owre selves in thought, word, and deed, within the lymitts of owre calling in all dutifull obedyence, to owre prince and superiours, for conscience towards God, and teach men both by word and example so to walke; but that all that wylbe saved must forsake the false church, and by repentance come under Christ's obedience, to serve and worship God aright in his true church, we hold it so true a doctrine as that there is no other meanes or promise of salvation; nether may we eyther neglect the true service of God nor practise of anie part therof, or have fellowship with the works of darknes, though the prince should inhibit the one and commaund the other; no, herein we shew no disobedience to magistrats, whose displeasure we must rather undergoe, than fall into the hands of the everlyving God who will abide no halting. For the warrant of those things we have the doctrine of the prophetts, Christ, and his apostles, who teach us in this case to suffer persequution as they that feare him that can cast both soule and bodye into hell fyre; and if the magistrate punish us for wel doing, we are far from resistance, willingly undergoing unto death theire displeasure. But God forbid they should be guylty of owre innocent bloud by such sclaunderous reports, without due examinacion of the truth. It is these wicked false prophetts that trouble the land, that oppose the magistrat's power against Christ, civill against spirituall, prince against subjects.

11. *That the presbiterie or eldership may for some causes, after admonition, if there ensue not reformation, excommunicat the queene.*

We detest that antichristian power of that person or presbiterye usurping aucthoritie over the whole church, as you and others do exercise in your popish courts, secret classes,[1] devised synods of priests, as though they were lords over the heritage. The true officers of Christ usurp no tyrannicall jurisdiction over the leaste member, neither do anie publique thing without the consent of the whole congregation, much lesse may the presbiterie excommunicat anie person by theire sole power, seing Christ hath gyven this power to the whole church, and not solye to the presbiterie.[2] The prince also if he wilbe held a member of Christ or of the church, must be subject [B iv *verso*] to Christ's censure in the church.[3] That

---

[1] For the classical movement, see Roland G. Usher, *The Presbyterian Movement in the Reign of Queen Elizabeth as Illustrated by the Minute Book of the Dedham Classis*, 1582—1589 ; Richard Bancroft, *Dangerous Positions*, and also his *Survay of the Pretended Holy Discipline* ; Matthew Sutcliffe, *A Treatise of Ecclesiasticall Discipline*. Another work, and one of the best, is Miss Edna Bibby's unpublished Manchester University thesis, " The Puritan Classical Movement of Elizabeth's Reign." [1929]. Patrick Collinson's dissertation, " The Puritan Classical Movement in the Reign of Elizabeth I," University of London, 1957, is an excellent piece of research.

[2] Barrow means by presbytery the eldership or governing body of the church, the session or the consistory. Above the local presbytery was the classis and the synod.

[3] This courageous statement was not calculated to please the queen or any of the guardians of her prerogative. To Archbishop Whitgift, or Sir Christopher Wray, Chief Justice of the Queen's Bench, the queen was the source of law, and her will made excommunication possible, rather than making herself the object thereof.

congregation, then, wherof the prince is a member, may excommunicat the obstinat offendors therin, without exception of person read of in the whole booke of God; yea, great injurye to Christ his church, and to the prince it were, to exempt them from the meanes of theire owne salvation, for which end this power is only gyven, and ought to be so exercised; neither doth it derogate, diminish, or take away anie part of the magistrat's power or aucthoritie, except you would have no lawefull magistracye that is not of the church, or that the spirituall power of Christ in his church should disanull the magistracy, which were divelish doctrine.

12. *That the Church of England, as it now standeth by lawe established, professeth not a true Christ, nor true religion, that it hath not ministers indeed, nor sacraments indeed.*

As for your religion, church, sacraments, *etc.*, we have before shewed the forgerye of them, unto which former articles we referr the reader.[1] Only now we must take away Balaam his stumbling block, which he layeth before men, as though we denyed the true Christ, perfect God, and perfect man, of his twoe natures subsisting, not confounded but united, *etc.* Yea, we confesse there is but one bodye, one spirit, one Lord, one faith, one baptisme; and that this Christ is in all places and the same for ever, howsoever the false church may challenge interest in the lyving child. But that these parish assemblies denie him to reigne over them, yea, to be anie true Christ unto them, by theire deeds it is manifest; for doe they not put the reede of the pope's canons in his hand, in steade of the scepter of his owne holy worde? Do they not make him a minister of an other Testament, by bynding him to this theire popishe apochripha liturgye, and all theire other devises made, or to be made? Do they not make him a priest, a sacrifice, to all the prophane and ungodly? To conclude, do they not hereby denye and abrogate all his offices in his church, of kingdome, priesthoode, and prophecye, and his whole anointing in the flesh?

---

[1] Probably a reference to *A Breefe Sum of Our Profession.* See also [" The True Church and the False Church "], *A Collection of Certain Letters and Conferences,* pp. 67-70, and separately printed in the present volume. Compare further the fourteen points refuted by Robert Some, *A Godly Treatise, wherein Are Examined and Confuted Many Execrable Fancies,* A iv *recto.* See also the twelve articles and their refutation at the conclusion of this treatise.

John Greenwood

THE BRIEF SUMME OF A CONFERENCE,
HAD THE 9 DAY OF THE 3 MONETH [MARCH 9, 1589/90], BETWEENE
MR. [WILLIAM] HUTCHINSON, ARCH-DEACON, AND ME JOHN GREEN-
WOOD, PRISONER IN THE FLEET, HAVING BENE KEPT CLOSE NOW A
YEARE AND A HALF, BY THE BISHOPS' SOLE COMMAUNDEMENT.[1] THE
PERTICULER DISCOURSE WHEROF, WERE BUT UNPROFITABLE TO RE-
LATE, NEITHER WILL I TRUST MY FRAILE MEMORYE THERIN.

Mr. Hutchchinson [*sic*] said he came by vertue of commission
in her majestie's name, to confer, *etc.*

I denying to make answere to anie thing, untill I might have
indifferent witnesse by, and the matter to be written downe, ob-
teined to have pen and ynke, and Mr. Calthrop, a gentleman and
prysoner to be witnes. I desired Mr. Hutchinson to set downe the
end of his comming, and I would make answere thereunto; whereuppon he wrote with his owne hand to this effect.

Memorandum, that I, Mr. Huthchinson, being desired by
Mr. Greenwood to set downe the end of my comming, shew it him
to be by vertue of commission, yet not to examine him, or anie way
to hurt him, but to confer with him about his seperating of himself
from the Church of England, if I might reduce him, *etc.*

I, John Greenwood, not desiring Mr. Hutchinson his comming,
yet am most willing of anie christian conference, where it shall be
free aswell to oppose as answere, and on both sides the matter to
be recorded in writing. The cause that I will not otherwise reason,

---

[1] This statement indicates that Greenwood had been a close prisoner in
the Fleet prison from September, 1588, to March, 1589/90. He was
arrested on October 8, 1587, kept in the Clink for thirty weeks (*circa* May
5, 1588), and then brought before Newgate Sessions, found guilty of the
law of 23 Elizabeth, c. 1, removed to the Fleet upon an execution of £260,
where he probably enjoyed the liberty of the house. But this kind of
restriction was changed to " close " imprisonment about September —
December, 1588. It is possible that during the summer of 1592 he may
have been bailed. Sir George Paule, biographer of Whitgift and comp-
troller of his household, states that Barrow and Greenwood were liberated
on July 18, [1588]. This is certainly erroneous for Barrow, and very
likely for Greenwood also, but it is probable that some Brownists were
liberated at this time.

is, for that I have been wickedly sclaundered, and our cause falsly reported by Doctor Some and others, *etc.*[1]

Mr. Hutchinson then brought forth certaine articles of theire collections, reading them unto me; also he shewed me Dr. Some's sclau[n]derous booke, where he turned to the positions the author had falsly affirmed to be ours.[2]   Having read his articles, he demaunded whether I approved or disalowed of them.   To the articles I said they were theyre owne collections and not ours; and as for Mr. Some's booke, it was full of lyes and sclaunders.   But I willed him, if he would confer, to set downe some position under his hand, which I would assent unto, or els disprove.   Still he would have me to answere some of those articles, *etc.*   But at length he willed me to set downe some cause whie I would not come to theire church: whereuppon I worte [wrote] thus.

The parish assemblies in England, consist of all sorts of profane people, generallye subject to this antichristian ministerie, lawes, courts, worship, etc. And therfore are not the true apparant established churches of Christ. [C i verso]

To this he first answered, that if the parish assemblies were a false church, then every member therof was a member of the false church, which were dangerous for me to affirme; I desired him first to denye or affirme, the argument being generall, and after infer what it pleased him; at last he made this answere in writing with his owne hand.

Hutchinson: Your unsufficient argument hath two defaults in it.
    1. the sequell of your argument is not true; 2. your first assertion cannot be prooved.

Greenwood: I will replie uppon your second exception, as order requireth.   That your parish assemblies consist of all sortes of profane people, *etc.*, is thus proved.

They were all by the blowing of her majestie's trumpet at her coronation

---

[1] Dr. Robert Some's *A Godly Treatise Containing and Deciding Certain Questions* (1588); and *A Godly Treatise, wherein Are Examined and Confuted Many Execrable Fancies* (1589).   George Gifford had replied in manuscript to Greenwood, but had not published his book yet.   *A Short Treatise against the Donatists of England* was entered in the *Stationers' Register* on May 4, 1590, and presumably was published in the same month.

[2] See the table of fourteen articles in *A Godly Treatise, wherein Are Examined and Confuted Many Execrable Fancies*, signature A iv *recto*.

in one day[1] receaved without conversion of life by faith and repentance, and they and theyr seede ever since generallie receaved to your sacraments without anie seperation from the world; therfore they now consist of all sorts of profane.

Hutchinson: Most of them are now departed by death, which then were so received.

Greenwood: Therfore I included their seede to stand in the same estate not separated from the world, and so could not be ekklesia [a church], a people called out.

Hutchinson: I know not what you meane by seperation.

Greenwood: You know what BADAL[2] signifieth, and as light is seperated from darknes, so must the church from the profane.

Hutchinson: What meane you by profane?

Greenwood: Atheists, men without the knowledg or feare of God, togeather with the papists, hereticks, and all other infidells. Answere, I pray you, directly to myne argument.

So he began with long circumstances to write, I perfectly remember not what words, but to this effect.

Hutchinson: Mr. Greenwood affirmeth, that because the people were converted from poperie by her majestie's trumpet at her coronation, therfore they consist of all sorts of profane, with certaine such like words.

Greenwood: You falsefie my former argument and make no sufficient or direct answere to it; answere directly.

Hutchinson: The Church of England receaveth none to their sacraments but such as make publike declaration of their faith; therfore consisteth not of, or alloweth any profane people, *etc.*

Heere we had much to doe about declaration of faith, he said they in everie assemblie had a general confession of sin, and other confessions of faith, and so were not to be called profane. To which [C ii *recto*] I answered the papists also had their confessions, as the Creed and *Pater Noster*, which they repeated

---

[1] Elizabeth's coronation occurred on January 15, 1558/9. I believe Greenwood means that the Act of Supremacy in May, 1559, converted the people by legislative enactment, and also the Act of Uniformity, which went into effect from and after the Feast of the Nativity of St. John the Baptist (June 24, 1559).

[2] In Hebrew " bad " means separation, and " badal " means to divide, separate, distinguish, differ, select.

daily in their meetings, yet could they not for that verball confession be accompted the true church.

Mr. Hutchinson said the popish church was the church, though with manie corruptions; and when I demanded whither the true church or no, he said they were the church of God. To which I answered, if it were not the true church, it was the church of the devill. At which they were displeased I should judg so uncharitablie. Well, still I denied theyr saying over their service to be a true and sufficient confession to make them Christians, affirming they might teach such a verball confession to a parrat.

Hutchinson: Wil you judg men's harts? Even their godfathers doe make a confession for their infants.

Greenwood: That is even such confession as the rest, a babling over certayne words without knowledg; neither can there anie confession be made for infants, but in mockerie. I judg not their hearts, but I know they are not able to give accompt of anie faith, except the verball repeating certayne words taught them by rote. But I will answer your former objection.

Your parish assemblies never published their conversion of life with knowledg and fruites of repentance, seeing they had no doctrine to call them before they were all without exception receaved; yet are all they and their seed of your church; therfore you receave and allowe the profane, etc.

This argument is not fullie set downe, because Mr. Hutchinson tooke up the paper, neither was it answered.

Whiles I was writing this last position, Mr. Huth: [Hutchinson] was dilating from the 3 of Mathew, how Jhon Baptist receaved them that came to his baptisme with small confession, and no knowledg of their former life; yea, that the Phariseis and Saduceis were baptised, *etc.*, also the eunuch verie speedily, *etc.*

Greenwood: You falsifie the text, and deceave the people; where can you prove that the Phariseis and Saduceis were baptised of Jhon?

Hutchinson: Heerupon Mr. Hutchinson turned to the 3 of Mathew and began at the fifth verse to read: " Then went out to him Jerusalem and al Judea; and they were babtised of him, confessing their sinnes."

Greenwood: Were all Judea and they of Jerusalem baptised?

John Greenwood

Hutchinson: No, none but they that confessed their sinnes were baptiz[ed].

Greenwood: This maketh against your self that none were receaved to Jhon's baptisme but such as confessed their sins, for with you all the world is receaved as membres of your church, and theyr seed baptised.

Heere he would have made the people beleeve I would have none receaved to the doctrine of the [C ii *verso*] church, but they which were alreadie called, I told him he must put difference betwixt the hearing of doctrine, and receavinge to be a member of the church, and to the sacraments. He demanded whome I accompted a member of the church. I said such as both by word and practise joined themselves (in the service of God) into the fellowship of the true church, *etc.* Then he demanded wherin the service of God consisted; I said in the whole obedience of his wil: he yet demanded wherin chieflie, *etc.* I answered I would not be catechized, but desired him to bring some more evident profe that the Phariseis and Saduces were baptised. He said the whole chapter proved it; I desired him to draw some one argument from some one verse: so he began againe and read the seventh verse.

Hutchinson: "Now when he saw manie of the Phariseis and Saduces come to his baptisme, he said unto them, generations of vipers, who hath forwarned you, *etc.*" Againe in the eleventh verse John said, "In deed I babtize you, unto amendement of life, *etc.*" First (saith he) they were forwarned to flee from the wrath to come 2. they came to his baptisme 3. the text saith, *Ego baptizo vos, etc.* All these prove they were baptised.

Greenwood: In that he calleth them generations of vipers, it is evident they obeied not his forewarning, neither were baptised. 2. their comming to his baptisme proveth not that they were baptized, 3. that same *Ego babtizo vos* is not referred to them: so that everie way you falsely made cohærence in the text; wheruppon he willed me to read it.

I then tooke the booke, and breeifly collected from the whole discourse thus; Jerusalem and all Judea came to Jhon's ministerie and all that confessed their sinnes were baptised; but when he saw the Phariseis and Saduces come unto his baptisme,

he called them generations of vipers, and therfore baptised
them not. For this disjunctive sentence, " but when he saw
the Pharises, *etc.*", sheweth an exception, that he baptized
not all that came to him in the wildernes, neither would he
have called them generations of vipers, if he had baptized
them. Abowt these matters we had much adoe, which because his next comming was onlie to cavill about the same, I
will refer it to our second conference.

It must be remembred that Mr. Hutchinson made promise
to me to proove the church of Rome the true church when
he came againe. Further remember, that these matters about
the Phariseis' and Saduces' baptisme were not written, and
these positions and awnsweres which were written, Mr.
Hutchinson would needs carrie them away, and would neither
have the witnesses to keep them, or me ever to see them or
consider of them. And [C iii *recto*] though I through much
adoe had gotten him to give them into the witnesses' hands,
yet so soone as I was gon and lockt up, Mr. warden's man
was sent to the gentleman for them, whoe deniing to deliver
them without our consents, Mr. Hutchinson sent the archbishop his pursyvant for them, which Mr. Hutchinson the
last day of our conference denied in the presence of manie
gentlemen. So that either the pursyvant Watson[1] made a
lie, or els Mr. Hutchinson cannot be excused. But for that
which I have written, I refer it to the witnesses for the truth
therof, yea, the positions and answeres to the writing which
Mr. Hutchinson hath kept from me.

[CONFERENCE No. 2 — MARCH 17, 1589/90]

THE SUMME OF THE SECOND CONFERENCE HAD
BETWEENE MR. HUTCHINSON, AND ME, JHON GREENWOOD,
THE 17 DAY OF THE 3 MONETH.

The 17 day of the 3 moneth [March 17, 1589/90] I was sent for
out of my chamber, and brought into the porter's lodg in the

[1] This is the same Watson who brought Barrow from the Clink to Lambeth
Palace on November 19, 1587.

Fleet, where I found Mr. Hutchinson, and one whose name I after understood to be Doctor Bright;[1] these two were closely locked in that no man might heare our conference, onely one of Mr. warden's men, besides my keeper, came in; so soone as I was come and willed to sit downe with them, Mr. Hutchinson began to make rehearsall of one point of our former conference, to this effect.

Hutchinson: Mr. Greenwood, you know the last time I was with you, I prooved unto you that Jhon Baptist receaved to his baptisme the Phariseis and the Saduces, mentioned in the 3 of Mathew, which you did not agree unto. The proofes that I brought were manie. First the text saith, " they came to his baptisme." 2. he saith, " I baptise you, *etc.*" How stand you yet minded in this point, proceding further to repeate mine answeres, but I brake it of[f], and made replie.

Greenwood: It is verie true that we dissented in this doctrine, and I disprooved all your alligations then brought to proove that they were baptised; I will not stand now to call into question our conference then had; only for that this was not them [then] set downe in writing, I beseech you if you remaine still of minde that they were baptised, set it downe under your hand, and I will either assent unto it, or denie it for just cause.

Hutchinson: I will doe so, but if you will denie it, set downe your denial.

Greenwood: So I will when I see what you will affirme.

[Hutchinson]: Then Mr. Hutchinson willed the warden's man to write thus. Mr. Hutchinson saith that Jhon Baptist did baptise the Pharises and Saduces mentioned in the 3 of Mathew, whome he calleth " generations of vipers."

Greenwood]: Mr. Greenwood he saith that Jhon Baptist did not admit the Phariseis and Saduces whom he there calleth, " generations of vipers," to his baptisme.

Hutchinson: It is expressed in the text that they came to be bap-

---

1 Dr. Bright. A friend of Dr. Hutchinson. One wonders if this could be Timothy Bright, M.D., rediscoverer of shorthand, author of the work, *Characterie, An Arte of Shorte, Swifte, and Secrete Writing by Character* (1588), and of *A Treatise of Melancholie* (1586). He was interested in religion, issued *An Abridgement of John Foxe's Booke of Acts and Monumentes of the Church* (1581 and 1589), seems to have been in London from 1586 to 1591, abandoned the medical profession to take holy orders, and was presented by the queen to two rectories in Yorkshire.

tised, because the text saith, " they came to his baptisme."

Greenwood: I denie the sequele of your argument, and your collection from the text I affirme to be untrulie gathered, for *ad baptismum* is not *ad baptizandos*,[1] that is, to be baptised.

Hutchinson: They came to his baptisme, and he repulsed them not, what is this but that they were baptised.

[C iv *recto*]

Greenwood: Baptisme is there understood for Jhon's whole ministration, not onlie of the seale of baptisme, but of his doctrine also.

Hutchinson: Then they came to Jhon's whole ministerie, therfore to his bàptisme, seing his baptisme was a part therof.

Greenwood: Alter not the question, I know they came to see all, as unworthy hearers and seers: but you must proove that they were baptised.

Hutchinson: They came to be baptized, did they not?

Greenwood: This is not the question, neither can you proove that they came therfore; I told you the last day manie came to see a reed shaken with the winde, some to cavill, and not to be either instructed or baptised; but you must proove that they were baptised, els you say nothing.

Hutchinson: I will take him in his owne words and wrap them up togeather; and thus he began to write with his owne hand.

[Hutchinson]: Mr. Hutchinson replieth that the words *ad baptismum suum* cannot be otherwise understood since that the exhortations following doth plainly declare they did offer themselves to be baptised, and he doth not bring it to proove that they were baptised, but to force Mr. Greenwood to shew whither they were expulsed by Jhon, considering they made offer of themselves. If *epi to baptisma* may not be understood of baptisme, but of the other part of Jhon's ministerie, which was teaching and exhortation, as Mr. Greenwood supposeth, then

---

[1] In Matthew 3: 7, the Greek text is " to his baptism." Greenwood believes that the Pharisees and Sadducees came as onlookers, as curiosity seekers, and that they would not seek baptism for themselves, not only because Jesus called them a generation of vipers, but because they were too strongly attached to the traditions of the elders.

John Greenwood

epi to baptisma is *ouk epi to baptisma* ["to the baptism" is "not to the baptism"].

Greenwood: You falsifie the Scriptures, wrest my words, denie your former affirmation, and seeke by al meanes to intangle by setting on foote new questions; I have often proved unto you that their comming unto Jhon's ministerie as unworthy beholders, did not proove they were baptised, neither did I say that *ad babtismum suum* was understood onlie of his doctrine, but of his whole in ministerie [*sic*], wherof his baptisme was a part, yet they were not baptised for coming to see him; and where you say you brought it not to proove they were baptised, it is manifestlie untrue, both by this and our former conference; againe, till you have prooved that they were baptised, you say nothing.

Hutchinson: Mr. Hutchinson prooveth that they were baptised, because Jhon saith afterward, *Ego baptizo vos*.

Greenwood: These words, *Ego baptizo vos*, are not spoken to those Phariseis and Saduces, but generallie to such as Jhon baptised, for it followeth " he that cometh after me, *etc.*, shall baptise you with fire and the Holie Ghost," Luke 3: verses 15, 16, which cannot be solely referred to the Phariseis, though they had beene [C iv *verso*] baptised, but this is a summe of a severall doctrine.

Hutchinson: Jhon Baptist in his exhortation saith unto them, " who hath forwarned you to flye from the wrath to come, *etc.*", this sheweth they came to [be] baptised.

Greenwood: Still you would alter the question, neither doth this proove that they were baptised, or yet that they did repent; but rather on the contrarie Jhon publisheth their obstinacie to all the people and threatneth them with the judgments of God.

Dr. Bright: They might repent upon his exhortation, and so be babtised.

Greenwood: There is no mention that they did repent.

Dr. Bright: Yes, these words which Mr. Hutchinson repeated, *Ego baptizo vos*, proveth it.

Greenwood: I have often shewed that those words are not spoken to them but to all such as were baptised by Jhon, *etc.*

Hutchinson: Jhon Baptist knew none of their conversations before or after, therfore he stirred them up to bring forth fruite worthy repentance, not that he see their fruites; and so me thinkes this and that receaving of the eunuch to baptisme so sodainlie, doth teach us, not to debar anie from the sacraments, whatsoever their life hath beene, yea, though we knew it not, they offring themselves and making declaration of faith.

Greenwood: In the true church none can be debarred from the sacraments that make with knowledg true confession of their sins, and promise obedience to the word of God, and to be ordered by Christ's ordinances; but I see no such confession made by these Pharises, neither yet by your communicantes. As for the eunuche we shall shew an other manner of confession than the verball repetition of certeine words used in your church.

Dr. Bright: Why, doe you thinke our people have not made a true confession of their sins, and promised amendment publikelie? *etc.*

Greenwood: No, your parish assemblies were never receaved into the true faith to submit themselves unto Christ's ordinances by true confession with knowledg and understanding, for that confession they made or make, is but a verbal repetition of words as one might teach a parrat.

Dr. Bright: Some doe understand what they say though all doe not; will you forsake the church because some are ignorant?

Greenwood: Neither doe those that understand what they say bring forth fruits, neither are they seperated from the unbeleebers [*sic*], neither is that confession of words which anie of you have made a sufficient confession to make you a church, but the most part are atheists and know not what they say.

Dr. Bright: What, have none of us made a true confession of faith? I never heard the whole profession we make denied before, neither that [D i *recto*] the most part doe not know what they professe, though I grant there be some such.

Greenwood: No, not with amendment of life; for you remaine one bodie with the infidels, and denie in deed the true profession and practise of the gospell, and subject your selves to the popish courtes and cannons.

[Greenwood] Heere we brake of[f] in some displeasing wordes, I desiring Dr. Bright to write, if he would reason orderly; he said he came but to beare Mr. Hutchinson companie.

Then I demanded of Mr. Hutchinson if he had brought all his proofes he had to proove that the Phariseis mentioned in the 3 of Mathew were baptised, he said yea, I said then I would oppose what reason I had to prove the contrarie; he said it was preposterous, yet he was content, *etc.* So I set downe two reasons thus.

Greenwood: In the 7 chapter of Luke, the 30 verse, the Holy Ghost setteth downe that those Scribes and Phariseis mentioned in the 3 of Mathew were not baptised, 2. that Jhon Baptist ought not to call them generations of vipers whome he receaved to his baptisme.

Hutchinson: The place of Luke is not to be understood of those Phariseis mentioned [in] Mathew 3.

Greenwood: Yes, the verie doctrine it self of our saviour Christ going before in the 7 of Luke is evident to be drawen from their contempt of Jhon's ministerie, Mathew 3.

Hutchinson: Nichodemus beleeved and manie other of the Phariseis.

Greenwood: That's not the question. The question is whether the Phariseis mentioned in the 3 of Mathew were baptised by Jhon or no; Luke saith they were not baptised of him.

Hutchinson: I will answere that of Luke, and take him in his owne wordes; so he wrote with his owne hand thus.

Mr. Hutchinson saith the 7 of Luke doth not proove that these Phariseis mentioned, Mathew 3, or that none of the Phariseis were baptised. The argument drawen from that place is of manie particulars, and the place of Luke is not generally but indefinitely conceived.

Againe wheras Greenwood prooveth by the 7 of Luke, that the Scribes and Phariseis mentioned in the 3 of Mathew came not to be baptised or (which is the other part of Jhon's ministerie) to heare his doctrine, but to gaze on him, and to see him as a spectacle, it is contrarie to the words of Mathew 3, *ad baptismum suum.* And therfore the Phariseis mentioned in the

7 of Luke cannot be understood of the Phariseis [in] Mathew 3. To the other, that Jhon Baptist ought not to call them generation of vipers, though it need no answere, yet it is false because [D i *verso*] Christ called Peter Sathan, and his disciples men of litle faith, and an unfaithfull nation, Paule [called] the Galatians *insensatos*,[1] etc.

[Greenwood] Whiles I was about to write myne answere to these things, Mr. Hutchinson would needs be gone, promising againe at his next comming to proove the church of Rome the true church: so I was constrained to set downe myne answere afterwards, which is this.

Our saviour Christ in the 7 of Luke setteth downe two sorts of people which came to John's ministerie, the one of such as heard and obeid his doctrine, and were baptised, the other of such as heard and saw, but obeid not his doctrine, neither were baptised. Of which sort chiefly the Scribes and Phariseis are note[d] unrepentant despisers. Therfore I mervell Mr. Hutchinson could so falsifye my words to excuse himself of open error, and affirme that I should say the Phariseis did not heare but onlie gaze upon him, seing I said they did heare but did not obey, neither were baptised. Further in the 7 of Luke, our saviour speaking indefinitelie and generallie of Jhon's ministerie, and of the Phariseis' contempt, and that they were not baptised of him, it were open contradiction to say they were baptised, and injurie to the Holie Ghost except you can shew by expresse words that some of them were baptised by Jhon. As for Nichodemus, he was not called to the faith by Jhon, much lesse baptised by him.

To the last point, Mr. Hutchinson his examples of Christ's reproof of Peter, or of his other disciples, *etc.*, as also Paule's reprehension of the Galathians, doth rather confirme my former assertions them [than] infringe it, seing they were reprooved for the present committing and standing in sin, and not upon their repentance. So that still I affirme it were contrarie to all the Scriptures to call them generations of vipers, who had publikelie made confession of their sin, till they againe transgressed, wherof there is no mention either of their conversion or transgressing after the confession of these Phariseis, Mathew 3.

---

[1] Galatians 3: 1. " Insensatus " is foolish or senseless. Paul's words were: " O insensati Galatae."

But at the first this controversie might have beene ended with this, that Jhon receaved none to be baptised, but such as were wonne by doctrine, and made publike confession. So that either the Phariseis were not baptised, or els they repented: and then heere is no shelter for Mr. Hutchinson's evasion, to proove by their example that all the land might in one day be received to their sacraments at the beginning of her majestie's reigne, without knowledg and true conversion, and so remaine a church of atheists and idolaters ever since. God call forth his elect from this fellowship.

[D ii *recto*]
CONFERENCE No. 3 — MARCH 18, 1589/90]

A SUMME OF THE CONFERENCE HAD IN THE FLEET THE 18 OF THE 3 MONETH [MARCH 18, 1589/90] BETWIXT MR. HUTCHINSON AND DR. ANDROES[1] OF THE ONE PARTYE, AND HENRY BARROW CLOSE PRYSONER THERE ON THE OTHER, SO NEERE AS HIS FRAYLE MEMORIE COULD CARY AWAYE.

They being set downe in the parlor with one gentleman whom they brought with them and three of theire owne servants, I being entered and come unto them, they desired me to sit downe with them, and that we might all be covered, *etc*. I demaunded to what end.

Hutchinson: Your chamberfellow, Mr. Greenwood, hath told you the cause of owr comming.

Barrow: He told me that some had bene with him yesternight,[2] but told me not the cause of your comming unto me this day.

Hutchinson: We come to the same end, to confer brotherly with you concerning certaine positions that you are sayd to hold. Having Some his booke [Doctor Robert

---

[1] Lancelot Andrewes, later to become Bishop of Chichester, Ely, and Winchester, was one of the ablest students of languages, Biblical and church history, and patristics.
[2] The conference with Hutchinson on March 17. This statement suggests the meeting was late afternoon or evening.

Some's book][1] and certaine articles of the bishops before him.

Barrow: I desire nothing more than christian conference, but having bene two yeares and well nye an half kept by the bishops in close pryson,[2] could never as yet obteine anie such conference, where the booke of God might peaceablie decide all owr controversies.

Andrewes: Whie, the booke of God cannot speake, which way should that decide owr controversies?

Barrow: But the spirit of God can speake, and which way is that spirit tryed or discerned but by the word of God?

Andrewes: But the spirits of men must be subject unto men, will you not subject your spirit to the judgment of men?

Barrow: The spirit of the prophets must be subject to the prophets, yet must the prophets judg by the word of God. And for me I willingly submit my whole faith to be tryed and judged by the word of God, of all men.

Andrewes: All men cannot judge, who then shal judge of the word?

Barrow: The word, and let every one that judgeth take hede that he judge aright therby. "Wisdome is justified of her children."[3]

Andrewes: This savoreth of a pryvat spyrit.

Barrow: This is the spirit of Christ and his apostles, and moste publique they submitted theire doctrines to the triall of all men by the word. So do I.

Andrewes: What, are you an apostle?

Barrow: No, but I have the spirit of the apostles.

Andrewes: What, the spirit of the apostles?

Barrow: Yea, the spirit of the apostles.

Andrewes: What, in that measure?

[D ii *verso*]

Barrow: In that measure that God hath imparted unto me, though not in that measure that the apostles had by

---

1 Most likely *A Godly Treatise, wherein Are Examined and Confuted Many Execrable Fancies* (1589).

2 From November 19, 1587, to March 18, 1589/90, is a period of two and one third years, lacking one day. Barrow's statement, made just nine days after Greenwood had said that he had been a close prisoner one and a half years, indicates that Greenwood received more lenient treatment.

3 Matthew 11: 19. Luke 7: 35.

141

John Greenwood

	anie comparison, yet the same spirit. There is but one spirit.
Hutchinson:	Well, you will confer then, and we come to confer with you if you will.
Barrow:	I am most willing of anie conference that may be to the glory of God and owr edefying.
Hutchinson:	Well, let us go to it then. What say you to these propositions? *Having the bishops' articles, and Some's booke in his hand.*
Barrow:	For Some's booke I disclaimed it, and sayd the man had greatly injured me. For anie propositions that I hold I was desirous to set downe myne owne propositions, and never required either the bishops or Doctor Some to set them downe for me.
Hutchinson:	I was at the great Commission a yeare agoe, where you did set downe with your owne hand your owne answeres.[1]
Barrow:	Then did you see the bishops offer me the greatest wronge that I suppose was ever offred to anie Christian in anie age. I was brought out of my close pryson and compelled there to answere of the sodaine unto such articles as the bishops in theire secret councell had contrived against us. I could not be admitted anie furder respite or consideration, neither anie present conference with anie of my brethren, neither yet so much as a copie of myne owne answers, though I most earnestly and humblie besought the same, but have ever since bene kept in most streight emprisonment without companie, ayre, or comfort, never hearing of anie kinde of conference untill now; but have in the meane while bene grevouslie sclandered, blasphemed, and accused, by sparsed articles, printed priviledged books,[2] in theire pulpets, in open Session, and unto owre honorable majestrats.[3]

[1] Barrow's Fifth Examination of March 24, 1588/89 " before certeyne Commissioners ther unto especially appointed by her Majestie." This statement corroborates the conclusion that the correct dating is March 24, 1588/89.
[2] Dr. Robert Some's books were printed by George Bishop, " Deputie to Christopher Barker, Printer to the Queene's most excellent Majestie."
[3] Sir Christopher Hatton, Lord Chancellor of England, and Sir William Cecil, Lord Treasurer of England, were the two men to whom Robert Some dedicated his book, *A Godly Treatise, wherein Are Examined and Confuted Many Execrable Fancies* (1589).

142

Hutchinson: We will not heare your complaints because we can-not redresse your complaints.

Andrewes: For close emprisonment you are most happie. The solitarie and contemplative life I hold the most blessed life. It is the life I would chuse.[1]

Barrow: You speake philosophically but not christianly. So sweete is the harmonie of God's grace unto me in the congregation, and the conversation of the saints at all tymes, as I think my self as a sparrow on the howse toppe when I am exiled from them. But could you be content also, Mr. Androes, to be kept from exercise and ayre so long togeather? These are also necessarie to a naturall bodye.

Andrewes: I say not that I would want [lack] ayre. But who be those saincts you speake of, where are they?

Barrow: They are even those poore Christians whom you so blaspheme [D iii *recto*] and persequute, and now most unjustly hold in your prysons.

Andrewes: But where is theire congregation?

Barrow: Though I knew I purposed not to tell you.

Hutchinson: They are a companie of sectories as you also are.

Barrow: Know you what a sectorie is?

Hutchinson: I know you to be sectories and schismaticks.

Barrow: What, both? It should seeme you know not what a sectory is. But it is evident that your church is deeply set, both in schisme and apostacye.

Hutchinson: A sectory and a schismatick are both one.

Barrow: That is not so. A schismatick is ever cut from the church, a sectory is not so.

Hutchinson: They are both one, and come indifferently of the word *schidzo, scindo, findo*.

Andrewes: There is a difference betwixt *schisma* and *[h]airesis*, a *schisme* and an *heresie*: the one signifying *election*, the other a *rent*. But I never heard of anie difference

---

[1] This statement seems somewhat unkind, patronizing, and tactless, but I believe Dr. Andrewes was emphasizing his own belief in the value of contemplation and was stressing that which could be a blessing even in adversity. For a different interpretation, see William Pierce, *An Historical Introduction to the Marprelate Tracts*, pp. 127-9, where he refers to these words as a "piece of brutal cynicism." Barrow does himself credit in his reply — truly a gem.

betwixt a *schisme* and a *sect*, both comming of one word.

Barrow: Though they both come of one roote, yet is not a *schisme* and a *sect* all one.

Here they would needs have a Greek dictionary and greatly wished it. So I sent for Scapula,[1] which being fetched, did not satisfie us concerning this point.

Andrewes: *Secta* in Latine is the same that *schisma* in Greeke.

Barrow: I denie that; there is a difference betwene a *sect* and a *schisme*.

Andrewes: *Secta* coms of *seco*, to cut, and *schisma* of *schedzo*, to cut, what difference.

Barrow: I take the use of the word *secta*, rather to be of *sequor*, to follow,[2] because *secta*, a sect, signifieth *via*, a way, and great difference appeareth in the Scriptures betwixt a schismaticke and a sectory. A sectory is allways in the church, a schismaticke allwayes out of the church.

Andrewes: Where finde you this in the Scriptures ?

Barrow: I finde it I Corinthians 3 and Hebrews 10. In the one place *sectories*, in the other *schismaticks*, described.

Andrewes: The sectories I. Corinthians 3 are schismaticks.

Barrow: That cannot be; they were cheif teachers of, and in the church of Corinth, where the apostle reproveth them because some held of, and followed one teacher, some of an other, as if one had held of Paul, another of Apollos.

Andrewes: There contentions are called *schismata*.

Barrow: What of that; yet you see these were sectories, and schismaticks are they which have cut themselves from the church, Hebrews 10, by leaving the fellowship.

Hutchinson: I Corinthians 11. The apostle saith that schismes are amongst [D iii *verso*] them. Therfore in the church.

Barrow: What is that to the purpose; I hope you will not say that he can be a schismatick untill he have rent himself from the church. There shalbe heresies and

---

[1] Joannes Scapula, whose *Lexicon Graeco-Latinum Novum* was published in Basel in 1580.

[2] Barrow seems to have the better of the argument here. *Sectum*, as a neuter past participle of *secare*, to cut, refers to a cutting from a plant, but *secta* derives from *sequi*, to follow.

schismes in the church, yet no hereticke or schismaticke untill they be eyther convinced and remaine
obstinate, or else have cut themselves from the
church, by forsaking the fellowship.

Andrewes: Augustine saith that an heretick breaketh the faith,
a schismatick charitie.

Barrow: A schismatick also breaketh the faith, by departing
from the communion of the church.

Andrewes: A schismatick may depart from the church, and yet
hold the faith.

Barrow: They cannot hold the faith which forsake the fellowship of the faith.

Andrewes: You speake ignorantly; sondry schismaticks have not
erred.

Barrow: I speake truly and as the Holy Ghost speaketh in the
last verse of the 10. to the Hebrews. " But we are
not of the withdrawing unto destruction, but of faith
to the conservation of our soule."[1] Here you see
the keeping of the faith, set opposite against the
departing from the fellowship.

Andrewes: Loking uppon my Testament, [h]uposolēs,[2] withdrawing. What is this to schisme ? The place you
would alledge is higher up in the chapter.

Barrow: This is the place which I would now alledge, what
say you unto it, is not that withdrawing from the
fellowship schisme ? Can anie with-draw from the
fellowship and yet kepe the faith ? Is there anie
salvation out of the church, or salvation without
faith ?

Andrewes: What [!] Is there none but a true faith, never read
you of anie other ?

Barrow: Yet acknowledg I but one faith, as there is but one
God, *etc.*, which faith no schismatick can have; and
as for this false faith, devills and hereticks may also
have such faith. But you will not say that an heretick doth hold the faith, neither yet doth a schismatick hold the faith.

Andrewes: Do not hipocrits make a shew of faith and yet they
have no faith ? What faith is theirs ?

[1] Hebrews 10: 39.
[2] Probably hupostolē, from hupostellō ; to evade, shrink, withdraw. See
Hebrews 10: 39.

145

Barrow: There is no comparison betwixt hipocrits and schis-maticks, the one whilest he standeth making shew of the true faith both by life and profession, so far as we can judge; the other making open breach of faith. But after the hipocrite is once discovered, I say then he also appeareth to have no faith.

Hutchinson: These are but *logomachiai* [logomachies], strife about words; shal we begyn to reason to some purpose.

[D iv *recto*]

Barrow: If we may have indifferent notaries that they may justly set downe what passeth on ech side, so that we may eyther of us have a copie therof, the better to expend and consider of ech other's reasons, I am very willing at anie tyme or place so to reason.[1]

Hutchinson: Here is one that can write: and called one of his men.

Barrow: He is no such wryter as I would have. Furder I would have some witnesses, because you are two, and I am but one.

Andrewes: Rather than that shall be a hinderance, I will goe up and reason with Mr. Greenwood, and leave you two togeather.

Barrow: That is not my meaning, I had rather you taried still. Only because you are two and I but one, therfore your testimonie may the rather be taken against me.

Ynke and paper being brought, and manie entred into the parlor, we were first to set downe and agree of a prop[osition], which, after much discourse to and fro, Mr. Hutchinson set downe after this maner.

Hutchinson: The parish church of St. Bride is a true church,[2] to which anie Christian may joyne in theire publique prayers and sacraments as they are by lawe now established.

Barrow: The parish of your St. Bride, as it consisteth of a confuse multitude of all sorts of people, mingled to-geather in one body, standing under a false minis-terye in idolatry and disorder, is not a true estab-

[1] In the margin are the printed words: "These speches were at the beginning of our conference which my memorie serveth not [to] place aright."
[2] The parish church of St. Bride's stands on the south side of Fleet Street, between Bride Lane and Salisbury Court. It was a rectory until about 1507, when it became a vicarage. The vicar from 1573/4 to 1591/2 was Roger Foster. In the 1586 listing, Mr. Goodman is the parson.

lished church of Christ, and therfore not such as anie true Christian ought to joyne unto in theire prayers and sacraments, as they stand in this estate.[1]

[Andrewes]. Here Mr. Andros moved that seing the question was agreed upon, and the tyme now far spent, we might depart untill an other tyme.

[Barrow]. But I seing much companie gotten in, and nothing more heard against me than this proposition, desired them to say somwhat unto it in that tyme that remayned.

[Andrewes]. First therfore Mr. Androes found much fault with my proposition, as disordered and unlearnedly set downe, and therfore deserved no answere.

[Barrow]. I sayd that if it were true it suffised me, and unlesse they could disprove it, it must still stand in force against them. Here we had also much adoe about owr order of reasoning, whither it should be after their schole maner, by logicke or no. I desired to reason after a christian maner, according unto truth, though not in logicall formes, where after some discourse of the necessitie and vanitie of the arte of logicke, I said I would not bynde the majestie of the Script-[ure] to logicall formes, whereabout we should have more vain cavilles, and spend more tyme, than about the discussing of the question; and that my conscience could neither be convinced or instructed with anie syllogismes so much as with the weight of reason and force of truth. [D iv *verso*]

Wherefore at length they condiscending unto me, denied with one consent my whole proposition as false and untrue. I also denied theire proposition as altogeather false, and willed them to make profe of it. But still urdging me to prove myne, I condiscended so to doo.

Barrow: In my generall proposition are conteined fower principall heads. Namely,

1. The confuse commixture of al sorts of people.

2. Theire antichristian and unlawfull ministerye.

3. Theire false and idolatrous maner of worshipping of God, and of theire whole ministration both of the word and sacraments, *etc.*

4. And theire popish and antichristian order and ecclesiastical government.

---

[1] This general proposition occurs frequently in Barrow's writing. It goes back to *A Breefe Sum of Our Profession* and to *Four Causes of Separation*. The four points are membership, ministry, worship, and discipline.

John Greenwood

From all which severall heads infinite reasons may be drawne. But because all these cannot be handled at once, I will begyn with some one of them. And as order requireth (if it please you), I will begin to shew that this people, as they stand in these parishes in this confusion, *etc.*, are not in this estate capable of the sacraments and ministery of Christ.

Andrewes: Order requireth that you should rather begin to disprove owr ministerie first.

Barrow: There must be sheepe before there be a flocke, a flocke before there be a shepheard.

Andrewes: A flocke and a shepheard are relatives.

Barrow: There must be a flocke before there can be a shepheard, because the people must chuse the pastor.

Andrewes: That is a devise of yours.

Barrow: Will you call the commandement of Christ my devise?

Hutchinson: Your whole proposition is denied, prove that.

Barrow: My proposition being so large, I must begyn with some one part therof; I will first therfore begin with the people of this parish.

Barrow: *Argument 1. The people of this parish are a confuse companie of infidells, idolators, ignorant, prophane and open wicked; therfore no such communion to which a Christian may joyne in theire prayers and sacraments in this estate.*

Andrewes: Infidells, what infidels? Know you what infidells are?

Barrow: I take them to be unbeleivers, such as have no true faith.

Andrewes: What, because they have no true faith, therfore infidells?

Barrow: Yea, because they have no true faith, therfore unbeleevers or infidells.

Hutchinson: We receave no infidells into owr church, if you meane by infidells *apistoi*, without faith.

Barrow: I meane by infidells, men without faith, *apistoi*.

Hutchinson: What, know you what *a* is here, it is *a* privative.

Barrow: And so I understand it; men distitute of faith. [E i recto]

Andrewes: Can you put no difference betwixt infidells and idolaters, what thinke you the papists to be infidells?

148

Barrow: I know the word infidell to be more large, yet hold I all idolaters infidells, and the papists infidells, because such grosse idolaters.

Andrewes: We thinke more reverently of the papists than so, though they be idolaters.

Barrow: But Moses and Paul think so of all idolaters, though Israelites, though Jewes, though apostataes; saying that what they offer, they offer unto devills. Leviticus 17, Deuteronomy 12, I Corinthians 10.

Hutchinson: Will you call hipocrits, infidells? Because we receave some hypocrits, therfore infidells?

Barrow: Hipocrits whilest they make and hold the same profession and faith with us cannot by us be discerned, or judged by the church, untill the Lord furder discover them, by breaking out into some error or transgression. But infidells are such as eyther are never come, or are fallen from the faith: of which sort I affirme all the people as they thus stand in your parishes to be.

Hutchinson and Andrewes: We denie that, prove it.

Barrow: They stand one with the world, uncalled forth unto the faith. Therefore they are such.

Andrewes: W[h]at new phrase is this, *stande one*? What meane you by stande one?

Barrow: The phrase is not new but usual through all the Scriptures.[1] I meane by standing one with the world, that they remaine one body with the world and the world with them, uncalled forth unto the faith, *etc*.

Hutchinson and Andrewes: We denie it: they stand not one with the world.

Barrow: I thus prove it. *They stande one with this whole land, and with all the wicked and abhominable persons thereof. Therfore they stand one with the world.*

Hutchinson and Andrewes: We denie both the antecedent and consequent.

Barrow: In proving the land to be of the world, the consequent will of necessitie followe.

---

[1] The expression is not usual in Scripture. I know of only one instance — in John 1: 26 : "there standeth one among you, whom ye know not." Even this instance does not support Barrow's generalization.

F

John Greenwood

Andrewes:	We denie this land to be of the world.
Barrow:	That land and people that are not truly called out and gathered unto Christ are still of the world. For owr saviour saith unto his disciples: " I have chosen you out of the world, *etc*." John 15. But this land hath not as yet bene truly called out and gathered unto Christ. Therefore it is of the world and the world of it. For I am [E i *verso*] sure it is neither holyer nor better than Israell and Judea were at the comming of owr saviour.
Hutchinson and Andrewes:	Our land is truly called and gathered unto Christ, and so are the people of this parish.
Barrow:	*Christ's church allwayes consisteth of a holy free people, seperat from the world, rightly called and gathered unto Christ, walking forth in faith and obedience; but the people of this parish and generally of the land have not as yet bene thus seperate from the wicked of the land, neither as yet bene thus gathered unto Christ, but stand mingled togeather with all the wicked, etc., as theire present estate sheweth. Therfore they are no people capable of the holy ministerie and sacraments of Christ, etc.*
Hutchinson and Andrewes:	The people of this parish, as also of the other parishes in the land, have bene and are truly called unto Christ, neither is there anie open wicked receaved into, or suffred in the church.
Barrow:	*Al the land at this day is of your church without the exception of anie one person. But I am sure you will not say but there are manie wicked in the land. Therfore you are not seperate from the wicked.*
Hutchinson:	I know no such wicked as you speake of. If you know anie, you shall do well to complaine that they may be cast out.
Barrow:	Alas, I know none other. But whie were they thus receaved? Or how should they be cast out?
Andrewes:	There were two cast out the last Sunday [March 15] here in London. Therfore we seperate the wicked and keepe them not amongst us as you say.
Barrow:	And had you no more apparantly wicked but two worthie to be cast out?
Hutchinson and Andrewes:	We know no more.

150

Barrow: That is well; I report me to all your gaoles, *etc.* And were not these two cast out by the power of anti-christ, by some chancellor or commissarie, or some of that crewe?

Andrewes: What if they were?

Barrow: Then you cast out Sathan by the power of Sathan.

Andrewes: Prove that?

Barrow: That were to digresse from the present question, which is not whome and howe you now cast out, but whom and how you receaved and kepe in your church, which I affirme to be all the prophane multitude of the land, without anie true seperation at the first, and so you continue.

Andrewes: That is not so; I tell you we excommunicated two the last day.[1] Therfore we have seperation.

Hutchinson: We denie your assertion, we received not all, or anie prophane into owr church at anie tyme.

[E ii *recto*]

Barrow: *In Queen Marie's reigne all the land was fallen into open apostacie and idolatrie. In this estate were they all found at the begynning of owr Queen Elizabeth's reigne, and so all at one instant uppon her first setting upp this religion received into the body of your church,[2] had this ministerie set over them, these sacraments administred unto them, etc., in your parishes as they now stand. Therfore all the prophane were received into your church without choise or seperation.*

Hutchinson: There were none then receaved but such as made true profession, and we can neyther requyre nor discerne more.

Barrow: *They could make no true profession that had no knowledge of truth. But the people at that tyme had no knowledge of the truth. Therfore they could make no true profession so sodenlye.*

Hutchinson: They all had knowledg of the truth. They repented and sorrowed for theire synnes, as appeareth in the " Confession."[3]

---

[1] This conference of March 18 fell on a Wednesday. Therefore, Andrewes is referring to the last [Sabbath] day, March 15.

[2] Elizabeth's accession was November 17, 1558, the Act of Supremacy on May 8, 1559.

[3] The " General Confession " is found in both the morning prayer and evening prayer of the *Book of Common Prayer*.

Barrow: Thus I prove that they had neyther true faith nor repentance. *None can have true faith and repentance but such as are called therunto by the preaching of the gospell; but all this people were received into your church without the preaching of the gospell going before; therfore they were received into your church without true faith and repentance;* for all were received into your church at one instant, this ministerie at the first dash set over them all, *etc.*

[Andrewes] Here Mr. Androes began a large discourse, that the Jewes had two maner of excommunications, the one of the heathens, the other of the publicanes. The one they banished from comming into their temple, the other they suffred to come thither, yet abhorred they theire companie and conversation in civile things. And here would needs know of me which of these were the greater.

Barrow: Your question is to no purpose, neither is your assertion true. The Jewes had not two kinds of excommunication; they did not excommunicate the heathen. And in that they abhorred the companie of the publicanes in civile conversation whilest they admitted them to the temple, they synned.

Andrewes: " Let him be unto thee as a heathen and a publicane."[1] Is ther not two kinde [*sic*] of excommunications mentioned amongst the Jewes, one to the heathen, another unto the publicane?

Barrow: No; there is no excommunication of the Jewes mencioned. The heathen they could not excommunicate, because they were never in communion with them. The publicanes they did not excommunicate, because they still admitted them unto the temple.

Andrewes: I will shew you in Scripture that the Gentiles were not suffred to enter into the temple; therfore they were excommunicate. And the other was a civile discommuning. [E ii *verso*]

Barrow: It should seeme you know not what excommunication is. They were never admitted to enter into the temple; therfore they were not excommunicat. For none can be excommunicat but he that hath bene in communion. But the heathen was never in

[1] Matthew 18: 17.

152

communion. As for this civile discommuning of such as are still held members of the church, it is a most ungodly devise; for to cast out or abhor in owr common meats such as the Lord receiveth unto his table, were verie unchristian.

Andrewes: You understand not the place. Did not owr saviour Christ there speake of excommunication, willing them to have such as refused to heare the church in detestation, as the Jewes held theire heathens and publicanes, whom they excommunicat?

Barrow: Oure saviour there speaketh not of the excommunication of the Jewes, but of the excommunicat Christians, willing all his disciples to shunne and eschue such as heare not the church, as the Jewes did the heathens and the publicanes, to have neither spirituall nor civile communion with them. But what is all this to the purpose, what answere do you make to my former reason?

Hutchinson: Which reason? You have as yet made none, but proved the same whith [with] the same.

Barrow: This reason. All the people of the land were received into the church at one instant; [they] had this ministrie and these sacraments, *etc.*, without being called unto faith and repentance by the preaching of the gospell. Therfore they were received into your church without true faith and repentance, because it is impossible to have true faith and true repentance without the preaching of the gospell going before.

Andrewes: Was not the eunuche as sodainly received into the church, had the sacraments administred unto him, with as little knowledg as they?

Barrow: No, he was called by the preaching of Phillip,[1] and had more knowledg than anie of these people, or well nigh anie of theire teachers then had, being all generally plunged in apostacy and idolatry immediately before.

Andrewes: Could he bewray greater ignorance, than to doubt of so plaine a place, as none in the Scriptures could be more manifest. " He was wounded for our transgressions, he was broken for our iniquities, the chas-

---

[1] Acts 8: 26-40.

tisment of our peace was uppon him, and with his stripes we are healed,"[1] of whom else could this be understood but of Christ?

Barrow: I not loking upon the place as Luke recordeth it, Acts 8, espied not then how craftely Mr. Androes falsefied and misaledged the text;[2] yet I added this: " He was led as shepe unto the slaughter, and like a lambe domb before his sherer, so opened he not his mouth."[3] My answere therfore hereuppon was, that it was no ignorant question. But that [E iii *recto*] the greatest Rabbine of those times might well have asked the question, seing it is so common a thing in the prophetts, to have figured manie things that came unto Christ in theire owne persons, as appeareth every where in the booke of Psalmes, and also in this prophecy, and almost in all other. Is it not said in this prophet, " Behold, I and the children that thou hast given me, are as signes and wonders in Israell."[4] Might not this question then be well asked whither the prophet spake it in his owne person or of an other?

Andrewes: It was a most ignorant question. Could anie beare or be broken for owr transgressions but Christ only?

Barrow: But the prophet might be led as a sheepe unto the slaughter, *etc.* And therfore the question was according unto knowledge, and such as without knowledg could not be moved; or unlesse it were knowne, that text not be understood. This eunuche was a godly and zealous proselite before Phillip met with him.

Andrewes: What, will you say godly before he had the knowledge of Christ?

Barrow: Yea, I say godly, and that before he knew that Christ was exhibited, and come in the flesh.

Andrewes: Then belike in that estate the eunuche might have bene saved, if so be he had dyed before he had heard that Christ was come in the flesh and ascended.

---

[1] A marginal printed note is: " Mr. Andros read the place out of Esai " [Isaiah 53: 5].
[2] The point is that Andrewes referred to Isaiah 53: 5, but in conversing with the eunuch, Philip read Isaiah 53: 7. See Acts 8: 32.
[3] Isaiah 53: 7.
[4] Isaiah 8: 18.

Barrow: Yea, I doubt not therof.

Andrewes   That is heresie, will you set that downe under your
and   hande ?
Hutchinson:

Barrow: Yea, that I will, and abide by it also to be truth, and
                     prove both you hereticks if you obstinatly affirme
                     and teach the contrarye.

Andrewes: Whie then there were two faithes, two wayes of
                     salvation, one for Jewes, an other for Christians.

Barrow: It followeth not; there was but one faith, one salva-
                     tion, common to all believers from the begynning;
                     " Christ to day and yesterday, and for ever the
                     same."[1]   The Jewes believed in Christ to come, the
                     Gentiles then in Christ come; both in Christ; both
                     saved by faith in Christ.   The Jewes that had not as
                     yet seene the person, nor heard of the ministerie of
                     Christ, dying in that estate were undoubtedly saved.
                     The Lord bare much and a long tyme with the Jewes,
                     and gave a tyme of removing these things.

Hutchinson: The eunuche made a true profession when he con-
                     fessed Jesus to be the sonne of God, and was then
                     baptised.   Therfore owr people making as good
                     confession, whie should they not [E iii *verso*] also as
                     sodainly be received to the sacraments and ministerie ?

Barrow: It hath oft bene sayd that your people do not, neither
                     could make so good a confession as the eunuche be-
                     cause they had not the preaching of the gospell going
                     before theire confession, neither shewed they such
                     fruits of faith as the eunuche did, who was a true
                     worshipper of God before.

Andrewes: The gaoler in the Acts was as sodainly called, bap-
                     tised, and shewed no more fruites of faith than these
                     did.[2]

Barrow: That is not so; he washed the apostles' stripes, ad-
                     ministred comfort unto them, and foode unto them
                     after that he and his howse-hold had heard and be-
                     leived the word preached.   But I never heard of anie
                     church erected in this manner, without the word
                     preached going before as yours is.

[1] Hebrews 13: 8.
[2] Acts 16: 23-33.

155

John Greenwood

Andrewes: They had the word preached in King Edward's time [Edward VI, 1547—1553].

Barrow: What boted that, when they all fell to idolatrie in Queen Marie's time [1553—1558], and all without being called to repentance by the gospell, were received into your church, *etc.*

Hutchinson: The confession they made was sufficient.

Barrow: That is denied and proved insufficient, because it was not wrought by the preaching of the gospell going before.   Answere that reason.

Hereuppon Mr. Hutchinson toke the pen and ynke and wrote to this effect.

Hutchinson: The confession of sinne that is publiquely made in the Church of England, is sufficient to enable all such as say it sincerely, to the ministerie and sacraments of the church.

Barrow: That verball confession that is prescribed and used in the Church of England, is not sufficient to enable the people that say it, or say *Amen* unto it, unto the ministrie and sacraments of Christ; neither could they make anie true or sincere confession, without the preaching of the word going before, to call them thereunto.

Uppon this issue we for that tyme ceased; they affirming this verball confession in this maner sayd, to be sufficient to enable all the people so saying it over, and I for the reasons above said, denying the same.

Mr. Hutchinson put up the paper wherein these arguments and propositions were wrytten into his bozome, but promised me a copie; whereunto I condiscended, so that upon the next conference I might keepe the paper.

There arose controversie betwixt Mr. Andrewes and me concerning these words *parochia* and *dioikēsis*,[1] he affirming them to be all one; I, to be very dyverse; the one signifying, vicinity; the other, disjunction of habitations; he alledging the ancyent use; and I [E iv *recto*] both the ancient and present: affirming all to be corrupt.

---

[1] *Paroikia*, a sojourning, an ecclesiastical district, a parish; *dioikēsis*, administration, the inhabiting of distinct places, the jurisdiction of a bishop.

Mr. Androes also in reasoning with me oft swore by his honestie, for which I reproved him for swearing unlawfully and making his faith an idole. But he said I knew not what an oth or an idole meant.

Mr. Androes also used this word *luck*. I sayed there was no fortune or *luck*; but all things came to passe by the providence of God. To proove *luck* he torned in my Testament to the 10 of Luke, verse 31, *kata svgkurian* [by chance], *etc*. And torned in a leafe uppon the place, and as he was going out willed me to consider of it. Which is no more than to come to passe,[1] although sodainly or unloked for to us, yet by the direction and providence of God unto us; without which a sparrow falleth not uppon the ground. So that though the heathens abused this word, to chance and fortune, yet is it both contrary to christian faith, and not the first and proper signification of the word.

[CONFERENCE No. 4 — APRIL 13, 1590]

A SUMME OF SUCH CHEIF POYNTS AS WERE HANDLED IN THE SECOND CONFERENCE, BETWIXT MR. HUTCHINSON, DOCTOR ANDROES, ON THE ONE PARTIE, AND JOHN GREENWOOD AND HENRY BARROW, PRISONERS IN THE FLEET, ON THE OTHER PARTIE, UPPON THE 13 OF THE 4 MONETH. THE DISCOURSE WHEREOF ORDERLY TO SET DOWNE WE CANNOT, ALL THINGS WERE SO DISORDERLY HANDLED THERIN BY THEM WHO SOUGHT NOTHING SO MUCH AS TO OBSCURE AND TURNE AWAY THE TRUTH BY THEIRE SCHOLE LEARNING, MANIFOLD CAVILLS AND SHIFTS, SHAMELES DENYALL OF MANIFEST TRUTHES, AND MOST UNCHRISTIAN CONTUMELIES, SCOFFES, AND REPROCHES AGAINST OWRE PERSONS.

[1] Luke 10: 31 begins : " And by chance there came down a certain priest that way." Barrow is contending that this phrase merely means " to come to passe," to occur, to happen. There are seven Scriptural passages in which the word " chance " occurs, but they are not strong supports for the idea of chance, luck, fortune. Andrewes' best example would have been Ecclesiastes 9: 11 : " but time and chance happeneth to them all." I suspect Barrow's reply would have been that this was not the counsel of the Holy Spirit but the philosophy of Koheleth, the cynical preacher. See John B. Bury, " Cleopatra's Nose," in *Selected Essays of J. B. Bury*, ed. Harold Temperley (Cambridge, 1930), pp. 60-69.

F*

John Greenwood

1. First they hold, but especially Doctor Androes, that the Scriptures now ought not to decide controversies, because the Scriptures cannot speake.

2. That the Scriptures ought to be judged and interpreted by the ancyent fathers' wrytings, and not by other Scriptures, or the circumstances of the text.

3. That because the spirits of the prophets must be subject to the prophets, therefore the wrytings of these dead men ought to judge and interpret the Scriptures.

4. That the Scriptures ought to be interpreted and expounded by logick.

5. That no man may preach the word, or interpret Scriptures, but he that hath an office in the church.

6. Being pressed with Acts 13, verse 15, and theire owne note uppon the same in theire Geneva Bible, he utterly rejected both that translation and the notes thereuppon, saying it was inhibited to be used in theire church.[1]

7. They further said, that Paul was a mynister of that synagogue, because he was a Pharisey.

8. There is no church where there is no administracion of sacraments. Being pressed that the pastor alone cannot make a church, neither that upon the death or deposing of the pastor, at which tyme the church for a season is without sacraments, as also that the host of the Israelites were a long tyme in the wildernes without sacraments; they only answered unto the last, and said, that the Israelites were not without sacraments at anie tyme, because they alwaies had the pillar of fire.

9. Being shewed that this pillar was no sacrament of the covenant prescribed by God to be used of the church, they still affirmed that the church could not be said to be without the [F i *recto*] sacraments, whiles they had these sacramentall signes.

---

[1] Verse 15 reads : " Ye men and brethren, if ye have any word of exhortation for the people, say on." The marginal note to this sentence in the Geneva Bible (1560 edition) says : " This declareth that the Scripture is given to teache and exhorte us, and that thei refused none that had giftes to set forth God's glorie and to edifie his people." This flatly contradicts Andrewes' belief that only office-holders could preach and interpret the Scripture. Andrewes' reply is ineffectual.

10.   They held that Christ after his death descended into hell.[1]

11.   Doctor Androes indevored to proove it by Colossians 2, verse 15, because Christ is there said to have triumphed over the principalities and powers; his consequent and collection being denyed and shewed to be a popish dreame, and to have no groundworke or warrant from this place, he sought to escape by denying the English translation, which saith: " And hath tryumphed over them in the same cross," because it is in some copies " tryumphing them in himself."[2]

12.   Being pressed that Christ's spirit was in the hands of his father, Luke 23: 46, his bodie in the grave, therfore he could not after his death descend into hell.   To this Doctor Androes answered, that his soule being in the hand of God might be in hell, because the hand and power of God was every where.   It was then said that Christ's soule was in paradise, and that all the soules of the blessed were then by that reason in hell aswell as his, yea, Christ his soule now might so be said to be in hel likewise, because the power of God is every where.   But Christ having finished all his suffrings, and performed them upon his crosse, John 19, had now nothing to do in hell.

There remayned an argument at our last conference without answere, which was this.

None can be called to a true profession of faith, without the preaching of the gospell going before; but all the people in these parishes were receaved into your church without the preaching of the gospell going before; therfore they were receaved without a true profession.

13.   Doctor Androes here denyed the minor, and said the people were not receaved into theire church and had the sacraments delyvered unto them before they had bene taught half a yeare.[3] Being demaunded what the people in the meane while were to be esteemed, whether faithfull or idolatrous, whether members or not members of theire church; he said, they were neither to be

---

1   This doctrine occasioned great disputes among interpreters of the creeds and Scripture.   The Anglican Church maintained it in the third of the Thirty-nine Articles.   See Thomas Rogers, *The Catholic Doctrine of the Church of England, An Exposition of the Thirty-Nine Articles*, ed. J. J. S. Perowne, pp. 59-62.   See also Hugh Broughton, *An Explication of the Article Katēlthen eis adou*, directed against Archbishop Whitgift, and the reply thereto, *Master Broughton's Letters* (*Short-Title Catalogue* 3864).

2   Wiclif has " in hym silf."   In Tyndale it is " in his owne person."   Cranmer has " in his awne person."   The Geneva Version, which Dr. Andrewes rejects, has " in the same *cross*."   The Rheims Version is " in him self."   The King James Version has " in it."

3   That is, from November 17, 1558, to May 8, 1559.

esteemed faithfull nor unbelievers, neither members nor not members, but they where [were] all this while in membring.

14. Being demaunded what those preachers were to be esteemed, whither ministers or not ministers unto this people, they answered that they were ministers.

> Argument 1. *There can be no minister but unto a flocke; but here by your owne saying was no flocke at this tyme. Therfore these could be no ministers unto them.*

15. They here denyed the major, and affirmed that there may be a minister without a flocke. [F i *verso*]

> Argument 2. *A shepheard can be no shepheard over goates or swyne, but only over sheepe; the ministerie of Christ cannot be set over infidells, or over anie people to take chardge or cure over them, untill those people be called unto, and have made profession of the faith.*
>
> *But here the people were not as then called unto, neither had made profession of the faith. Therfore the ministerie of Christ could not at that tyme be set over them, in that estate.*

16. They still denied the major, and gave this reason therof, because the unbeleevers might heare the ministerie of the church.

> Wee graunted that the unbeleevers might heare the ministerie of the church, but from hence it followeth not that they had interest in the ministerie before they were members of the church. It is one thing to heare the ministerie of the church, and an other thing to be a member of the church.

17. Then they brought Paul's example to prove that a ministerie might be set over infidells, because he was said to be the teacher of the Gentiles, and all the apostles willed to goe and teach all nations.

> To this it was answered, that Paul stood no minister, neither tooke government or chardge over anie heathen which were not called to the faith, and joyned to the church, still putting difference betwixt teaching the heathen the truth, and exercising a ministerie over them.

18. They alledged I Peter 1, that the apostle there tooke chardge and care over strangers.

> It was answered that those strangers were Jewes, called to the faith, dispersed through manie regions, as the next verse, I Peter 1: 2, and James 1, sheweth.

19. Paul wrote himself a father of the Corinth[ian]s: " though ye have manie teachers, yet have ye but one father."

> It was still answered that those Corinthians were beleevers.

Argument 3. *There can be no communion betwixt the beleevers and unbeleevers, therefore the infidells can have no communion with the church in the ministrie thereof, or in anie spirituall action.*

Being demaunded by them what we meant by communion, we answered, such communion as is spoken of, Acts 2: 42, in doctrine, in prayer, in the sacraments, in mutuall communication in all christian duties, and how none were receaved to this communion, before they were joyned as members unto the church. [F ii *recto*][1]

Argument 4. *There can now be no pastor over anie people by the rules of Christ's Testament, but where a mutuall covenant is made betweene the pastor and the people, he bounde to teach, guide, and governe them, they againe to obey him in the Lord. But the infidells have made no such covenant with the pastor; therfore, etc.*

20. Doctor Androes said, the pastor ought not to governe; that he himself was a pastor, yet no guyde or governor of the flocke; and that in the church there were governors over the pastors, as bishops.

We answered that the word bishop or overseer was a generall name, common to the pastor, teacher, and elders, which name importeth government and care. Philippians 1: 1, Acts 20: 28.

21. Doctor Androes here said, that the word " bishop " was not common unto either the pastor, teacher, or elders, but unto other higher governors.

We answered, that unto their ministerie the name of a bishop did not indeed accord, but only unto their lord bishops, and desired some proofe of this their assertion out of the word of God.

22. Unto which they answered, that all their ministerie was by positive lawes.

We then said that it must needs follow, that all their religion and worship was pollitick also, and that ministerie which Christ hath not prescribed in his Testament is antichristian.

At length, after manie bitter and reprochful speaches against us, we returned againe to our former discourse, and framed this argument unto the rest.

Argument 5. *The people now are to make choice and proofe of their pastor. But thei without the faith cannot make choice of theyr pastor. Therfore, etc.*

Here they said that this and all owre other positions were fond

---

[1] Mistakenly E ii in the text.

[absurd], vaine, and foolish; and this was all the answere we could get of them.

Mr. Hutchinson at the breaking up requyred me, Henry Barrow, to set downe some reasons whie I refused to joine unto their church, that the people present might be satisfied; wheruppon I set him downe under mine hand as followeth.

> The reasons whie I, Henry Barrow, cannot joine
> with the Church of England, yeilded by me the
> 13 of the 4 moneth.   [F ii *verso*]

1. The people as they stand are not called orderly to the faith, but stand mingled togeather in confusion.
2. The ministerie set over them is not the true ministerie of the gospell which Christ hath appointed to his church in his Testament.
3. The administration and worship of this church is not according to the word of God.
4. The ecclesiasticall government, courts, officers and cannons are not according to the Testament of Christ, but new and antichristian.

> Untill all these points be eyther approved by the word of God, or reformed, I cannot consent to joyne unto this church in this estate.

> These things I witnesse and subscribe.
>
> *H. Barrow.*

I, John Greenwood, being demaunded by Mr. Hutchinson whether I would set downe myne hand unto this, or ells yeild some other cause of my dislike, refused to do either of both, untill he had prooved the church of Rome to be the true church of Christ as he had twise promised, and at neither of his commings would performe.   [F iii *recto*]

A BREIF ANSWEARE TO CERTAYNE SCLAUNDEROUS ARTICLES AND UNGODLIE CALUMNIATIONS SPARSED ABRODE BY THE BISHOPS AND THEIRE ADHERENTS AGAINST DIVERSE FAITHFULL AND TRUE CHRISTIANS, HER MAJESTIE'S LOYALL AND LOVINGE SUBJECTES, TO CULLOUR THEIRE OWNE UNGODLY AND TYRANNICALL DEALING WITH THEM, AND TO BRING

A Collection of Certaine Sclaunderous Articles

Article 1. *They hold that the Lord's Praier or anie sett prayer is blasphemy, and they never use anie prayer for the queene as supreame head under Christ of the Church of England.*

Answeare. We hold that the Lord's Praier (so commonly called) is sacred and canonicall Scripture, conteyning a most absolute and perfect rule and growndworke wherby all faithfull prayers ought to be framed, gyven by owr savyour Christ for the instruction and confirmation of his disciples that theire prayers might be according to the will and glory of God.

But that the very forme of words as they are in theis petitions were gyven and instituted as a sett and stinted prayer, or that owre saviour Christ and his apostles have ever used it in that maner, we finde not in the Scriptures, where we see theire prayers according to theire present occasions, *etc.*, set downe in other words, and no mention made of such prescript and lymited saying of this as they requyre and enjoyne. Moreover, if they were as ignorant what belongeth to true prayer, or of the true use of this forme for prayer as they seeme, yet even theyre owne practize in theire pulpyts and liturgies doth excuse us thus far forth and condemne them.

For her majestie we praye both publiquely and pryvatly, day and night at all tymes and places according to owre duties as becommeth us, and, godwilling, wyll not cease so to do whilst owre lyves shall last.

Article 2. *That all set prayers or stinted prayers, or read service, are but meere babblinge in God's sight and plaine idolatrie.*

To this we answeare that we are taught in the Scriptures
(*a*) that God is a spirit and wilbe worshipped in spirit *(a)* John 4 and truth; we finde further in the Scripture and in owr selves (*b*) that God gyveth to all his children, and hath *(b)* Rom. 8: 26 gyven to us his Holy Spirit to help owr infirmities and to teach us to pray according to his will in his worde; we are also there taught (*c*) that we neede no man to *(c)* I Jo. 2: 27 teach us but as the same anoyntinge teacheth us of all things. Moreover, we finde not anie such devised prayers or stinted service prescribed to the church by those excellent and perfect workemen, the appostles;

---

[1] There is a manuscript version of this " A Breif Answeare " in Harleian MSS. 6848, ff. 22 *recto* — 29 *recto*. See also Ellesmere MS. 16 b. at the Huntington Library; compare also Harleian MSS. 6848, ff. 83 *recto* — 84 *recto*.

John Greenwood

(d) I Cor. 3: 11, 12, etc.
Matt. 15: 9

Coll. 2: 20

Gall. 5: 1

(d) neyther yet anie commaundment [F iii *verso*] or authoritie gyven by them unto the church to make, bring in, ympose, or receive, anie such stinted, devised, and apochripha service where only the worde of God and the graces of God's spirit ought to be heard. For these causes we esteeme and refuse all such devised liturgies as superfluous, will not[1] worshipp inventions and traditions of men, besids and contrary to God's revealed worde, to the graces of God's spirite, and to

Reve. 10: 4
I Thess. 5: 19

owr christian libertie. Wherfore we wonder at the ignorance of theise blynde Pharesies, which knowing neither the right ende, use, nor meanes of prayer themselves, yet dare in this maner teach, correct, and quench the spirit of God in others by ymposing the chaffe and leaven of their own lypps upon the whole church, yea, as a sacryfice upon God himself will he nyl he.[2]

Article 3. *They teache their is no head or supreame governor of the church of Christ; and that the queene hath none authoritie in the church to make lawes ecclesiasticall.*

(a) Ephes. 1: 22, 23

We hold Christ to be the only (a) heade of his church, and the greatest princes in the world to be but members

(b) I Pet. 2: 13

of his church. We hold her majestie to be (b) supreame governor of al persons' estats and causes whatsoever with in her dominions. We renounce the pope and all popishe jurisdictions over eyther conscience, queene, or contrye, and we acknowledg no other prince, potentate, or power forreigne, or domestical, ecclesiasticall or civill, to have anie superiour or equall authoritie within her majestie's dominions. We hold Christ to be the

(c) Deu. 18: 15
Matt. 17: 5
Acts 3: 22
(d) Heb. 3: 6

only (c) lawgyver in his church, and that he hath already (beinge the (d) sonne, and as faithfull in his howse as his servant Moses in his tabernacle) established sufficient lawes for the government of his church

(e) 1. Cor. 2: 16

unto the world's end in his last (e) will and testament; which no prince, nor all the princes in the world nor

(f) Gal. 3: 15
(g) Deu. 4: 2
Rev. 22: 18, 19

the whole church may (f) alter, (g) add unto or take from, upon the paynes contayned in the Scriptures. But both prince and people ought with all their en-

[1] In some copies the word " not " is blotted out in printer's ink. Two readings are possible : 1. will worshipp, inventions ; 2. [we] will not worshipp inventions and traditions of men.

[2] Willy-nilly, that is, will he, n[ot w]ill he ; whether he is willing or not.

devour, as farr as the Lorde hath gyven them knowledg and meanes, to put the same in execution.

Article 4. *They teache that a lay man may beget faith, and that we have no neede of publique administration.*

We know not what you meane by your popish termes of lay men, we holde al true beleyvers ecclesiasticall and (*a*) spirituall, yea, and that anie such beleyver may beget faith, and for evident proofe therof referr you to these places [F iv *recto*] of Scripture. Luke 10: 1, *etc.*, Luke 8: 39, Acts 8: 4, Acts 11: 19, *etc.*, Acts 18: 26, 1 Corinthians 14 entier, I Corinthians 7: 16, Philippians 2: 15, 16, 1 Peter 3: 2, 1 Peter 4: 10, 2 Timothy 2: 2, 1 Thessalonians 5: 11, *etc.*, James 5: 19, 20, which shall eyther instruct or convince your [*sic*] herein. Yet hold we the publique administracion of the word by pastors, teachers, and the prophets in the church by far, and without all comparyson more excellent, more blessed, and more to be desired, and judg your synne and iniquitie by so much the more heynouse and even come to the full, in that you so bitterly with all your gall and spyte resist the Holy Ghost, by hindring us his servants from proceeding to so heavenly and gracious a meanes of owr salvation, and earnestly with all your forces oppose your selves against God, in that you will neither enter your selves into his kingdome nor suffer such as would.

(a) 1. Pet. 2: 5
Rev. 1: 6

1. Thes. 2: 15, 16

Mat. 23: 13

Article 5. *They condemne all comming to churche, all preaching, all institution of sacraments, and say that all the ministers are sent by God in his anger to deceave the people.*

The Lord condemneth, and we according to his commaundement shunne all false churches, false and deceitfull preaching, and false institutions of sacraments, and we believe as the Lord hath said (*a*) that all false ministers are sent of God in his wrath to deceave the people, of which sorte we protest, your publique parrish assemblies as they stand in this confusion, disorder, and idolatrie, your publique preaching, sacraments, and ministrie to be, and are ready by the manifest evidence of God's undoubted word to approve the same to your faces, if anie christian audience or indifferent tryall might be granted.

(a) 2. Thes. 2: 10, 11, 12
Rev. 13: 13, 14
Rev. 19: 20

John Greenwood

Article 6. *They affirme that the people must reforme the church and not tarye for the magistrate, and that the primative churche sued not to courts or parliaments, nor wayted uppon princes' pleasures; but we make Christ to attend uppon princes, and to be subject to their lawes and government.*[1]

(a) Jos. 6: 26
Jere. 51: 9, 26

We goe not about to reforme your *(a)* Romish bishop-ricks, deanes, officers, advocates, courts, cannons, neither your popish priests, halfe-priests, ministers, all which come out of the bottomlesse pytt. But we leave those

(b) Jer. 50: 15, 16
Rev. 18: 6
(c) Luke 17: 20

(d) Zach. 4: 6
Isay. 40: 10
Jere. 17: 5
(e) Mat. 3: 3, 8

merchantmen and their wares with the *(b)* curse of God uppon them untill they repent. We are also taught in the word, that the [F iv *verso*] kingdome of God commeth not by *(c)* observation, neither is brought in by the *(d)* arme of flesh, but by the spirit of God, and by the power of his worde *(e)* working in the harts of all Christ's faith-full servants true repentance from deade workes and all things that displease the Lord, even as sone as they are reproved unto them by his worde, as also a true conver-sion of theire harts and soules unto the Lord, with an earnest love, continuall zeale, and ready desire to put in practise what soever the Lord sheweth them to be

(f) Luke 9: 59, etc.
(g) Luke 14: 18, etc.
(h) 1. Cor. 14: 38
Rev. 22: 11
(i) Mat. 15: 12, etc.
Gal. 1: 10

his will in his worde without all *(f)* delaye or *(g)* excuse whosoever forbyd or commaunde the contrarye. We are to obey God rather than men, and if anie man be ignorant, let him be *(h)* ignorant stil. We are not to stay from doing the Lord's commaundement *(i)* uppon the pleasure or offence of anie.

Article 7. *That the Booke of Common Prayer is a pregnant idole and full of abhominations, a piece of swyne's flesh, an abhomination to the Lorde.*[2]

We have shewed in owr answeare to your second article what we thinke of all apocrypha and devised liturgies, when they are brought into and emposed uppon the church. But seinge you are so zealous for the sylver shryne of your Diana, and wayle for your portuise [portas, breviary], we affirme it to be as you report a (PREGNANT IDOLE) which hath in it an infinite sorte of

---

[1] Albert Peel and Leland H. Carlson, *The Writings of Robert Harrison and Robert Browne*, pp. 151-170. See also " Certen Wicked Sects and Opin-ions," in the Appendix.

[2] This idea and similar phraseology appear first in *Four Causes of Separation.* See also " Certen Wicked Sects and Opinions," in the Appendix.

idols, and is full of abhominations and bytter fruite.
As may appeare by the double idols of your solempne
and double feasts of your Hollomas,[1] Christmass,
Candlemass,[2] Easter, Whitsontyde, Trynitie Sonday,
etc. Your Lady dayes,[3] Saints' dayes with the Eaves,
feasts, fasts, and devised worshipp unto them, which fill
a great part of your booke. Also your Lents, Rogacions,[4]
Ash-Wensdayes with the bitter cursings and commina-
tions. Your mawnday[5] holy Thursdayes, your Good
Frydayes with their peculiar worshipps. Your devision
of the yeare into your Advent, Septuagesima,[6] Easter
and Trinety Sonday with theire collects and worshipps
servinge to every weeke in the yeare, yea, to every day
in the weeke, except such feasts and dayes as are above
named. To all which you add your blasphemous abuse
of the Scriptures, shredding and rendinge them from
theire naturall sence and true use, to bende and applye
them to your idole feasts and dayes; your abhominable
collects over, for, and to the deade, your celebrating
dayes to angells, as your Michaell's day,[7] your making
archangells there and making Michael a creature. As
also your high prophanacion of the sacraments, perverting, changing, and corrupting the holy institution
of Christ with your popish devises, signes, godfathers,
godmothers, with theire ridiculous dialogue betwene
priest, cleark, godfathers, godmothers, and the infant,
[G i *recto*] and the rashe, undiscreete, and unpossible
vowe of the saide gossipps. Your purifications, and
churching of the woman, with her offring then for her
self, and at the christnings (as they call it) for the childe,
your hastie baptisme by the midwifes, your bishopping
or second baptising of children. Neither is the other
sacrament [Lord's Supper] free from your pollutions; it

---

1 Hallow-mas. All Saints' Day, November 1.
2 February 2.
3 March 25. The Annunication of the Blessed Virgin Mary.
4 Rogation Days are the three days before Ascension Day, which occurs
on Thursday. During the procession, litanies or rogations were chanted.
5 Maundy Thursday was the day before Good Friday. Associated with
that day was the distribution of food in maunds or baskets. On the
Continent the name was Holy Thursday.
6 The third Sunday before Lent.
7 September 29.

is sold for two pence a head, the institutucion of Christ broken and changed in the delyvery, a stagelike dyalogue betwene priest, cleark, people, added, new apochrypha lawes and injunctions added, to the priest to stand at the north end of the table, *etc.*, to the people to kneele, verse and collect in their appoynted tymes and tornes. Moreover, your popish and idolatrous housling the sick with this sacrament, thus prostituting and selling both sacraments to the open unworthie and their seede; as also your popish maner of visiting and pardoning the syck, wherwith this your booke swarmeth, as with sondry peculiar errours, which were even a wearynes to report, much more to confute.

Yea, we doubt not but that these which we have named do appeare to all men which have anie sparke of light in them, to be most grosse idolatries and heinouse blasphemies, as wherby the honour which is due to God is gyven to creatures, God is worshipped after the devices and fantasies of men, and not after his revealed will in his worde, God's name highly taken in vayne, the holy Scriptures prophaned, the sacraments sacriligiouslie abused, yea, even the office of God taken from him and gyven to an impiouse priest.

If you doubt of anie of these things, let your portuise, this service booke, be but brought and tryed by the worde of God (wheras now it is sett upp as the idole of indignation and Dagon's stump[1] above the worde of God), and you shall finde these things to stand thus and worse than we report.

And now you should not thinke it strange that it is termed a peice of swyne's-flesh; let it be brought to the old usuall mass-booke, and see if you finde it not a collop of that fowle mezeled hogg,[2] howsoever it hath lighted into some conning cook's handling that hath finely mingled and interlarded it to the pollecies of

[1] Dagon's stump refers to the national idol-god of the Philistines, after he had fallen on the ground, with his head and the palms of his hands cut off. See I Samuel 5: 1-4.
[2] Collop of that fowle mezeled hogg. A collop is a piece of flesh, a slice of bacon, or an aggregate of meat cut into small pieces. Such meat taken from a foul hog, infected with measles, is putrid, offensive, and filthy.

theis tymes that it might please both sorts, aswell the
new forward Protestants of theis dayes, as those that
lyked the old relygion (as they terme it) best. Innova-
tion (especially to Christ's Testament) was then (as well
as now by owr polletique devines) held dangerous to the
common wealth. Well, as we sayd, you shall finde it a
peyce, nay, a pyg, of that swyne, now growen to a
greater age, even to the encrease that you see; and [G i
verso] wee doubt not, if you bring it to that beast the
parent, it wil acknowledge as much, yea, we have
crediblie hearde by some of no small accompt, that
the pope's holynes himself hath offred to ratifie this
booke, ministrie, *etc.*, if so be we would receave him
as our arch-bishop. And this you know that swyne's-
flesh was forbidden by God's lawe both to sacrifice and
dyet. It was an abhominacion both to God and man
as then, and surely if it were so in the tipe,[1] it is much
more now in the substance.

Article 8. *They say it is a greater synne to go to the church
to publique prayers, than for a man to lye with his father's wife.*
The first is grosse idolatrie and high synne against the
whole first table; the seconde is an horrible abhominacion
against the lawe of God and of nature, not so much as
to be spoken or thought of by anie chaste or christian
hearte, much lesse in this maner compared. But it is
even shame to heare or repeate those things you are not
ashamed to publish, much more which manie of you
commyt in secret.

Article 9. *Those that will not refraine from our churches,
preaching or service, they gyve unto the devyll and excommunicate.*
As we meddle not, neither have anie thing to do to judge
them that are (*a*) without, so receave we none as (*b*)
members of our congregation,[2] but such as having left
all false assemblies where God is not rightly worshipped,
joyne themselves unto us to serve God togeather accord-

(*a*) 1 Cor.5: 12
(*b*) Acts 2: 41, 42
2 Cor. 6: 17

1 Type; in the symbolic representation or prefiguration.
2 This congregation is first mentioned in October, 1587, when Greenwood
and others were arrested. It continued as a conventicle until September,
1592, when Francis Johnson was chosen as pastor, John Greenwood as
teacher, Daniel Studley and George Kniveton as elders, Christopher
Bowman and Nicholas Lee as deacons.

ing to his worde, and to leade our lyves in his holy faith
and feare. If anie of these fall into (c) errour, apostacy,
idolatry or anie other knowen synne, and will not be
reduced by christian admonitions, exhortations, *etc.*,
therunto belonging, such obstinat offendors then, we
togeather (according as we are commaunded of God)
by the power of our Lord Jesus Christe (which he hath
(d) left unto his church), (e) delyver unto Sathan in the
name of our Lord Jesus Christe, for the humbling of the
flesh, that their soules might be saved in the day of our
Lord Jesus; this beinge the last remedy God hath
appointed, the last duetie we can performe to them for
their salvation. The neglecting wherof as it should be
to their hurt, so should it be to the chardge of the (f)
whole church before the Lord, who is a jelouse God,
even a consuming fyre. [G ii *recto*]

Article 10. *They hold it not lawfull to baptise children*
among us. They never have anie sacraments among them.
We neither condemne nor neglect the sacraments, being
ministred by a lawfull minister to the faithfull and their
seede according to Christ's institution. In that we
refuse your sacraments, it is for your wilfull prophaning
and prostetuting them to all commers, for the defaults
of your assemblies, worship, ministrie, and the heinouse
breach of Christ's institucion, *etc*. In that we have no
sacraments amongst us, it is not by our default (whose
soules gaspe and bray after them) so much as by your
barbarous crueltie and tyrannicall dealing with us, who
will not suffer us to assemble not so much as to see one
annother's faces by your goodwills, hunting, pursuing
them abroad, persecuting, confiscating, shutting upp
close prisoners them you get into your hands. Wherfore we with the prophet David even crye out unto our
God against such wylde boares as thus destroy the
tender vines, against such cruell tyrants as persecute
us into the wildernes, and keepe us from the comfort
of the worde and sacraments in the assemblie of the
saints by their open force and pryvie sclaunders.

Article 11. *They refuse to take an oth to be examined.*
We refuse not reverently to sweare by the holye (a)
name of God before a lawfull magestrat uppon just

(c) Rom. 16: 17
1 Tim. 6: 3,
5
Tit. 3: 5
2 Tim. 3: 5
2 Thes. 3: 14

(d) Mat. 18: 17
2 Cor. 2: 7,
10
(e) 1 Cor. 5: 4

(f) Josu. 7: 12
& 22: 16,
17, 18
1 Cor. 5: 6
Heb. 12: 29
2 Pet. 2: 4,
5

(a) Deut. 6: 13
Jer. 4: 2
Heb. 6: 16

170

occasion according to the worde of God. But we have just cause to refuse that ungodly rash and unlawfull oth, (*b*) by or with their booke, *etc.*, offred and enforced by theis bishops at their pleasure uppon every occasion to every one that commeth before them after the manner of the Spanish Inquisition, expreslye contrarie to the word of God, the lawes of this land, and derrogatorie to her majestie's prerogative royall, her crowne and dignitie.[1]

(b) Amos 5: 14
Zeph. 1: 5
Matt. 5: 34,
35, 36, 37
Mat. 23: 16,
etc.

Article 12. *They will not marrie amongst us in our churches, but resort to the Fleet and to other places to be married by one Greenwood and Barrow.*

We finde not in the Scriptures the gyving and joyning in matrimonie to be an action of the church, neither to be restrayned or to belong to the minister's or pastor's office. Wherfore, seing the action is meerely civile, wee see not whie we may not after the (*a*) examples of the godly in the Scriptures marrye in all (*b*) places, at all tymes in the Lord by the direction or [G ii *verso*] consent of parents (unlesse it be by their owne manifest defaults), before faithfull witnesses, *etc.* Neither have the men (whome you here untruly sclander) taken uppon them to marry anie, or executed that office otherwise than togeather with other faithfull to wytnesse the same and to praise God for it.[2]

(a) Ruth 4: 9,
10, 11, 12
John 2: 1, 2
(b) Heb. 13: 4
1. Cor. 7: 9
1. Tim. 4:
3

---

1 The oath *ex officio mero*. On November 19 and 27, 1587, before Archbishop Whitgift and the High Commissioners, Barrow refused to put his hand on the Bible and swear. There is a Ph.D. thesis at Radcliffe College on the oath *ex officio* by Mary Ballantine Hume (Mrs. John MacArthur Maguire), "The History of the Oath *ex officio* in England," Radcliffe Thesis H 922. The oath was as follows : "You shall swear to answer all such Interrogatories as shall be offered unto you and declare your whole knowledge therein, so God you help." See Lambeth MSS. 445, f. 438. See also Charles Dodd's *Church History of England* 1500—1688, ed. Father M. A. Tierney, III, 129 note.

2 This espousal of civil marriage, of course, challenged the ecclesiastical monopoly of the Established Church, the canon law, and the civil law. Barrow and Greenwood, or possibly Greenwood only, had witnessed the marriage of Christopher Bowman in the Fleet, in 1588 or 1589.

John Greenwood

Psalm 52

> 3. *Thou dost love evill more than good, lies more than to speake the truthe.* Selah.
>
> 4. *Thou lovest all wordes that may destroy, o deciptfull tongue.*
>
> 5. *So shall God destroy thee for ever, he shall take thee and pluck thee out of thie [thy] tabernacle, and root thee out of the land of the living*: Selah.
>
> *Let the lying lips be made dumbe which cruelly, pryvely, and spitefully speake against the righteous.* Psalm 31: 18.

Yet as greate paynes as these men have taken by theyr close imprisoning, open rayling, and pryvie sclaundering to convince owr errors and instruct owr consciences, they have left out and not acquainted you all this while with the greatest heresie we hold, and that is, that her majestie hath as good right to the personages [parsonages],[1] gleabe lands,[2] bishopricks, prebendaries,[3] and all other cathedrall collegiat church lyvings, as her majestie's father of most famouse memorie, King Henry the Eight, had to the abbies, and that it shalbe as greatly to the glorie of God, the good of Christ's church, the benefit of her majestie and the whole land, to dissolve theis now, as the dissolucion of the abbies was in the tyme of her majestie's father. The abbies and theis had both one originall, they sprang all from one fountayne. Now the Scripture *(a)* saith one fountayne sendeth not out bitter and sweete water, men gather not grapes of thistles. As for *(b)* tythes, they belonged to the Leviticall preisthode, and to the service of that temple, and therfore ought now to be abolished. Set stipends have no stay to leane upon in the Scriptures except *(c)* Micha his priest help to prop them upp.[4] Owr savioure Christ *(d)* and his apostles perswaded to sufficiencie but appointe not neither will them to *(e)* condicion for anie certentye. This is the matter that

(a) Jam. 3: 11, 12
Mat. 7: 16

(b) Nom. 8: 18, 24
Heb. 7: 12

(c) Judg. 17 entier
Judg. 18, 19, 20
Jude 11
(d) Mat. 10: 8, 9, 10

---

[1] That is, the portions of land, offerings, and tithes set aside for the maintenance of the parson.

[2] Glebe lands were those portions of lands assigned to a clerical incumbent as a part of his benefice.

[3] That is, prebends, or lands and stipends, attached to a cathedral or collegiate church.

[4] This exception relates to Micah, who employed a Levite as the priest for his house, and paid him an annual stipend of ten shekels of silver, food and clothing (Judges 17: 10).

172

boyleth in thier stomacks, and will by no meanes be 1 Tim. 6: 8
(e) 2. Cor. 2:
17
digested, this is hit [it] that toucheth to the quicke, and 1 Thess. 2: 5
maketh all the sylver saints in this land aswell tything
priests as hyred lecturers thus to bestur them, least their
portions should be reproved; they would gladly have
their portions improved, the one sorte in seeking to have
persona- [G iii *recto*] -ges impropriat restored,[1] the other
sort in suing to have the bishoppricks reformed by convert-
ing their lyvings from them to their servants the preachers.
Both labour in vayne, Dagon of the Philistims cannot
stand before nor with the arke of God, the head and the
hands are cut of[f], the stump must follow after. The
stone that was cut without hands hath smytten and
broken their image, even that stone which these evill
buylders refused, wherat they stumble and are offended, 1. Pet. 2: 8
Zach. 4: 7
is appointed the cheife of the corner; his poore saints Mat. 21: 16
whome they so despise and persecute shall bring it
forth with shouting and joye, and crying " grace,
grace " unto it, maugre [notwithstanding] all their
turning of devices; yea, even the children in the street
shall welcome Christ into his church, saying, Hosanna Luke 19: 27
to the sonne of David, when he shall take vengeance of
his enemyes, and of all such as would not that he should
reigne over them. That nation and kingdome which
will not serve hym shal perish, and those nations Isay. 60: 12
shalbe utterly destroyed, for all the kingdoms of the
world are owr lord's and his [are] Christ's and he shal Revel. 12: 15
raigne for evermore.

There is no counsell, nor strength, nor pollycy against the Lord.[2]
Be wise therfore now ye kinges, be learned al ye judges of
    of the earth.
Serve the Lord in feare and rejoyce in trembling.
Kisse the sonne least he be angry and ye perish in the way,
    when his wrath shall sodenly burne.
Blessed are all that trust in hym.[3]

---

[1] An impropriation was a benefice controlled by a lay person or corporation.
[2] Proverbs 21: 30.
[3] Psalms 2: 10, 11, 12.

173

John Greenwood

Expect theyr other conferences with all possible speed:[1]

FINIS

[G iii *verso*] blank
[G iv *recto*]   *Faults escaped in the printing*
For thruth read truth.   [A iii *recto*]
And for wne reade owne.   Page 3.   [A iii *recto*]
For aimisse reade amisse.   Page 4.   [A iv *recto*]
For them reade then.   Page 11.   [D i *verso*]
For babtised [Baptisme] reade baptised.   Page 12.
   [B iii *verso*, or C iv *verso*]
For note reade noted.   Page 13.   [D i *verso*]
[G iv *verso*] blank

---

[1] Thus far Barrow and Greenwood have reported their conferences with Hutchinson and Andrewes. This promise refers to their conferences with Thomas Sperin, John Egerton, and Mr. Cooper [probably — Coper, in *A Collection of Sclaunderous Articles*, A 4 *verso*], which are in *A Collection of Certain Letters and Conferences.*

A COLLECTION OF CERTAIN LETTERS AND CONFERENCES LATELY PASSED BETWIXT CERTAINE PREACHERS AND TWO PRISONERS IN THE FLEET

When *A Collection of Certaine Sclaunderous Articles Gyven out by the Bisshops* was published, about May or June, 1590, the final page (G iii *recto*) included a promise: " Expect theyr other conferences with all possible speed." The publication of *A Collection of Certain Letters and Conferences*, about July, 1590, was the fulfilment of this promise. It is a treatise of seventy-five pages, printed in the Netherlands, at Dort, and consists of four parts.

1. A statement to the reader.

This is very likely by Robert Stokes or Arthur Billett, who refers to certain arguments presented to the Reformists or Presbyterian leaders about September, 1588.

2. A summary of three conferences.

The first conference was held on March 14, 1589/90, when Thomas Sperin visited Barrow in the Fleet prison. The second conference was held on March 20, 1589/90, when John Egerton and Sperin conferred with Barrow and Greenwood. The third conference was held on April 3, 1590, when a Mr. Cooper joined Sperin in another conference with Barrow and Greenwood. Both Barrow and Sperin participated in all three conferences.

3. Letters of Barrow, Greenwood, and Egerton.

A consequence of the second conference with Thomas Sperin and John Egerton was a series of seven letters, four from Barrow and Greenwood to Egerton and three replies, written in April and May.

John Greenwood

4. " The True Church and the False Church."

This is a description of the true church and a characteriza-
tion of the English parish churches as companies of prophane
and ignorant people. There are eleven faults or errors charged
against the established churches.

This section was written about September, 1588, and
delivered as a challenge to the Presbyterian leaders, Thomas
Cartwright, Walter Travers, William Charke, and William
Floyde [or Fludd]. Since these arguments had been unanswered for more than a year and a half, they were inserted
into the present treatise. Inasmuch as they do not belong
in the present treatise, they are printed separately under the
year 1588, with the title, " The True Church and the False
Church."

This volume was secretly printed at Dort in the Netherlands. The printer was unknown to Barrow and Greenwood,
but Robert Boull testified that " one Hanse " was the printer.
The manuscript reading may be Hanse or Hause, and this
name may be a given or surname. Perhaps the printer may
have been Hans Stell, but we cannot be sure. Robert Boull
prepared the copy and arranged for the printing of 500 copies,
and Robert Stokes paid the costs and transported the books
in his cloak-bag to England. Arthur Billett served as "cown-
ter " or counter for this impression, and probably performed
duties of examiner and proof-reader.

Once the books had arrived in England, some were delivered to one Mychens. Greenwood's maidservant, Cycely,
brought copies to the prisoners, and Stokes and Billett and
Boull very likely aided in the task of distribution. This book
was rare in 1590, because of the danger of owning, selling,
lending, or reading it, and since that time has become rarer.

*   *   *   *   *   *   *

A COLLECTION OF CERTAIN LETTERS AND CONFERENCES LATELY PASSED BETWIXT CERTAINE PREACHERS AND TWO PRISONERS IN THE FLEET

1590

[Dort]

[A 2 *recto*]

TO THE READER.

Considering the reformist preachers are now become the bishops' trustie actors in their most conning and cruell enterprises, who erewhile would make the world believe that they neither pleaded for the bishops, [nor] tooke their ministrie from them, [nor] submitted it unto them, or subscribed unto their proceedings, nor would ever oppose against the truth or anie part therof, muchlesse be at the commaundment of their lords the bishops to persequute Christ's afflicted, or be partakers in their innocent bloudshedding; againe, that they pitied the ignorance of those that went to[o] far, and charitablie sought to reduce them. I thought it therfore my duetie (that the truth of these things might appeare) to give thee to understand how they have behaved themselves in this busines, and what was the power of their weapons in conference against those men, whom they have so reprochfully published in their pulpits and writings to be silie men, whot [hot] spirited, ignorant, Brownists, schismaticks, *etc.*, to the intent thou mightest equallie consider of both sides (by these few things discussed betweene them) the estate of their controveries, as also how manie of these prisoners' arguments against th[e]ir church, ministrie, and administration lie uppon them unanswered. For the conferences, the truth of them thou maist perceive in certaine letters which passed betwixt them,[1] how carefullie and upon what sure ground the prisoners related them. And if thou finde not such pith or substance in the matters discussed betwixt them of weightie doctrines as might be expected of such men, thou must consider and mayest perceive that these preachers were loth to have the sore touched, but by evasions sought alwaies to darken and torne [turn] away the truth with indirect answeres and conning distinctions.

And to make the matter more evident, I have at the latter end

---

[1] There are seven letters in all. Of these, four of the letters are from Barrow and Greenwood, and the three replies are written by John Egerton.

anexed certeine arguments, given their cheif teachers long agoe to have answered by writing,[1] the which they have (as these prisoners report) closely put up, and with an evill conscience spoken evill in their pulpits, in stead of consent and repentance. Which course of rayling and denying of free conference thou seest they still are wholy bent to proceed in, how unchristian soever it be, thinking therby their auditorie shall still be held in false reportes and blindnes; sufficiently satisfied uppon these men's wordes to persequute these poore afflicted prisoners, who love not their lyves unto death, that the truth might [A 2 *verso*] come to light to thy salvation. And (to my grief) I must desire thee to remember, that the preachers are to nothing more unwilling, than to grant these sillye men a free conference, making no scruple in the meane time to speak all maner evill sayings of them, unconvicted by them of anie error or crime, which bewrayeth both their corrupt wayes wherin they walke, that may not be brought to triall, and also their spirit to be voide of true christian love, howsoever they pretend outward holines. As thou findest God give thee grace without partialitie to valewe and esteeme the truth of God, not after men's persons, but as the cause it self requireth; and the peace of God shall rest uppon thee forever.

[Page 1 — A 3 *recto*]
[CONFERENCE No. 5 — MARCH 14, 1589/90]

THE SUMME OF THE CONFERENCE BETWIXT MR. THOMAS SPERIN[2] AND ME HENRY BARROW UPPON THE 14 OF THE THIRD MONETH[3] IN THE FLEET, AS NERE AS MY ILL MEMORIE COULD CARIE AWAY.

Sperin: First Mr. Sperin signified unto me that he was sent by

1 Printed separately in this volume as " The True Church and the False Church."
2 Thomas Sperin (or Speryn) was rector of St. Mary Magdalen Church on Milkstreet from 1577—1592. He is not listed with the 42 clergymen appointed by the Bishop of London to confer with the prisoners. Perhaps his name was added to the list, which Barrow and Greenwood printed in *A Collection of Certaine Sclaunderous Articles Gyven out by the Bisshops*, signatures A 4 *verso* and B 1 *recto*.
3 March 14, 1589/90. Barrow consistently regards January as the first month.

the Bishop of London[1] to confer with me concerning certeine things that I was said to hold, namely, that there
was no church in England.[2]

Barrow: I answered that for the Bishop of London I had nothing
to do with him, neither he with me; what I hold concerning their Church of England the bishopps knew long
agoe, and never as yet would grant either publicke or
private conference, where the booke of God might quietly
decide the controversies betwixt us; but they had imprisoned me in close and most streight imprisonment now
two yeares and well nigh an half,[3] besides manie more
greevous injuries offred unto us, as publishing us heretikes,
schismatiks, Anabaptists, recusants, turbulent, sedicious,
and what not in their pulpits, privileged bookes,[4] sparsed
libells, accused us for such unto our most honorable
magistrates[5] at publicke sessions, *etc.* Therfore I had
just cause to suspect anie conference that he could send
unto me, considering his manifold mischeivous practices
against the gospell and true servants of Christ continually.

Sperin: Hereuppon Mr. Sperin protested his comming to be in love
to confer brotherly and christianly with me, not unto my
harme or prejudice anie kinde of way, and began in some
faint termes to defend the Bishop of London [John Aylmer]
to be learned, grave, wise, *etc.*

Barrow: I said that could not be, he was a grievous enemy unto the
trueth, to Christ, and his saintes, now holding above sixty

1 John Aylmer (1521—1594), consecrated Bishop of London on March 24,
1576/77. See John Strype, *Historical Collections of the Life and Acts of
the Right Reverend Father in God, John Aylmer* (Oxford, 1821), p. 19.
For adverse comments see Martin Marprelate's *The Epistle,* and *The
Epitome,* conveniently available in William Pierce, *The Marprelase Tracts,*
1588, 1589, pp. 13-171.

2 That is, the Church of England was a false church. Hence, the Barrowists
contended that no true church existed in England. In 1588 Robert Some
sought to refute this point in his *A Godly Treatise Containing and Deciding
Certaine Questions,* pp. 34-37.

3 From November 19, 1587, to March 14, 1589/90, would be almost two and
a third years — lacking five days. Greenwood's imprisonment had continued for two years, five months, and six days.

4 Three of Robert Some's books, appearing in 1588 and 1589, were printed
by George Bishop, deputy to Christopher Barker, who was printer to the
Queen.

5 Barrow is referring to such privy counselors as Lord Burghley, Christopher
Hatton, and Lord Buckhurst, before whom he appeared on March 18,
1588/89.

of them in sondry prisons[1] without cause, lawe, or conscience. Yea, I affirmed him to be an apostata, a persecuter of that truth he sometime gladly acknowledged and defended, and therefore his name was grievous and hatefull unto me; and furder I demanded of Mr. Sperin his name, which being understood, I willed him from henceforth to [page 2 — A 3 *verso*] use his owne name unto me, for so I would not denie anie kinde of conference at anie time, which was in my power to grant; but I said that I merveled to see him come now in the bishops' name, because I had heard he had sometymes bene otherwise minded.

Sperin: To this he answered that he ever thought reverently of the bishopps, both for their learning, as also because her majestie hath authorised them.

Barrow: I shewed their unlawfull antichristian beastlike power and authoritie, as also their barbarous havock they exercised in the church, confounding and subverting all God's ordinances, and setting up their owne devises in steade therof. And therfore they that reverence theis men call Christ execrable, and worship the beast.

Sperin: Here Mr. Sperin objected against me the place of Jude, that I despised government, and spake evill of them in authoritie.[2]

Barrow: If the things I have spoken be true, or that their authoritie be not of God (both of which I affirme and will approve by the word of God), then you greatly injure both this Scripture and me.

Sperin: Their authoritie is of God, in as much as it is of the prince.

Barrow: The prince cannot make lawfull that which God forbiddeth, namely, to have and exercise both ecclesiasticall and civile authoritie, as this man doth from whom you come.

---

[1] There are 52 prisoners listed in *A Collection of Certaine Sclaunderous Articles*, signature A 4 *verso* and B 1 *recto*. For a detailed discussion of prisoners, see Frederick J. Powicke, "Lists of the Early Separatists," *Transactions of the Congregational Historical Society*, I, No. 3 (July, 1902), pp. 141-158. See also the Barrowist petition to Lord Burghley, about April, 1590, which lists 59 prisoners, in Lansdowne MSS. 109, f. 42 (no. 15), and in Strype, *Annals*, IV, 127-130. See also the Appendix for lists of the prisoners.

[2] Jude 1: 8.

Sperin: I justifie not his ecclesiasticall authoritie, but that authoritie he hath from the prince.

Barrow: If he be a civile magistrate, whie is he called a bishop, and usurpeth an ecclesiasticall function ?

Sperin: May not civile magistrates be called bishops ?

Barrow: I never read that they were so in the New Testament, yet I acknowledg they are called shepheards in Ezekiel and Micah,[1] but this man we speake of was sometimes a parson of a towne, if not of more than one, then an archdeacon, now a lord bishop,[2] which offices by their use appeare, and by the lawes of our land are held, to be ecclesiasticall.

Sperin: Much is to be given to the prince's authoritie.

Barrow: We will afterward speake of the prince's authoritie; let us first enquire of theis their offices.

Sperin: I will not here reason furder of them.

For there were manie in the windowes, and by this time was my keeper retorned with paper and inke, which he was a litle before sent for.

I had forgotten to insert certeine speech we had concerning the church. I told Mr. Sperin that I never denied that Christ had his church in England, but that church was seperate and [page 3 — A 4 *recto*] gathered from the prophane of the land, and now in great persecution under the malignant church. He then demanded of me what I thou[g]ht of their parish assemblies; I answered that as they stood in this confusion and idolatrie, they could not be held the true established churches of Christ. Now the inke and paper being brought, Mr. Sperin set downe this proposition.

Sperin: *The parish assemblies which have preaching ministers who for life and doctrine are unreproveable, and which themselves professe the true faith and christian obedience, are churches.*

Barrow: Hereunto I set downe this other proposition.

Your parish assemblies as they generallie consist of all prophane, wicked, etc., mingled togeather in one bodie, worshipping God

---

1 Ezekiel 34: 2 and Micah 5: 5.
2 Bishop John Aylmer (1521—1594) became the private chaplain about 1541—2 to the Marquis of Dorset, in Bradgate, Leicestershire. In 1553 Aylmer was appointed archdeacon of Stow, in the diocese of Lincoln; in 1562 he became the archdeacon of Lincoln. The former was valued at £24 per annum, the latter at £179 and 19 shillings. In March, 1577, he succeeded Edwin Sandys as Bishop of London.

G

after the devises of men, standing in subjection to the anti-christian power and courtes of the bishops, etc., though they have a preaching ministrie, yet are not the true established churches of Christ.[1]

I denied also his proposition, namely, that there were anie such parishes which made such profession of faith and obedience, and had such a minister as he spake of, which he endevored to prove thus.

Sperin: *They are as lawfull churches of Christ, as the assemblie of beleevers in Corinth was a lawfull Church of Christ. But that assemblie was a lawfull church of Christ; I Corinthians* 1: 2.

Barrow: Your first proposition is denied.

Sperin: What soever was necessarie to the decerning[2] of the church of God in the assemblie of Corinth, is in our assemblies.

Barrow: It is still denyed.

Sperin: The profession of faith and obedience, ministrie and sacraments, were the necessarie pointes wherby to discerne that church, but theis we have in as good or better maner than they.

Barrow: It is not so with you; you have not theis things in such maner as the church of Corinth had.

Sperin: I will insist uppon my parish in Milkstreet. It maketh such profession of faith, hath such a ministrie of the gospell, *etc.*

Barrow: It maketh not such profession, nor hath such a ministrie of the gospell.

Sperin: Some of the church of Corinth erred in chief points of the faith, denying the resurrection, *etc.* They erred in maners, being gyven to fornication, incest, oppression, drunkennes, their ministrie were vaineglorious, mixing and teaching their doctrines with the words that man's wisedome affordeth, deli-[page 4 — A 4 *verso*]vering their sacraments after a corrupt and evill maner, *etc.* Yet for all theis faultes they were pronounced by the Holy Ghost the church of God. But in my parish in Milkstreet we hold no such opinions or errors, we have no such faultes either

---

[1] This is a recapitulation of the four causes which Barrow constantly stresses: false membership, false worship, false government or discipline, and false ministry.

[2] Decerning — distinguishing, discerning.

in life or maners, nor in our ministrie; so ours is much more the church of God.

Barrow: It is verie preposterous to reason of the ministracion of, and in the church, before you have proved your parish to be an established church, which you see I deny, and require you to prove. In all this you have reasoned from a church to no church, and so no comparison betwixt them, nor sequell of your argument. The best church that ever was or shalbe whilest it consisteth of mortall men is daily subject to manie errors, which faultes being shewed in the glasse of God's word, it by and by washeth and purgeth them away in that fountaine which is opened to the howse of David for synne and uncleanenes; sondrie of the church of Corinth erred in manie of theis things, the whole church in some, as in the abuse of both the sacraments, the neglect of their ecclesiasticall censures. But the church of Corinth uppon the apostle's admonition by one letter repented, shewed great sorrow, and amended. But now for your parish, it consisteth of a confuse companie of prophane, atheists, covetous, gluttons, vaine, light, ignorant, and wicked people of al degrees and estates, of each sexe and age, they being all generallie without the knowledg, faith, or feare of God, without care of this life or of the life to come; to all which you indifferently administer and sell your sacramentes, delyvering them in a false maner not according to Christ's Testament. Your whole ministrie and ministracion is false and antichristian. Furder, you have neither the freedom to practise Christ's Testament, nor the power or will to redresse anie thing that is amisse emongst you, but either runne to the antichristian power and courtes of the bishopps, or els continue obstinat and carelesse in your synnes. Thus you see no comparison anie way betwixt the church of Corinth and your parish.

Sperin: I know the contrary to this, I both know and visit all the housholders and their families, and I admit not anie to the sacraments which have not knowledg and make true profession of faith.

Barrow: I know this I have said to be true, and that you have and do admit some to your sacraments which have no such knowledg and make no such profession of faith.

Sperin: What is true profession ?

Barrow: Where faith and obedience are joyned to the word of God.

Sperin: They all make true profession and beleleeve [*sic*] accordingly; who [page 5 — B 1 *recto*] so doth not, I seperate him from the sacraments.

Barrow: Their ungodly life and false maner of worshipping of God shew, that they neither professe nor beleeve aright; furder, this your maner of suspending or seperating, is as popish as the rest, even the instrument of that foolish shepheard; where finde you in all Christ's Testament that one man may seperate anie alone ?

Sperin: I do it with the consent of the people.

Barrow: How should that be when they know not of it. Do not you it by vertue of your idole service-booke, and by that power your lord the bishop alloweth you ? For Christ never gave anie such censure as this suspencion to his church, or such power to anie one man to seperate anie from the sacraments, which is not pronounced excommunicat.

Sperin: Paul to the Thessalonians willeth that such as are found disobedient should be noted with a letter, and his companie [should be] avoided that he might be ashamed.[1]

Barrow: You alledg not the text right, neither doth the apostle there meane of suspencion: It is wonderfull how you and some others that have written of, and seemed to seeke reformation, dare thus apparantly innovate the Testament of Christ, by bringing in your devises into the church and putting them in stead of a scepter into Christ's hand, making him to reigne by them, and exercise them over the soules of men.

By this time manie being gotten into the parlour and more into the wyndowes, we thought it meete to remoove up to the chamber where I lie. Being come thither and set downe, I willed Mr. Sperin to finde out and applie his place of the Thessalonians, which he did. It was II Thessalonians 3: 14 and could serve nothing for suspencion. The place not being furder enforced or stood uppon by Mr. Sperin, I called back againe to the point where we left, or rather where we began, *viz.*, that he should prove his parish in Milkstreet to be a true established church of Christ. And theruppon I set him downe this argument in writing.

---

[1] Sperin is misapplying the text. In II Thessalonians 3: 14, Paul wrote: "And if any man obey not our word by this epistle, note that man, and have no company with him, that he may be ashamed."

> *In your congregation in Milkstreet you have no holy or orderly communion nor true ministerie of the gospel, no christian power, freedome or order. Therfore no true established church of Christ.*

Sperin: Here Mr. Sperin affirmed againe his parishioners to be a faithfull, holie, free people, walking orderly according to the gospel, and proved it thus; because he doth administer the sacraments to none but unto such as he knoweth faithful, saying that he knoweth all the parishioners, both men and women to be [page 6 — B 1 *verso*] such, except one houshold, neither did he admit anie of their servants to the communion before they came to him and fetched his token, at which time he examined them.

Barrow: Were not all the parish of your church, and did not you administer the sacraments unto them all and to their seede, even the first day you were made their pastor ? How could you then have this assurance of their faith ?

Sperin: They had before a faithfull and godly man to their pastor (naming Mr. Paget)[1] by whom they were instructed, therfore ther was no cause that I should doubt of their faithfulnes.

Barrow: I wene that man still lyveth. Thus you buy and sell, chop and change, your ecclesiasticall offices and lyvings of your church as horses in a faire; he was even as unlawfull a minister as your self, he shewed himself a hireling in that he forsooke his flock.

Sperin: Why is it not lawfull with consent of the flock, uppon some occasions to remove ?

Barrow: But the priestes of England come and goe at their owne pleasure as best is for their gayne, without the privitie or goodwill of the people; he shewed himself a hireling both at his entrance and departure, so could he no way justifie or approve this whole parish unto you. But let me ask you a question, how found Mr. Paget this parish ?

Sperin: Peradventure they had a preacher before. But why aske you ?

Barrow: For this reason, because in Queen Marie's time they were all apostate and fallen to idolatrie; at the beginning of

---

[1] This is probably Eusebius Paget (1551 ?—1617), but I have found no statement that he ministered to the church on Milkstreet in the 1580's. John Paget (*ca.* 1575—1640) and Ephraim Pagett (*ca.* 1566 or 1575—1650) began their ministries after 1590. The latter served as rector of St. Edmund the King from 1601—1626, and perhaps longer.

Queen Elizabeth's reigne they were all found in that
estate, and by the first sound of her trompet all made
Protestantes, had this ministrie set over them, the gospell
and sacraments immediatlie administred, even in the same
parishes and estate as they now stand. So that I would
know of you whether this people in this estate were a fit
flock or congregacion to receive the ministrie of the gospel
and sacraments or no; and also whether anie preacher
(how conning soever) can make this people, which contynue in the same estate, without anie repentance or
amendement of their former doings, the true church of
Christ or no.

Sperin: Neither did they all apostate in Queen Marie's daies,
neither do I thinke they therby forsook their Christianitie,
or were no church.

Barrow: Idolatrie was then publikly set up and exercised in their
church, all the parish resorted and gave outward obedience
to the same, such as refreined were eyther forthwith persecuted unto the death, or out of the land; therfore I may
affirme that all the parish that remained were generally
apostate, and so found and recei-[page 7 — B 2 *recto*]
ved in that estate of this ministrie to theis sacraments, and
so successively have they continued to administer unto
them for the wage of Balaam.[1] Now that in this time of
popery and idolatrie they could be no church, the whole
first table of the lawe sheweth plainly. There is but one
God, one spirit, one faith, one Christ, one church, one
ministrie; Christ is not devided, he is not here and there,
neither doth he communicate with antichrist or idols.
There must needs then be a seperation made of the faithfull from the unbeleevers, idolaters, prophane, before there
can be a flock or fit people for the Lord. There must
needs also be a flock before there can be a pastor or true
ministrie erected or exercised; but as yet your parish in
Milkstreet was never thus seperate from the prophane of
the land, or prepared to receive or exercise the ministrie
of Christ. Therfore both people and ministrie are still
in confusion and disorder, and cannot be held the true
established church of Christ.

---

[1] Jude 1: 11 ; Numbers 22, 23, 24.

Sperin: They are seperate from the prophane, neither suffer I anie such to communicat there.

Barrow: They still stand in the same estate and confusion that they were first received at the beginning of our Queen Elizabeth's reigne, even all the parish that now dwell there, or hereafter shall dwell there, without exception of anie person, all are of your church, none all this while seperat, no, not one put from emongst you; therfore you stand in the same estate that the rest doe, even one body with all the wicked of the land, unless you also think that there are none wicked emongst you, none wicked in the land.

Sperin: I know none wicked in all my parish.

Barrow: What, not one wicked all this while? Sure you then have a more excellent church than ever was on the earth. But trow you are none wicked in all the land, with whom you stand one body (for all are of your church); will you justifie also all the parishes of England?

Sperin: I will justifie all those parishes that have preaching ministers.

Barrow: And what think you of those that have unpreaching ministers?

Sperin: I think not such to be true churches.

Mr. Sperin was here requested to set downe this under his hand, but would not.

Barrow: Surely theis preachers are wondrous men, they can do more than ever our saviour Christ or his apostles could do [page 8 — B 2 *verso*] with their preaching, that in al places wheresoever they become [be come? or become ministers?] can eftsoones[1] immediatly make that church which erewhile was none, the true church of Christ, and that all the parish without exception of anie one person, and that even as sone as they are become ministers of the same. But what if that parish where an unpreaching priest is, make the same profession that the other doe that have preachers, are they then no churches?

Sperin: Yes, if they make the same profession of faith, then I hold them churches also.

Barrow: That they do. All the parishes in England have the same confession, creed, and English service-booke read, as the

[1] Eftsoones — a second time, again.

papists also have the same creedes, *Pater-nosters*, pistles, gospels, and much of this service-booke; therfore they are all of the church, and so we are againe where we began, and all the land of your church, without seperacon or exception of person; for all the land maketh this confession after this maner.

But we have enough now spoken of theis parishes; let us come to the ministerie of your Church of England, what shall we think of the unpreaching ministrie, is it a ministrie or no ?

Sperin: It is necessarie that the church should have the Scriptures read, and that by a minister.

Barrow: You answere not the point; the question is, whither they be ministers or no.

Sperin: I thinke they are ministers.

Barrow: Pastors they cannot be, because they cannot teach; which Mr. Sperin consented unto. Yet adventure they to deliver, and the parishes to receive, their sacraments, which none but pastors can do. They also both possesse and supply the roomes [places] of parish-parsons. But I would now see how you can approve your owne ministrie by the Testament of Christ; which he endevored to do by this proposition.

Sperin: *My ministerie is from God, with the approbation of the assemblie of the church where I am.*

Barrow: That cannot be, you were presented by your lord patron, instituted by your lord bishop in some place at his appointment, not in the presence of your congregation, they were not called, neither had they anie thing to do with the action, they must take of force such an one as is thrust uppon them by theis lords the patron and bishop; they have neither consent nor discent [dissent], nor anie thing to do in this action; they can neither chuse nor refuse nor put away for anie fault that their parson can commit, be it never so heynous; be he an heretike, conjurer, adulterer, drunkerd, [page 9 — B 3 *recto*] they can for no error or crime put him away, they must joyne unto him in prayer and sacraments untill the bishop remove him. Thus have ye not that approbation even of this people you speake of, which though you had could nothing availe but rather overthrow your ministerie, they being as yet ungathered to Christ, and therfore neither may in this estate chuse a minister, nor anie exercise a ministerie unto them, without heynous sacriledge. But this your ministerie both in your entrance, office, and whole administration is antichristian, your entrance being by the patron and bishop, your office to be a towne priest or parish parson, your administracion according to the prescription and limitation of your lord the bishop, to whom you have sworne your cannonicall obedience.

Sperin: The patron doth elect by consent of the people, who have yeilded their right unto him, as unto the wisest and worthiest emongst them, and so they approve his choise.

Barrow: Whether the patron had that power and priviledg of the people or no is doubtfull; I thinke rather [it is derived] of the pope. But that he doth it without their privitie, and maugre [in spite of] their wylls, it is evident; for be the patron an hundreth miles of[f], be he a childe, a woman, yet they both may and will gyve the benefice without the knowledg, privitie, or consent of the parish. Now which way can either this election be justified by the Testament of Christ, or be joyned unto the ministerie of Christ?

Sperin: I make lesse matter of my ordinacion than of my ministerie.

Barrow: Yet without a true calling you cannot exercise anie true office.

Sperin: The calling is not the substance of the ministerie.

Barrow: Thus whilest you professe science you make shipwrack of faith, and with your logick put away the Testament of Christ. Christ saith that he which ascendeth into the shepefolde anie other way is a thiefe and a spoyler;[1] and in an other place: no man taketh this honour to himself, but he that is called of God, *etc.*[2] Christ hath ordeyned to every office lawes for the giftes, lif, and conversation of the officer, for his probation, election, ordinacion, administracion. He which wanteth the calling of Christ unto the ministrie cannot have or exercise anie ministerie in the church; but you want [lack] the calling of Christ unto your ministrie; therfor the ministerie you exercise is not of Christ.

[1] John 10: 1.
[2] Hebrews 5: 4.

189

G*

Sperin: I have the true calling of Christ unto my ministrie in my conscience. [page 10 — B 3 *verso*]

Barrow: The conscience only is assured, and resteth upon the word of God. But your calling unto this ministerie cannot be warranted by the word of God, but is found therby to be unlawfull and antichristian; therfore, *etc*.

Sperin: I stand not uppon my outward calling by the bishop so much as uppon my inward calling and the consent of the people.

Barrow: But the people, you said erewhile, consented to the election of the patron, the ordinacion of the bishop, *etc*. Therfor their consent was unto and in evill, and so can no way justifie your ministerie, neither have the people anie power to make anie other or better election, all of them standing under the antichristian yoke of theis Babilonish bishopps.

Sperin: I will not stand to justifie the calling of the bishopps; I have a better calling than the calling of the bishopps.

Barrow: But what then thinke you of the calling of theis bishops ?

Sperin: I confesse it to be unlawfull.

Barrow: Set downe that under your hand.

Sperin: To what end; that were to bring my self into danger.

Barrow: Are you afraid to witnesse unto the trueth ? Well, but being unlawfull, how chance you were not afeared to receave it and still to reteine it ?

Sperin: I did it in ignorance, I have since repented it.

Barrow: Which way could you be a true minister that knew not so much as the true entrance unto a true ministrie; how durst you adventure to administer before the Lord, and take the care of the soules of men in this ignorance ? Furder, how can you be said to have truly repented that calling which you still reteine, still administring by the same the bishop's licence, and still standing under his yoke and obedience ?

Sperin: I attribute much to the civile magistrate, I do it because of the civile magistrate that authoriseth the bishop.

Barrow: But may the civile magistrate either commaund anie thing contrary to the commaundement of God, or if he do, is he to be obeyed therin, or can he excuse you before the tribunal of Christ for the breach of God's lawes ?

Sperin: Why, then you affirme that the queene and the parliament

190

do wickedly in gyving this power and authoritie unto the bishops. Will you write that?

Barrow: Yea, that I will by the grace of God whilest I have breath,[1] and seale it with my blood also (if so God will), it being directly contrary to the Testament of Christ as your self confesseth, and yet continue to do contrary to your owne conscience. O take heed, God is greater than your conscience.[2] It is a fearefull thing to fall [page 11 — B 4 *recto*] into the hands of the living God.[3]

Sperin: I thanke God I have his calling unto my ministrie, which is the inward calling, being approved by my gyftes unto my flocke, so that though there were error in my outward calling (which I have repented), yet my ministrie is not disanulled.

Barrow: With what conscience can you now call that an error in a true calling, which even now you confessed to be a false calling? Is not this to diminish, excuse, and hide your synne? Call you this true repentance, how can you be thought, or dare you affirme, to have repented this error in your entrance into your ministrie, when you still pleade for and justifie that calling by the civile magistrate, when you confesse it repugnant unto, and condemned in the Testament of Christ, how can you be said to have repented it when you still reteine it, stand and administer by it, and joyne unto such as still enter that way? Neither in deed have you anie other calling unto your ministerie in your church: make it therfore either good or evill, lawfull or unlawfull, by the word of God, let us bring it to the triall.

Sperin: I stand not so much by their calling as by the calling of God, by whom I am enabled to my ministrie.

Barrow: This is Anabaptisticall to justifie open transgression by the inward conscience or giftes; might not anie thus usurpe the civile magistrate's office also by their inward

---

[1] Although Sperin prudently refused to put in writing his views on the appointment of bishops, Barrow is not one to claim a like privilege. He abhorred expediency as a policy, and too often he cast discretion aside. That he is not indulging in merely brave talk is evident from his fearless pronouncements on the subjection of the queen to the censures of the church, and his denunciation of " such blasphemous titles, popish prerogatives and dispensations, as SUPREME HEAD OF THE CHURCH " (*A Brief Discoverie of the False Church*, pp. 242-247).

[2] Compare I John 3: 20 and Job 33: 12.

[3] Hebrews 10: 31.

gyftes, wisdome, knowledg, fitness, *etc.*, but God hath ordeined a lawfull calling to every lawfull office, which may at no hand be severed from the office, which calling who so wanteth and taketh honour to himself to administer, *etc.*, breaketh the boundes of God and usurpeth. You have no gifts which you have not received of God, God knoweth his owne giftes which he hath given to every one best whom he seeth meete and hath appointed to the ministerie, unto such he alwayes gyveth a lawfull calling unto the ministerie; wherfore, you must eyther approve your calling by the word of God, or els be held an usurper, for all your giftes.

Sperin: The bishops tolerate manie thinges with us.

Barrow: They allow nothing but their owne proceedings, neither doth the land receive or alow anie other.

Sperin: I say not allow, they may suffer that they allow not.

Barrow: Here is good worke emongst you, they tolerate with you, and you subscribe unto them; thus are you togeather in conspiracie against Christ.

Sperin: Will you say that Mr. Egerton and Mr. Gardiner[1] are not true ministers of the gospell because they have no such calling as you require? [page 12 — B 4 *verso*]

Barrow: I require no other calling than Christ enjoyneth, which calling if they want (as I am sure they do) I dare affirme that they do not serve Christ in the ministrie of the gospell, all extraordinarie offices and callings therunto being now ceased.

Sperin: All the churches and learned in Europe give us consent and allow us for ministers.

Barrow: But untill you approve your selves such by the word of God, it will nothing availe you.

Sperin: Our giftes and doctrines approve our ministrie. Did you ever heare Mr. [Stephen or John?] Egerton and Mr. [Richard] Gardiner?

---

[1] Both are mentioned in the list of preachers appointed to confer with the prisoners (*A Collection of Certaine Sclaunderous Articles*, signature A 4 *verso* and B 1 *recto*). I think that Thomas Sperin is speaking of John Egerton, although Stephen Egerton is a possible choice. There is a Richard Gardener, staunch Presbyterian, in whose home the leaders met in October, 1590, to discuss whether Cartwright should reveal Presbyterian secrets during his imprisonment (A. F. Scott Pearson, *Thomas Cartwright*, p. 316). He is probably the same Mr. Gardner who is listed as the preacher at Whitechapel Church (Albert Peel [ed.], *The Seconde Parte of a Register*, II, 184).

Barrow: You still oppose your giftes against God, and hold the faith in respect of men's persons. The men you speake of I never heard in their ministerie, but I know them by their ministerie to be notable sectories and false teachers.

Sperin: They be men of singuler giftes, and how can you gyve out this of them and know them not, neither ever heard them teach.

Barrow: I am taught to know the tree by the fruit, a false minister by his antichristian entrance, office, and administration, all which are notably found uppon them and uppon you all; neither will I say that the one of them bought his benefice, or that the other hath bene convinced of false doctrines by his owne auditorye sondry times.

Sperin: The first hath repented that, and you have the other but by hearesay; they are knowne to be learned men, and such as teach sound doctrines.

Barrow: My hearesay hath better proofe than your [sic] know; but how can theis or anie of you teach sound doctrine sincerely in a false ministerie? Balaam, and the Pharises, and Satan himself, had and hath as great giftes and learning as they or anie of you. But if we would come even to this preaching you boste of, I suppose more corrupt teachers cannot be found in anie age than these, they teaching nothing almost truly, much lesse sincerely.

Sperin: I teach Christ Jesus very God and very man, and him crucified, and that truly.

Barrow: I will not presse you with anie argumentes drawne from your false entrance and administracion, all which undoubtedly convince that you cannot preach Christ soundly, yet is there no heretike that holdeth not some trueth. But this I affirme and will approve that you deny the whole anointing of Christ in his three offices of king, priest, and prophet, and therfore you deny Christ be to come in the flesh[1], and cannot preach him soundly; I graunt indeed that you preach him crucified in [page 13 — C 1 *recto*] your sermons and church, buffeted, skourged, crowned with thornes, by rayling, blaspheming, and imprisoning his faithfull witnesses and servants dayly at all handes, you preach him blindfoulded by drawing

---

[1] The same language was used by Barrow against Robert Browne. Browne quotes Barrow, and Dr. Bancroft quoted Barrow and Browne in his sermon of February 9, 1588/9. See *Four Causes of Separation*, footnote 1.

a vaile over his face, that the people should not see to the end of his ministerie, not one of you either priest or people as yet knowing what belongeth to a true profession, a true communion, a true office, or a true entrance, much lesse to [a] true administration: Christ crucified you all abhorr, you can not abide his crosse, you will not suffer or abide by anie trueth, but dayly seeke new cavills, distinctions and evasions to hide anie trueth which bringeth danger, or to avoide the crosse of Christ, and therfore you shall not reigne with him. It were an infinite thing to reckon up the diversitie of opinions, sectes, errors that are found emongst you of the ministrie, it being almost an unpossible thing to finde two of you of one judgment, or anie one of you constant to your selves, except it be in evill; one preaching one doctrine in one place, and another the quite contrary in another place, yea, some of your chief teachers have preached *palinodan*[1] concerning your ministerie and sacramentes of your church. But I would now know what office these men you speake of, or your self, do execute.

Sperin: Mr. Egerton is a doctor, Mr. Gardiner and my self are pastors.

Barrow: Your Church of England hath no such office as the teacher's office, it hath no other than universitie doctors, which are not in anie office, or therby ministers. I wene also he hath a dumbe minister, one that cannot preach for his pastor; so that he is a hireling curat and no christian teacher.[2] As for Mr. Gardiner and your self, you be parish parsons, and therfore cannot be held christian pastors.

Sperin: I deny your argument, it followeth not because they are termed parsons, therfore they are not pastors.

Barrow: Both the name and office are diverse, therfore not the same.

Sperin: The parson is called in Latine *Rector Ecclesiae*, which name properly agreeth to the pastor.

Barrow: Your Latine name is popish, one of the names of blasphemie written uppon the heades of the beast, for Christ

---

[1] From *palinodia*, a retracing of one's path.
[2] In a list for 1586, Dr. Egerton is specified as the preacher at St. Anne in the Blackfriars. His curate is a Mr. Die, who is also listed as the preacher at St. Bartholomew the Great.

hath appointed many to the office of governing and overseeing, and not the pastor only. And therfore this name is not proper to the pastor. [page 14 — C 1 *verso*]

Sperin: The pastor should governe the church.

Barrow: But the pastor is not to governe it alone, there are others joyned in commission with him, therfore he cannot in this maner be called the *rector*[1] of the church, though he be a governour emongst the rest. But the office of a parish parson is as greatly diverse from the office of a pastor, as the name is, for if Mr. Foxe say true,[2] they were first created when the metropolitane bishops sprang up, as baylifes unto them; furder, I never read in the New Testament that the pastor of a church should be so stinted and limited by other ministers, as you are by your lord bishop, his chanceller, commissary and arch-deacon; I marvell what ecclesiasticall offices theis men that thus rule over so manie pastors and churches also, have.

Sperin: Though the parson be called *Rector Ecclesiae*, yet he doth not governe alone, there are others joyned with him.

Barrow: Who be theis? I never heard of anie such.

Sperin: The church-wardens and sidemen, *etc.*

Barrow: What! are these governours also?

Sperin: Yea.

Barrow: To say the trueth, neither the one nor the other do governe, but stand in most miserable and servile subjection to the bishops and to their substitutes; or if this government should be their owne (as you surmise), most antichristian it is, and such as no true pastors or elders may execute in the church of Christ. But are you not afeared, Mr. Sperin, thus to glose and counterfet to cover these marked souldiours of the beast, with the names and titles of Christe's officers? Wil you set downe this under your hand?

Wheruppon Mr. Sperin set downe this proposition.

Some parsons may be pastors, Ephesians 4. Some church-wardens and sydemen may be elders, 1 Timothy 4. But those that cannot preach are no pastors, and those church-wardens that cannot governe are no elders.

Barrow: Those are wonderfull governours as ever I heard of, I had

1 Rector — one who rules, guides, directs, leads, or instructs.
2 John Foxe, *The Acts and Monuments of John Foxe*, ed. Josiah Pratt, 4th edition, I (1877), introductory section.

thought theis church-wardens had rather bene the collectors or deacons of your church, because they gather and dispense the almes of your churches. But now to your parsons, they have a diverse and discrepant 1. name. 2. office. 3. entrance unto their office both in election and ordination, 4. administracion, 5. maintainance or lyving. For all which reasons severed, and joyned, none of your parsons can be true pastors.

Sperin: The name of pastor is of no moment, for they are also called governours and overseers, as well as pastors.

Barrow: But this name of pastor is only peculiar and doth distinguish the office of the pastor from others, and so doth neither the name [page 15 — C 2 *recto*] of elder nor overseer,[1] but being in counsell and government common to him with others, are also gyven indifferently to him with other. Therfore this name of pastor is of great monent [*sic*] and can neither be altered nor spared, as wherby the wisdome of God doth both distinguish and expresse the office, therfore if you take away or change this name, you also take away and change the office, no other name that can be devised by man sufficing to distinguish and expresse this office, as this doth.

Thus the time not suffering to follow or urge the other pointes alledged against this office, we for this time ceased; Mr. Sperin making promise to come againe, and if he could to bring some other with him. [page 16 — C 2 *verso*]

CONFERENCE No. 6 — [MARCH 20, 1589/90]

THE SUMME OF A CONFERENCE HAD BETWENE MR. SPERIN AND MR. EGERTON OF THE ONE SIDE; AND HENRY BARROW AND JOHN GREENWOOD OF THE OTHER SIDE, IN THEIR CHAMBER WHERE THEY WERE KEPT CLOSE PRISONERS IN THE FLEET, UPPON THE 20 OF THE THIRD MONETH, 1590 [MARCH 20, 1589/90].

---

[1] Elder or presbyter (priest) and overseer or episcopos (bishop) are here equated by Barrow, who rejects any theory of episcopacy *iure divino* as advocated by Richard Bancroft.

Mr. Sperin comming before Mr. Egerton more than half an houre, and not being certaine of Mr. Egerton's comming, they not staying thereuppon, straight wayes entred speech.

Sperin: I would know the causes of your forsaking our church.

Barrow: Whye, have you forgot all our last conference? I then shewed you manie causes.

Sperin: I tooke it, because all the people were received into the church at the beginning of her majestie's reign (without anie proofe of their faith or due order) was the cause.

Barrow: The unworthines and confusion of the people, togeather with the unlawfull ministrie, ministration and ecclesiasticall government now exercised emongst you, were alledged for causes.[1]

Sperin: But neither our ministrie or people are such now.

Barrow: All the land in the beginning of her majestie's reigne were compelled and received into your church in one day[2] from open apostacie and grosse idolatrie, without the preaching of the gospel going before, this self same ministrie set over them, and [the] sacraments administred unto them, in this estate wherein they are now founde and remaine.

Sperin: I know not what then was done, I was but eight yeares old,[3] neither suppose I that you can remember it. Therfore I will not meddle therewith.

Barrow: I reason from the first gathering and planting of your church, which I proove unto you to be unlawfull, and contrary to Christ's Testament. For it was never read there, that anie church hath bene gathered and planted by civile force and without the preaching of the gospel going before; or that all so sodenly and confusedly were received into the church.

Sperin: I will not justifie their doinges then. But now I affirme all my people to professe.

Barrow: How should they professe, when they stand in the same estate and transgression they then did?

---

[1] These oft-repeated four causes constitute a main theme and summary of Barrow's teaching: a false worship, a false ministry, a false membership, and a false discipline or government.

[2] May 8, 1559, with the enactment of the Act of Uniformity and the Act of Supremacy. The Act of Uniformity went into effect on June 24, 1559, the Feast of the Nativity of St. John the Baptist.

[3] Therefore Thomas Sperin was born in 1551 and would be 39 years old — about the same age as Barrow. Sperin died in February, 1591/2.

John Greenwood

Sperin: I denie that. They which were then unbeleevers do now
beleeve. [page 17 — C 3 *recto*]

Barrow: That cannot be.

Greenwood: But before you proceede further, it is necessarie that
Mr. Sperin either justifie or disalowe of the gathering of
the church then.

Sperin: I will not justifie that gathering by constraint.

Greenwood: Set downe that under your hand.

Sperin: What neede that, you heare I say it.

Barrow: But for the better prooceeding, set it downe under your
hand, or else defend it, and we will disproove it.
Where uppon Mr. Sperin set downe this proposition under
his hand.

Sperin: *I do not maintaine that church that was gathered, and as it was
from papisterie compelled to be Protestants in the beginning of her
majestie's reigne.*

Barrow: I will proove that your parishes still remaine in the same
estate, as they were then gathered.
*Your parishes now consist of the same people and their seede, as yet
no seperation made, still remaining under the same ministrie,
worship, sacraments, courts, ecclesiasticall government. Therfore
they are in the same estate.*

Sperin: Most of these that at the beginning of her majestie's reigne
were received into the church, are dead and changed, and
new come into their roomes.

Greenwood: You have them or their seede.

Sperin: Once in twelve yeeres lightlie [likelie ?] the most part of
the parish changeth, as I by experience know, some goinge,
and others comminge.

Greenwood: But none come but such as then were received, or
their seede; for they go but from one parishe to another,
all the parishes being one bodie, one church.

Barrow: I would have you answer unto my former proposition,
wherein I have shewed your parishes to be in the same
estate, wherin they then were planted.

Sperin: I deny that. For neither all the people remaine, neither
are they the same people, for they were then unbeleevers,
and now they that remaine beleeve or professe the faith,
now they willinglie professe faith, which then constrained-
lie confessed faith.

Barrow: This distinction of Augustine will deceive you, for how should the unlawfull and ungodlie actions of anie past, be justified by his faith following. Faith doth not justifie but forsake transgression. Againe, how should they be said to have faith, or to have left their sinnes, which still continue in the same confusion, disorder, false ministrie, false worship, false government. [page 18 — C 3 *verso*]

Sperin: They doe not so.

Barrow: I will proove all this in due order. And first that you have the same people and their seede in the same confusion.

Greenwood: All the land is now of your church.

Sperin: It is not so.

Barrow: All the queene's naturall subjects that dwell in anie parish are of your church, because everie parish is of your church.

Sperin: All the queene's subjects that dwell in our parishes are not of our church.

Barrow: They are of the parish. Therfore of the church.

Sperin: There dwell manie papists that are not of our church.

Barrow: Even those papists are of your church. And thus I proove it.

None but those of the church may offer in the church or have anie communion with the saints, or have anie interest in the ministrie: But the papists communicate with your church and have interest in the ministrie, in that they contribute together with the parish unto the ministrie.

Therfore the papists that dwell amonge you are of your church.

Sperin: Whie [?] is it not lawfull for the minister to be maintained with the goods of unbeleevers. [?]

Barrow: Unbeleevers have nothing a doe, neither are bound to the maintenance of the ministrie. This contribution is called in the New Testament a dutie and communion of the saints, an offering and sweete odoure unto God. [Romans 15: 26, 27 and Philippians 4: 18]. But unbeleevers may have no spirituall communion with the saints, neither may offer with them in the church, neither have interest or anie thinge to do with the ministrie. Therfore [the unbeleevers] may not be bounde, nor received to contribute unto the maintenance of the ministrie.

Sperin: I denie that.

Barrow: Whie, it is prooved by all these reasons. Further, it is expresslie forbidden, Leviticus 22: 25, that the priest might not receive anie maner of offering, were it never

199

John Greenwood

so perfect, at the hand of a stranger.   Therfore much lesse may the minister of Christ.

Mr. Sperin in reading the text would give no judgment of it, untill he had further considered therof.

Barrow: I will proove it by a necessarie reason unto you.   None that was not a Jewe, or come unto the faith, might enter into the temple, much lesse contribute or offer in the temple.

At this time Mr. Egerton entered, whoe beinge set downe with them and made acquainted with the present discourse, they proceeded as followeth.

The place of Leviticus being read again and further enforced [page 19 — C 4 *recto*][1] thus:

The oblations of the wicked are an abhomination unto the Lord. But the tithes and contributions of the papists are oblations of the wicked.

Therfore they are an abhomination, etc.

Sperin: But may not the minister receive anie gifts of unbeleevers ?

Barrow: Yea, they may receive or inherit civile things, that are given by, or belonged to, unbeleevers.

Sperin: It is written, 1 Corinthians 10 [10: 27]. If the unbeleevers bidd you to a feast, *etc.*, eate, making no question.

Greenwood: We doubt not but all Christians may receive in private or civill respects, the goods or benevolence of unbeleevers.   But you must put difference betwene that contribution in communion, to and with the church, and civile and private benevolence.

Sperin: *The apostle, Galatians 6 [6: 6], willeth all that are taught in the word to communicate of their goods unto them that teach them. But the papists are taught by us in the word. Therfore they may contribute unto us in our ministrie.*

Greenwood: This place is to be understood of such as are received into, and taught in the church, and not of all them that are without the church, and heare the ministrie therof. The apostle gave not this rule to them.

Barrow: The recusant papists are not instructed of you, the other papists are both instructed, and they and their seede admitted unto the sacraments.   But all contribute and pay tythes and so are all of your church.

[1] The numbered pagination is sometimes wrong. In the original edition page 19 and page 20 are both numbered 20

Sperin: In my parish I admitt no papists or open unworthie unto the sacraments.

Greenwood: Your parish hath as yet made no seperation from the papists or prophane of the lande. Therfore you do not seperate the unworthie.

Sperin: They are now beleevers, that before were unbeleevers; they now professe willinglie that before professed by constraint; and if ther be anie wicked, I put them from the sacraments.

Barrow: You so fix your eyes upon your owne assertions, as that you give no eare to other men's reasons. How oft hath this bene denied and disprooved unto you; you have never as yet made anie seperation, but still remaine in the stepps and sinnes of your fore-fathers, neither have you anie power to seperate anie from amonge you.

Sperin: I have power, and doe put the wicked from the sacraments. [page 20 — C 4 *verso*]

Barrow: What, your selfe alone?

Sperin: Yea, with the consent of the church.

Barrow: I shewed you the last day what kinde of instrument your suspention and puttinge from the sacraments is; you and your parish have not the power to excommunicat anie.

Sperin: This is not true. We have power, and do excommunicat.

Barrow: It is then by the power of the bishops and not by the power of Christ.

Sperin: It is not by the power of the bishopps, but by the power of Christ.

Barrow: That is not so, you have neither power from Christ, nor from the bishopps, to excommunicat anie: you have leave in your service-booke to suspend from your sacrament, but not to excommunicat without the bishop.

Sperin: We do excommunicat without the bishop.

Barrow: Then your church hath two maner of excommunications

Sperin: That followeth not, the bishopp's excommunication is but an approbation of ours.

Barrow: That is not so. The bishop hath power to excommunicate when and whom he will of your parish, and that without your privitie or consent. Moreover, the bishopps do excommunicate by a Latine writt;[1] but if your excommunication be such, then is it antichristian, if it be after another maner, then have you two sorts of excommunications in your church.

Sperin: When anie deserveth to be excommunicated, then I and the church-wardens present such to the bishop, and he excommunicateth them.

Barrow: Then the bishop excommunicateth, and not you; you are but as they that give evidence and information to the judg. The bishop is the judg.

Greenwood: The bishop doth not excommunicate upon your information, neither for anie sinne, how heinous soever. But only for not appeeringe at, or disobeying their courts. Moreover, as the Ordinary doth excommunicat, so doth he absolve whom he list, without the privitie of your congregacion.

Egerton: ⎞ The bishop his excommunication is but a civile dis-
Sperin: ⎠ communion.

Barrow: ⎞ What, will you make the excommuncation of your
Greenwood: ⎠ church a civile action? We never heard of anie such excommunication, until Cooper and Gwalter[2] published their conceites therof.

Egerton: ⎞ May not the civile magistrate approve the excommuni-
Sperin: ⎠ tion of the church?

Barrow: ⎞ Yes, but the civile magistrate may not excommunicate
Greenwood: ⎠ anie, as your bishopps do; and that as you say, by vertue of the civile authoritie. [page 21 — D 1 *recto*]

Sperin: The bishop doth not excommunicat, he doth but approve our excommunication.

Barrow: Whye, erewhile you confessed that you did but present your sheepe to the wolfe, and that the bishop did excommunicat: and we prooved that the bishop did both excommunicate and absolve whom and when he would in your parish, without your privities or consents; as also that your church hath none other excommunication, than that of his.

---

[1] Latin writs of excommunication, and of other purposes, are discussed in Robert Phillimore, *The Ecclesiastical Law of the Church of England*, II, chapters IV, V, VI, X, XI. See Felix Makower, *The Constitutional History and Constitution of the Church of England*, and Edward Cardwell, *Synodalia*, 2 vols.

[2] Thomas Cooper, *An Admonition to the People of England*, pp. 141-4. Rudolph Walther [Gualter], of Zurich. See his *Biblia sacrasancta*.

Sperin: We have the same excommunication that they had in the church of Corinth. 1. Corinthians 5.

Barrow: You have neither such a faithfull people gathered out of the world unto Christ, neither have you the power of Christ, neither do you it after that holie order of the church of Corinth. But you are driven to runne unto your lord the bishop, who doth it of his sole authoritie, by his commissarie in forme of a Latine writt, which you are compelled to reade and publishe in your parish church. How can you call this that excommunication they had in the church of Corinth.

Sperin: We excommunicate in the name and power of Christ, as the church of Corinth did.

Barrow: That is not so, it is don in the name and power of the bishop, and not in that maner as is expressed. 1. Corinthians 5.

Sperin: The bishopp's power is civile, but this action ecclesiasticall.

Barrow: And may a civile person execute anie ecclesiasticall office or action?

Greenwood: Do you hold the bishopps, their commissaries and substituts, meerly civile, and not ecclesiasticall?

Sperin: Yea, I hold them meerly civile, and not ecclesiasticall.

Barrow: Write that, and set it downe under your hand.

Sperin: So I will: and tooke unto him penne and inke.

Egerton: Whye so, what neede it to be written?

Barrow: That we may the better know, wherof we reason and hold to the point.

Greenwood: This is a needfull point to be set downe in writing. For if the bishopps and their substituts be meerly civile, then you have as yet no church, no ministrie, no sacraments.

Egerton: Their offices and actions are civile, as we esteeme them.

Sperin: I hold them meerly civill and not ecclesiasticall, because they are constituted by the prince, and not by Christ in his Testament.

Barrow: Write that, let us have it set downe.

But he delaying because of Mr. Egerton, Mr. Barrow set downe as followeth. [page 22 — D 1 *verso*]

The bishopps, commissaries and their substitutes are merely civile and not ecclesiasticall, because they are constituted by the prince, and not by Christ in his Testament.

This beinge written was read and shewed unto them, but duringe the time of drawing them to this proposition, and the writinge therof, Mr. Greenwood enforcing the conclusions and sequell that would ensue therof: Mr. Sperin here began to retract his proposition and quallifie it by puttinge in this word (*as*) insteede of (*because*) so that now, he alloweth them, both civile and ecclesiasticall officers.

Barrow: What, may the bishopp execute both civile and ecclesiasticall offices ?

Sperin: Whye not ?

Barrow: Because it is contrarie to the ordinances of God, who hath appointed unto these divers and distinct offices, divers persons to execute the same.

Greenwood: Let him that hath an office waite on his office.

Sperin: Their civile authoritie is of the prince.

Barrow: It is not therby justified, seing it is unlawfull for any ecclesiasticall officer to execute also a civile office, or for one man to have both an ecclesiasticall and civile office at once.

Egerton: David was both a king and a prophet.

Barrow: What then ?

Egerton: He executed both a civile and ecclesiasticall office therby.

Barrow: That is not so.

Egerton: A prophet was an office of the temple.

Barrow: None but a Levite might be a minister of the temple.

Sperin: But sundrie have executed both.

Barrow: Moses and Samuel did so for a season, but it was by expresse warrant from God's mouth; neither continued they so to do, neither gave they example, or may be presidents [precedents] for us to do the like, without the like warrant. Make therfore your bishopps either whollie civile, or whollie ecclesiasticall, let us know what to hold them ?

Egerton: They are ministers.

Barrow: And they are civile magistrates, lords of the parliamenthouse, justices of peace, judges of civile causes, *etc.*

Egerton: Though their power be mixt, yet is it not simply unlawfull.

Barrow: By the word of God it is symplye unlawfull for anie one man to execute both a civile and ecclesiasticall office at once.

Greenwood: This mixture is the misterie of iniquitie, and the power of the beast.

Egerton: Though they have civile offices, yet keepe they the ministerie, and their ministeriall actions are good. [page 23 — D 2 *recto*]

Barrow: This is strange doctrine, that one man may administer both in civile and ecclesiasticall offices at once. May a civile magistrate intermeddle with the ministrie in the church, or a minister of the church execute anie civile magistracie? What a confusion were this.

Egerton: Their civile authoritie doth not abolish their ministeriall actions.

Barrow: The civile magistrates may not intermeddle with the execution of the pastor's office, as they do in delivering their sacraments, no more than Uzziah might burne incense.[1]

Egerton: The example doth not hold. The bishops were ministers before they were civile magistrates.

Barrow: Yet the doctrine holdeth: that the civile magistrate may not administer in the church, neither one man execute such diverse offices.

Egerton: Though it be unlawfull, yet their ministeriall actions are not unlawfull.

Barrow: *It is not lawfull for a civile magistrate to administer in the church whilest he keepeth his civile office. But the bishops are civile magistrates, and keepe and execute their civile offices.*
Therfore it is not lawfull for them to administer in the church whilest they keepe their civile offices.

Egerton: Your argument is not good; you put that in the conclusion, which you should have put in the second proposition.

Barrow: I regard not the forme. If it be unlawfull for them to administer, then their ministeriall actions are unlawfull.

Egerton:⎱ The consequent of the major is denied.
Sperin: ⎰

Barrow: It of necessitie followeth. For God only wilbe served in his church by his owne ministers and in the ministrie, by such as he hath appointed and called thereunto, all

[1] II Chronicles 26: 16-19.

strange ministries and their ministeriall actions being an abhomination unto him.

Greenwood: All their actions are accursed in the Lord's sight that presume to offer in his church in an office whereunto they are not called of God, and their ministerie under the curse of Korah's censure. Numbers 16: 40.

Egerton: The bishopps are not under that curse; for they are ministers.

Barrow: What, and civile magistrates also?

Sperin: The bishopp's office, as it is given of the prince, is civile; as they superintend divers flockes and pastors, they are ecclesiasticall officers.

Barrow: This is a rare distinction to make one and the self same [page 24 — D 2 *verso*] office both civile and ecclesiasticall. I never heard that the office of a bishop was civile, or of anie such office in the church of God as a lord bishop. And seing we are entred into speech of their ministrie, I would faine know what ecclesiasticall office they execute in your church.

Egerton: They are pastors.

Barrow: Whye, each of them doth superintend and oversee divers, yea, many hundreth flockes and pastors. These are strange pastors as ever I heard of.

Egerton: I say not as they are bishopps they are pastors; but as they were ministers of the gospell before; which ministrie they have not lost by being bishopps.

Barrow: Your meane when they were parish-parsons. But that office they have forgon when they were made bishopps.

Egerton: That is not so.

Barrow: The office of a parson and the office of a bishop are divers and distinct offices of your church. One man cannot be both a bishop and a parson.

Egerton: A bishop may be a pastor [—] as you call it a parson.

Barrow: Then a man may execute divers offices of your church at one time. This was never heard of in the church of Christ since the apostles' time.

Egerton: Might not the evangelistes also execute divers offices, after the apostles' time?

Barrow: I have not read that they did. But you hold not your bishops evangelistes, yet they by your saying execute divers ecclesiasticall offices at one time. As to be parsons and lord bishopps, both which are distinct and divers offices of the church. Hold you it lawfull for one man to exercise diverse offices of your church at one time also?

Egerton: To execute divers offices is unlawfull.

Barrow: But the office of a lord bishop and of a parish parson are diverse offices of your church which one man exerciseth. Therefore their ministeriall actions in these offices are unlawfull.

Egerton: These offices are not so diverse to disanull their first ministrie which they had when they were preachers.

Barrow: These offices are so diverse as one man cannot execute them both, but he must of force do the one by his substitute. Moreover, the office of a lord bishop doth abolish and swallow up the other. For he cannot be both an overseer of so many churches and pastors, and be a private peculiar pastor of one church too.

Egerton: The bishopp's office is but a civile addicion which he joyneth unto his former ministrie. [page 25 — D 3 *recto*]

Barrow: Whye, you see the office of a lord bishop is one of the chief ecclesiasticall offices of your church, and this office is wholye conversant in ecclesiasticall affaires.

Egerton: They are peeres and lords of the parliament house.

Barrow: Yea, but spirituall lords by virtue of their ecclesiasticall office. Therefore the office of a parish-priest and of a lord bishop are diverse and distinct offices of your church.

Egerton: Yet are they not so diverse as by taking the office of a bishop they loose their first ministrie.

Barrow: *Everye ministrie in the church is belonging unto and in regarde of an office, neither can be otherwise, or longer executed, than in that office to which it belongeth. But the bishops have resigned that ecclesiasticall office wherunto their first ministrie belonged.*

Therfore when they keepe not that office they cannot keepe that ministrie.

Egerton: The bishopps have not resigned their first office.

Barrow: It is manifest that they have. For it is impossible that they should be both superintendents over so manie churches, and execute the pastor's office over one church togither.

Egerton: Though one man execute diverse offices, his actions are not simpl[i]e unlawfull.

John Greenwood

Barrow: What a monstrous confusion and commixture of all God's ordinances is made by this doctrine of yours. God hath utterly forbidden anie one man to manage both a civile and ecclesiasticall office at once. You (notwithstanding the bishopps exercise both civile and ecclesiasticall authoritie, and execute many ecclesiasticall offices of the church) yet in this estate would have their ministeriall actions lawfull.

Egerton: Though to exercise diverse offices be unlawfull, yet it is not so unlawfull as to disanull their ministeriall actions.

Barrow: I have proved that ecclesiasticall ministrie and ministration to be unlawfull, which hath no foundation in God's word. But this their mixt ministrie and confused ministracion hath not only no warrant in, but is found expresslie contrarye to, the whole word and ordinances of God. Therfore this their ministrie and ministeriall actions are simplie and utterly unlawfull.

Egerton: Though a tyrant be an unlawfull magistrate, yet may his actions in his regiment be lawfull.

Greenwood: You must make difference betwene the usurping of a civile office in a common-wealth by a tyrant, and the usurping of an ecclesiasticall office in the church.

Barrow: There is no comparison betwixt the regiment of a tyrant in a common-wealth, and the ministration of an usurper or [page 26 — D 3 *verso*] wretched person in the church. With the first, we which are but subjects have not to meddle, either to place or displace, but to obey in the Lord such civile magistrates as are set over us of the Lord. The second, namely, of all ecclesiasticall offices, we have the sole choise and oversight; power to create, power to depose; neither are we to suffer anie unlawfull ministrie or ministration. But now to speake simplie of the regiment of a tyrant as considered in itself, it is altogither unlawfull unto himself, because he usurpeth that office by intrusion, contrarie to the lawe of God, and shall therfore accompt before the Lord.

Egerton: But in asmuch as the bishopps were once lawfull pastors, they cannot loose their first office and ministrie; and so their ministeriall actions (as preaching of the word and ministration of the sacraments) are still lawfull.

Barrow: They manie wayes have forfeited their ministrie and place, if so be it were so, by taking and executing two offices, by taking other ecclesiasticall offices, and those such, as they cannot execute their pastorall office whilest they keepe them. Therfore they can be no pastors, neither their administrations of the word and sacraments, whilest they remaine in this estate, lawfull.

Egerton: They may notwithstanding these other offices, execute their pastoral offices; as to preach the word, and minister the sacraments; which are the chief things of the pastor's office.

Barrow: They can not do these thinges duely, in asmuch as they cannot duely attend and watch over their peculiar flock, whilest they keepe these other offices. But I would faine know of you, when they had this true pastorall office wherof you speake so much? For surelye if ever they were true pastors, they are now wondrouslie apostate.

Egerton: When they were first made ministers.

Barrow: Your ministerie is large. Do you not meane when they were first made parish-parsons?

Egerton: They were then pastors, when they were such parsons as you terme them.

Barrow: You hold then the parson's office to be the pastor's office.

Egerton: Yea.

Barrow: I will let passe their having manie parsonages, as also the insufficiencye of sondrie that professe the same. And only shew in generall why a parish-parson cannot be held a true pastor, according to the gospell and Testament of Christ.

The parish-parson hath not the (1) *name* (2) *office* (3) *calling to his office* (4) *administration in his office,* (5) *power* [page 27 — D 4 *recto*] *nor that* (6) *maintenance of his living that a true pastor hath.*

Therfore a parish-parson cannot be called or held a true pastor.

Egerton: The antecedent is not true.

Barrow: Let me prove it. First you see they have a diverse name, the one a parish-parson, the other a pastor.

Egerton: No man of knowledg will now call them parsons.

Barrow: This is the peculiar and proper name belonging to their office. Therfore reserved as dounge to be cast in their faces by all have that [*sic*, that have] knowledg. Yea, it is an open marke to everye one that hath knowledg

209

wherby to discerne them from true pastors. The true pastor will never beare the marke and caracte[1] of the beast of antichrist.

Egerton: The name is of no moment. What shall we call a parson ?

Barrow: A parson, or Baal's priest.

Sperin: A parson is called *rector* in Latine.

Barrow: And I shewed you the last day, that this Romish name was one of the names of blasphemie written uppon the heades of the beast.

Egerton: The parson hath sondrie names in the Scripture: as an elder, an overseer, a steward, *etc.*

Barrow: But none of these names do distinguish his office, as the name of pastor doth. But if we come to their office we shall finde it as strange as the name therof.

Sperin: Prove that.

Barrow: If Mr. Foxe say truly,[2] the parson's office tooke beginning when the metropolitane bishopps sprong, and were as their baylifes. But it is the same office that was and is executed in the Romish church. Therfore not the pastor's office.

Egerton: It is not the same office.

Barrow: The self same. You take it as they left it, as also all the ministrie you have beside. Only you put in new men in those old offices.

Egerton: The entrance and ministration is quite changed: the priestes were massing and sacrificing priestes, prayed for the dead, worshipped saintes, *etc.* So do not we.

Greenwood: So do you also, your whole worship being changed but out of Latine into English.

Egerton: We do not so.

Barrow: We shall hereafter have occasion to discusse these matters when we come to handle your ministration. Only we still finde the office of the parish parson the self same that then it was, and this none know better than they that have the [page 28 — D 4 *verso*] giftes of the same benefices. But I will draw an argument from some doctrine.

In the church of Christ there is no ecclesiasticall office above the pastor.

---

1 Caracte — sign, mark, characteristic.
2 John Foxe, *The Acts and Monuments of John Foxe*, ed. Josiah Pratt, 4th edition, I (1877), introductory section.

But in your church there are sondrie ecclesiasticall offices above the parson.

Therfore the parson's office is not the pastor's office.

Egerton: The apostle's office was above the pastor's office in the church of Christ.

Barrow: But that was temporarie and but for a time. We reason not what was, but what now is in the church since extraordinarie offices ceased. We reade of no office in the church of Christ above the pastor's office. Therfore it cannot be the office of a parson.

Egerton: A true pastor may exercise his office under another ecclesiasticall office above him.

Barrow: *God hath instituted no ecclesiasticall office above him. Therfore he may exercise his office under no ecclesiasticall office above him.*

Egerton: I deny the argument. Those thinges are not now simplie unlawfull, which at some times were lawfull.

Barrow: That is verie false. All things are now simplie unlaw-
Greenwood: full which are forbidden in the word of God as the Leviticall priesthoode and all extraordinarie ministries now are, which yet sometimes were lawfull.

Egerton: Did not sondrye pastors and ministers exercise their ministrie under Diotrophes ?[1]

Barrow: Never that I ever heard of. But if they had, should it therfore be lawfull ?

Egerton: But if the pastor should execute his office under another ecclesiasticall office, should he therfore be no true pastor ?

Barrow: A true pastor cannot execute under another ecclesiasticall office in the church of Christ; therfore the question is vaine, the thing being unpossible.

Egerton: But if there be anie office above him, should he therfore cease to be a pastor ?

Barrow: What so ever ecclesiasticall office is now above the pastor is antichristian, neither is he a true pastor that exerciseth his office under such.

Egerton: I deny that.

Barrow: *Whatsoever ecclesiasticall office is not expressed in the Testament of Christ is antichristian.*

---

[1] III John 1: 9. Since this is the only place where the name occurs, it would seem that Egerton is reading into the text more than is found therein.

John Greenwood

But there is no mention of anie ecclesiasticall office to be now above the pastor's office in the Testament of Christ.

Therfore al such offices as are above the pastor's office, are antichristian.

Egerton: I deny the major. All ecclesiasticall offices that are above the pastor's office are not antichristian.

Barrow: You may aswell denie the whole ministrie of the New Testa-[page 29 — E 1 *recto*]ment, and bring in anie other. But thus I prove it:

Christ hath left a perfect ministrie. Therfore nothing may be added unto it.[1]

All other ministries are antichristian save that which Christ hath left in his Testament.

But Christ hath left no such ministrie as these in his Testament. Therfore, etc.

Egerton: Though Christ hath left a perfect ministerie, yet all things that are added unto it are not antichristian.

Barrow: Yes, all new ministries are antichristian and he of antichrist that executeth, standeth under or justifieth them. For he that bringeth in a new ministrie taketh Christ's office and sitteth in his place and is that antichrist spoken of the apostle, 2 Thessalonians 2, and by our saviour Christ, Matthew 24, and all that stand under such a new devised ministrie stand under antichrist.

Mr. Sperin here would have denyed the bishop to be antichrist. But Mr. Egerton willed him never to denye that, which they had agreed uppon.

Barrow: Do you hold the faith in respect of men's persons? Shal no more be trueth than you have agreed uppon?

These doctrines following were holden and affirmed by Mr. Egerton in discourse with Mr. Greenwood as Mr. Barrow was writing other arguments and assertions.

(1) Egerton: *That the true church may be without the power of Christ to censure and redresse.*

Greenwood: I never read of anie such church in the Scriptures. Christ hath given to everie church his power to censure and redresse.

Egerton: Though we want discipline, yet we have the power of Christ by the scepter of his word in doctrine.

---

[1] In the text this sentence is in roman type, contrary to the usual practice of printing syllogisms in italic.

Greenwood: By the word discipline you turne away the whole practise of the gospel, neither are you governed by Christ his scepter, howsoever you may take his word in your mouth.

(2) Egerton: *That the name of a bishop spoken of, I Timothy 3, is only peculiar unto the pastor and teacher; because it is said, verse 2, he must be apt to teach.*

Greenwood: Though some particular rules in that generall doctrine be only spoken of the pastorall and teacher's office, yet it is evident by the whole scope of the place, that there are also [p. 30 — E 1 *verso*] rules given for other elders, which are also called bishops in sondrye places of the Scriptures.

(3) Egerton: *That no man may preach the word without an externall calling.*

Greenwood: Giftes of interpretation are sufficient calling to speake of the word in the congregation, in due order and place.

Egerton: That is not so.

(4) Egerton: *We abstaine from excommunication, because we have no elders as yet.*

Greenwood: The church is never without the power to excommunicate.

(5) Egerton: *Our pastors only now want [lack] some censurers.*

Barrow: The least member of the church that is a communicant hath as much interest in all the censures of the church as the pastor, and have equall power according to the rules of the word, to censure the pastor for errour or transgression, as the pastor hath to censure them.

[LETTER No. 1 — *ca.* APRIL 10, 1590]
[p. 31 — E 2 *recto*]
TO MR. EGERTON DELIVER THIS.

Almightie God, whose spirit is one, and joyneth in one all his elect vessells, in his good time bringing them forth from darknes to light, give you and us to be of one minde, and of one judgment in the trueth, to the glory of his owne name, our rejoycing in his mercies for ever, and the present conversion of manie, to the obedience of Christ

213

H

John Greenwood

Seing it hath pleased God, after our long imprisonment, once of late to send you unto us (by what meanes, or to what further purpose, we yet know not) to give us a beginning and an entrance into the discussing of his trueth, by some kinde of conference: which, because it was not with that harmonye that it may please God to effect, if your heart as ours be set to know his will, and to proceede by one rule, even the rule of his authenticall Testament, we are moved to write unto you, rather by your modest, honest, and sober behaviour shewed to us the Lord's most unworthie witnesses, than for anie procurement of peace to our selves. For most of all we desire your salvation, and with all the good of manie, by the measure of spirituall guyftes gyven you, and as we trust, you will bestow them to the furtherance of his church. Yet in your last conference,[1] (to speake the trueth), we found your spirit in no loving consent to the truth, but dangerouslie corrupted, or at least set to oppose with poysoned distinctions by vaine philosophie, yea, against that trueth your self would not insist to denie, whether to trye our strength or to abuse the hearers, or for endangering your self. Yet against al these Paul saith we cannot [do] anie thing against the truth but for the truth ?[2]

We have since often merveiled we heard no more from you, or of your estate, which then was made manifest to be without promise, whiles you exercise a ministeriall function under antichrist, in a false office, unto a confuse assemblie of all sorts of people, one with the world. Whereuppon, hearing no further yet of you, we thought it good, in tender care of your salvation, and for the advancement of the Lord's trueth, to shew you, so neere as our fraile memories could collect, the summe of such arguments or positions and answers as passed betwene us, having set downe nothing but that, wherof we have the positions to shew under wryting at that present, and honest witnesses to testifie our uprightnes herein.

And least you should otherwise conceive, that we should some wayes injurie you, we have sent you a copie to peruse; and if you make yet anie other answere to our assertions, than there is conteyned, we freely gyve you libertie so to do. But cheiflie the end of our wryting is, to [p. 32 — E 2 *verso*] stir you up not to

---

[1] March 20, 1589/90.
[2] II Corinthians 13: 8. The Genevan version reads: " For we can not do anie thing against the trueth, but for the trueth." The King James version reads: " For we can do nothing against the truth, but for the truth." Barrow and Greenwood give a literal translation of the Greek.

leave the matter thus, considering the seriousnes therof, but eyther yeild therunto, or procure some more large and free place and time to make our mynds plaine and faith open one to another, that the truth may appeare, and they that depart from the same, be knowen.   And the same we wryte unto you herein, we hereby offer to all the rest of your fellow ministers, our hearts (as the Lord knoweth), being open to all men to their good, and the glory of our God the Father of our Lord Jesus Christ.   Only the Lord delyver us from unreasonable men, and suppresse all his adversaries and opposers against his glorious truth, Amen.

Most desirous of your fellowship in the faith of Christ.

HENRY BARROW
JHON GREENWOOD

[REPLY No. 1 — APRIL 14, 1590]

TO MR. BARROW AND MR. GREENWOOD

The Lord Jesus open our eyes to see the truth, and sanctifie our tongues and pennes to declare the same.

I receyved a letter from you, and also a [report of our] conference in writing.   Touching your letter, this I answere.   First for those poysoned distinctions you mention, if you had named them, I hope no poyson would have appeared in them, except it had come from the contagion of your owne spirits.   Secondly, for vaine philosophie, if you meane therby (for other I remember none) that help which God hath lent us by logicke to reason breiflie and plainly, you do but as Browne hath done, whose braynlesse reasons to prove the vanitie therof, are not only easie to be answered by other men, but also abundantly confuted by his owne practise, both in speach and writing.[1]

Touching your feined conference, this I say.   I finde in it some things wanting that were spoken, manie things expressed that

---

[1] In *A Treatise upon the 23. of Matthewe*, Robert Browne inveighed strongly against the misuse of logic. Believing that preachers had made logic an end in itself, and that they had made a fetish of the syllogism, he denounced them in these words: " But nowe their Logike hath helde them so long in learning what they shuld do, that they have done little or nothing at all." (Albert Peel and Leland H. Carlson, *The Writings of Robert Harrison and Robert Browne*, pp. 17, 18, 179).

were never spoken (no, not ymagined on my behalf) and most things that were spoken, perverted. Finally, I finde it so full of partialitie, so voyd of upright and true dealing, and so far out of order, that I have neither leasure, muchlesse anie lust to deale with it. And if you shall proceede to gyve out copies, I shalbe readye to disclayme you wheresoever I come, not only for men voyde of pietie, but even of civile honestie also.[1]

Now concerning a free conference, I have neither powre nor will to performe it; my reasons I reserve till further oportunitie. But if you will deale with me, do [p. 33 — E 3 *recto*] this: send me under your hand some six or seven (or as you thinke good for the nomber) of your cheif reasons, whie you refuse to come to our publique assemblies, brieflie and plainly concluded; and I will (by the help of God), as my leisure shal serve, set you downe my answere in the like sort under my owne hand, with reasons why you ought to come. This course if you like I will deale with you as I may, otherwise I will not meddle. Written the 14 Aprill, 1590.

Written by him, that not only desireth your good in the Lord, but also is ready by anie peaceable and christian course of proceeding, to furder the same.

I. [JOHN ?] EGERTON. So I write.

[LETTER No. 2 — *ca.* APRIL 17, 1590]

TO MR. EGERTON

More grace and feare of God unto you.

This your replie unto our letter we have received and read with litle comforte, perceiving therby even that smale sparke of hope (which began to appeare in you) to be utterly extinct; the bellowes

---

[1] If Egerton is correct in these criticisms, it follows that Barrow has given us a distorted or incomplete version of what transpired. It is easily conceivable that Barrow would clearly remember those points by which he had scored an advantage, and partly forget those discussions which were won by Egerton. But Barrow, though vehement at times, was an honest man with a sensitive conscience. I do not believe Barrow would consciously distort Egerton's views, judging from the detrimental frankness with which Barrow reported his own examinations before Whitgift and Burghley. For Barrow's reaction to Egerton's accusations, see his reply, dated *circa* April 17, 1590.

burnt, the drosse wil not be purged from the silver, that there might proceed a vessell to the fyner [finer or refiner] so that the founder should melt in vaine, where the Lord hath not made choise of the mettall. Greatly sorie we are to behold your fearefull estate, who not being able to approve the ministrie you exercise, by the word of God, yet to your owne furder judgment, and the seducing of manie soules, continue to plead for, and practize the same, for the feare of men and the love of the world to avoide persecution, submitting your self, your whole church, ministrie, and doctrines unto the professed enemies of Christ and of his gospell, such whom your self hath confessed to be antichristian: with whom you have not only sit [*sic*] amongst the other commissioners in Caiaphas' house,[1] but also by an especiall ticket,[2] according to their mandate, were sent out amongest the chosen bande of their guard to feight against the poore persecuted witnesses of Christ, yea, amongst the rest of your subornate [suborned] witnesses to lay in wayte against the blood of the saints; endevoring by the deepe learning of Satan to entangle them into the same counterfet walking with your self, as also by your sophisticall distincions to obscure and turne away the truth, perverting and confounding al God's ordinances, calling light darknes, and darknes light; labouring to perswade, that one man may execute both civile and ecclesiastical offices at once; yea, though he so do, yet his ministrie in both of them is lawfull. Likewise, that though [p. 34 — E 3 *verso*] one man executed sondry offices of the church at one tyme, yet this his ministerie in them all is lawfull also; yea, though the bishop execute a strange and tyrannicall ministerie, never read nor heard of in the Testament of Christ, usurping authoritie over so manie churches and pastors, possessing the very chaire of antichrist, corrupting and changing the whole ministerie and ordinances of the gospel, *etc*. Yet are they to be esteemed true ministers of Christ, and their ministeriall actions good.

Theis and sondrye other enormous and blasphemous doctrines you strowed emongst us, and sought to confirme them by these and such lyke poysoned distinctions. *Not simplie evell. Not simply unlawfull. Good in parte. Though it be unlawfull to execute diverse offices, yet are not his actions therein unlawfull. Though his office he*

1 Lambeth Palace.
2 Egerton is listed among the forty-two clergymen sent to the Separatist prisoners, but Thomas Sperin is not. Since Egerton was assigned to visit George Collier and John Sparowe in the Clink, it may be that he had received a special ticket to visit Barrow.

John Greenwood

executeth in the church be unlawfull, yet are his ministeriall actions lawfull. Of the substance of the essens, etc., without which you cannot reason, nor by the evident testimonie of God's word approve your doings unto all men.

Now let the christian, or but indifferent reader, judge of the leaven and poyson of theis distinctions and cavills, of what spirit they proced and by whom they are used, whither by you or by us. As for the opinions and name of Browne, there is no cause you should upbraid us therwith, he being a man with whom we had never anie thing to doe, neither may have in this estate of his apostacy. He is now a member of your church, toward whom (we thinke) you walke not according to Christ's rule, neither yet deale brotherly with him (much lesse as beseemeth a guyde and teacher of the church) thus to publish and raile of your brother Browne, without and before christian admonition and orderly censure.[1] But having thus behaved your self towards him that is so nere unto you, we must not think it strange if you multiplie your reproches uppon us, that are devided so far from you, as Sion is from Babilon.

Concerning that conference, or rather that summe of our conference, this we say. We, in all loving maner, sent it unto you to peruse and correct, or to shew your dislike wherein you judged it faultye; yea, we gave you free lybertie, if you disliked anie of those answers which you then made unto our reasons, to alter and chaunge them as your self uppon better advise should thinke meete; so loath were we to gyve you the least cause of offence, and so desirous to have the truth further brought to light, which if you had performed with that faithfullnes and modestie that beseemed you, and we expected in so high causes, then had you not gayned this just blame and publick infamie you now by these your dealing have brought uppon your self. But in steade of this, loe, you have pronounced the whole wryting which we [p. 35 — E 4 *recto*] sent, feyned; *some things there wanting which were spoken; manie things there expressed which were never spoken, nor imagined by you; and most things there spoken perverted by us; finally, you found it so full of partialitye, so*

---

[1] These comments of Barrow on Browne are interesting, since Barrow and his followers were frequently called "Brownists." Browne made his submission and recantation to Archbishop Whitgift on October 7, 1585. In the next two years the Barrowists came into public notice, and in 1587 they were first imprisoned by the Bishop of London and the Archbishop. The Barrowists, suffering imprisonment for their beliefs, regarded Browne's return to the Church of England as "apostacy."

*voide of upright and true dealing, and so far out of order, as you have neither
leisure nor lust to deale with it.*[1] First we say, there was no cause you
should expect to have every thing wrytten, that was then spoken,
both in regard of our fraile and slippery memories, as also that we
signified unto you our intent to be but to summe up the discourse
of such cheif pointes as were then handled, willingly passing by
other impertinent and lesse necessarie speaches. But yet, if you
can call anie to remembrance which may anie way benefit you, or
prejudice us, if you shall signifie them unto us, we will most willingly
insert them. For the order we will not greatly contend, because
it is of lytle moment unto us. Yet is there cause we should aswell
remember it as you, because we were both alyke in the action,
and had the propositions before us, which you knowe were written,
as the matters fell out in handling.

But now touching your other chardges of adding, perverting,
falsefying, *etc.* Surely if theis things stoode thus, great were our
sinne toward God and towards you. Yea, woe unto our selves, if
we should walke with such festered consciences. How should we
then appeare before God or men with comfort? Though the
measure of our gyfts be smale, yet God accepteth the worke of his
owne spirit. We need not, neither ever did defend his most plaine
and pure truth against the most subtile and malignant adversaries,
with lyes, falsefying, sclaundering, *etc.*, muchlesse in this action as
you chardg us. No [!] God is witnesse unto our consciences, with
what care and uprightnes we have set downe these things, being
guyltie to our selves of no such crimes as you accuse us. Yea, for
our further clearing herein, we have set downe no one poynt of
importance which we tooke not in wryting from your owne mouthes,
even before your eyes, and read it in your presence, and in the
hearing of sondry honest witnesses: which propositions and witnesses, still remaine to be produced in record of the truth, against
you or us, wherein we depart from the same. And surely much
better had you provided for your owne credit, and much more
impeached ours, if you had set downe some perticulers, wherin we
had thus falsified and perverted, before you had in this maner
reproched us, especially being requested therunto by us; who, not
trusting to[o] much to our owne memories, first sent our copie unto
the witnesses, then unto you, to correct or reprove what you dislyked
or thought amisse therein, we being alwayes ready and most
desirous to alter it, according [p. 36 — E 4 *verso*] to the truth. But

---

[1] These accusations are quoted from John Egerton's letter of April 14, 1590.

you, as though there were no judge in heaven, no witnesses in earth of the things that passed betwixt us, have most boldlye, without all feare, shame, or truth denied even what your owne mouth uttered, accusing us as voide of all uprightnes and true dealing, full of partialitie, *etc.*, and all to hide your owne corrupt estate, and the vanitie and weaknes of your defenses from the eyes of the world. Not being able, nor daring to produce or alledge anie one pointe in perticular, which we have eyther falsified or perverted, least you should be taken and reproved, as your associate Mr. Sperin was this other daye in the exceptions he tooke, both by theis written propositions, and by sondry eare witnesses that were present unto his face.

Yea, even of that heynous perilous proposition which you now so faine would call backe, *viz., that you had agreed amongst yourselves, that the bishops be antichristian.* Whereunto, though you were then enforced to yeild, through the inevitable powre of God his word, wherwith you were pressed; yet since, for the feare of men's faces, and to avoide persecution, you have both denied the undoubted truth of God, or that ever you spake the same, contrarye to your owne conscience; yea, for the preservation of your worldly estimation, and for this corrupt dissembled peace, you hold with your lords and bishops, you are not ashamed unto the rest of the vituperie wherwith you have laden us, to add theis most unchristian and undeserved threats; namely: *that you will disclaime us in all places whersoever you come, not only for* [being] *men voide of pietie, but even of civile honestie*; and all this without either fault of offence made you at anie time, unlesse to witnesse unto that truth which we have sene and heard, be so greivous unto you.

Also Mr. Egerton, what shall you gaine by this? Suppose you to buyld or repaire your credit uppon or by the ruynes of ours? Can you immagine to stay the course of that truth which God hath sent forth by so manie witnesses which heard you? Or can you think by these vaine threats to stop our mouthes from testifying or publishing this or anie other truth of our God unto all men, by all meanes? We feare not the curse causeles,[1] neither shunne we the light. Our religion and honestie we willingly submit, both in this or in anie other thing we affirme or doe, to the christian judgment of all men. The further you shall proceede in this intemperate and unchristian course, the greater shalbe your owne shame and judgement, when God shall returne the venome and

---

[1] See Proverbs 26: 2.

malice of your owne tongue into your owne bosome. In that you will neither meddle with the conference past, nor accept of anie to come, the reasons you reserve and keepe so secret, are manifest unto all men: namely, because your [p. 37 — F 1 *recto*] deeds are evill and cannot abide the fierie tryall by God's word: therfore seeke you by all meanes to hide them from the light; being for nothing so sorye, as that you cannot call backe that, which hath alreadye passed you; knowing that the further you meddle with it, and the more you stryve, the furder and faster you shal but entangle your self. Wherfore with one consent you and your fellow ministers, studie and stryve to suppresse that truth you cannot resist. But he whose eyes are like a flame of fyre, shall shortly discover your practises, and fight against you with that sword of his mouth.

As to your offer of answere by wryting unto six or seven of our cheifest reasons whie we refuse your publick assemblies, we hold it needles to trouble you with more, untill you have answered those unanswerable reasons, brought in one sentence of our former letter unto you against your owne counterfeit and antichristian ministerie,[1] which you were sayd to have derived from, and to exercise 1. under *Antichrist*: 2. in a false office 3. to a confuse assemblie of all sorts of people. All which severallie, and plainely, are proved unto you in that our conference with you; all which you have willingly balked, as also denied what your self in the sayd conference affirmed, and utterly refused all furder conference. Wherfore we cannot be induced to thinke, that you have anie meaning christianly and freely to discusse theis points by wryting; especyallie, since you could by no meanes be drawn to wryte at our being togeather, yea, you were afraide to speak what truth you knew. But we manifestly discerne this pretence to be but one of your sleights to uphold your crazed credit, and to withdraw us, and the eyes of others, from theis unrecoverable breaches, as though you had some better power or skill to defend your doings by writing, than either you have done or dare yeilde to do by free conference of mouth.

As to your disordered parish assemblies, wherein you will needs be still powred out in the error of Balaam for wage,[2] we have long since proved them wholly antichristian by sondry reasons, drawen

---

1 Barrow is referring to the first sentence of the second paragraph of his first letter to Egerton, beginning: " We have since often merveiled." This sentence contains the " unanswerable reasons," but Barrow wants Egerton to answer them nevertheless.
2 Numbers 22: 7-21. See also II Peter 2: 15, which characterizes Balaam as one " who loved the wages of unrighteousness."

H*

from the description of the true established church of Christ; which reasons, a yeare and a half since, were delivered unto some of your cheif ministers, wherunto we never yet received anie answere.[1] Wherfore we have no more to say unto you, but to desire you and them to looke to your estates, and no longer to seduce the people in the bye wayes of men's devises, to their assured destruction, and your owne fearefull reckoninge, except God give you repentance. Which grace that you may finde, we will not cease ever, so long as we may, to pray for you.

And this with unfeyned desire of your salvation, HENRY BARROW [and] JHON [p. 38 — F 1 *verso*] GRENEWOOD, close prysoners in the Fleet, for the testimonie of the truth of the gospell of our Lord Jesus Christ, to whom be glory for ever.

[REPLY No. 2 — MAY 4, 1590]

TO MR. BARROW AND MR. GREENWOODE

More truth and love, etc.

The question I named (to my remembrance) was, whether it were lawfull to come to our church assemblies, or no. But because that which you have chosen tendeth to the same end, I willinglie accept it. Your arguments are three, and may be thus concluded. That ministrie which is 1. derived from, and exercised under antichrist; 2. a false office; 3. in a confused people, is not lawfull. But such is ours. Therfore our ministerie is not lawfull. For answere wherof, I denie your assumption or minor proposition, and returne the same reasons upon your head thus. That ministerie which is 1. derived from and exercised under Christ; 2. in a true office; 3. amonge a faithfull people, is lawfull; but such is ours. *Ergo.* Prove your assumption and I will mine. In the meane time I

---

[1] Barrow and Greenwood are referring to eleven points or reasons, sent about October, 1588, to Thomas Cartwright, William Charke, William Floyde [or Fludd], and Walter Travers. See pages 67—70 of the treatise, *A Collection of Certain Letters and Conferences Lately Passed betwixt Certaine Preachers and Two Prisoners in the Fleet.* It is reprinted in the present volume, with the title, "The True Church and the False Church."

trust myne affirmation shalbe as authenticall as yours. Your letter came the second of this fifth moneth; and I write the fourth. *Valete; and estote sani.*[1]

He that wisheth your convertion.

I [JOHN?] EGERTON.

[LETTER No. 3 — MAY 5, 1590]

TO MR. EGERTON

Grace unto you from the Father of lightes, to see and yeild unto the truth.

Your letter of the fourth of this fifth moneth we have receaved, and perceive therby your controversie (touching the truth of that brief of our conference which we sent unto you) to be ceased.

And nowe your speach turned backe againe to the question there handled amongst us; which we hoped to have then beene thus far forth discussed and decided, that now you had no cause to denie or retract that, which there was enforced, and you condiscended unto; espeacially, without adding anie one reason unto your former, or disproving anie one reason brought by us; except peradventure you would have your owne bare affirmation [p. 39 — F 2 *recto*] be held as authenticall with us, as it is with your miserable auditorie, that have no power or freedome publickly to censure or reprove anie false doctrines that you publickly deliver.

But for the truth and proof of these assumptions we still refer you (as before we referred you) to a furder consideration of that summe of our said conference, with somme better heed and conscience. Where you shall finde these things you now denie sufficiently proved; and in effect wholy yeilded unto by your self. For if these your lordes arch-bishopps and bishopps be agreed upon amongst your selves to be that antichrist, how should that ministerie which is derived from them, and exercised under them, be held the true ministerie of Christ, except the same ministerie may be derived from, and exercised under two divers heades, and those so contrary as Christ and antichrist. Now that your whole ministerie is thus derived and held of your lordes these arch-bishopps and

---

[1] Farewell, and be sound in mind.

bishopps, we hope we neede not stand to prove, neither dare stand you to denie: not so mich [much] for breaking the oath of your canonicall obedience, which you have sworne unto them, as least you be therfore called before them, scilenced, deprived, imprisoned by them.

As to the people to whom you stand a minister, they were all by your owne confessions, immediatlie from idolatrie receaved by constreint into your church, without the preaching of the gospell goinge before to call them to the faith, or before anie christian voluntarie profession made by them in perticular, to witnesse their faith and true convertion. But it is manifest they all still remaine in the same confusion, disorder and servile subjection togeather with you unto these your lordes bishops, their courtes, officers, and canons. Unto which people, in this estate, you for the wage and hire of Balaam are powred forth, and administer the sacraments to them, by your lord bishop his commandement, and that in a doctor's office,[1] as you pretend; or els at such times flee touche,[2] and hide your self out of the way, withdrawing your self from their fellowship at such solemne feastes as this your Easter, *etc.*, when, by the lawes of your church, you were to administer the communion unto them. Thus you may see your naked deniall, nor all the conning anie of you have, wil not serve to cover, mich [much] lesse to cure, these Egiptian malignant ulcers that are founde upon the men that have the marck of the beast, and that worship his image. Wherfore we still exhort you, in the name and feare of God, not anie longer to strive against the prickes, or gnawe your tongue for grief, remayninge impenitent and hardened in your ungodly workes. But rather (whilest grace is offred) to purge your self through unfeyned repentance [p. 40 — F 2 *verso*] in that fountaine which is open to the house of David for sinne and for uncleannes, by forsaking your evill wayes and antichristian ministrie, and now yet at length taking up your crosse, to joyne your self unto the hole armye of saintes, that war in all faithfull and patient maner, under the conduct of the lambe, against all the trumpery and tyrannye of antichrist; that so you may have comfort and assurance unto your owne soule.

Which grace that you may find, and shew; we shall not cease hartely to praye, and by all the means we may, to procure unto you. In the meane time wishing you so to fare and prosper, as

---

[1] Egerton was a doctor.
[2] To flee touch is to make off or escape. Egerton branded this charge a lie.

your soule prospereth, and as you walke according to the rule of God's word.

Henry Barrow }
Jhon Grenewood } Prisoners for the truth of the gospell and witnesses against all antichrist's marcked souldiours and proceedings.

In that you received our second letter no sooner, you are to impute it to your owne absence, that could no sooner be spoken withall by our messenger, who was at your house to deliver it to you, upon the eighteenth of the fourth moneth, and at sondrie other times since.

Written this fifth day of this fifth moneth.

[REPLY No. 3 — MAY 6, 1590]

TO MR. BARROW AND MR. GREENWOOD

More truth and love to you, etc.

Because your letters [*sic*] received the sixth of the fifth moneth, hath in it as manie lyes, as myne to you (to my remembrance) hath lynes; I thinke it the best course to set them before you, to move in you some remorse; except it be with you as the prophet saith, *nescit impius erubescere.*[1]

Lyes.

1. 1. That my bare affirmations are held authenticall of my auditorye:
2. 2. That it was sufficiently proved the last conference, our bishops were that antichrist:
3. 3. That it was in effect wholy yeilded unto by me:
4. 4. That it is agreed uppon amongst our selves, that they be that antichrist:
5. 5. That I have broken my oath of canonicall obedience:
6. 6. That I have sworne canonicall obedience unto the bishops:
7. 7. That I dare not deny their authoritie, for feare of sylence, prison, *etc.*:
8. 8. That the people, by our owne confessions, were all received by constraint immediatly from idolatrie into our church, without preaching of the gospel:

---

[1] The wicked person knows not how to blush. This is probably a reference to Jeremiah 6: 15 and 8: 12.

9.   9. That all the [p. 41 — F 3 *recto*] people remayne still in the same disorder, confusion, *etc.*:

10.   10. That I am powred out in the wages of Balaam:

11.   11. That I administer the sacraments at the lord bishopp's commandement:

12.   12. That I hid my self at Easter:

13.   13. That I am bound to minister the Lord's Supper at Easter:

14.   14. That I have the marke of the beast:

[15.]   15. That I worship his image.

What shalbe thy reward, o thou lying tongue, *etc.* Without shalbe doggs, enchaunters, *etc.*, and all that loveth and maketh lyes.[1] If Barrow and Greenwood be so voide of grace, what should we thincke of that pitifull bande of seduced schismaticks. The Lord give you repentance, Amen. 5 [6] of Maye, 1590.

I. [JOHN] EGERTON

[LETTER No. 4 — MAY 11, 1590]

TO MR. EGERTON

Theyr poison as the poison of a serpent, as the deafe adder stopping his eare. Psalm 58.[2]

The Lord rebuke Satan and judge betwixt us. This your reprochfull letter of the sixth of this fifth moneth, we received the tenth of the same moneth. We fynde it so full of vanitie, vituperie, and blasphemie, as it deserveth none answere or speaking of, eyther in regard of the matter conteyned, or author thereof, were it not for the satisfying of others to whom these our controversies may come. Wherfore as your best profes either to convince us or to defend your self, have hitherto bene the naked assertions and false chardges of your owne mouth, without anie place of Scripture or waight of reason aledged, so when we shall make but a short and sudden demonstration of the truth of these positions which you have collected out of our letter, and as rashly pronounced, lyes; we doubt not, your present evill estate and bad dealing shall as sodenly lye open unto all men, and to your self also if you be not of those evill men and imposters the apostle speaketh of, that shall goe for-

1 Psalm 120: 3 and Revelation 22: 15.
2 The Geneva version of Psalm 58: 4 reads: "Their poison is even like the poison of a serpent: like the deafe adder *that* stoppeth his eare."

ward to the worse, seducing and being seduced, *etc.* [II Timothy 3: 13].

Touching your cattologue of lyes wherof you accuse us, we thus through the grace of God shall cleare our selves, and shew the truth of as manie as we acknowledge, *etc.*

[1.]   The first lye you chardge us with, is, *that your bare affirmations are held authenticall of your auditorye.* Our answere is, that you have drawen an absolute proposition from conditionall words.   [p. 42 — F 3 *verso*] We in our letter reproved you for not adding doctrine to your lypps, some proofe to your assertions, saying; that except you would have your owne bare affirmation to be held as authenticall with us as it is with your miserable auditorie, that have no power or freedome publicklie to censure or reprove anie false doctrine that you publickly delyver, *etc.* Here is in these words no untruth; be your doctrines never so blasphemous and pernitious, your church hath no power presently and publickly to censure you or them, but must joyne unto you still in prayer and sacraments, untill their Lord Ordinarie redresse the matter; or if he will not, they must then swallow all up, how impious soever they be. *Looke for this lawe in the booke of your advertisements in the articles for doctrine and preaching.*[1] Now howe far your

---

[1] See [England, Church of]. *Advertisements Partly for Due Order in the Publique Administration of Common Prayers and Usinge the Holy Sacramentes, and Partly for the Apparrell of All Persons Ecclesiasticall, by Vertue of the Queene's Majestie's Letters Commaunding the Same, the XXV Day of January, in the Seventh Yeare of the Reigne of Oure Soveraigne Lady Elyzabeth, by the Grace of God, of Englande, Fraunce and Irelande, Queene, Defender of the Faith, etc.* (London, [1565 ?]).
" First, that al they which shalbe admitted to preache, shalbe diligentlie examined for their conformytie in unitie of doctrine, established by publique authoritie." See A iii *recto.*
All licences for preaching granted by the archbishops and bishops in the province of Canterbury, with a date before March 1, 1564 [1564-5], are void and must be reissued. The cost is only four pence for writing, parchment, and wax. See A iii *recto* and *verso.*
" No parson or curate, not admitted by the bysshoppe of the dioces to preache, do expound in his owne Cure or other where, anye Scripture or matter of doctrine or by the way of exhortacion." See A iiii *recto.*
" That no curate or minister bee permitted to serve without examination and admission of the Ordinary or his deputy, in writing." B i *verso.*
" I shall not preache or publiquely interprete, but onelye reade that whiche is appointed by publique authoritye, without speciall license of the Bishoppe under his seale." See B iii *verso.*

doctrines are authenticall to that woefull people, that have no power in themselves to call them into question, to examin, trye, or censure them, judge you; yea, how authenticall you would have your owne bare affirmations esteemed, let these your three letters shew; where you have not added one reason to prove or disprove anie thinge you affirme or denie, but your owne bare word. But they must not be so with us, who meane to examin them by the Scriptures before we receive them.

The word *authenticall* peradventure we had not used, had not you gyven occasion in your former letter in these words. *I trust my affirmation shalbe as authenticall as yours.* Which presumptuous words you would not have used, if you had not thought well of your self, and some speciall authoritie to be gyven to your words. As for us, we seeke no credit furder than we speake according to truth; neither hold or would have anie thing held authenticall, besides or with the holy word of God.

2.

Scriptures in stead of lyes.
Rom. 18: 1 [*sic*, perhaps for 1.1]
Rom. 12: 6, 7, 8
1. Cor. 12 entier
Mat. 20: 25, 26
Luke 12: 14
Acts 20: 29
Mat. 18: 17

The second lye should be *that it was sufficiently proved in our last conference, that your bishops were that antichrist.* This we doubt not to affirme, and you cannot deny but your bishopps were there proved to usurpe both civille and ecclesiasticall offices and jurisdiction; that they hold and execute divers ecclesiasticall offices of your church at one time: as to be doctors, pastors, superintendents, lord bishops, lord arch-bishops; and these togeather with their civile offices being judges in courtes, justices of peace, manie lords palatyne, all lords of parliament, and states of the land. That they usurpe and exercise the whole power of the church, in making ministers, in the use of excommunication, hereby confounding and commingling the whole order of God, all the ordinances both of church and common wealth, and invert all the ordinances of Christ his Testament. It was there shewed and proved, that they which [p. 43 — F 4 *recto*] presume into Christ's place, usurpe his title and offices, are those antichrists or that antichrist; and

Danyel 11: 36 etc.
2 Thes. 2: 4
John 3: 29
Cant. 8: 12
John 13: 13
1 Pet. 5: 4

that your bishops usurpe Christ's place, in that they take and holde his bride unto them, making the whole church to heare their voice, and to beare their yoke of their antichristian burdenous traditions; that they

usurpe Christ his titles, Christ being the only Lord, _{1. Cor. 8: 6} _{Rev. 13: 1}
Arch-cheif, high Bishop of Bishopps, to whom all bishops
shall accompt. And therfore these titles are uppon
them but the names of blasphemye written uppon the
heads of that beast; that they usurpe Christ's offices, in
that they take uppon them to rule and oversee so manie Rev. 1: 13, *etc.*
pastors and churches, to walke in the middest of the James 5: 12 Psal. 74
seven golden candlesticks, to give lawes to the church, Dan. 7: 24
etc.

To be short, they were proved unto you to be that
antichrist or those antichrists (for we hope you will not
tye the title to the person of one man only) in that they
change and invert, yea, overthrowe and cast out al the
offices and ordinances which Christ hath appointed
unto his church, even the whole ministerie and Testa- Rev. 9
ment of Christ; and have in place therof brought in,
and set up their owne new forged antichristian ministerie of arch-bishopps, lord bishops, arch-deacons, commissaries, parsons, vickers, curatts, deacons or halfe
priests, even all the horned cleargie, Romishe officers,
popish courts, and innu[m]berable enormous canons Gal. 1: 6, 7, 8
and constitucions of antichrist. As also their newe 1. Joh. 4: 3
devised publique liturgie, wherby the whole worship Mat. 15: 9
and ministracion of your church, yea, wherby the
whole word of God is stinted and lymited to eaves,
and dayes, and houres, to fasts and feasts, *etc.*, what parts
and shredds therof they will have read, what parts suppressed and cast out, *etc.*

Now if all these evident concurring peremptorie
marks do not manifestly prove them to be that and those
antichrists, even that abhomination of desolation stand- Mat. 24: 15
ing in the holy place, let him that readeth consider.
And for your furder assurance, let us now ad unto their
barbarous havocke, their dayly and beastlike crueltye,
tyrannie, persecution and blasphemie of the truth and
servants of Christ, and you may then (the Lord opening
the eyes of your understanding) evidently see them to be Revel 13 and
that monsterous beast, spoken of in the Revelation. 17
Judge now in your self which way you could or can with
all the learning you have or want, withstand these
reasons, or how all the false prophets that flowe from

and guarde the throne of antichrist, can finde anie phisique or baulme for these wounds of the beast.

3. & 4.

So then your third and fourth lyes; [3.] *that it should be in effect wholy yeilded unto by you* 4. *and agreed uppon amongst your selves that the bishops are antichrists.* [p. 44 — F 4 *verso*] We hope will not prove so incredible; especially when they shalbe confirmed to your face (as they were unto your fellow, Mr. Sperin's) by sondrye credible eare witnesses that were present, if you continue so shameles to denie it.

5.

Unto your fifth lye, *that you have broken the oath of your canonicall obedience.* We answere that you greatly mistake the matter, we never so sclaundered you; we always thought you overwell observed that ungodly oath. Our words in our letter were, that " we neede not stand to prove that your ministerie was derived from, and exercised under theis bishops, neither durst you stand to denie it; not so much for breaking the oath of your canonicall obedience which you have sworne unto them, as least you should therfore be called before them, *etc.*" Here leaving the whole estate of the bishops, who were proved by us, and confessed by you, to be antichristes, as also passing by the present estate of your owne ministerie, which is derived from and exercised under them, and therfore proved unto you to be antichristian, unlesse it and you may belong unto, and stand under two divers heads, and these so contrary as Christ and antichrist. But all these waightie matters you willingly passed bye (after the maner of all timeserving Pharises) and picking a quarrell at these three points in fifth, sixth, and seventh lyes: the worst we wish you is, that you had never made, or els had now broken this ungodly oath, and that you had clearly cast off their antichristian yoke, and had delivered your soule from them, and that you durst indeede boldly speake and stand against their antichristian authoritie and ungodly proceedings: we are willing upon theis condicions, for your so great good, to suffer more than a lytle reproche.

6.

The sixth lye should be *that you have sworne canonicall obedience unto the bishops.* We finde the lawes of your

church to be, that none be suffred to preach or administer in your church, or be made full priest, except
he first sweare his canonical obedience unto his Ordinarie,[1] diligently to appeare at his courts, and to observe
their decrees: none may preach without the bishop's
licence, or if he speake against anie thing by publicke
authoritie established, or by the same authoritie that
shalbe established in your church hereafter. These
lawes we finde generall, and no particuler exception to
the same; therfore we see not how or whie you should
more be exempt from this oath, license, lawes, than the
rest of your brethren and fellow priests. Furder, you
do preach and administer after these orders and canons
prescribed by your lords the bishops; therfore it is likely
you have taken the same oath and licence, or that which
is all one, it is most sure you stand under the [p. 45 —
G 1 *recto*] same antichristian lawes and yoke.

We will beleve your seventh to be a lye when you shall [7]
have forsaken your antichristian ministerie, which you
now execute, *etc.*, and speake and suffer boldly and
sincerely against the bishop's authoritie and proceedings:
till then you must beare with us if we esteeme you as we
finde you, and gyve no credit to your ambiguous
speaches, wherby we know not whither you will or will
not speake against the bishop's authoritie.

This your eighth lye, *that the people by your confessions were* 8.
all received by constraint ymmediatly from idolatry into your
church without preaching of the gospell,[2] you have marred
by the figure of *Omission*, in an evill conscience leaving

---

1 See " The Ordinal, Being the Form of Making, Ordaining, and Confe-
crating Bishops, Priests, and Deacons, together with the Form of Con-
secration of a Church, An Office of Institution of Ministers," in *The Book*
of Common Prayer. The candidate for the office of the deacon is asked
by the bishop: " Will you reverently obey your bishop, and other chief
ministers, who, according to the canons of the church, may have the
charge and government over you; following with a glad mind and will
their godly admonitions ? " To this the candidate replies, " I will en-
deavour so to do, the Lord being my helper."
For the candidate to be admitted to the order of priesthood, the question
is the same, with the addition of the phrase, " and submitting yourselves
to their godly judgments." The answer is, " I will so do, the Lord being
my helper."
2 That is, by the enactment of the Act of Uniformity and Act of Supremacy
on May 8, 1559, when Queen Elizabeth constrained her people to make
the abrupt change from Catholicism and idolatry to Anglicanism.

out the one half of your matter, least if you had justly reported it, you might have bene ashamed to have called it a lye; seing it should to all men appeare a most manifest truth, confirmed by the times past and present. Let us therfore help you out with the rest, that the lye may be more notorious.   It followeth in our letter thus. *To call them to the faith or anie christian and voluntarie profession made by them in particuler to witnes their faith, and true confession.*   Now you have your whole tale, let us see with what face or truth you can denie this.   At the first planting of your church in the begynning of our Queene Elizabeth's reigne, and for your confession we have the effect of this under your fellow Mr. Sperin his hand, which being read before you and reported unto you, you neither gainsayed it in anie thing, neither would or could stand to justifie their order in the first establishing of your church.

9.   Your ninth lye is, *that all the people remaine still in the same disorder, confusion, etc.*   That litle which you here also by the same figure in all evill conscience suppresse, would have done better in this place than " *etc.*", and peradventure might so have cleared the pointe, as it might have saved both you and us from the imputation of this lye also.   The words that lacke are these, *and servile subjection unto these your lord bishopps, their courts, officers and canons togeather with you.*   Put it now togeather and see if you can denie it, or anie part of it. It is manifest you still have and reteine all the same people or their seede in the same confusion, false worship, the same antichristian ministerie and ordinances, no seperation, no reformation as yet made: this, that our conference, but the present estate of your church best of all sheweth.[1]

10.   And these things standing thus, your tenth lye will likewise prove a truth to your furder chardge, *viz., that you are poured out in the wages of Balaam.*   Seing you still administer to this prophane miscelyne people in this confusion, subjection for their hyre, *etc.*, we need not doubt with the Apostle Jude to say that you are powred

[1] This, which our conference has revealed, but which the present estate of your church best of all revealeth or sheweth.

out in the error of Balaam for wage; and with the
Apostle Peter, that for-[p. 46 — G 1 *verso*]saking the
right way you have gone astray, following the way of 1. Tim. 6: 5
Balaam of Bozor,[1] that loved the wage of iniquitie, John 10: 12, 13
thinking that gayne is godlynes, making marchandise Rev. 2: 14
of the word like an hireling. Yea, it were no hard
matter to prove, that you maintaine the doctrine of
Balaam that taught Balac to set a trap before the
children of Israel, to eate things sacrificed to idoles
and to commyt fornication,[2] if your sitting in commission in Caiaphas' hall with that old false prophet
of London,[3] your finger in his bloudye mandate by
name and especiall ticket,[4] your subtile conference
with Christ's persecuted servants in their prysons, and
your continuall clamors in your pulpit, were duely
skanned.

That you do or ought to administer the sacraments at 11.
your lord bishop's comaundement, is manifest in that
you are full priest. Everie full minister of your church
ought, by the lawes of your church, and may deliver
the sacraments. That we here urdge not your lord
bishop's late edict unto all curats or hireling preachers
that were full ministers, to that effect.

That you hid and with drewe your selfe from the fellow- 12.
ship and communion of your parishioners and flocke at
your last Easter,[5] leaving them to the ministerie and
conduct of your dumbe pastor, is to be proved by manie
witnesses, and the words of your owne wife and servants
unto our messenger that was to delyver our letter unto
you, if you might have bene then founde.

And that you and all the curats and full priests in 13.
England are by the lawe of your church bound to

---

1 Beor is the modern form. II Peter 2: 15 mentions Bosor.
2 Numbers 22, 23, 24, and 31: 16. Revelation 2: 14.
3 John Aylmer, Bishop of London, member of the High Commission, meeting
  in Lambeth Palace.
4 Although Egerton is listed in Bishop Aylmer's order of February 25,
  1589/90, he is there assigned to confer with George Collier and John
  Sparowe (or Sparrow) in the Clink. The difficulties which Thomas Sperin
  encountered in coping with Barrow during the first conference on March
  14 may have led to Egerton's special assignment on March 20. Egerton
  is referred to as a doctor, Sperin as a pastor.
5 April 19, 1590.

administer the communion at Easter, peruse your portuis or service-booke better.

14. That *you have the marke of the beast* and that [it is] in the foreheade is manifest; in that the arch-bishops and bishops are proved [to be] that antichrist, that beast, and you stand a waged minister under them by their licence, in their kingdome.

15. That *you worship the beast his image* is as manifest; in that you administer by the constitutions and decrees of their devices, service booke or liturgie, which is set up in al your churches; unto and by which you burne your incense, joyne and applie your doctrines and preachings, els could you stand no minister in their market.

Thus may you see all your lyes retourned home to their resting place to the land of Shinar,[1] even your owne bozome, from whence they proceeded; thus may you see your self taken and ensnared, even in every word that hath come out of your mouth; thus may you see, the furder and more you strive against the truth, the furder and faster you entoyle [ensnare] your self. How much better therfore were it for you to wash your self in that fountaine which was shewed you, Zachariah 13, and with the false prophet there, to be ashamed of your vision and rough gowne to deceave; acknowledging [p. 47 — G 2 *recto*] these wounds to be given you in the house of your lovers, than thus to fulfil the words and

Rev. 16: 10 judgments of God in your self, in gnawing your tongue for griefe, and casting the poisoned darts of your virulent tongue at the innocent, even them that seeke your good.

Take heed and be warned, you were told of these judgments, and may see how they are daily more and more fulfilled uppon you; take heed you be not judged of your owne mouth, and be shut out with those lyers, doggs, and enchanters you mention. Your lyes you see whither they are retourned, and uppon whom they rest. How you have barked at and bitten, not only us, but all the deare servants of God, and faithfull witnesses of Christ, speaking out of the mouth of that

[1] The land of Shinar was the place where the descendants of Noah began to build the city and tower of Babel [confusion]. See Genesis 11: 1-9.

dragon, and of that beast, and of that false prophet, by this blasphemie in your letter appeareth. The enchanters you speake of, are those false prophets that do their miracles before the throne of the beast; those merchant-men, that helpe to decke and adorne the harlot, the false church; those mediciners, that seeke to heale the wound of the beast; those deceivers, that by the effectuall working or [*sic*, of] Satan in all power, and signes, and lying wonders, seduce such as receive not the love of the truth, that they might be saved; those sorcerers, that did al their miracles in Egipt, still to kepe the people of God in bondage and to hinder them from their jornye toward Sion, that resist the truth as Jannes and Jambres withstood Moses,[1] whose madnes as it was made k[n]owen unto all men, so shall yours also be. As you have alledged, these lyers, doggs, enchanters, shalbe rejected in the buylding of Sion, shalbe shut out of the heavenly Jerusalem, the church and bryde of Christ; but the beast shalbe taken, and with him the Rev. 19: 20 false prophet that did these signes before him, in which he deceaved them that receaved the marke of the beast, and that worshipped his image; these two shalbe cast alive into that lake of fyre burning with brimstone. Be warned therfore and tremble, consider of your estate. God send you of his grace. This eleventh of this fifth month.

HENRY BARROW
JOHN GREENWOOD.

Except your letters hereafter be ceasoned [*sic*] with more gravitie and grace, we shalbe unwilling to receive anie more of them, or at the least forbeare anie further to answere or followe you in this untemperate course; leaving you to the judgment of God for all the wicked sayings you shall speake against the servants and truth of Christ, which you cannot impunge [impugn, withstand]. [p. 48 — G 2 *verso*]

---

[1] II Timothy 3: 8.

John Greenwood

THE SUMME OF A CONFUSE CONFERENCE HAD THE 3 OF THE 4
MONETH, BETWIXT MR. SPERIN AND MR. COOPER, JOHN
GREENWOOD AND HENRY BARROW IN THE FLEET.

At the first, being set downe at the table, Mr. Sperin used certaine
speach openly in way of prayer.

Greenwood: Whie do you here take uppon you to offer up the
prayers of us all without our consent, we not being
met togeather to that purpose *homothumadon* [with one
accord] but as you know differing in judgment, and
disalowing your church and ministrie.

Sperin: I used it for my self and such as would joyne unto it.

Greenwood: If for your self, it was to[o] pharisaicall, and not to
have bene publicke. As for us, you know we would
not joyne unto it.

Sperin: All actions ought to be undertaken with prayer going
before.

Barrow: But prayer ought to be made with one accorde, where
with one mynde and one mouth they may praise God
the Father of our Lord Jesus Christ. Romans 15: 6.

Cooper: Christ and his apostles used prayer when they reasoned
with the adversarie.

Barrow: That is not so. Where finde you that?

Greenwood: Your prayers and all your actions are accursed in this
popish ministrie you execute.

Sperin: None will say so but such schismatickes as you, that
have rent your selves from the church.

Barrow: It should seeme you know not what either a schismaticke or the true church is. Have we so largely
disprooved your church unto you at your former
being here, yet you now call us schismatickes, not
being able to approve your church.

Sperin: You never could disprove our church.

Barrow: We proved it unto you to consist of a confuse assemblie
of prophane people, received immediately from open
idolatrie uppon one day by constreint without anie

236

instruction in the word of God going before into your church, this ministrie, sacraments, worship, set over them, which you confessed and would not approve.

Sperin: It is not so; I never denied it to be a church.

Barrow: Will you now denie it? I will produce your owne hand against you. And fetched a paper where indeed that proposition was not but some argumentes insuing theruppon.

Wheruppon Mr. Sperin began to insult. *The proposition indeed being under his hand in an other paper, which I then remembred not.*

Barrow: There are manie witnesses of this assertion. But I will bring you [p. 49 — G 3 *recto*] unto it by circumstances, or convince it by profe. Did you not denie to meddle with that time, because neither you nor I were of age to remember it?

Sperin: That is true.

Greenwood: You then confessed, (and it is manifest) that all the people were then received to the sacramentes, without anie convertion by doctrine.

Barrow: You confessed also that this was done by force, and did not alowe therof.

Sperin: Neither doo I now alowe of it, if it were so.

Barrow: Whie should you make question of so cleare a thing? We proved it; as also that all your parishes now consisted of the same people and their seed, had still the same ministrie, worship, government, *etc.*

Sperin: I then denied and still denie, that the people or ministrie are the same.

Cooper: There is now great alteration in the faith and knowledge of the people over [what] was then.

Greenwood: Had you not then a ministerie set over an ignorant people, and have you not the same ministerie over the same people and their seed now?

Sperin: }
Cooper: } The people are now wonne to the faith.

Greenwood: But have you not still the same ministrie which was then set over them in this disorder and confusion? Hath there since bene anie seperation or amendement emongst you? Remayne you not in the same sinnes still? What change can you shew us?

237

John Greenwood

Barrow:	Are not all still of your church? Or what wicked man of the land is not of your church?
Sperin:	Such schismatickes as you, are not of our church.
Barrow:	You know neither what a church or schismaticke is. You can neither prove your church, nor shew us [to be] schismatickes.
Sperin:	You are such schismatickes as were in the church of Corinth and are spoken of, 1 Corinthians 1: 10.
Barrow:	You reade there of no schismatickes in the church of Corinth, neither understand you that Scripture aright.
Sperin:	I will reade the text. *Now I beseech you bretheren by the name of our Lord Jesus Christ that yee all speake one thing, and that there be no schismes emongst you. But be you kint [knit] togeather in one minde and in one judgment.* Are not here schismatickes spoken of?
Barrow:	What then?
Sperin:	Then were there schismatickes.
Barrow:	It should seeme you know not what a schismaticke is, that can put no difference betwixt a sectorie and a schismaticke. The [p. 50 — G3 *verso*] apostle there speaketh of sectories, and not of schismatickes.
Sperin:	The apostle there speaketh of schismatickes, such as were vaine glorious and despised them that taught sincerelie.
Barrow:	The apostle there speaketh of sectories, such as you are: that sought to drawe the people after them, and to have them to follow, heare, and relye uppon themselves; so that some would heare one man, some an other, according to their ytching humors: which sectories were teachers in the church; neither doth the apostle there speake of schismaticks. A sectorie is alwayes one that raiseth factions in the church; a schismatick is he which draweth from the fellowship, and rendeth or severeth himself from the church, of whom you reade, Hebrews 10.
Cooper:	The word schisme is a generall word, and is read *promiscué*.
Barrow:	That is true. A sect also is conteined under the word schisme.
Sperin:	The apostle useth the word *schisma*. Therefore they were schismat[ics].

238

Barrow:	Can you not yet learne a better construction of this word schismes in this place? Mr. Cooper hath taught you a better construction. You will not say that these were cut from the church?
Sperin:	Whie not?
Greenwood:	The eleventh verse of the first chapter of the Epistle [to the Corinthians] sheweth that they were of the church, *for it hath bene declared unto me (my brethren) that there are contentions emongst you.*
Barrow:	They were famous teachers of and in the church, therfore they were not cut off, or schismaticks.
Cooper:	I Corinthians 11: [19, 20]. It is said that there shalbe schismes and heresies emongst them.
Barrow:	I grant well: what of that, therfore hereticks and schismaticks are of the church. You will not conclude so?
Cooper:	Schisme and a schismatick are *coniugata* [etymologically related].
Greenwood:	By your logicke and prophane artes you pervert the trueth of the Scriptures.
Sperin: ⎱ Cooper: ⎰	Logicke is a helpe to the understanding of the Scriptures.
Greenwood:	You make it a cloke for your wickednes, with shiftes to torne [turn] away the trueth.
Barrow:	You can put no difference betwixt a schisme and a schismatick, the offense and the offender.
Sperin:	There cannot be schisme, but there must be a schismaticke.
Barrow:	But may not the apostle speake of a schisme where he speaketh not of a schismatick.
Greenwood:	There may a schismatick arise in the church, and yet not be of the church: as antichrist is said to arise in the church of God, yet is not of the church. He cannot be a schismatick, untill he have cut himself from the church.
Sperin:	The apostle saith there were schismes and schismaticks emongst them, for some held of Paul, some of Apollo[s], some of Cephas. But Christ is not devided. [p. 51 — G 4 *recto*]
Barrow:	The apostle there speaketh of such sectorie teachers and people following them, as thus were led into

partes and factions of such teachers as boasted of their giftes, and of the nombers they had baptized, and that followed them. Yet all this sheweth, in that they were still teachers and baptized, that they were still of the church, and not schismaticks. But if you had judgment dulie to consider of this place, you should finde the faultes there reproved to be found mich [much] more rife uppon the teachers of your church than they were in Corinth, where are almost so manie sectes as teachers.

Sperin: It is understood of such Brownistes and schismatickes as you are.

Barrow: It is your custome to blesse Christ's enemies and blaspheme Christ's servants. We are no Brownistes, we hold not our faith in respect of anie mortall men, neither were we instructed by him or baptised into his name, untill by such as you we were so termed. Schismaticks we are not: we hold communion with all Christ's servants in true faith and love: only we have separat our selves from the false church and false ministrie, which we have proved you to be.

Greenwood: Browne is an apostata, now one of your church; you receceive [*sic*] all such apostataes from Christ; we never had anie thing to do with Browne, neither are we members of your church.

Sperin: You were somtime a minister of our church, were you not? And now are gonne backe.

Greenwood: Seing this matter concerneth me, I pray you give me leave to shew them what kinde of ministrie I then had, and whie I left it. I was somtimes indeed a minister of your church, after your popish orders; but finding my ministrie to be wholie unlawfull in the verie office, entrance, and administration, by the rules of Christ's Testament, I, according to the commandement of God, Zechariah 13, Hezr. 2. [Ezekiel 2][1] and as manie places as commaund to absteine from evill and to do that which is good, by repentance left it.[2]

---

[1] The reference to Ezra 2 seems to be a misprint or a mistaken citation.
[2] Greenwood gave up his ministry in [Rackheath ?], Norfolk, in 1585. He served as rector of Wyam, Lincolnshire, 1582-3.

Cooper: Because there were some corruptions in it, will you therfore forsake your whole ministrie?

Greenwood: My ministrie was wholy evill, both in office, entrance, and administration, so that I left it not for some corruptions. But if you can prove it to be a true and lawfull ministrie, though with some corruptions, wherof I may repent and yet keepe my ministrie, I will willingly go out of pryson with you, and labour in it againe.

Cooper: And if you can prove it wholie unlawfull, I will leave my ministrie and come and sit with you in pryson.

Barrow: It is not in your power so to do, repentance is the gift of God.

Greenwood: It is written, Revelation 16: [10, 11], that when the sinnes of the false church shalbe discovered, the ministers therof shalbe so far from repen-[p. 52 — G 4 *verso*]tance, as they shall gnawe their tongues for sorrowe, and blaspheme the God of heaven. Let us then have penne and ynke, that our reasons and answers may be set downe.

Cooper: To what purpose? You seeke writing buth [*sic*] to catch.

Barrow: We seeke writing to avoide sclander, and that the trueth might the better appeare, when both our reasons and answeres are set downe.

Cooper: It were but to spend time. I will not write.

Greenwood: Let us growe to some head: we will write though you will not. Let me shew you my ministrie that I had in your church, I pray you. I was first made deacon by the Bishop of London, to no peculiar congregation: afterward made full priest by the Bishop of Lyncolne, you know after what a popish order.[1]

Cooper: Because there might be some defaultes in your entrance, do you therfore think all your ministrie unlawfull?

Greenwood: If I had no true entrance unto the ministrie, and yet should exercise a ministerie, I were in the nomber

---

[1] Greenwood was made a deacon in the year 1581, when John Aylmer was the Bishop of London, and was ordained a priest August 8, 1582, when Thomas Cooper was the Bishop of Lincoln.

John Greenwood

of those whom Christ pronounceth thieves and murderers, John 10.

Cooper: Though there be defaults in your entrance, your ministrie may be lawfull. You must prove your whole ministrie unlawfull.

Greenwood: My ministrie was unlawfull, both in the entrance, office, and administration: therfore wholie unlawfull.

Sperin: ⎱ Our ministrie is not wholie unlawfull in the entrance,
Cooper: ⎰ office, and administracion.

Greenwood: I will beginne with myne entrance, which I thus prove to be wholie unlawfull. *There was no flocke called me to the ministrie. Therfore I could have no lawfull calling to exercise anie ministrie in anie office unto them.*

Cooper: You might be a minister and exercise your ministrie unto them, though you were not called by them; because you might offer your giftes unto them, and so be a minister by an inward calling.

Greenwood: Though this be no answere to my argument, yet let it be set downe in writing.

Wheruppon this proposition was set downe.

Cooper: *It may so fall out some times that a man, not being called of the flocke, may yet offer his ministrie unto the church; and that shalbe a sufficient calling for him to be either pastor or doctor, because ther is an inward calling.*

Greenwood: Do you hold that by an inward calling a man may exercise an office in the church of God without an outward calling therunto? If I should hold it, I should quicklye be drawne forth for an Anabaptist.

Cooper: With theis circumstances he may. As a man indued with giftes should offer them in pitie and compassion unto an ignorant people.

Greenwood: But whither [whether] doth he offer himself as a minister, or as no minister unto them? [p. 53 — H 1 *recto*]

Cooper: He offreth himself as a minister by an inward calling.

Greenwood: He could not offer himself as a minister unto them, because he had neither office nor calling unto the ministrie before.

242

A Collection of Certain Letters and Conferences

Cooper: Sperin: }	He may be a minister, pastor, or teacher before he be chosen of a flocke, because he may have an inward calling.
Greenwood:	No man can be an officer in the church, except he have a true outward calling therunto.
Cooper:	You hold him no true minister, without he have a perfect calling.
Greenwood:	I pleade not for perfect outward calling, but for a true outward calling.
Cooper:	Then you grant that though there be some defaults in his outward calling, yet he may be a true minister.
Barrow:	We are so far from looking for a church or ministrie without faults here in this life, that we affirme ther can be no church or ministrie here without fault.
Green- wood: Barrow: }	But you goe from the question: we reason not of a perfect, but of a true outward calling, without which there can be now no true minister in the church. Answere therfore directly to the argument, either denie or affirme.
Cooper: Sperin: }	We will answere by distinguishing: and repeated their first proposition. That a man by his inward calling might be received as a minister of the people, without an outward calling.
Greenwood:	Then you denie my proposition, *that of necessitie everie true minister must have a true outward calling to his office.*
Sperin:	A man may be a minister without a true outward calling in an extraordinarie time, having an inward calling.
Greenwood:	The rules of Christ's Testament are now perfect, and perpetuall in all times: therfore there is no such extraordinarie time, that anie man may take upon him a ministrie without a true outward calling according to the rules of the word.
Sperin:	Luther and Calvin, *etc.*, were true ministers in theis extraordinarie times without a true outward calling.
Green- wood: Barrow: }	We are not now to contend about their ministrie, they are now dead: will you oppose their ministrie against the rules of Christ's Testament? We affirme no man can be a true minister, without a true outward calling therunto.

243

John Greenwood

Cooper: We do affirme that ther may be a ministrie without a true outward calling. But by circumstances.

Greenwood: This is contrarie to your former assersion: that ther might be a minister without an outward calling at all, *ut supra*. [p. 54 — H 1 *verso*] Answere therfore directly, yea or no.

Cooper: His offring, his guifts unto the people, and their receiving of him is some outward calling.

Greenwood: Hold you this a true and sufficient outward calling?

Cooper: For such times as theis, I hold it a true and sufficient outward calling.

Barrow: An unbeleeving people cannot call or elect a minister. But you confesse the people to be such.

Cooper: He may be a minister to the people, they accepting of him, before they be called to the faith. How els would you have them called to the faith?

Greenwood: Not by placing Christ's ministrie over an unbeleeving people. The infidels ought to heare the word, but cannot chuse a minister.

Cooper: Thus he may be a minister. *The people, what people soever, before they be called, are to take this man thus offring himself as a teacher unto them by his inward calling, as a minister in the office of pastor or teacher.*

Barrow:
Green-
wood: } May the sacraments then be delivered to an unbeleeving people?

Cooper: Not before they be taught.

Greenwood: Is anie of the flocke and yet incapable of the sacraments, or may there be a pastor and a flocke and yet no sacraments delivered?

Cooper: As they are instructed they are to have the sacraments delivered unto them.

Barrow: But all your people receive the sacraments, all being baptised without the exception of anie, either hereticke, witch, or conjurer and their seed before they were instructed, and you stand ministers unto such.

Sperin: This is but your sclander; we stand ministers to no such.

Barrow: Let the prisons and estate of the land be searched whether ther be no such to be found: all the land is

244

	baptised in your church, and you stand ministers to all the land in high sacriledge.
Sperin:	I deliver the sacraments to none, but unto such whose faith I knowe.
Barrow:	It should seeme you know not what faith is, or unto whom to deliver the sacraments: what wicked person is ther in your parish, or in the whole land, that is not baptised and received to your sacraments?
Sperin:	You judge uncharitablie of the whole land. I pray what thinke you of your self when you were of our church.
Barrow:	I then was as you now are, and went where I was ledd away unto dumbe idoles by such as you are.[1]
Cooper:	You abuse the Scripture. The apostle there speaketh of the heathen and of stockes and stones.[2]
Sperin:	We leade you not to idoles, neither to worship images; theis are your sclanders. [p. 55 — H 2 *recto*]
Barrow:	I abuse not the place, neither sclander you. We are ledd unto idoles when we are ledd unto such ministers as you, which stand for that [which] you are not in the church, and are idole shepherds and ministers, Zechariah 11. Againe you leade us to open and grosse idolatrie; as the worshipping of dead saintes and angells; yea, your selves worship images, even that image of that beast.
Sperin:	These are but your railings and sclanders. We worship neither angells, nor saintes, nor the image of the beast.
Barrow:	You give unto angells and dead saintes in your church and solemnlie indict [proclaim] an eave, a day, on the one a fast, on the other a solemne feast, with an especiall worship devised of purpose unto peculiar saintes and angells, the day proclaimed and kept holie. Call you not this idolatrie, do you not now worship saintes and angells?
Sperin:	We do not worship them though we use theis ceremonies.
Barrow:	You shew your self a man without sence or shame. I purpose not at this time to meddle with your grosse

[1] I Corinthians 12: 2.
[2] Compare I Corinthians 8 and Jeremiah 3: 9.

245

I

idolatries, it were from the purpose and an endles worke. Let me now shew you how you worship the image of the beast. You worship and use in your worship the constitucions and devises of these antichristian bishopps, as your service-booke, *etc*.

Sperin: You speake you know not what. You know not what the image of the beast is.

Barrow: Yes, I knowe that speaking image of the beast which is set up in all your churches, even the humane constitutions of all theis antichristian bishops; which and wherby, you and all your people worship. This I affirme to you and unto all the world, to be the image of the beast: that *eikōn*. All devises of men brought into the worship of God are idoles: as your Apochripha writings in stead of God's spirituall worship.

Sperin: That is not so; how prove you that?

Barrow: I prove it by the second commandement. *Thou shalt not make to thy self anie graven image or idole.*

Sperin: Loe, you understand not the second commandement; it speaketh only of stockes and stones, *etc*.

Barrow: See what a good teacher you are that understand not the lawe, and yet would be a teacher of the lawe. The second Commandement is not only understood of worshipping creatures, but of all maner false and devised worship, when we worship God after the devises of men.

Sperin: It is not so, you understand not this commandement.

Greenwood: Christ himself so expoundeth it, Matthew 15. *You worship me in vayne, teaching [for] doctrines men's precepts.* [p. 56 — H 2 *verso*]

Barrow: You are ignorant of theis doctrines, are unworthie to be a pastor: for anie thing I have seene in you, you understand no Scriptures.

Cooper: You have verie shamefullie perverted the place to the Corinthes, which is spoken of dombe idoles, stockes, and stones.

Greenwood: He used not the place of the Corinthes at all, but onlie spake according to that phrase. So that if his doctrine be true the place hath no injurie.

Cooper: He used the place.

Barrow: It is not so; I alleadged not the place: but onlie spake according to the phrase. We are commaunded to speake with holie wordes, and as the words of God.

Cooper: Speake of your conscience whether you meant not to use the place.

Barrow: I use not to speake against mie conscience in or for anie thing. I have told you how I ment to use the place. Neither can it be otherwise collected from mie speach. But read you never, that our saviour Christ and his apostles have used places in the prophets and psalmes, and otherwise applied them than they were in their context?

Cooper: Those the apostle there spake of, were the idolls of the heathen, and to the heathen people, and therfore can not be applied to us.

Greenwood: All idolls are of the same nature and in the same detestation with the Lorde, whether they be blockes, or stockes, or spirituall idols, which are more subtile.

Barrow: I have shewed your idolatrie to be grosse enough: as the worshipping of saints, angells, keeping holie dayes and holie eaves unto them, holie fasts and holie feasts. But it were a wearines to rip up your popish, Jewish, heathenish ministrations.

Cooper: Theis are but rayling and foolish wordes.

Greenwood: I pray you follow them no furder. Let us be no longer ledd away with their cavills, and by shifts from our present purpose; els we shall conclude of nothing.

Barrow: I pray you then go to it againe. For I am wearied with them, and will no more deale with such unreasonable men.

Cooper: I can no longer stay, I must be gonne.
And so he arose upp, and would have broken of[f].

Greenwood: Wil you openlie declare that you had no purpose to edifie your selves or us? Wherfore then did you come, will you conclude of no pointe of doctrine? Answeare this argument, I beseech you.
Every true minister of the church must have election, approbation, and ordination, in and of a true congregation of Christ.

John Greenwood

> *But you have not such election, approbation, ordination.*
> *Therfore you are no true ministers of Christ.* [p. 57 —
> H 3 *recto*]

Cooper: We have election, approbation, ordination, in a christian congregation.

Greenwood: That is not true. For neither have you a people trulie called and gathered unto Christ, nether were you chosen and ordeyned by the people, but by the bishop.

Barrow: Here must be noted your unconstancie, that agree not unto your self. Erwhile you defended your ministrie by your inward calling without anie outward calling; and now you justifie your outward calling. But let me not trouble you: follow your argument.

Cooper: I had the people's acceptation when I was made minister.

Greenwood: The people's acceptation was but your agreement with them for your wadges.

Cooper: That is not true. I could have mie wadges without the people's consent by law.

Greenwood: The lawe alloweth a curate but tenne pounds by yeare, but that will not content you. You must therfore compownd with the people for more.

Barrow: You could not have the people's acceptation, when you were made minister, you had no flocke then.

Greenwood: Before you had a flocke Mrs. Lawson[1] got a lycens for you from the arch-bishop to preach in that parish.

Barrow: What office do you exercise in your church, Mr. Cooper? Are you a pastor?

Cooper: I am no pastor, I am a doctor.

Barrow: Ther is no such office in your church. Everie parish is but allowed his parson or vickar; endowed curats or such doctors are but the parson's substitutes to help a dumbe or plurified parson.

Cooper: We have the doctor's office in our church.

Barrow: It is evident you have not.

---

[1] Probably Mrs. [Margaret ?] Lawson, known as Dame Lawson, wife of Thomas Lawson. See William Pierce, *An Historical Introduction to the Marprelate Tracts*, p. 156; see also his book, *The Marprelate Tracts*, pp. 30-32, 98, 208, 269, 356. Bishop Cooper denounces her in *An Admonition to the People of England*, pp. 39, 56.

Greenwood: You were made minister by the bishop before you came to your parish by Powles [St. Paul's Cathedral].[1]

Cooper: I was made minister to a flocke.

Barrow: That could not be, seinge you are no parson. You were made minister to anie that would hire you.

Greenwood: You are those *asteres planetai*, those wandring starres Jude speaketh of,[2] like the Levite that ran from place to place wher he might get the best wadges.

Cooper: ⎱ You falsly applie the Scriptures against us. We are
Sperin: ⎰ not those *stellae erraticae* Jude speaketh of.

Barrow: Yes, and in the error of Balaam being powred fourth for wadge. How manie parishes have you beene at, runninge from one to an other. [p. 57 — H 3 *verso*][3]

Sperin: ⎱ Is it not lawfull for a minister upon some occasions
Cooper: ⎰ to remove from one congregation unto an other?

Greenwood: That minister that forsaketh his flocke is an hireling, commeth but to robbe and spoile. But you both are placed in, and removed from your flocke without the consent of your flocke; and are silenced in your flockes by the bishopps, by whom you were made priests.

Cooper: ⎱ We had not our ministerie from the bishop but from
Sperin: ⎰ a congregacion.

Greenwood: What congregation was that, when each of you have had so manie?

Sperin: ⎱ What if we were made by a congregation of ministers?
Cooper: ⎰

Greenwood: How can that be, can there be a pastor of pastors, or a congregation of pastors? You were made ministers by the bishops and not by anie christian congregation.

Sperin: ⎱ We had not our ministerie of the bishops but by
Cooper: ⎰ consent of a congregation.

Greenwood: Thus I prove you had your ministerie from the bishop. By the bishop's calling you administer and by none other. Therfore.

Cooper: ⎱ We had not our ministrie by the bishops onlie.
Sperin: ⎰

Greenwood: By the bishop's callings you administer, and without

---

[1] Perhaps the parish referred to was " St. Gregorys by St. Paul's."
[2] Jude 1: 13.
[3] This should be p. 58. From this point on the pagination is wrong — one less than the correct number.

the bishop's calling you cannot administer. Therfore by the bishop's calling onlie.

Sperin: We have the approbation of the congregation also.

Barrow: You have not. Your curats (as is said) are made ministers *in nubibus*,[1] without anie flocke. Your parsons are nominat by the patron, and made by the bishop. Thus t[h]rust upon the flocke without either the knowledge, privity, approbation, or choise of the people.

Sperin: The patron's choise is the people's choise.

Barrow: How can you saie the patron's choise is the people's, when they have neither privitie, consent nor assent. Be the patron a woman, an infant, an ideote, have he forty benefices and those in all the parts of the lande, such as he hath never seene or knowen, yet doth he present, and the people must accept.

Sperin: I had the approbation of the flock before I went unto the bishop, and was a minister before I was at the bishop.

Barrow: You could not have your parsonadge before you had bene at the bishop, neither be a minister without the bishop. Were you not a minister before you came to your flocke? Answere directlie.

Sperin: I was made minister by a bishop before I had the approbation of the people.

Barrow: What truth or agreement is in your speach? Even now you said your [*sic*] were a minister before you came at the bishop and had the approbation of your flocke before. Now you say (which indeed is true) [p. 58 — H 4 *recto*] you were made minister by the bishop before you had the approbation of the people.

Sperin: I meant the Bishop of London. I had the approbation of my flocke before I went to him.

Barrow: We reasoned all this while of the bishopps indefinitely, and not of anie one bishop more than of an other. But to what end serveth now the approbation of the people, when you are made full minister before.

Sperin: I was a minister in part, but no full minister before I had the approbation of the people.

Barrow: See how you intangle your self. How can you make

---

[1] In the clouds.

this agree unto your second proposition, [namely,] that you were made minister by a bishop before you had the approbation of the people.

Sperin: I hold not my self a minister in the sight of God by the bishop's ordination, untill I have the people's approbation.

Barrow: God seeth and knoweth all his workes from before all beginnings. God knoweth all that he hath appointed and set apart to the work of his ministrie, even before he made them or in their cradles. So that God in his fore knowledg maie ordaine chosen vessells unto his ministerie, which yet in the sight of men are not to be held ministers, untill they have that lawfull calling which God hath prescribed ther-unto, which calling, seing you want, you are to be held no minister in the sight of men also. Moreover, the bishop without the approbation of your flocke ordeyned you a minister. Now which way should you not hold your self a minister after their orders; or to what end served the ordination of the bishop, if you were not then made minister?

Here Mr. Cooper hasted away and said he could no longer tarie. Wherupon we ended this general conference. Yet notwithstanding (the chamber dore being locked, and no porter neere to let them out) Mr. Cooper used speach to the standers by which after followeth.

We have omitted one especiall pointe that fell out in our conference, not perfectly remembring the due place where it should come in.

Cooper: If you would not have a ministrie sett over the un-believing people, how should the unbelieving people be called unto the faith.

Greenwood: We shall shew you an other order to call the people to the faith according to Christ's Testament. And not without warrant, to sett the ministery of Christ over an unbelieving people, to the perverting of all God's ordinances, and committinge of sacriledge, having no promise of anie action you do in that estate.

Cooper: Which way would you then have them called, if they should not be instructed. [p. 59 — H 4 *verso*]

Greenwood: Both the magistrate ought to compell the infidells to heare the doctrine of the church, and also with the approbation of the church to send fourth meete men with gifts and graces to instruct the infidells, being as yet no ministers or officers unto them.

Barrow: Furder everie Christian is bounde both in his familie and conversacion to call others by all meanes he may, unto the faith.

Cooper: What if the church be where ther is no magistrat? Is there alwaies a magistrate?

Barrow: Yea, the church cannot be without a magistrate, neither can ther be a common wealth or estate without a magistrate. There is alwaies a magistrate, though not alwaies a christian magistrate.

Cooper: Ther is not alwaies a magistrate.

Barrow: Without a magistrate there can be no society, no trade, no calling had.

Cooper: Ther hath not beene alwaies a magistrate over the church.

Greenwood: The church hath alwaies beene in some common wealth or other. Ther can be no common wealth without a magistrate.

Cooper: What magistrate was ther in Habell's time?[1]

Barrow: When the church and all the world was in Adam's household he no doubt was a father, a magistrate, a teacher, a governour.

Cooper: Ther was no magistrate over the churche befor the lawe.

Barrow: That is not so.   Was not Melchisedeck a magistrate?

Cooper: Melchisedeck was a figure of Christ, not an ordinarie king.

Barrow: Doth not the Scripture say he was a king of Salem?

Greenwood: Was not Abraham a magistrate over the church?

Cooper: Abraham was no magistrate.

Greenwood: He was a magistrate over his household, his household was then the church.

Barrow: Was not Joseph a magistrate, thinke you?

Cooper: Over the Egiptians after the heathen maner.

---

[1] Abel, second son of Adam and Eve. Genesis 4: 2.

Barrow: Heathens maie be lawfull magistrates over the church also. But Joseph was a magistrate over the church.

Cooper: He was not a magistrate over the church.

Barrow: He was a magistrate over all Egipt and over all Pharao his servants. But the church was then in Egipt emongst Pharao his servants. Therfore he was a magistrate over the church, as plentifullie appeareth in the history; his brethren acknowledged him their lord.

Greenwood: It was so prophecied of him before, as the visions and dreames declared.

Cooper: Joseph was a figure of Christ.

Barrow: What then ? So were all the kings of Juda — therfore no magistrats ?

Greenwood: Moses also was a civile magistrate over the church before the lawe. [p. 60 — I 1 *recto*]

Cooper: He was an extraordinarie magistrate, he was not chosen by the people.

Barrow: Whie is everie magistrate to be chosen by the people ? Was not the ordinance of God a sufficient calling to the magistracy ?

Greenwood: Moses was both called of God, and approved his calling unto and before the people of Israel.

Cooper: Moses was a prophet; therfor he could be no ordinary magistrate.

Barrow: David also and Salomon were prophets, yet you will not say that they were not ordinary magistrates.

Greenwood: Every prophet was not a minister of the temple in the priest's office.

Cooper: The prophet's office was a ministeriall office.
Sperin:

Barrow: None but Levites might be ministers of the tabernacle. But ther were manie prophetts which were not of the tribe of Levi. But what is this to our purpose ? Was not Moses, Joseph, and theis others civile magistrates ? Mr. Cooper, will you confesse your error ?

Cooper: They were no ordinarie magistrates.

Barrow: It is evident they were civile magistrats, and ordinary, and excellent magistrats according to the revealed

253

I*

will of God.   But you will yeild unto no truth, but cavil perverslie against the evident Scriptures.

Amongst mich [much] confused speach that passed betwixt Mr. Sperin and me Henry Barrow.   After that our conference was broken up in following his last assertion: *that he held not himself a minister by the bishop's ordination untill he had the approbation of the people.*

1.   He first confessed the bishop's ordination to be a civile constitution.

2.   Then that the bishops by the prince's commandement may ordeyne ministers by their sole authority; because Timothi and Titus did ordenie [ordain] elders alone.

3.   When it was alleadged that Timothi and Titus did ordeine them according to the apostle's constitutions and as the apostles themselves used to do, which alwaies was by the free election of the flocke, 1 Corinthians 4: 17, Acts 14: 23, he said that Timothi and Titus, as also the apostles, were ministers alone, without the people's election.   And that the word *cheirotonesantes*,[1] Acts 14: 23, has relation unto the apostles, that lifted up their hands before they laid them on; and not unto the people, that lifted up their handes to signifie their approbation in the election.

4.   He said that if so be this Acts 14 were to be understood of the people's election, yet ther were no more places to prove that the [p. 61 — I 1 *verso*] people ought to chuse their ministers.   Being demaunded what he thought of Acts 1 and Acts 6, of 1. Timothy 3 and Titus 1, he said that Acts 6 was but of deacons onlie, and as for the other places they proved not that the people might chuse their elders.   Being demaunded who then were to make choise and probation of the elders, he said that Timothi and Titus in those chapters.   Being asked who now was to succeed Timothi and Titus, seing they had left no heires apparant behind them: he said the bishops were to chuse and ordeine them, who now being old

[1] Stretching out the hand.   Hence, to appoint to an office of the church.

and able to take no more paynes, were to governe over manie churches, as they did.

5.   Being asked of 1 Timothy 3, verse 10, who was to chuse and make probation there, he confessed that the church; being asked whether that rule of probation belonged not also, and were spoken of elders in like maner, he said no, but onlie of deacons: being asked if the word hosautos[1] in the eighth verse had not relation unto the same chusers and gave not now rules unto them concerning deacons also; and how he could by that chapter make anie distinction, or shew whie the former rules concerning the chusing of elders should not aswell belong unto the church, as theis concerning deacons; or whie if the former belonged unto Timothi, theis also should not belong unto Timothie; he answeared still that the church was to chuse deacons, but not elders.

6.   In furder discourse of theis rules for the gifts, maners, and rules of the conversation and life of theis elders, which were such as could be knowne unto, and examined by none, but by the church where they lived, which shewed that theis rules of their election were given unto the church, wherin Timothie was rather to help and instruct the church, than anie way to plucke away the power, authoritie, and interest of the church: he answeared that Timothi could onlie best try the gifts and learning of theis ministers, and therfore the choise and approbation were given to him onlie. Being demaunded whether ther were not manie rules concerning sondrie christian vertues of manners, conversation towards all men, of the governing of themselves, of their wives, children, families, which belonged and were common to the teaching and governinge elders, which the church wher they lived, could only best judge: He said that 1. Timothi 3 and Titus 1 were onlie written and understood of pastors and teachers because it is ther said a bishop must be *didacticos*,[2] which is only peculier unto the pastor and teacher. Neither would he

---

[1] Hosautos, likewise. I Timothy 3: 8.
[2] Didacticos — apt at teaching. I Timothy 3: 2. II Timothy 2: 24.

yeild though it were shewed him, that the name and care of elders were common unto all aswell the governing as teaching elders, that most of the rules accorded unto them indifferently, Acts 20. Furder that he could shew no other rules in the Testament of Christ for the election of [p. 62 — I 2 *recto*] the governing elders than there.

7. Wherupon he fell into this grosse opinion also. That those elders and deacons were one office. Not understanding Romans 12: 8, 1. Timothy 5: 17, Philippians 1: 1.[1]

8. Retorning againe unto the bishops, being demaunded by what warrant they may usurpe this inordinate power over all the churches. In processe of speach he was driven to acknowledge it onlie to be by the prince's authoritie, and not by the Testament of Christ, and so held them to be meerly civile. Being demaunded what then he thought of their ministerie and sacraments which they delivered; he awhile denying that they medled with the sacraments or ministrie; in the end being pressed, because they in all the parishes of their diocesses did and might at their pleasure preach and deliver the sacraments, whether the church and parson would or no; yea, they will make the parson follow them with the cupp and booke; yea, the bishop will scilence, suspend, or remove what minister or parson he list. Here Mr. Sperin said that the bishop did not, neither should administer anie sacraments in his parish.

Thus with one breath he affirming and denying, graunting and retracting, I told him that I would not from hencefourth anie more reason or confer with him untill he brought a better conscience with him.

To conclude, seing he neither understood the Scriptures wherof he so bouldlie affirmed or denied, seing he understood not the verie first doctrines and beginnings of Christ, as the doctrines of laying on of hands, of election, ordination, *etc.*, neither yet knewe so mich [much] as the offices that belonged to the church of Christ, he was altogeather unworthie and

---

[1] Philippians, not Philemon.

unfit to be a teacher or exercise anie government in the church of Christ. Saying that God would er long shew who were fitt ministers to drawe neere unto him.

He said unto me that I medled which [*sic*, with] more than I needed, and that I did but take a wolf by the eares.[1] I said that he abused and understood not that proverbe, also that I did not *immiscere alienae liti*.[2] That it was a matter of mine owne salvation that I stood for, in refusing all subjection or communion with antichrist and his detestable enormities; that everie true Christian ought to contend for the maintenance of the faith that was once given unto the saints. Revelation 14: 9, *etc.* Jude 3.

Mr. Cooper to shift off the answeare of our arguments wherwith he was pressed, when he perceived the issue of them, he rose from the table and brake off [the] conference with us, pretending hast to be gonne: but the dore being lockt, he turned him to two gentlemen which sate behind as hearers of our conference, and fell a perswading of them. Wherupon I John Greenwood left Mr. Barrow and [p. 63 — I 2 *verso*] Mr. Sperin in conference still, and went to give eare to Mr. Cooper, whose deceipts I fownde so pernitious and doctrines so fowle that I againe replied upon him, and received certaine errors from his mouth, some wherof I shall heare insert with mine answere in breife, not following our whole discourse.

1. Cooper: A private man ought not to make question our [or ?] doubt of the minister's outward calling, but if he find comfort in heart by his doctrine, he ought to approve of his ministrie, what calling soever he have.

Greenwood: This is sweete doctrine that you sowe here; hath not the Lorde given as great commandement to avoide false prophetts as to heare and obey the true messen-

---

[1] A saying used by the Greeks and Romans. As used by Augustus, in reference to his position in Rome, it meant that it was equally dangerous to hold on or let go. Robert Burton observed that "he that goes to law, as the proverb is, holds a wolf by the ears" (*Anatomy of Melancholy*, ed. Floyd Dell and Paul Jordan-Smith [New York, 1938], p. 70). See also Antipho's statement: "I've got a wolf by the ears, as they say, can't let go and can't hold on," "Phormio," Act III, *Terence*, trans. John Sargeaunt, Loeb Classical Library (London, 1912), II, 59.

[2] To meddle or interfere with the seashore that belongs to another.

gers, and all true messengers therupon approving their sending to all men's consciens by the evident testimonie of God's reveyled [revealed] will, shall not the flocke know their pastor, yea, chuse and call their pastor ?

Cooper: If one come into a congregacion and heare one preach, he ought not to make question of the minister's calling, or refuse his doctrine.

Greenwood: If one come so, and before know that that preacher hath a false outward calling, yea, that he hath no office in a true church but is a false prophet, he offendeth in hearing of him, especially in a false church, for ther is no false teacher but teacheth some truth, *etc.*

2. Cooper: A man may be a true minister to a people uncalled, and they are a true church or faithfull congregation *potentia* though not *actu*.[1] And he may be an officer or minister unto them, they being a true church *potentia.*

Greenwood: This is such doctrine as I never heard, that a pastor can be ordeyned and exercise the duties of a pastor, to a church that as yet is not. But your ministers most sacrilegiouslie give them the sacraments also in this estate.

3. Cooper: Though the minister do deliver the sacraments to the open knowne unworthie, and so commit sacriledge, yet maie a private man communicate with the minister, and the partie not be partaker of their sinne.

Greenwood: If I associat a theife and communicate in his evill, shall I not be guiltie, how mich [much] more if I reprove not this transgression against God, and absteine from their fellowship till they repent, or by due order be censured.

Bartlet: Here Mr. Bartlet,[2] a gentleman, said it was not well we had not some more orderlie conference about theis weightie causes that the truth might appeare.

Greenwood: You see they will not come to anie pointe of doctrine to con-[p. 64 — I 3 *recto*]clude anie thing, we have long made sute to have some free conference and never

---

[1] Virtually though not **actually**.
[2] Evidently a witness or listener.

	could obteine anie, but are lockt up close prisoners.
Cooper:	They denie our church and ministrie, and therfore are not to be disputed with.
Bartlet:	Yet their reasons would be seene and convinced orderly; if they deserve it, then to suffer punishment.
Greenwood:	We have often shewed causes whie we hold your church and ministrie to be false, and not to be joyned with of [by] anie that wilbe saved: as for example. [1.] you have not a people rightlie gathered unto Christ, but stand one with the world, so that your parishes cannot be called EKKLESIA [*sic*],[1] a people called fourth 2. you have set a popish ministrie over this whole lande 3. you most sacrilegiously give the sacraments in this order to all commers 4. you worshipp God after men's devises and not according to Christ's Testament. 5. you have not the power or freedome to redresse sinne by due censure, being all subject to theis wicked courts, *etc.*
Bartlet:	Theis thinges would be answeared and convinced.
5. Cooper:	We graunt the things they seeke are good, and manie of us have written and taught fullie the same, but they seeke them not by due order.
Greenwood:	This is not true, you are limited what to preach, to conforme your doctrines to theis antichristian orders, and still practize contrarie if you write or teach anie truth. And as for us we seeke to do the will of God after the same order that all true prophets, Christ, and his apostles have taught and practised for conscience towards God: to have no fellowship with that ministerie and church which rejecteth Christe's Testament, and will not be guided by him and his ordinances.
6. Cooper:	We professe and teach trulie all the articles of faith.
Greenwood:	The papists teach the same articles in generall wordes, but nether you nor they, ether teach the particular doctrines, our [*sic*, or] practise the same truly. But both you and they denie speciall doctrines of our justification.
Cooper:	What article of faith do we not trulie teach?

---

[1] The separated — those called out, the body of believers, the church.

John Greenwood

Greenwood: You teach that Christ descended into hell after his death and buriall.[1]

Cooper: We hold it not, neither teach it, manie of us have taught and written against it; you therfore do us wrong to chardge us with it.

Greenwood: It is set out with priviledge as an article[2] of your faith and received and redd in all your parishes. [p. 65 — I 3 *verso*]

Cooper: Though the governours of our church sett it out and we can not help it, yet we are not to be chardged with it.

Greenwood: Besides that you daylie communicate with them that do hold it (if not reade it to the people), you have subscribed to this and all other such errors in your church of late, as I heare.

Here Mr. Cooper was smitten with mutenes and the gentleman said, have you donne so?

Cooper: He careth not what he saith of us.

Greenwood: Will you denie it? I will bring witnes to prove it unto you before tomorrow at 8. of the clocke, if you denie it.

Cooper: I will not make you acquainted with my private actions.

Greenwood: I desire not to knowe your private actions, but this is a publique matter of your subjection to antichrist in your whole ministerie against your conscience; but it seemes your deeds ar evill, and therfore you would hide them, least they should be reproved of the light.

The gentleman [Bartlet] said it was thought [that] we held some error about the Lord's Prayer, as they call it: wheruppon I shewed him our judgment in writing, and said that we would not continue in anie error to our knowledg. And when he read that we said it could not be called the Lord's Prayer, because

---

[1] The two viewpoints on this article of the Apostles' Creed were that: (1) this article proves that Christ delivered the souls in hell from the power of Satan; (2) this article was blasphemy. This latter viewpoint was held by the Separatists.

[2] The third article of the 39 Articles pertains to this doctrine. " As Christ died for us, and was buried; so also is it to be believed, that he went down into Hell."

	he never prayed it, Mr. Cooper tooke exception thus.
Cooper:	It may be called the Lord's Prayer in respect he taught it his disciples.
Greenwood:	This proveth it cannot be called the Lord's Prayer, for doctrine is one thing, and prayer is an other. Prayer is a powring fourth of our hearts unto the Lord, according to our present wants; doctrine is an instruction of others; so that it cannot be called the Lord's Prayer.
Bartlet:	But this troubleth us that you hold it not lawfull to say over those wordes in prayer, *etc*.
Greenwood:	You see that we denie no man to use the verie wordes, all or anie part of them in prayer, by explication, or application, according to our present occasions, as anie other Scripture.
Cooper:	What is the meaning of that explication or application.
Greenwood:	Explication and application is meant thus: as when I desire that the pope and such ministers of poperie might be suppressed, I say: do this, Lord, for the advancement of thy kingdome. Let thy kingdome come, *etc*.[1]
	And without this explication or application to say over the whole wordes conteyning all things that can be praid, were but abuse of that forme of prayer, seing they that so praye cannot understand what he (that [who] is the mouth of all) asketh, for we cannot [p. 66 — I 4 *recto*] pray for all things at once, but that which is within the compasse of our faith; otherwise it is but babling.
Cooper:	For the whole church it may be said over as a praier.
Greenwood:	All praier must be of faith for such things as are within our knowledge, and as we knowe the church to be in present neede of, and those things to be particularly craved at God's hand, els we do but babble as the papists do.
Cooper:	I grant that al our praiers ought to be of faith and expressing our present necessities. Yet ought we

---

[1] Greenwood means that it is permissible to use the phrase "let thy king-dom come," or any other part of the Lord's Prayer, so as to apply it to one's own thought or phrase. By explication he means to explain, to unfold or amplify the meaning.

John Greenwood

everie day to say over the Lord's Praier for the whole church.

Greenwood: This is popish doctrine, and such praier were super-stitious babling, *etc.* [p. 67 — I 4 *verso*]

[The rest of this treatise, pages 67-70, is a description of the true church, a denunciation of the false Church of England, and a listing of eleven reasons why the Church of England is not the true church. Since these arguments were written in 1588, they are printed separately, with the joint works of Barrow and Greenwood, for 1588, with the title, " The True Church and the False Church."]

X

LETTER TO WILLIAM CECIL, LORD BURGHLEY
SEPTEMBER 13, 1590.

Barrow and Greenwood seemed to believe that Lord
Burghley would prove friendly to the Separatists' cause.
They must have become somewhat disillusioned after their
appearance on March 18, 1588/9, before the Privy Council —
including Lord Burghley himself, because they were remanded
to prison and Barrow was rebuked by the Lord Treasurer.
But they still hoped for aid from Burghley, and in 1590 seem
to have secured his permission to present to him a treatise
representing their views. The result was a drawing up of a
work entitled *The First Part of the Platforme*, which they included with their letter of September 13, 1590. Lord Burghley
replied within two or three days with a sharp retort that he
disliked their ideas, and expressed his determination to have
nothing to do with the prisoners. With a heavy heart Barrow
and Greenwood replied on September 18, begging his pardon
if they had offended him, requesting a general conference on
disputed points, and as a last resort desiring permission to
leave England to join with a foreign church.

The original letters are preserved at Hatfield House,
Hertfordshire, in the Cecil Papers, Volume 167, ff. 100 *recto*
and *verso* and 102 *recto*. They are calendared in the Historical
Manuscripts Commission, *Calendar of the Manuscripts of the
Most Honorable The Marquis of Salisbury, K.G.*, Part IV
(London, 1892), pp. 74-5. Although the letters are clearly
dated the 13th and 18th " of this 9th month," the editor has
inserted the dates November 13 and 18. But Barrow and
Greenwood regard January, not March, as the first month.
Consequently, the correct dates would be September 13 and
18. As a bit of confirmatory evidence, the endorsements in a

different hand are 13. 7 br. 1590 and 18. 7: br. 1590. These would apply only to September.

The letter of September 13 is printed in *Mr. Henry Barrowe's Platform*, where it is appended to " The First Part of the Platforme " (E 3 *recto* — I 2 *recto*).

*   *   *   *   *   *   *

LETTER TO WILLIAM CECIL, LORD BURGHLEY, LORD HIGH TREASURER OF ENGLAND

SEPTEMBER 13, 1590

Right Honourable, we have, as our fraile memories and smale measure of knowledge would suffer, in the middes of many encombrances in this our miserable imprisonment, drawen an unperfect discourse[1] of such weightie causes, as we were desirous (when God should call us thereunto) to make knowne unto her majestie or some of her honourable counsell. And now by your Honor's speciall desert and gratious allowance occasioned, we most gladly relate and present the same unto your good lordship onely: as to one, whose rare wisdome we know most able to discerne, whose care to defend and preserve the innocent accordinge to right. Wherefore, we most willingly put both this weightie cause and our owne wofull lives in your hand, to be preserved to some equall triall from our enemies' rage, like to be encreased hereupon, in that it so nerely toucheth their estimation and worldly prosperitie.[2] And howsoever these high causes of God (which have not bene hetherto looked into since the first defection from the sincere practise of the gospell in the primitive church) may seme strange unto your Honor at the first vew [view], especially if thei be weighed with humane reason; yet beinge examined by that arch type and true patterne of Christe's Testament, we doubt not but your Honour shall see with us how far the present state is swarved from the inviolable order prescribed, especially if your Honor vouchsafe but to looke into the office, entrance, and administration of this ministry, you shall see it, as some of their owne writers have confessed and none can deny, to be derived by

1 This is Barrow's *The First Part of the Platforme*, printed in volume III.
2 Barrow's enclosed treatise advocated the elimination of such officers as deans, sub-deans, prebendaries, and vicars ; the abolition of the spiritual courts administered by the archbishops, bishops, and archdeacons ; the disendowment of the Church of England, and the redistribution of ecclesiastical lands.

succession from the pope. Who, though he were expelled with many of his enormities, out of this land by her majestie's most royall progenitour,[1] yet remained these offices, lawes, courtes, worship, *etc.*, untaken awaye
Jeremiah 51: 26 or suppressed. Notwithstandinge that the Lord of hostes had said they shall not take a stone of Babell for a corner, nor a stone for foundations, for it shall be desolate for ever. So that it is impossible antichriste's ministerie should build or serve in the true church of Christ, he himselfe havinge instituted and ordeined an other ministry in his Testament, and forbidden and accursed all such as have not their warrant from thence. It is then our purpose, right Honourable, to make plaine in our treatise, that when the pope was expelled, his ministry and orders which came out of the smoke of the bottomles pitt were still reserved and set up in stead of Christe's ministry and ordinances, and so still remaine. Which their ministry beinge found antichristian must by the prince be abolished and suppressed, that God's wrath be not kindled against this whole land for the wilfull violating and defacinge of God's ordinances, bowinge downe unto, endowinge and maintaininge of such bitter plantes of antichriste's graftinge. Neither will it suffice to say that the martyrs in Quene Marie's daies stood in these offices in King Edwarde's daies,[2] seinge it were great impietie to justify iniquitie by the example of fraile man, no man livinge without errour, for that were to set the martyrs of Christ against Christ, either to build our faith wholy upon men, and cast aside the Testament, or els rippe up their ignorances to maintaine some sinne in our selves, even presumpteously to tempt God, to continue obstinate in knowne sinne, which far be it from us, seinge the spirit of God teacheth us [or, teache thus], that neither martir nor angell from heven may warrant any [thing, crossed out] which

[1] Henry VIII, by the Act in Restraint of Appeals (1533), the Act for the Submission of the Clergy and Restraint of Appeals (1534), the Act concerning Ecclesiastical Appointments and Absolute Restraint of Annates (1534), the Act concerning Peter's Pence and Dispensation (1534), and the Supremacy Act (1534).
[2] This is a reference to the argument used by Gifford in *A Short Treatise*, p. 82, and refuted by Barrow in *A Plaine Refutation*, pp. [153-157].

Christ in his word condemneth, nor may withdraw us from the evident rules of Christe's Testament or any jote therof, must lesse from the whole true ordinances and governement of Christ in his church. Neither would they have stood in those offices, if they had knowne it, for they suffered unto death for the truth they see, teachinge us so far to follow their example as thei followed Christ.[1] Neither nede this matter now trouble us, seinge all countries about us have suppressed the bishops and their courtes with all that rable and many other abhominations which flow from those fountaines, and remaine still with us. The learned of the clergie of this land also have written and cried out for the utter abolishinge of these offices. So that it is of all confessed the prince ought to suppresse and abolish all such offices and orders, as cannot be approved by the word of God.

Shall this famous land, then, right honorable, lye still in the knowne dregges of popery under God's wrath for the same ? Shall a few pompeous prelates for their owne private lucre, pride, and idlenes, with hold the practise of Christe's Testament and mislead the whole land to eternall judgement ? Shall her majestie's most loyall subjectes be persequnted [persecuted] and miserably made awaye in prison for not bowinge downe to these confessed abhominations ? Shall her majestie and her most honourable counsell be thus made guiltie of innocent bloud by sufferinge the bishops in this un-christian procedinges ? God forbid. Especially the Lord alluringe her majestie and the counsell both with spirituall promises and present heapes of earthly treasures (with much peace and happines to the whol land) for the redresse hereof, without injurie unto, or

---

[1] In the printed volume, *Mr. Henry Barrowe's Platform,* which includes *The First Part of the Platforme,* there are three gaps in this sentence, with the following explanation: " Those wordes were spoiled by ill accident in my custodie ; but the reader may gather the sense or help himself as he may: For I am now where I cannot have another coppie to perfect it: but our hope must be that London, Amsterdam, or Leyden will supply all such defects (*Mr. Henry Barrowe's Platform* [London ? 1611], signature I 2 *verso*). These hints about custody of copies, location in the Netherlands, and devotion to Barrow suggest that Francis Johnson may be the compiler, using the pseudonym of Miles Micklebound.

just complaint of any her subjectes, so highly shall they be contented. So that if this be not now received, beinge put thus by God's providence into your Honor's handes, it will be received in the age to come, what soever become of our miserable bodies, it will be looked upon. It is God's word that hath now discovered it, which goeth not out in vaine, nor returneth fruitles, but surely effecteth his owne will in his appointed tymes.

We have then further in our discourse, right honourable, taken away some of these silver smithes' deceitfull objections, beinge redie upon the dispense of our lives to make (by the assistance of God's spirit) all appeare mist, chaffe, and dounge [dung], that they can alledge for themselves in this their estate. The other part of our treatise, [showing] how this should be effected, what the true ministry of Christ is, how it should be erected, and brought in, we have purposely reserved till we know your Honour's pleasure, for the discussinge of these which must be agreed upon, before we can procede to the other.[1] And then upon your honour's acceptation (though we are more willinge and have more nede to hear and learne, than to instruct and speake), we shall to the utmost of our power make your Honour pertaker of that truth God giveth us to see. Even of these thinges also which are to be abolished we have yet refrained to mention some, which necessarily follow upon the rest, and will bringe yet more present benefit unto her majestie of earthly wealth, an unutterable somme. Not meaninge the universities, for they standinge in her majestie's will to use at her pleasure, may be employed to the maintenance of teachers and studentes in the knowledge of tounges and other honest christian and lawful artes, [but we do desire] the monkish orders and prophane learninge, with all unlawfull artes, abolished

---

[1] This would seem to be sufficient evidence that the second part of the platform was never written because of Lord Burghley's dislike of the first part. The compiler [Francis Johnson ?] of the book, *Mr. Henry Barrowe's Platform*, queries whether there ever was a second part and confesses he has never seen it, though he had made diligent inquiry.

and suppressed.[1] If any thinge shalbe [objected] against the pointes we have written, we besech your Honour their reasons may be set downe, and be discussed either by publicke conference under notorie, or in private before your Honour with whom your lordship shall thinke mete or by writinge. Yea, if your Honour shall be willinge to hear any of the doctrines discussed by the Scriptures, your lordship may procure some of the learned, whom your Honour may best trust in such buisines, and call us to triall in your owne audience, without makinge them acquainted with the end of the question, least thei deale partially, and so seke to trouble and not to edify, as their custome is.

In the meane tyme, by reason of our longe close imprisonment, we (having had no exercise to our bodies, aire, or thinges nedefull even for the preservinge of life allowed us now this three yeares in effect,[2] our bodies weake, and our memories impaired and greatly broken, as also in no smale perill to be indirectly hastened to our grave by our adversaries in this prison, as they have heretofore endeavoured), most humbly besech your Honour, we may be placed at some honest man's howse, where your Honour please to appoint, or [where] we can provide, puttinge in sufficient bondes [for our appearance] when and where we shall be called to any lawfull triall.

Thus besechinge almightie God by his owne Holy Spirit to direct your lordship in these weightie affaires, yea, to draw forth your honourable yeres in health, safetie, and prosperitie, to your owne endlesse comfort and good of this whole land, craving perdon for our boldnes, and givinge most humble thankes for your honourable compassion alredie shewd, we in all due

---

1 This qualification about the universities was made by Barrow, partly because Dr. Robert Some had accused him of advocating that Queen Elizabeth abolish the universities of Cambridge and Oxford (*A Godly Treatise, wherein Are Examined and Confuted Many Execrable Fancies*, signature A 3 *recto* and pp. 1-4). Lord Burghley was Chancellor of Cambridge University and Robert Some was appointed Master of Peterhouse in May, 1589, and served as vice-chancellor in 1590 and 1591.
2 Greenwood's imprisonment began October 8, 1587, and Barrow's began on November 19, 1587.

reverence take our leave, untill we further understand
your Honour's will.

From the Fleete the 13 of this 9 moneth.

Your Honour's most humbly
in the Lord to command
John Grenewood
Henry Barrowe

Endorsed

To the right honourable their singuler
good lord, the Lord Burleygh, Lord
Treasorer of England, one of her majestie's most honourable Privie Counsell.

Folio 100, *recto* and *verso*   [In another hand along the margin]
Cecil Papers, Vol. 167   13. 7 br. 1590
at Hatfield House,   Grenewood and Barrow
Hertfordshire.   [September 13, 1590][1]

---

[1] In the Historical Manuscripts Commission, *Salisbury Manuscripts*, Part
IV, pp. 73-5, this letter is incorrectly dated November 13.

XI

LETTER TO WILLIAM CECIL, LORD BURGHLEY, SEPTEMBER 18, 1590

Having received your lordship's aunswere in dislike of our writings and causes, togither with your refusall to have any thinge to doo with us,[1] it brought no small dismaye and heavines unto our sorowful soules, thus to have offended your Honor, and deprived our selves of your lawful helpe and defence. Wherby we are nowe lefte and exposed to the violent hands of our adversaries, who wille nowe sone [soon] shorten our mortall lives, and make speede to devowre the pray [prey] thei have taken. But yet our chiefest griefe is to beholde this moste heavenly and blessed cause, which the Lorde by our weake and contemptible bodies hath offred to your Honor and this whole lande, to be, peradventure through our defaltes and insufficient handeling, rejected and caste away with out furder inquirie or trial. As to our selves, Right Honorable, we moste humblie, even with all submission, crave your Honor's perdon for any thinge we have offended you, being of no worldly thing more lothe than to give your lordship or any of our honourable magistrates the leaste cause of offence or dislike. And as to our writings or any thing we houlde wherein your lordship is not of one judgment with us, we no furder houlde them than thei shall be founde consonant to God his holy worde, neither furder or otherwise perswade them, than upon that trial thei shall be approved, moste humbly and gladlie submitting our whole faith and lives in all that we have saied, written, or doone unto any christian trial or censure by the worde of God, which we in all things desire to make the lanterne to our feete, the grounde of our faithe. Protesting not wittingly to open our mouthes against any parte of God his sacred truth, but moste redely to yealde therunto and to revoke whatsoever we shall be shewed to houlde contrary to the same. Wherfore, Right Honorable, in the tender care and love you have of our soules, as the laste petition that ever we are like to make to your lordship,[2]

---

1 This is Burghley's reply to Barrow and Greenwood's letter of September 13 and Barrow's *The First Part of the Platforme*.

2 In the following year, 1591, Barrow dedicated his book, *A Plaine Refutation*, to Lord Burghley, and included a five-page dedicatory address to him.

we moste humblie and instantly, even in the name and mercy of
that greate sheapherd that sought us all out when we ran astraye,
beseache of your Honor, before our weake bodies retourne to duste
(which through the inhumane usage we have indured are not likely
long to continue in this life). That we might yet be allowed some
peaceable and christian conference in loving and sober maner,
where these hie and weighty matters in controvercy may by the
worde of God be discussed and decided, our reasons be duely
expended and aunswered, our doubtes by the Scriptures assayled,
and we by the evidence of God's worde convinced and instructed
and not by such hostilitie, slaunder, reproche, persecution, close
emprisonment, cruel commissions and judgmentes, which are
meanes rather to abalienate [alienate] than any waye to perswade
the soule and conscience. This christian course have we in all
meaknes sought even by all meanes at our adversaries' hands: yea,
if so be thei would not graunte us this conference in the lande, or
to live in peace by them under baile as other her majestie's loial
and faithful subjects, that yet for the peace and comforte of our
sowles and bodies thei would soffer us to depart the lande to some
foreigne churche.[1] This peaceable course as the uttermoste thing
that we with good conscience can any way devise or consent unto,
we stille moste humbly beseache of your lordship. That all former
hostilitie, violence, quarels, complaintes, *etc.*, layed aside, we may
at length with one accorde meete togither in christian loving and
reverent maner to enquire the wille of our God, which being
brought to lighte we may all both high and lowe as the children
of our heavenly Father peaceably and joyfully condiscend therunto, and reste in the same. Thus may your Honor easely quenche
and appeace much unnatural strife and debate, reduce such as
erre, unite us all in the truthe, and moste highly advance the
gospel of our Lorde Jesus Christe to the glory of God, the unspeakable benefite of this whole lande, and to the endles comfort of
your oun soule and praise, both with God and men: which that
your Honor may happely accomplish, as also to continue your
accustomed favoure and mercy to Christe's poore afflicted ser-

---

[1] Barrow and Greenwood frequently request a conference, but this is the
first instance of a request to leave England — most likely for Holland.

Letter to William Cecil, Lord Burghley

vants, we shall not cease to praye even whilest we have breathe.
The 18th of this 9th month.[1]
Your Honor's moste humble and bounden in the Lorde

$$\left.\begin{array}{l}\text{Henry Barrowe}\\ \text{John Grenewood}\end{array}\right\}\begin{array}{l}\text{Close prisoners}\\ \text{in the Fleete}\end{array}$$

Endorsed

To the Right Honorable their verie good lorde,
the Lorde Burleigh, Lord Treasorer of England
and of her majestie's most honorable Privie Councel.

18. 7: br [September] 1590
Henry Barrow
John Grenwood
prisoners in the Fleet.

---

[1] September 18, 1590. In the Historical Manuscripts Commission, *Calendar of the Manuscripts of the Most Honorable the Marquis of Salisbury, K.G., Preserved at Hatfield House, Hertfordshire*, Part IV, pp. 73-5, the date is erroneously given as November 18. Barrow and Greenwood always count January as the first month and September as the ninth month.

APPENDICES

A. Separatist Petitions

B. Separatist Beliefs

C. Separatist Prisoners

D. A Chronological Summary

A. SEPARATIST PETITIONS

1.

THE TRUE COPYE OF A LAMENTABLE PETITION DELIVERED TO THE QUEENE'S MAJESTYE THE 13 OF MARCH, 1588 [1588/89]

This petition is to be found in Harley MSS. 6848, ff. 18 *verso* — 20 *recto*. It is printed by Arber in his book, *An Introductory Sketch to the Martin Marprelate Controversy*, 1588-1590, pp. 35-38. Arber has " consideration," " vesing," " snot," and " endinges," but the correct readings are " commiseration " [18 *verso*], " vexing " [18 *verso*], " not " [19 *verso*], and " enemyes " [20 *recto*]. Mr. Arber gives the date as March 13, 1588, and suggests that the manuscript was seized on July 18, 1588. This is incorrect, since the correct date of the petition is March 13, 1588/89. Therefore, the date July 18, 1588, is impossible. Furthermore, the reference to nineteen months of imprisonment brings us to 1589 as the correct year, and this is confirmatory evidence against Arber's statements. Also, Arber has the wrong reference, Harley MSS. 6848, f. 7, but the folios are 18 *verso* — 20 *recto*. If one takes the trouble of checking folio 7, he will find no evidence for Arber's statement. Mr. F. J. Powicke seems justified in his statement that, after examining some of Arber's references, " what revealed itself was so surprising and disappointing as to shake at once my confidence in his trustworthiness." See F. J. Powicke, *Henry Barrow, Separatist* (1550 ? — 1593) *and the Exiled Church of Amsterdam* (1593 — 1622), pp. viii, 287-325, 348. After checking the dating of two other items in Mr. Arber's *An Introductory Sketch*, pp. 38, 40, I find that he is wrong in both cases.

The purpose of this " Lamentable Petition " was to plead for the redress of outrageous wrongs, for a speedy trial, for

277

John Greenwood

the revocation of the bishops' cruel decrees against the saints of God, and for a hearing before the queen herself or the Privy Council. The twelve petitioners were very bold in pressing into her majesty's presence, and in complaining of great persecution. Because of their boldness, Christopher Bowman was imprisoned for more than three years in the Wood Street Counter ; John Nicholas was committed to the Gatehouse at Westminster for more than three years ; and John Sparewe (or Sparrow) was imprisoned in the White Lion and the Clink for more than four years, without indictment or examination or trial. All were imprisoned on the order of the Privy Council.

Although the petitioners were harshly treated, the " Lamentable Petition " was a success. Five days later, on March 18, 1588/9, Barrow and others of the Separatist brethren were examined by the Privy Council. Six days later, on March 24, 1588/9, both Barrow and Greenwood were examined by a special commission consisting of five of the greatest judges in England and three of the leading ecclesiastical officials in the Church of England. The petitioners were heard, but they remained in prison nevertheless.

* * * * * * *

THE TRUE COPYE OF A LAMENTABLE PETITION DELIVERED TO THE QUEENE'S MAJESTYE THE 13 OF MARCH, 1588 [1588/9].

The Lord of heaven and earthe, that hathe so wonderfully hitherto preserved and established your Majesty in your earthly kingdom, that you should now advaunce his spirituall kingdome befor all the nations of the earthe, that God whom you have suche cause to love, honor, and serve, enclyne your royall harte (which hathe ever bin pytifully affected even towardes her greatest enemyes) to some christian commiseration and speedy redresse of the outragious wronges and most extreame injuryes wherewith sundrye of your most faythfull and true harted subjects have bin a longe tyme and are at this present especially oppressed in all places by the bishops of this lande, but principally by the bishops of Canterbury and London, for the true profession and practize of the ghospell of our Lord Jesus Christe, as we are alwayes ready to approve befor God and men, if we might be but produced to any christian and equall tryall.[1] Which ghospell thoughe your Majesty have most graciously published to the eyes and ears of all men throughe all places of your kingdome, inhibitinge none but incytinge all to the faythfull obedience and syncere practize thereof; yet these professed enemyes of all righteousnes, will not only not enter them selves into the kingdome of God, but forbydde others that woulde, with deadly hatred and extreame rage, persecuting all those that upon conscience towardes God and care of their owne salvation, in humble and peaceable maner seeke for reformation for these antichristian burthens and popishe abhominations, which the bishops, for the maintenance of their proud estate, with a strong hand imposed upon the consciences of men, contrary to the expresse rule and truthe of the ghospel of Christ. Daily spoilinge, vexing, molestinge, hurtinge, pursuynge, imprisoninge, yea, barringe and locking them up close prisoners in the most unholsome [19 *recto*] and vyle prysones, and their deteyninge them, without bringinge them to their answers, untyll the Lord by death put an ende to their myseries. Some they have haled [hauled] from their honeste labors in their trades,

---

1 Many of the Separatists were thrown into jail and kept there without trial, without bail, and even without some of the prison liberties accorded to the baser type of criminal. Some of the Separatists remained in prison for more than five years without a trial of any kind, without beds, or even straw to sleep on, and without food except from family and friends.

and caste them loden hands and feete with boultes and fetters of yron in to cold and noysome prysons, close prisoners.[1] Some they have cast into the " Little Ease ": some they have put into the " Myll," causinge them to be beaten with cudgels in their prysones:[2] others in the nighte tyme they have apprehended and drawen out of their houses, yea, out of their beddes ffrom their wiefes,[3] shuttinge them upp close prysoners, separating them most ungodlye from their wiefes, children, famylies, callinges, trades, laboures, to their utter undoinge, and the affamishemente of their poore wiefes and children.[4]

All this barbarous havocke they make without regard of age, sexe,[5] estate, or degree, as may appeare by the lamentable estate of those which remayne, and by the deaths of others by them murthered in the prisons,[6] whose bloud cryeth out from under the aulter: some of us have bin kepte prysoners these nineteen monethes for hearinge the Scripture read unto us in one of our houses upon a Lorde's day morninge in all godly and peaceable maner.[7] Neyther have we bin all this tyme once produced to our answere, or had either errour or cryme objected against us. Others of us, after they have ben kepte close prisoners half a yeare without any

[1] Quinton Smythe was " taken from his labours, cast into the dungeon with irons, his Bible taken from him by Stanhoop " [Dr. Edward Stanhope, chancellor to the Bishop of London].

[2] John Purdy, who refused to hear the priest in the Bridewell prison, was cast into the " Little Ease " and beaten with cudgels. The " Little Ease " was a hole too small for standing, stretching, or sleeping. He was also forced to grind in the mill.

[3] Roger Jackson was " taken out of his bed from his wyef in the night and committed close prysoner " in the Counter Poultry. Thomas Legate was taken out of his bed and committed close prisoner, without a warrant.

[4] This language is similar to that in *A Collection of Certaine Sclaunderous Articles*, signature A ii, *recto* and *verso*.

[5] Roger Waterer was eighteen years old. Nicholas Crane was sixty-six. Margaret Maynard, Alice Roe (or Row) and Edith Burroughs were aged widows.

[6] At least six had died. John Chandler, who had a wife and eight children, had died in the Counter Poultry. George Bright, who commended a faithful Christian at his indictment, was imprisoned for his boldness and died in the Wood Street Counter. Nicholas Crane, Margaret Maynard, and Alice Roe (or Row), all aged, had died of the prison infection in Newgate. Richard Jackson died in Newgate also. Robert Griffin (or Griffith), prisoner in the Wood Street Counter, was bailed, " being very sicke."

[7] From October 8, 1587, to March 13, 1588/89, is a period of seventeen months and five days. Even if all of October and all of March are counted, the period is still eighteen months. Perhaps the petitioners may have been mistaken in calculating the time. Conceivably, the original petition in March had seventeen months, and if the copy was made a month or two later, the number may have been changed. Possibly, a " 17 " in the original petition may have been miscopied as " 19 ".

cause or pretence of cause, as yet knowen, unles for refusinge to take an othe ministred by them *ex officio*, they have at lenght[h] brought forthe to Newgate sessions,[1] ther endyted, condemned, and imprisoned uppon the statute of recusancye made for the papistes,[2] the auncient enemyes of Christ, your royall person, [19 *verso*] and the realme, notwithstanding that we refused not any parte of the word of God, neither to be truly enstructed in the same, most hartely detesting all Romish trumperyes and all heresies whatsoever, being always readye, and still most humbly desiringe to render an accounte of that faythe that is in us, doinge or leaving undone nothinge for which we have not expresse warrante in the worde of God. Yet have we not (lying in prysons uppon execution of these great sommes unto your Majesty) enjoyed that benefite of the liberty of the house [prison] which the law alloweth, and [which] they afforde to the most daungerous and pestilent papistes in that behalf, but have ben agayne shutte upp close prysoners these thirteen weekes,[3] to the great empeachment of our healthe, and hazard of our lives, and so styll remaynethe, no cause as yet shewed thereof.

Neither yet here hathe their malyce ceassed, but during this tyme of our close imprisonment, wher we might neither speake nor wryte for our selves, have they in their pulpyts published and denounced agaynst us, raylinge and most falsly slaundering us even in your Majestye's presence, accusinge us of many daungerous, erroneous, and heynous crymes, whereof yet unto our faces they never durst produce anye, seeking herby to bringe us into your Majestye's indignation, and to drawe out your sword of justice

---

1 John Greenwood was imprisoned for thirty weeks in the Clink, from October 8, 1587, to about May 5, 1588, then brought to the Newgate Sessions, indicted, found guilty, and committed to the Fleet prison, upon execution of £260. Henry Barrow was imprisoned for twenty-four weeks, from November 19, 1587, to about May 5, 1588, indicted, found guilty, and committed to the Fleet upon a like sum.

2 23 Elizabeth, *Caput* I. " An Act to Retain the Queen's Majesty's Subjects in Their Due Obedience." This Act was directed against Catholics, and penalized those who said, sang, or heard mass. As such, it was a " statute of recusancy made for the papists." But the Act also specified that " every person above the age of sixteen years, which shall not repair to some church," shall forfeit £20 for each month which he or she shall so forbear.

3 This statement indicates that Barrow was a close prisoner in the Gatehouse for a period of twenty-four weeks (November 19, 1587, to May 5, 1588), then was brought to trial, committed to the Fleet about May, 1588, and kept as an ordinary prisoner for about seven months. About December 12, 1588, he was put into close imprisonment and remained so for more than four years until his death.

(which is geven for the defence of innocentes)[1] agaynst innocentes
and so bringe that guyltles blood, which they have shed, uppon your
Majesty and the whole land, by drawing you into their quarrell
which they have against Christ Jesus and all that truly professe
his name, as may more appeare when their dealinges with the faythfull servauntes of God shalbe more looked into. But we hope that
God, which hath hitherto kept your Majesty, will also deliver you
from those evell men and their evell wayes, yea, and put into your
royall harte to revoke all their cruell decrees agaynst the sayntes
of God, in whose name we most humblye besche your Majesty
to cause us and our accusers to be brought forthe either befor your
highnes or some of your honorable and trusty counsell [Privy
Council],[2] befor whom yf we be founde to have committed any
thinge either worthy of bondes or this handelinge, we desyer no
mercye, but to the example and terror of all others to receyve
condigne punishment to our desertes; but if we be found innocent,
then to be freed from the cruelty of these men, and to be receyved
into your royall and gracious protection, for which cause God hathe
even placed you in this highe throne of dignitye.

In the mean while, and whyles we lyve, we shall not ceasse to
solicitte the Lord our God for the continuance and encrease of all
his blessinges uppon you in this lyef, and the full fruicion of them
in the worlde to come, ther without empechment of any enemyes,
to raygne with Him for ever in his heavenly kyngdome. Amen.
Amen.[3]

[1] In the examination of March 18, 1588/9, Barrow said to Lord Burghley:
" It is a woeful thing that our prince's sworde should thus be drawen
against her faithful subjectes."
[2] The petition was successful. A hearing for Barrow was held five days
later, March 18, 1588/9, before the Privy Council, and before a special
commission on March 24, 1588/9. Other Separatists were also heard,
because Christopher Bowman was committed to prison on March 17
and John Greenwood was examined, about March 24. On March 18
Barrow saw twelve of the brethren, including Christopher Bowman,
John Nicholas, and John Sparrow, in a withdrawing chamber at the
Court at Whitehall, just prior to his examination by the Privy Council.
Bowman, Nicholas, and Sparrow were committed because they delivered
this petition of March 13 to the queen. According to Robert Some,
these men were very bold in pressing into her majesty's presence.
[3] There is a reference to " A Lamentable Petition " and to the petitioners.
See *Calendar of State Papers, Domestic, Elizabeth and James I, Addenda*,
1580—1625, p. 275. The writer, a Jesuit spy, says: " Some meane
persons have been committed [to prison] for presenting supplications to
the queen on church matters. They were referred to the Archbishop of
Canterbury." See also Public Record Office, State Papers, Domestic,
Addenda, Elizabeth, volume XXXI, no. 33. The date of writing is
June, 1589.

2.

CHRISTOPHER BOWMAN'S PETITION TO THE RIGHT HONORABLE THE LORD BURLEIGH, LORD TREASORER OF ENGLAND

[MARCH, 1589/90]

This petition is found in Lansdowne MSS. 109, item 8, folio 23. With eleven other petitioners, Bowman had pressed into her majesty's presence on March 13, 1588/9, in order to present " A Lamentable Petition " on behalf of the Separatist prisoners. On March 17, Bowman was imprisoned in the Wood Street Counter, and at least two other petitioners were also imprisoned — John Nicholas and John Sparrow. After one year, in extreme sickness, want, and penury, Bowman appealed to Lord Burghley for release. His petition was denied, and he remained in prison until 1592. He was present at the organization of the Separatist church in September, 1592, was elected deacon, was arrested about March 4, 1592/3, and examined on April 4, 1593. Later he was released (or exiled), and proceeded to the Netherlands.

* * * * * * *

CHRISTOPHER BOWMAN'S PETITION [MARCH, 1589/90]

To the Right Honorable the Lord Burleigh
Lord Treasorer of England.

In pittifull distresse desirhith your Honor, your suppliant, Christofore Bowman,[1] that wheras he, with a xi [eleven] others, delivered a petecion to her Majestie in March was twelv moneths,[2] purportinges [sic] ther humble request for release of certine presoners,[3] committed for practizinge God's woord, wherupon it pleazed some of the Honorable Previe Councell to comite them presoners, emonge which your orator was committed to Woodstret Counter, wher ever sinc the xviith of March was xii moneths,[4] he haith ben deteyned, lyinge in the hole of the same Counter, in extreme want and penury, beinge of late vizited with extreme sicknes, which encreaseth so mightilie upon him, that he is in present perill of death, which in so vile and contagiouse a place can hardly be prevented. In concideration wherof your orator, beinge a very poor man, havinge charge of wief and children, maie it pleas your Lordships of your lenitie and aboundant pittie, to taike corinzavacon [consideration or commiseration?] of your orator's lamentable case, and to vouchsafe forthwith to enlarge him of his said impresonment, and he shall praie to the almightie for your Honor's preservacon.[5]

[1] Christopher Bowman was a resident of Smithfield, about twenty-nine years old, and a goldsmith.

[2] We do not know all twelve, but Bowman, John Nicholas, and John Sparrow were three of the petitioners who were imprisoned for about three or four years each because they presented the "Lamentable Petition" to the queen. On March 18, 1588/9, Barrow saw twelve of the brethren in a withdrawing chamber at Whitehall — very likely the petitioners.

[3] On October 8, 1587, twenty-one Separatists were arrested and imprisoned. Of these ten were released, but the remaining eleven remained in prison. By May, 1589, four had died, fifteen additional persons had been imprisoned; of this latter group of fifteen, two had died, and three had been bailed. Thus, there were seventeen prisoners in May, 1589, and the number was about the same in March.

[4] March 17, 1588/9. Bowman has been a prisoner for a year, lying in the hole of Wood Street Counter prison.

[5] The endorsement on his petition reads: "The humble petecion of Christofor Bowmane, presoner in Woodstret Counter. He with XI [eleven] other were committed by the lords of the [Privy] Counsell about a yeare paste for practising the woord of God. He remaynes prisonner in the Counter in Woodstrete in the hole, by the contagiousing wherof he is lyke to perishe. He humbly prayes in pitye of his estate to be enlarged."

284

3.

TO THE RIGHT HONORABLE THE LORD BURLEIGHE, LORD TRESURER OF ENGLAND

[*circa* APRIL, 1590]

This is a petition to Lord Burleigh from fifty-nine prisoners, who request that they might be bailed.   If this request cannot be granted, they ask that they might all be together in one prison, Bridewell, or in " anie other convenient place." It is also a request for a free and christian conference, either public or private, where impartial judges and witnesses may learn the truth of their beliefs and practices.

The petition gives the names of eight prisons and lists the prisoners in each.   It also lists the names of ten prisoners who have died, four of whose names have been added for the first time to those previously deceased.

The original petition is Lansdowne MSS. 109, folio 42, number 15.   It is printed by John Strype, inaccurately, in *Annals*, IV, item number 61, pp. 127-130.   Strype dates this petition 1592, but 1590 is the correct date.   What is annoying is that Strype omits sentences and sections without telling the reader.   What is even more annoying in this petition is that the omitted material casts reflection upon the bishops or puts the petitioners in a reasonable or favourable light.

This petition is printed in Daniel Neal, *History of the Puritans*, I, 431 f. (1822 ed.), and in I, Part II, 351 f. (1837 ed.). Neal has evidently copied Strype, whose work preceded his by twenty-three years, inasmuch as he has the same omissions and commits the same mistakes as Strype made.   Neal begins the petition with one long sentence — about six printed lines — which is really a summary of the whole petition.   Evidently he has incorporated the clerk's summary or endorsement into the main text.

* * * * * * *

K*

TO THE RIGHT HONORABLE THE LORD BURLEIGHE
LORD TRESURER OF ENGLAND

[*ca*. April, 1590]

The almightie God that hathe preserved your Lordship unto
theis honorable yeares in so highe service to our sovereigne prince
and to the unspeakable comfort of this whole land, gieve your
honorable hart some tender compassion and carefull consideration
in equitie of the poore afflicted servaunts of Christ. That before
the Lorde pleade against this land for Abell his innocent bloode
that is shedd in the severall prisons, your Honor may open your
mouthe for the dumbe in the cause of the children of destruction:
yea, may open your mouthe and judge righteouslie, and judge the
cause of the afflicted, as the people of Israell, when they went to
warr, first made peace with God and removed all occasions wherbie
his wrathe might be incensed, least he should fight against them
in battaile. For if this suppression of the truthe, and oppression
of Christ in his members, contrarie to all lawe and justice, be with
out restraint prosequuted by his enemies in the land, then not
onlie the voyce of the persequuted shall daylie crye from under
the altar for redresse, but God's wrathe be soe kindled for the
sheddinge of the bloud of man, the innocent bloude, even the
bloude of his owne servaunts (of whom he hathe said, " touche
not mine anoyneted "),[1] that thoughe Noe [Noah], Daniell and
Job should praye for this people, yet should they not deliver them.
Miche [much] less will our jealous God open his eares to the cryes
of those which see his servaunts murdred in their eyes, yea, ayde
and arme the persequitors therunto, and yet stop their eares
against all their sutes and complaints as thoughe the matter per-
teyned not unto them. But God forbid this should fall out thus.
Your honorable commisseration may prevent God's wrathe from
your self and from this whole land by tymelie redresse therof. For
surely the Lorde will shew mercy to all that shewe mercye.[2] Pleasethe
it then your Lordship to understand that we her majestie's most
loyall, dutifull, and true harted subjects, to the nomber of three-
skore persons and upwarde, have contrarye to all lawe and equitie

1 Psalms 105: 15 and I Chronicles 16: 22.
2 Strype omits this sentence and also the preceding three sentences (*Annals*,
IV, 128).

beene emprisoned,[1] separate from our trades, wives, children, and families; yea, shut up close prisoners from all comforts, manie of us the space of two yeares and an half[2] upon the bishopps' sole commaundement, in great penury and noysomnes of the prisons, manie ending their lives,[3] never caled to tryall, some haled fourthe to the Sessions,[4] some cast in irons and dungeons,[5] some in hunger and famyne. All of us debarred from anie lawful audience before our honorable governors and majestrates, and from all benefite or help of the lawes, dailie defamed and falslie accused by priveledged pamphletts,[6] private suggestions, open preachings, sclaunders, and accusations of heresie, sedition, schisme, and what not. And above all (which most neerlie touchethe our salvation), they keep us from all spirituall comfort and edefying by doctrine, prayer, or mutuall conference[7] (if it were possible) to destroy our soules also. All this (with mich [much] more cruelty than can be expressed), they daily inflict upon us, not being able all this tyme to convince us of cryme or errour, nether will suffer us to come to anie due tryall by lawe, or graunt us anie free christian conference, not suffer us to have anie meanes of relieff when they have shutt us

---

1 About May, 1589, there were seventeen persons in prison. By February 25, 1589/90, there were twelve former prisoners and forty new prisoners, for a total of fifty-two. In the course of the next month, eight new prisoners were added, two more were re-imprisoned, but three, who are missing in the list for April, 1590, have been bailed or released. Thus, there would be fifty-nine prisoners. In October, 1587, twenty-one or twenty-two were arrested ; in May, 1589, fifteen new names of prisoners appear in the list ; in February, 1589/90, thirty-eight new names are listed ; and in April, 1590, another eight have been apprehended. Thus, at least eighty-two Separatists were arrested.

2 This enables us to date this petition as *ca.* April, 1590, by reckoning from October 8, 1587. " Manie of us " refers to Edith Burroughs, George Collier, John Greenwood, and George Smalles, who had been in prison since October 8, 1587. Barrow's imprisonment began on November 19, 1587, and approximates two and a third years.

3 Ten had died, including two widows who were approximately sixty years old.

4 Barrow and Greenwood, and possibly others, were brought to Newgate Sessions.

5 Quintin Smythe and Roger Waterer were put in irons, and John Purdy was put into " Little Ease " and compelled to grind in the " Mill." Christopher Bowman complained of " lyinge in the hole " in the Woodstreet Counter prison.

6 Robert Some's two books were printed by the G.B. [George Bishop], Deputy to Christopher Barker, Printer to the Queen's most excellent majesty. John Strype has " published," which is a misreading for " priviledged " in the manuscript.

7 Strype has an " *etc.*" after the word " conference." He then skips the next 108 words — parts of three sentences — and continues: "And seeing for our conscience only."

up close,[1] but so lett us lye as men buryed quicke, free amongst the deade. Wherefore, right honorable, seing the conscience is not convinced or perswaded by the sworde, but by the infaylable testimonie of Gode's holie worde, and seing for our conscience onlie we ar deprived of all comfort; we most humblie beseeche and intreat your good Lordship that some more mitigate and peaceablre [*sic*] course might be taken herin that some free and christian conference might be graunted us publiquelie or privatly before your Honors or before whom it would please you, where our adversaryes may not be our judges, but our cause with the reasons and profes of bothe sides might be recorded by indifferent notaries and faithfull wittnesses. And if anie thing be fownde in us worthye of deathe or bandes, let us be made an example to all posterities. If not, we intreate for some compassion to be shewed in equitie according to lawe for our relieff. That in the meane tyme we may be bayled to doe her majestie's service, and walcke in our calings to provide things needfull for our selves, our poore wives, desolate children, and families, relying upon us, specially to the instruction and salvation of our soules.[2] Or ells that we might be prisoners togeather in Bridewell or anie other convenient place at your Honor's appoyntement, when we might provide such relieff by our dilligence and laboures as might preserve liff [life], to the comfort both of our soules and bodies. And if your Honor will not of your self graunt us this sute, yet we most humblie entreate that your Honor will make the rest of her majestie's most honorable Privie Councell acquayneted with our distressed estate, and togeather graunt us some present redresse. That we may so live to serve her majestie, your Honors, and our countrey under her, against all her enemies ether outwarde or intestine, with our uttermost powers and forces. And in the meane while and whilest we live we shall not cease to pray for the preservation of our deare sovereigne, your Honors, and of the whole land.[3]

[Here follows " the names of your Honor's poore suppliants, prisoners " — fifty-nine persons in eight prisons. There is also a list of ten persons who have died. These sixty-nine names are given in Appendix C 10, and need not be repeated here.]

[1] Henry Barrow, Edward Boyes, William Denford, Roger Jackson, Thomas Legate, and Christopher Roper suffered "close" imprisonment. John Purdy, Quintin Smythe, and Roger Waterer suffered what was worse than "close" imprisonment by enduring irons, "Little Ease," and the "Mill."

[2] These last nine words are omitted by Strype.

[3] The last two sentences are omitted by Strype. Neal omits the last three sentences.

4.

TO THE RIGHT HONORABLE THE LORDES AND OTHERS OF HER MAJESTIE'S MOST HONORABLE PRIVIE COUNCELL.

August 27, 1590

This petition is in Lansdowne MSS. 64, item 19, folio 61. It was printed by John Waddington in his *Historical Papers* (*First Series*). *Congregational Martyrs* (London, 1861), pp. 110-112. Mr. Waddington has modernized the spelling, and his reproduction is substantially correct, but he has " express " for " expose," " sorrowly " for " souccorles," and has omitted eight words.

The date is established by the endorsement and also by the reference to the length of imprisonment — " wel nigh three whole yeares cast and detayned and enclosed in sundrie most noysome and vile prisons."

The endorsement reads: " 27 August, 1590. To the Lords of the Councell. Certen persons imprisoned in diverse prisons L [fifty] [LX ?] in number, whereof some have remayned there three yeares and not called to tryall.

" Pray they may bee released, to lyve uppon their trades, or relieved otherwise, being as they are with close and contagious imprisonment like to perishe."

*   *   *   *   *   *   *

August 27, 1590

Most lamentablie expose unto your lordships right noble and honourable: her majestie's poore distressed and innocent subjects, their most miserable estate, that have to the nomber of above three skore persons,[1] being for the space manie of them wel nigh three whole yeares[2] cast and detayned and enclosed in sundrie most noysome and vile prisons, used with al inhumanitie, debarred from al comfort or accesse of their nearest friendes, wives, *etc.*, kept from their honest trades, and al other meanes of relief, to their utter undoing, and affamishment of them, their desolate wives and souccorles children, al benefite or help of the lawe shup up against them, noe peaceable order taken, or hope of redresse offred, but daylie newe injuries accumulate upon them, to the unspeakable miserie of their bodies and discomfort of their soules. Soe that sundrie of them have by this usage ended their sorowful dayes.[3] The rest that remaine, through want of relief and noysomnes of the prisons, are like fourthwith to followe, and yeild up their innocent lives, under this cruelty, to the pulling downe God's wrath upon the whole land for the bloud of his servants, except the same God in mercy encline your honorable harts to some compassion, to looke upon their unchristian usage, to examine the cause and add some redresse; that if they be fownd guiltie of anie such cryme as deserveth bands or death, they then may speedilie be produced and have judgment according to lawe, and not thus unmercifullie be deteyned in perpetual and lingring close

1 In April, 1590, the list of prisoners numbered fifty-nine. This statement implies that no new prisoners had been confined, no deaths had occurred, no one had been bailed or released unconditionally, and that the requests in the petition of April, 1590, had not been granted. But it is likely that about ten persons had been bailed, with about forty-nine still in prison, if the manuscript reading is L. It could possibly be read as LX.

2 From October 8, 1587, to August 27, 1590, would be "wel nigh three whole years for Edith Burroughs, George Collier, John Greenwood, George Smalles, and Henry Barrow."

3 Ten had died since October, 1587: George Brightie, John Chandler, Nicholas Crane, Richard Jackson, Margaret Maynard, John Purdy, Alice Roe, Thomas Stephens [or Thomas Freeman], Jerome Studley, and Henry Thomson.

imprisonment, without anie tryal, until they be made awaye. But if, according to their protestation, they be fownde unblameable of anie such cryme or offence, then they may have your Honors' accustomed gratious favor, and the benefite of true subjects.

And in the meane while they all most humblie and instantlie, even for the love and mercy of Christ, beseech your Honours, that for the preservation of their lives, their wives and children, they may, by your good and gratious meanes, be presentlie restored to their painefull labours in their honest trades, or els by some other meanes be relieved before your Honors goe out of the citie. Wherebie they may, according to their bownden dueties, serve their sovereigne prince and your Honors, live dutifullie and orderly in their calings to the glorie of God, which you shal highly advance therebye, and their poore wives and children, as also al that love and feare the Lorde in the land, be bownde to praise God for your Honors' christian compassion, and fatherlie care in [the] cause of the innocent, and to pray for the encrease of al God's blessings and graces upon your Honors for the same.

B.   SEPARATIST BELIEFS

5.

CERTEN WICKED SECTS AND OPINIONS,

MARCHE 1588 AND 1589

This important document is Harley MSS. 6848, ff. 83 *recto* — 84 *recto*. It is significant because it reveals details of the meetings held by the Separatists, the times and places, the nature of the services, the attitudes and beliefs on the Lord's Prayer, sacraments, and marriage. It also reveals details about the excommunication of Mr. Love and of his reasons for leaving the Separatists. This document further indicates the severe criticisms against the Anglican preachers. The Separatists insist on the right of laymen to preach the gospel, and they deny that the queen has any power to appoint ministers. With Robert Browne, they teach that reformation should proceed without tarrying for the magistrate's permission.

Champlin Burrage has printed this document in *The Early English Dissenters in the Light of Recent Research* (1550-1641), II, 27-31. He has listed this item as a Barrowist deposition, but it is really a confession by three men who were either curious onlookers or renegades to the Separatists. Clement Gambell had been apprehended at a conventicle on October 8, 1587, but he was not imprisoned, and " vacat " appears after his name on the manuscript. John Dove, an Oxford graduate, seems to have attended an occasional meeting, and Mr. Love had forsaken the Separatists and had been excommunicated.

Burrage has omitted about fifty to sixty lines of material. What is surprising is the fact that he has omitted important and interesting material. It is true that some of the omitted manuscript material is difficult to read, but the omissions seem arbitrary and unpredictable.

This document reveals that the authorities had seized Separatist manuscript treatises from Roger Jackson and Quintin Smyth. The treatises and the confessions provided material which was used in questioning the Separatists in the examinations of March, 1588/9. It may be that Clement Gambell's information led to the arrest of Roger Jackson, inasmuch as Gambell had been a servant of Anne Jackson, who is probably the wife of Roger Jackson. Both Jackson and Smyth were harshly treated in prison, the former kept in " close " confinement and the latter cast into the dungeon with irons.

*   *   *   *   *   *   *

[Endorsement]

[Title]   The manner of the assemblie of the secret conventicklers together with some collections of there [their] opynions.

Confessed by Clement Gambell[1]

In the somer tyme they mett together in the feilds a mile or more about London. There they sitt downe uppon a banke and divers of them expound out of the Bible so long as they are there assembled.

Confessed by Clemente Gambell

In the wynter tyme they assemble them selves by five of the clocke in the morning to that howse where they make there [their] conventicle, for that saboth daie, men and woemen together, there they contynewe in there [their] kinde of praier and exposicion of Scriptures all that dai. They dyne together, after dinner make collection to paie for there [their] diet, and what mony is left somme one of them carrieth it to the prisons where any of there [their] sect be committed.

Confessed by John Dove[2]

In there [their] praier one speketh and the rest doe grone, or sob, or sigh, as if they wold wringe out teares, but saie not after hime that praieth, there [their] praier is extemporall.

1 Clement Gamble's name is found in the first list of Separatists arrested on October 8, 1587. See Public Record Office, State Papers, Domestic, CCIV, item 10. After his name in the manuscript appears the word " vacat," which indicates that his arrest was vacated, nullified, or made void. He was evidently willing to testify freely, and he provided much information for the authorities. He was a servant to Anne Jackson, whose husband may be Roger Jackson, and whose son may be Richard Jackson, who died in Newgate.

2 John Dove (1561—1618) was a student at Christ Church, Oxford, received his A.B. degree in 1583, his M.A. in 1586, and his B.D. in 1593. In 1588 or 1589 he attended one or more meetings. Evidently he was willing to testify, and he provided valuable information. At this time, he was about twenty-seven years old and a recent Oxford graduate. From 1594 to 1613 he wrote eight published books and sermons, two of which were appeals to English Catholics, and in 1606 he wrote *A Defence of Church Government*, which was pro-Anglican. The *Dictionary of National Biography* includes seven of his works but omits *A Sermon Preached at Paule's Crosse, the Sixt of February*, 1596 [1596/7]. [London, 1597].

Separatist Beliefs

In there [their] conventicles they use not the Lord's Confessed by Clemente Gamble
Prayer, nor of any forme of sett praier, for the Lord's
Praier, one who hath ben a dailie resorter [to] there
[their] conventiclers [conventicles ?], hath [*sic*] this yeare
and a half on the Saboth daies,[1] confesseth that he never
h[e]ard it said emongest them, and this is the doctryne
of the use of it in there [their] pamphletts, to that which Taught in one of there [their] wrytinges taken from Sm[y]th[3] of the Blackfriers
is alledged, that we ought to saie the Lord's Praier,
bycause our savior Christ saieth, when you praie do
you praie thus[2] and so forth, we [the Separatists]
answer he did not saie, rede this [thus ?] or praie these
words, for that place is otherwise to be understood,
namelie, all our peticions must be dyrected by this
generall doctryne, neither can we gather that there is
set downe all Christ's words but rather a brief somme
of doctryne.

For thuse [those ?] of set or stynted praier (as they terme
it), this they teach that all stynted praiers and redd
service is but babling in the Lorde's sight, and hath Taught in the same pamphlet
neither promise of blessing nor edification, for that
they are but cushyns for such idoll priests and athiests
as have not the spirit of God, and therfore to offer up
praiers by reading or by wrote [rote] unto God is
playne idolatrie.

In all there [their] metings they teach that there is no

---

[1] This takes us back to about October 8, 1587, when the Separatists were
first apprehended in a conventicle.

[2] Matthew 6: 9 reads: "after this manner therefore pray ye," which is
the same translation in the Tyndale, Cranmer, Geneva and King James
versions. The Revised Standard Version has: "pray then like this."
The Greek adverb *houtōs* allows for variation, gives latitude — in this
way, thus, like this, according to this model. But Luke 11: 2 in all the
versions mentioned has: "when ye pray, say." Luke is specific, pre-
scriptive, definite.

[3] This "Smyth" is difficult to identify. William Smyth was a clergyman
from Bradford in Wiltshire, but does not enter into the circle of Separatists
before 1592. There is an Andrew Smith who appears first in the lists of
prisoners for February and April, 1590. The best guess is Quintin Smyth,
who was a feltmaker from Southwark, who first appears in May or June,
1589, in a list of prisoners. He was "taken from his labours, cast into
the dungeon with irons, his Bible taken from him" by the Chancellor to
the Bishop of London, Dr. Edward Stanhope. This harsh treatment may
be explained partly by his possession and possible dissemination of
Separatist writings in manuscript.

John Greenwood

Confessed by Clement Gambell

heade or supreme governor[1] of the church of God, but Christe, that the queene hath no aucthoritie to appoyn[t] mynisters in the church nor to set downe any govermente for the church which is not directlie commanded in God's worde.

Taught in another of there [their] writing[2] taken from the for[e]said Smyth, confessed by John Dove

To confirm there [their] privat conventicles and expounding there, they teach that a pryvatt man being a brother may preach to begett faieth, and nowe that the office of the appostles is ceaseth [sic] there nedeth not publicque mynistres but every man in his owne calling was to preache the gospell.[3]

Confessed by Clement Gambell

Taught in one of there [their] former pamphletts

Taught in the same pamphlet

Confessed by John Dove

They condempne it as utterlie unlawful to comme to our churches in England to any publicque praier or preching of whome soever, for that they saie as the chirch of England standeth they be all fals teachers and falce prophetts that be in it, there [their] reason is for that our [Anglican] preachers (as they saie) doe teach us that the state of the realme of England is the true church (which they denye), and therfore they saie that all prechers of England be fals preachers sent in the Lord's anger to deceyve his people with lyes, and not true preachers to bring the glad tydings of the gospell, and all that come to our churches to publicque praier or sermons they accompt damnable soules.

Taught in one of there [their] former pamphletts

Concerning the aucthoritie of magistracye, they saie that our preachers teach we must not cast out pollucion out of the church untill the magistrate hath dissanulled the same, which they saie is contrary to the doctryne of the appostles, who did not tarry [for] the aucthoritie of the magistrate. They saie our preachers teach that we may not put the dissipline of the church in practise

---

[1] By law Henry VIII was the "supreme head in earth of the Church of England, called *Anglicana Ecclesia*"; and by law Elizabeth was "the only supreme governor of this realm, . . . as well in all spiritual or ecclesiastical things or causes, as temporal."

[2] This reference implies at least two writings in manuscript which were circulating in 1589 and very likely in 1588.

[3] Dr. Robert Some sought to refute this doctrine. He asserted that "no man, how able soever, may preach without an externall calling," and he refers to "Barrowe's rule" as Anabaptistical, leading to the "absurdities" that women might preach and that private men might insinuate themselves into pulpit and counsel chamber. Dr. Some concludes with a pun: "I doe not marvaile greatly at these arguments. They are sutable to Master Barrowe's propositions. Weake buildings have for the most part Greene wood for their groundsils" (*A Godly Treatise* [1589], pp. 23—26).

till the magistrat begynne. And therfore our preachers
be false prophetts for that we ought to reforme without
the magistrate if he be slowe, for that they saie the
prymityve chirch whose example ought to be our Taught in an
warrant sued not to the courts and parlyaments nor other of the[i]r
former wryting
wayted not uppon prynces' pleasur for there [their] taken from
Roger Jackson
reformacion. When the stones were reddy, they went
presentlie forward with there [their] buylding, wherof
they conclude against all our prechers, that you might
emong [enjoy] this worldie peace, you care not [you
are willing] to make Christ attend uppon prynces and
to be subject unto there [their] lawes and governmente.[1]
Touching the *Book of Common Praier* this is there [their] Taught in the
doctryne, let the great pregnant idoll, that booke of same pamphlet
taken from
your common praier, which is so full of errors and Roger Jackson
abhomminacions, be examined at every parte, wherof
when they have railed, calling the collects therin
hereticall, thus they conclude of it, neither can the
cunnyingest of you make the best parte of it other than
a pece of swyne's fleshe, an abhomminacion to your land
[lord ?], neither can the perswasion of your conference
[conscience] either justifie your worshipe, cleare or
satisfie others.[2]
Those who have ben of there [their] secret brotherhood, Taught in the
and seing there [their] errours do fall from them and same pamphlet
taken from

---

1 This material in the last two sentences is taken from Barrow's defence
  of the fifth article against Gifford. See "A Brief Summe of the Causes
  of Our Seperation, and of Our Purposes," printed in the previous volume.
  Since this material came from a pamphlet or manuscript treatise seized
  from Roger Jackson, it is evident that Barrow's controversy with Gifford
  was circulated in manuscript among the Separatists. See also George
  Gifford, *A Short Treatise against the Donatists of England*, pp. 103-106.
2 This paragraph is taken from the manuscript treatise seized from Roger
  Jackson. It is Barrow's reply to Gifford's answer to the first principal
  transgression. See "A Brief Summe of the Causes of Our Seperation,
  and of Our Purposes." Compare Gifford, *A Short Treatise against the
  Donatists of England*, p. 10. Gifford quotes Barrow as saying that the
  Book of Common Prayer was "a great pregnant idoll, full of errors, blasphemies, and abhominations."

Roger Jackson.[1] Confessed in Mr. John Dove's examination, a Master of Arte, who was at one of there [their] conventycles

submytt them selves to be partakers of publyque praiers and hering of Gode's worde, which they condempne as apostates, and they saie it is a great[er] synne to goe to our chirches to publique praier than for a man to lye with his father's wief.[2]

Confessed by Love[3] who is the partie who[m] they so used and by Mr. Dove who was present at this accion and was the first man who reveled this

And when as one of late forsoke there [their] conventickles they sent for him, and when he gave them many reasons whie he co[u]ld not hold there [their] opynions for good, as, namelie, that they rejected the Lorde's Praier, that they were dissemblers in that two of them had made a deede of gyfte of all there [their] landes to deceyve the queene, and a nomber of other reasons which he alledged to them, when they sawe they co[u]ld not wynne hime they gave hime over to the handes of Satan till he would submitt hime self to the chirch agayne, and they all kneling, he that gave that sentence made a praier to desyre God to ratiffie that censure against hime.

Wydowe Unyon,[4]

They held it unlawful to baptise children emongest us but rather chewse to let them goe unbaptized, as in

---

1 In the first list of the prisoners arrested October 8, 1587, the name of Anne Jackson occurs. Her name is not found in the next list of May, 1589, and the presumption is that she was bailed or released unconditionally. In the list for May, 1589, however, we find Roger Jackson named twice. The first one named is " taken out of bed from his wyef in the nighte and committed close prysoner." It is likely that this Roger Jackson is the husband of Anne Jackson, that he was found with a Separatist manuscript in his possession, and that he was regarded as an obnoxious and confirmed recusant, since he was committed to " close " imprisonment. It is ironical to learn that Clement Gamble, who confessed, was a servant to Anne Jackson. The second Roger Jackson is one who dyed in Newgate prior to May, 1589. Barrow speaks of that rare young man, Richard Jackson, who died in Newgate, and it is probable that Richard is a son or brother of Roger, and that the name has been confused. In fact, in two later lists Roger Jackson appears as " Robert."

2 This slur is difficult to believe. The Separatists would never condone incest. Barrow refuted this slander by describing it as " an horrible abhominacion against the lawe of God and of nature, not so much as to be spoken or thought of by anie chaste or christian hearte, much lesse in this maner compared."

3 Mr. Love was probably one of two persons excommunicated by the Separatists. The lay reader was T.L. [Thomas Lemar or Thomas Legate], and the time was about February, 1588/9. Barrow disagreed witht his action and disclaimed it because it occurred at a conventicle, and no minister or pastor was present. See Robert Some, *A Godly Treatise* (1589), p. 36.

4 Katheren Unwen or Unyen was a widow, thirty years old in 1588. She was first arrested October 8, 1587, and is listed as Catherine or Katherin Owin or Onyon. Her name is not found on later lists, and she was evidently released.

somer 1588 a child of one of theires, being twelve yeres of age, was knowne not to have ben baptized, and when the pore infant desyred the mother often that it might be baptized, she said it was borne of faiethfull parentes, which was enough for it, which child was by the Chauncelor of London[1] caused to be publiquely baptised, at a sermon made for that purpose the last somer, and the mother ranne awaie for feare of punishmente.[2] *(marginal note: one of there [their] chief conventickler[s], her child was baptized in St. Andrews in the Wardrope)*

It cannot be learned where they receyved the sacraments of the Lorde's Supper, and one who never missed there [their] metings of a yere and a half confesseth that he never saw any min[i]stracion of the sacrement nor knoweth where it is donne. *(marginal note: Confessed by Clement Gamble)*

For marriadges, if any of there [their] chirch marry together, some of there [their] owne brotherhood must marry them, as of late a cople were married in the Fleet.[3] *(marginal note: Confessed by Clement Gamble)*

---

[1] Dr. Edward Stanhope, Chancellor to the Bishop of London. The minister or parson at St. Andrew's in the Wardrobe was Arthur Williams.

[2] The Separatists did not object to infant baptism, but they did protest against baptism by false ministers. Nevertheless, it is surprising to find a child born in 1576 still unbaptized in 1588.

[3] Possibly Christopher Bowman and his wife. Bowman was imprisoned in the Wood Street Counter on March 17, 1588/9, and remained in prison until about the spring or summer of 1592.

6.

THE ASSERTIONS OF THE CONVENTICLES
LATELY APPREHENDED

[1589]

These " Assertions " are in Harley MSS. 6848, ff. 83 *recto*
— 84 *verso*. They are also in Ellesmere MS. 16 b. They have
been printed in *A Collection of Certaine Sclaunderous Articles
Gyven out by the Bisshops*, F iii *recto* — G ii *verso*, where they are
listed and defended. They are also given and refuted by
Richard Alison, in his book, *A Plaine Confutation of a Treatise
of Brownisme, Entituled*: A Description of the Visible Church
[*A True Description out of the Worde of God, of the Visible
Church*], pp. 113-119. Inasmuch as there are twelve articles,
they are sometimes confused with another set of twelve articles,
similar in subject matter but different in wording, which appear
with the heading, " A Briefe of the Positions Holden by the
Newe Sectorie of Recusants," in *A Collection of Certaine Sclaunderous Articles Gyven out by the Bisshops*, A iv *recto*.

The substance and much of the identical wording of these
" Assertions " are found in " Certen Wicked Sects and
Opinions," March 1588/89. Therefore, the real source for
these beliefs and practises is to be found in the confessions of
Clement Gambell, John Dove, and a Mr. Love, and also in
two or three Separatist manuscript pamphlets seized by the
authorities from Quintin Smyth and Roger Jackson. The
" Assertions " represent a summary of the confessions and
confiscated pamphlets.

The date of these " Assertions " is about December, 1589.
" Certen Wicked Sects and Opinions " give us a *terminus a quo*
of March, 1588/89. The printed version of these " Assertions,"
in *A Collection of Certaine Sclaunderous Articles Gyven out by*

the Bisshops, gives us April, 1590, as a *terminus ad quem*. But it seems possible to establish within a month or two the first appearance of these " Assertions." The clue is found in the phrase " Conventicles Lately Apprehended."

On October 8, 1587, twenty-two persons meeting in a con-venticle were arrested. From a list of twenty-six prisoners in May, 1589, we see that there are fifteen new names, of which eleven are living, two are dead, and two are bailed. All of these fifteen seem to have been arrested separately and at varying times, and not at a common meeting or time or place. Therefore, we may conclude that these prisoners are not relevant to the " Conventicles Lately Apprehended."

Our next list of prisoners brings us to February 25, 1589/90. Of the fifty-two names, forty are new. When were these forty apprehended ? The best answer is December, 1589, and the evidence rests upon Roger Waterer's testimony. On April 3, 1593, he stated that he had been in prison three and one-fourth years, or from January 3, 1590, if his figure is exact. If he had been in prison since December 3, 1589, he would have replied three and one-third years. If we allow for three weeks of latitude, both ways, his imprisonment occurred sometime between December 13, 1589, and January 24, 1589/90. For-tunately, we have independent testimony that helps in the solution of this problem. In his letter to Mr. Fisher, of Decem-ber, 1590, Barrow wrote: " I omit to relate here how many Doctor Stanhope hath caste into yrons in Nuegate and of the boy of fifteen yeares ould he there kept in a dongeon in yrons a whole yeare for this cause, which boy is yet there prisoner." Since this boy is Roger Waterer, and since Barrow is careful in designating time by expressions such as " well nigh two years," we may conclude that Barrow means a whole year. This would corroborate December, 1589, as the time of Waterer's arrest.

Roger Waterer testified or confessed that he was " in an assembly in a garden howse by Bedlem, wher James Forrester

John Greenwood

expounded." Inasmuch as both Waterer and Forrester are listed for the first time as prisoners in February, 1589/90, we may conclude that one or two conventicles were discovered by the authorities in December, 1589, or January, 1589/1590.

* * * * * * *

THE ASSERTIONS OF THE CONVENTICLES
LATELY APPREHENDED.

[1589]

1. They houlde that the Lorde's Prayre, or any sett prayre, is blasphemy and they never use any, nor pray for the queene as supreme head under Christe of the Church of Englande.

2. That all sett prayres or stinted prayers, or reed [read] service are but mear bablinge[1] in the Lorde's sighte and playne idolatry.

3. They teache that ther is noe head or supreme governor of the churche[2] but Christe, and that the queene hath noe authoritye to governe in the churche, or to make lawes ecclesiasticall.

4. They teach that a private lay man may preache to begett fayth[3] and that we have noe need of publique ministers.

5. They condemne all commynge to churche, all preachinge, all ministration of sacraments, and [say] that all the ministers are sent by God in his anger to deceyve the people with lyes, etc.[4]

6. They affirme that the people muste reforme the churche and not tarry for the magistrates and that the primytive churche sewed [sued] not to courts nor perliamentes nor wayted upon princes' pleasures for reformation, but we make Christe to attende upon princes, and to be subject unto the[i]r lawes and governmente.[5]

7. That the *Booke of Common Prayre* is a great pregnant idoll and

---

[1] This phrase is used frequently in articles and questions directed against the Separatists.
[2] They deny the legal title given to Henry VIII and Elizabeth.
[3] Taught in a Separatist pamphlet or manuscript of *ca.* 1588, confessed by John Dove, and refuted by Dr. Robert Some in *A Godly Treatise* (1589).
[4] See " Certen Wicked Sects and Opinions," ninth paragraph.
[5] *Ibid.* This doctrine is taught in 1582 by Robert Browne in " A Treatise of Reformation without Tarying for Anie," in Albert Peel and Leland H. Carlson, *The Writings of Robert Harrison and Robert Browne*, pp. 151-170.

full of abhominations, and a peec of swyne's fleshe[1] and an abhomination of the Lorde.

8. They say it is a greater sinne to goe to churches to publique prayres, than for a man to lye with his father's wife.[2]
9. Those that will not refrayne from our churches, preachinges, and service, they give up to the devell and excommunicate.[3]
10. They houlde it not lawfull to baptize children amongest us. They never have any sacramentes ministred amongest them.[4]
11. They refuse to take an othe to be examinede.[5]
12. They will not marry amongeste us in our churches but resorte to the Fleete and other places to be marryed by Greenwoode and Barrowe.[6]

[1] A striking phrase, a foolish utterance, and a cause of much trouble. This phrase is found first in *Four Causes of Separation*. It is also used by Barrow in his first reply to Gifford's first answer, which is included in "A Brief Summe of the Causes of Our Seperation, and of Our Purposes," which is printed in the previous volume. This latter treatise was first printed in 1591 as pages 1-20 of, *A Plaine Refutation of M[aster] G[eorge] Giffarde's Reprochful Booke*.

[2] This assertion was strongly denied by Barrow and the Separatists. It may have originated with John Dove, who " confessed " it. Dove may have been a curious visitor, or he may have been an informer. His writings after 1594 are a strong defence of the Anglican church.

[3] The company of T. L. [probably Thomas Legate, but Thomas Lemare is a possibility] excommuncated two persons, one of whom was probably Mr. Love. Barrow disclaimed this action, since no minister or pastor was present. See Robert Some, *A Godly Treatise* (1589), p. 36.

[4] As soon as the Separatists organized their church in September, 1592, with a pastor and teacher, they observed the sacraments of the Lord's Supper and Baptism.

[5] The Separatists disliked oaths in general and the *ex officio* oath in particular. Frequently they agreed to speak truly, or to state that they had spoken the truth *after* they had learned what the questions were. They refused to run the risk of incriminating themselves by swearing to answer to any questions that might be proffered.

[6] This statement helps to date the present document. Barrow and Greenwood were indicted about May, 1588, and transferred from the Gatehouse (Barrow) and the Clink (Greenwood) to the Fleet.

C. SEPARATIST PRISONERS
7.
SEPARATISTS ARRESTED AT A CONVENTICLE
[OCTOBER 8, 1587]

This important document is found in State Papers, Domestic, Elizabeth, volume 204, item 10, in the Public Record Office. It is significant for two reasons. First, it provides us with the names of twenty-two persons who were arrested at a private conventicle. This is the earliest list of Barrowist prisoners that we possess, including two clergymen, Nicholas Crane and John Greenwood. Secondly, it provides us with the correct date of the arrest, October 8, 1587. In the rare tract, *The Examinations of Henry Barrowe, John Grenewood, and John Penrie, before the High Commissioners, the Lordes of the Counsel. Penned by the Prisoners Themselves before Their Deaths*, there is contained " A Brief of the Examination of Me Henry Barrowe the 19 of November, 1586. Before the Arch Bishop, Arch Deacon, and Dr. Cussins: as Neere as My Memorie Could Carry: Being at Lambeth." In the first line Barrow begins by saying: " The 19 being the Lord's day." In 1586, November 19 was Saturday. In 1587, November 19 fell on Sunday. Furthermore, numerous references to the length of imprisonment prove that 1587 is the correct year. In his biography, *Henry Barrow, Separatist*, F. J. Powicke has used 1586 as a starting point instead of 1587. Consequently, the dating of Barrow's examinations is incorrect (pp. 16, 19, 20, 24). Not only Powicke, but also Henry M. Dexter and many other writers have been misled by the original mistake for which the anonymous editor may be responsible, in giving 1586 instead of 1587 as the year of Barrow's first examination. With the anchor date of October 8, 1587, correctly established, it follows that Barrow's first examination six weeks later fell on November 19, 1587, and his second examination, eight days later, fell on November 27, 1587.

*   *   *   *   *   *   *

[October 8, 1587]

[The names of certain Brownists (Barrowists) taken at a Conventicle in Henry Martin's house, October 8, 1587, and examined in the Episcopal Palace, London, on the same day.]

8⁰ *die mensis Octobris* 1587.
In palacio episcopali London.

Brownestes.

1   Crane a minister mad[e] by Bishop Grindall[1] when he was Bushop [*sic*] of London, and before that he was a student in lawe in the Inner Chauncery. Called for beinge at privat conventicles this daye in Henry Martin's howse in St. Andrewes in the Wardropp.[2]   He saieth that all the booke (meaninge the comon booke, is not gospell).[3]

2   Henry Martin,[4] of the same secte.

3   George Smells,[5] of the same sect.
     for beinge at [p]rivat conventles.

---

[1] Nicholas Crane (1522—1588), was ordained a priest by the Bishop of London, Edmund Grindal, in April, 1562.   He was a nonconformist, held Presbyterian views, lived in Roehampton, Surrey, was active in establishing a presbytery at Wandsworth, Surrey, in 1572.   Martin Marprelate's book, *The Epistle*, was printed at the home of Mrs. Crane in East Molesey, Surrey, but she was *not* the wife of Nicholas Crane, as often stated.   She was Mrs. Anthony Crane, and her second husband was George Carleton. See Julia Norton McCorkle, " A Note concerning ' Mistress Crane ' and the Martin Marprelate Controversy," Transactions of the Bibliographical Society, *Library*, XII, 4th series, 1932, pp. 276-283.   Burrage has misread the manuscript by his reading " Crane a minister mad[e] by 23 Grindall."   The " 23 " is " B " for Bishop.   Nicholas Crane died in Newgate in 1588.   See *A Parte of a Register*, pp. 119-124.

[2] St. Andrew's in the Wardrobe is south of St. Paul's and Carter Lane. The church was close to the King's Wardrobe, and was north of the Thames and Thames Street.

[3] That is, some portions of the *Book of Common Prayer* contain material that is unscriptural, or superstitious, or papistical.

[4] Henry Martin is not found on any later list of prisoners.   By 1603 he seems to have become a Johnsonian Anabaptist in the Netherlands.

[5] The manuscript is not clear.   It may be read as Snells, Swells, or Smells. The latter is the best guess.   He was a tailor, about thirty-four years of age, living in Finch Lane, near Cornhill and Thread Needle Street and the Royal Exchange.

4   Edward Boyce,[1] of the same sect.

5   Anne Jackson,[2] of the same sect.

6   George Collier,[3] of the same sect.

7   Katherin Owin[4] [Onyon, or Unwen].

8   Roberte Lacy[5] of St. Andrewes in Holborne, of the same sect. He refuseth to take an othe. Of Grey's Inne, gentleman.

9   Thomas Freeman of the parishe of St. Botulphe[6] with owt Aldersgate, of the same sect and a Brownest.

10   Edithe Burry[7] of Stepbunhits [or Stepbunhith].

11   Mr. Grenwood,[8] preacher, deprived of his benefice in Norfolke about two yeres past, takin at the said

---

[1] Edward Boyce, or Boyes, was a haberdasher, about twenty-seven years old, who lived on Fleet Street, in St. Bride's parish. St. Bride's or Bridget's church was about a mile west of St. Paul's, south of Fleet Street and north of Bridewell prison.

[2] Possibly the wife of Roger or Robert Jackson. Her servant was Clement Gambell, who made a frank confession to the authorities about the activities of the Separatists.

[3] George Collier, age thirty-two, was a haberdasher, living near Ludgate, in St. Martin's parish, less than a half mile west of St. Paul's. He was imprisoned in the Clink, in Southwark.

[4] Katherin Unwen, or Unyen, Onyon, Onion, a widow, age twenty-nine, both of the parish of Christ Church, near Newgate and Butcher Hall Lane, and of St. Andrew's in the Wardrobe. In 1587 she had a child eleven years old who was unbaptized. In the summer of 1588 the Chancellor to the Bishop of London, Dr. Stanhope, caused the child to be publicly baptised in St. Andrew's Church in the Wardrobe, against the wishes of the mother, who ran away for fear of punishment.

[5] Robert Lacy, gentleman, son and heir of William Lacy of Stamford, Lincolnshire, was evidently released after questioning. We hear of him six weeks later, on November 19, 1587, when he was with Barrow, very likely visiting Greenwood in the Clink. Barrow suggested Lacy as a surety for himself, and described him as a gentleman of Gray's Inn. There is a record of his admission on April 24, 1583, in Joseph Foster, *The Register of Admissions to Gray's Inn, 1521—1589, together with the Register of Marriages in Gray's Inn Chapel, 1695—1754,* p. 63.

[6] There were four churches with the name of St. Botolph: they were near Aldgate, Bishopsgate, Billingsgate, and Aldersgate. The latter church was on the west side of Aldersgate street. Freeman reappears on the February and April, 1590, lists of prisoners.

[7] Edith Burry, Burrough, Barrowe, Burrowghe, Borough, is described as an aged widow, of the parish of Stepney. The older forms are Stebenheth or Stibbenhidde. This parish was about two miles east of St. Paul's. She was committed by the Bishop of London, indicted, found guilty, and sent to Newgate.

[8] Greenwood was a curate in Norfolk, perhaps at Rackheath, near Norwich, about 1583—5. When he was asked at his examination in March, 1588/9, the question: "Are yow a minister?" he replied: "No, I was one after your [Anglican] orders." To the question: "Who disgraded yow?" he replied: "I disgraded myself through God's mercy by repentance."

privat conventicles in Martin's howse. He is committed to the Clincke.

12 Margaret Maynerd[1] of Bredstreet. She saieth ther is no church in England. She hath not bin at church theis ten yeres.
Committed to Bridewell.

13 Alice Re [Roe],[2] wydow. Of St. Andrewes in the Wardrop.

14 Agnes Wyman[3] of Stepney.

15 Roberte Griffith,[4] of the same sect.

16 John Chaundler[5] of Stepney, of the same sect.

17 Edmond Thompson[6] of Stepney, of the same sect.

18 Henry Thompson, Dunst[an] parishe [or Dnise — St. Denis] parish,[7] [eiusdem praedicte] of the same sect.

---

[1] Margaret Maynard was an " aged widow," about fifty-eight years old. She is listed as Maynerd, Meynard, and " Mother Maner." As a resident of Bread Street, near Cheapside, her parish church may have been Allhallows, St. Mildred, or St. Mary-le-Bow. As a recusant for ten years, and as one who believed that the Church of England was a false church, she was deemed incorrigible. Committed to Bridewell by Bishop Aylmer, she was indicted as a recusant, found guilty, sent to Newgate, where she died of the infection of the prison, sometime before May, 1589.

[2] Alice Roe, widow, about fifty-eight years old, was committed by Bishop Aylmer, indicted as a recusant, found guilty, and sent to Newgate, where she died of the prison infection before May, 1589. She is listed as Roe, Roo, Re.

[3] Agnes Wyman was probably released. We do not hear of her in any later activity.

[4] Robert Griffith, or Griffits, or Gryffin was imprisoned in the Wood Street Counter. By May, 1589, he had been bailed, being very sick.

[5] John Chandler was the husband of Alice and the father of eight children. Before May, 1589, he had died in the Counter Poultry, probably without any indictment or trial. His only " crime " was attendance at Henry Martin's house, listening to the reading of Scripture, and participating in a conventicle.

[6] Edmond Thompson, or Thomson, or Tomson, was released. He was arrested again about December, 1589, or January, 1589/90, because he appears on a list of prisoners in February, and also April, 1590, both times in the Gatehouse.

[7] Henry Thompson was kept in the Clink, is listed in May, 1589, as a prisoner, is not found on the list for February, 1589/90, is one of the ten deceased in April, 1590. He died about the autumn of 1589. In the manuscript are two words difficult to decipher. Burrage has read them as *eiusdem praedicte*. The reading is difficult, but it may be Dunst[an] par[ish]e or Dnise [St. Denis] par[ish]e. The former parish is in Stepney. We do not know the relationship between Edmond and Henry Thompson.

19   Roberte Redborne and Thomas Russell[1] — ser-
20   vantes to Mr. Boyce of the parishe of St. Brigitts
      in Flet Stret.

21   Peter Allen,[2] servant to Mr. Allen a salter, of the
      parishe of St. Botulphe nere Billingsegat, of the same
      sect, and at Martin's howse a foresaid at the con-
      venticle.

[22] Vacat Clement Gamble servante to Anne Jackson.[3]

---

[1] Robert Redborne and Thomas Russell were released, and they do not
reappear in the lists of Separatists. Their master, Edward Boyce, remained in the Bridewell until May, 1589, was transferred to the Clink as
a close prisoner. He was probably bailed before February, 1589/90,
and was apprehended again in December, 1592.

[2] Peter Allen was released. We do not hear of him again.

[3] In the manuscript the two names are crossed out.

L

8.

THE NAMES OF SUNDRY FAYTHFULL CHRISTIANS IMPRISONED

[MAY, 1589]

This list of prisoners is given in Harley MSS. 6848, ff. 20 *verso* — 21 *recto*. It is printed in Edward Arber's book, *An Introductory Sketch to the Martin Marprelate Controversy*, 1588-1590, pages 38-40. The list provides information about twenty-six persons, informs us that they were incarcerated in six prisons, and enables us to know which of the persons imprisoned in 1587 were still in custody. Seven persons who were imprisoned on October 8, 1587, still are in prison, and four have died ; there are fifteen new names, of which two have died.

Edward Arber gives the date May-June, 1588, but this is an error. John Fraunces has been in prison for ten months, William Bromell for twelve months, Jerome Studley for fifteen months, Henry Thomson and George Collier for nineteen months, and Edward Boyes has served nineteen months in the Bridewell and an unspecified time in the Clink. Computing nineteen full months from Collier's and Thomson's arrest on October 8, 1587, we arrive at May 8, 1589. If we accept June 8, 1589, as a possibility, the period would be twenty months, but it is clear that Thomson and Collier have served nineteen months. Therefore, we must conclude that Boyes, who is described as " now close prysoner in the Clynke," has served less than a month in his new prison after transference from the Bridewell. Conceivably, he served eighteen months, plus two or three weeks, or almost the equivalent of nineteen months, and has been in the Clink for two or three weeks. The date, May, 1589, is thus the best date for this list of prisoners.

Separatist Prisoners

The list is a Separatist document, hostile to the Bishop of London and the Archbishop of Canterbury, as well as to William Fleetwood, Recorder of London, and to Edward Stanhope, Chancellor of the Diocese of London. It was probably circulated among the Separatists and may have been used as a means of appealing to public sentiment.

There are three Separatists who are not listed but who are in prison. Christopher Bowman is in the Woodstreet Counter. John Nicholas is in the Gatehouse at Westminster, and John Sparrow is in the White Lion at Southwark or in the Clink. They were committed about March 17, 1588/9, for presenting " A Lamentable Petition " to the queen on March 13. The reason they are not included seems to be that this is a list of prisoners committed by Archbishop Whitgift and Bishop Aylmer, whereas Bowman, Nicholas, and Sparrow were imprisoned by order of the Privy Council.

*   *   *   *   *   *   *

L*

THE NAMES OF SUNDRY FAYTHFULL CHRISTIANS IMPRISONED
BY THE ARCHBISHOP OF CANTERBURY AND THE BISHOP OF LONDON
FOR THE GHOSPELL OF OUR LORD JESUS CHRIST.

[May, 1589]

1. JOHN GREENWOOD
   In the Fleete

2. HENRY BARROW
   In the Fleet

3. HENRY TOMSON

[26] GEORGE COLLIER[3]
   In the Clynke

4. JEROME STUDLEY
   In the Counter
   in the P[o]ultry

1. Having bin imprysoned by the Bishop of London thirty weeks in the Clynke for readinge a portion of Scripture on a Lorde's daye in a frynde's house, removed by hab[e]as corpus.[1]

2. Barrowe uppon the like, having bin close prysoner at the Archbishop's commaundement twenty-four weeks for not taking an othe ministered unto him *ex officio*. Wher [at the Fleet prison] they [Barrow and Greenwood] lye uppon an execution of 260li [brae] [£260] a peyce.[2]

3. Committed by the Bishop of London for hearinge a portion of Scripture in a frynde's house, read by the said Greenwood on a Lorde's daye, and have there remayned prisoners, nineteen moneths, without being brought to their answere.[3]

4. Committed for not swearinge before the Bishop of London, and hath remayned prysoner, fifteen monethes, having a

[1] Arrested October 8, 1587, Greenwood remained in the Clink until about May 5, 1588, then was brought to Newgate Sessions, indicted as a recusant, found guilty, and committed to the Fleet prison. The friend's house was that of Henry Martin, who lived in St. Andrew's in the Wardrobe. The fine or judgment against Greenwood was £260.

[2] Barrow was arrested November 19, 1587, remained in the Gatehouse until May, 1588, was brought to Newgate Sessions, indicted as a recusant, found guilty, and committed to the Fleet.

[3] Not numbered in the manuscript. Collier and Thompson were arrested October 8, 1587. A period of exactly nineteen months brings us to May 8, 1589.

wife and six children and nothinge but his labours in his callinge to susteyne them.[1]

5. CHRISTOPHER ROPER
   In the Counter
   in the P[o]ultry

5. Committed close prisoner by the Bishops of London.[2]

6. ROGER JACKSON
   In the Counter
   in the P[o]ultry

6. Taken out of his bed from his wyef in the nighte and committed close prysoner.[3]

7. EDWARD BOYES

7. Prysoner in Brydewell nineteen monethes, now close prysoner in the Clynke.[4]

8. JOHN CHAUN[D]LER

8. Having a wyef and eight children, died [in the Counter Poultry] for hearinge *ut supra*.[5]

In the Counter in Wood Street

9. ROBERT GRYFFIN

9. Bayled, being very sycke.[6]

10. GEORGE SMALLES

10. By Bishop of London, for hearing, *ut supra*, and hath remayned unbrought forthe.[7]

---

[1] Studley was arrested about February, 1587/8, and evidently was committed to the Counter Poultry for refusing to take an oath. He may have been the brother of Daniel Studley.

[2] The manuscript is bb., which is common for " bishops," but the reference is John Aylmer, Bishop of London. It would be helpful to know why Roper is committed a " close " prisoner. Was he in possession of Separatist pamphlets, that is, manuscript treatises ?

[3] Roger Jackson may have been the husband of Anne Jackson, who was apprehended October 8, 1587. Roger Jackson was in possession of Separatist literature — manuscript pamphlets — including Barrow's reply to Gifford. This may account for his " close " imprisonment. He was arrested about March, 1588/9.

[4] In the Bridewell from October 8, 1587, until about May 8, 1589, then to the Clink, where he may have been for less than a month. He may have been indicted as a recusant, found guilty, and committed.

[5] Arrested October 8, 1587, and died before May, 1589. He is the husband of Alyce. The phrase *ut supra* means " for hearing a portion of Scripture in a friend's house, read by Greenwood on a Lord's day."

[6] Also spelled Griffith, or Griffits. Prisoners who were " very sycke " usually died, but he does not appear on any list of deceased prisoners.

[7] His name in the manuscript could be read as Snells, Swells, Smells, or Smalls. Apprehended October 8, 1587.

11. GEORGE BRYGHTE	11. Committed from Newgate Sessions by the Recorder of London, for commendinge a faythfull Christian which was ther indited, this George dyed ther [in Wood Street Counter].[1]
12. THOMAS LEGATE	12. Comitted by [the Bishop of] London, out of his bed in the nyght tyme and now close prysoner.[2]
13. [WILLIAM] CLARKE	13. Comitted by the constable for sainge they did evell to enforce Master Legate without a warrant.[3]

[In Newgate]

14. MEYNARD	14. Aged widdowes first committed by [the Bishop of]
15. ROO [ROE]	15.
16. BARROWE [BURROUGHE OR BURRY]	16. London for hearing *ut supra*, after endighted and two of them dyed of the infection of the prysons.[4]

---

[1] This faythfull Christian may have been Barrow or Greenwood, during the trial at Newgate Sessions, about May, 1588.

[2] It is remarkable that Thomas Legate was seized at night without a warrant and that he was committed a close prisoner. The explanation may be that " T.L. and his company, in a conventicle in London, expounded Scriptures, conceived long prayers at a sudaine, and drew out the sworde of excommunication against two [including Mr. Love], which were sometime of, and had now left that brotherhood. No minister, as T.L. confessed, was then present in that fantasticall assembly. For proofe of this, *vidz.*, that excommunication may bee without a minister, T. L. quoted I Corinthians 5: [4, 5, 11, 12, 13], which place, if it be considered aright, is very directly against him.
Master Barrowe is not of their judgement in this: he did disclaime it " (Robert Some, *A Godly Treatise* (1589), p. 36). T. L. may be Thomas Lemar, but Thomas Legate is a prisoner in May, 1589, whereas Lemar is not. Dr. Some is writing before May, 1589. If the confessions of Clement Gambell, John Dove, and Mr. Love provided the information, as is most likely, then we may date the arrest of Thomas Legate about March or April, 1589.

[3] William Clarke evidently protested the arrest of Legate, about March or April, 1589, and was arrested. He is still in prison by February, 1589/90, but by April, 1590, has been bailed or released unconditionally.

[4] Margaret Maynard and Alice Roe died. Edith Burrough is on the lists of prisoners for October 8, 1587, May, 1589, February, 1589/90, and April, 1590. How soon thereafter she was released, we do not know, but she did not die in prison.

Separatist Prisoners

17. ROGER [RICHARD] 17. Dyed in Newgate.[1]
    JACKSON

18. NICHOLAS CRANE 18. A man of 66 yeares, havinge a wyef and
    chyldren, first imprysoned by [the
    Bishop of] London for hearing *ut supra*,
    after endighted and dyed of the in-
    fection of the pryson in Newgate.[2]

19. ALYCE CHAUNDLER 19. Wyddowe of the above named JOHN
    CHAUNDLER, bayled by Master
    [Richard] Yonge.[3]

20. JOHN FRAUNCES 20. Committed by [the Archbishop of]
    Canterbury: prysoner 10 monethes,
    having a wyef and children.[4]

21. ROBERT BADKINGE 21. Committed by [the Archbishop of]
    Canterbury, bayled by Master
    [Richard] Yonge.[5]

22. WYLLIAM DENFORD 22. Uppon the statute [for recusancy], close
    prysoner.[6]

[1] Barrow speaks of "that rare yong man, Rychard Jackson, who there died," and of the fact that no jury or inquest was permitted by Bishop Aylmer.
[2] See the footnote on him in "October 8, 1587 — Separatists Arrested at a Conventicle."
[3] She is not on the list for October 8, 1587. With a husband in the Counter Poultry, and with eight children, she may not have been imprisoned too long.
[4] John Frances, Francys, or Fraunces was arrested about July or August, 1588, and is still in prison in April, 1590. He was liberated thereafter, and does not reappear in the records.
[5] Badkinge, Badlinge, Batkine, Bodkin, or Badkyne, a tailor, living on Gray's Inn Lane. He was arrested before May, 1589, put in Newgate, bailed, and then arrested again about the end of the year. In February and April, 1590, he is imprisoned in the Fleet. He possessed one of Barrow's books.
[6] Denford was a schoolmaster, about forty-six years old, living on Foster Lane, near Cheapside and north-east of St. Paul's. He was evidently indicted and found guilty of violating 23 Elizabeth, *Caput* I, which not only enforced church attendance but also specified that any schoolmaster neglecting church attendance should be disabled and suffer imprisonment without bail for one year. He is listed as a prisoner in Newgate in Febuary and April, 1590. He was very likely released about May, 1590, after serving a full year's sentence. He was arrested again in March, 1592/3, and died in prison.

John Greenwood

23. QUYNTIN SMYTHE 23. Taken from his labours, cast into the dungeon with irons, his Bible taken from him by [Doctor Edward] Stanhoop [Stanhope].[1]
These ten last are in Newgate.

In Brydewell

24. JOHN PURDYE 24. Cast into " Little Ease," the " Myll," and beaten with codgels in that pryson, for refusinge to heare the preyst of that house. Committ[ed] by [the Archbishop of] Canterbury prysoner [?] monethes.[2]

25. WILLIAM BROMELL 25. Committed by [the Archbishop of] Canterbury, prysoner 12 monethes. And so forth.[3]

[26. GEORGE COLLIER][4]

---

[1] Arrested about March or April, 1589, and caught with Separatist pamphlets or manuscript treatises in his possession, Quintin Smythe was roughly treated by Dr. Stanhope, Chancellor to the Bishop of London. He was removed from Newgate to the Clink. Smythe was a feltmaker from Southwark, about twenty-six years old.

[2] Purdy was brutally treated in prison, and died in the Bridewell before February, 1589/90. Barrow described him as " grave, sober, and very godly and honest, and is to be well testified of all that knew him." His crime was a refusal to attend religious services in the prison chapel, as performed by an Anglican priest. His punishment was threefold: beaten with a cudgel " very extremely " ; compelled to grind in the Mill ; put into a torture hole, the " Little Ease," where he could neither stand nor stretch.
He was probably arrested in 1588. There is a blank in the manuscript before the word " monethes."

[3] Bromell, or Broomall, was arrested about May, 1588, was bailed or released, perhaps in the summer of 1589, is missing from the February, 1589/90, list of prisoners but reappears in the list for April, 1590, in the Bridewell prison.

[4] He is listed with Henry Tomson (no. 3), but is not numbered.

316

9.

A LIST OF PRISONERS, FEBRUARY
[1589/90]

This list of prisoners is taken from *A Collection of Certaine Sclaunderous Articles Gyven out by the Bisshops*, sig. A iv *verso* — B i *recto*. It includes forty-two preachers or visitors, fifty-two prisoners, and six prisons. The preachers are identified in the footnotes of *A Collection of Certaine Sclaunderous Articles Gyven out by the Bisshops*. Some of the prisoners are identified in previous lists and in separate footnotes, but most of them are briefly described here. There are thirty-eight new names, six names from the first October 8, 1587, list, and eight names from the May, 1589, list. Actually, there are twelve names which continue from the May, 1589, list, but four of them are also on the October, 1587, list, and are counted with the six names. It is interesting to note the names that are not found on the February, 1589/90, list. Boyes, Bromell, and Legate were very likely bailed, but Bromell and Legate reappear on the April, 1590, list. Henry Thompson, John Purdye, and Jerome Studley do not reappear, having died in prison. Alyce Chaundler and Robert Gryffin, previously bailed, do not reappear, but Robert Badkinge, previously bailed, does reappear. See Appendix, C 11, for an alphabetical listing of these prisoners.

*   *   *   *   *   *   *

John Greenwood

[PREACHER]	[PRISONER]	[PRISON]
Doctor Bancraft*	James Forester[1]	prysoners in Newgate
	John Francys[2]	
	Robert Batkine[3]	in the Fleete
Doctor Grant	Thomas Freeman[4]	in the Gatehowse
Doctor Wood	Thomas Settel[5]	
	John Debenham[6]	
Mr. Egerton	George Collier[7]	in the Clynke
	John Sparowe[8]	
Doctor Sallard	Edmond Nicolson[9]	in the Clynke

* All the preachers have been identified. See *A Collection of Certaine Sclaunderous Articles Gyven out by the Bisshops*, A iv *verso* — B i *recto*, *supra*.

1 James Forester, or Fawrestier, a physician and Master of Arts. He matriculated as a sizar at Clare College, Cambridge, in 1576, proceeded B.A. in 1579/80, and M.A. in 1583. He copied out, from the original manuscript, Barrow's book, *A Brief Discoverie of the False Church*, and prepared it for printing. The original manuscript was brought out of prison sheet by sheet, by Daniel Studley, who also smuggled blank sheets to Barrow in the Fleet. Studley brought the copy to Forester, who was paid for his efforts by Robert Stokes. At a conventicle in a garden house near Bedlem [Bethlem or Bethlehem Hospital] about December, 1589, Forester expounded the Scripture, according to the testimony of Roger Waterer. Thomas Mitchell was influenced by Forester to accept the Separatist teachings. About 1593 Forester withdrew from the Separatists and returned to the Church of England, was indicted and convicted March 21—23, 1592/3, for publishing seditious writings, 23 Elizabeth, *Caput* II, acknowledged his errors, and saved his life. In 1594 he published *The Pearle of Practise, or Practisers Pearle for Phisicke and Chirurgerie*.

2 Previously identified.

3 Previously identified.

4 Previously identified.

5 Thomas Settel, or Setle, or Settle, born about 1555, matriculated at Queen's College, Cambridge, ordained by Edmund Freake, Bishop of Norwich, and served a parish church in Boxted, Suffolk. He was cited in 1586 before Archbishop Whitgift, imprisoned in the Gatehouse, very likely was released, apprehended again about December, 1589.

6 John Debenham, or Father Debnam, named as a prisoner in the Gatehouse on the February and April, 1590, lists. He died in prison, presumably before 1593.

7 Previously identified.

8 John Sparowe, or Sparrow, or Sparewe, born about 1533, a fishmonger, together with Christopher Bowman and John Nicholas, and perhaps with nine other perons, delivered " A Lamentable Petition " to the queen on March 13, 1588/89. On the order of the Privy Council, he was committed to the White Lion prison in Southwark and then to the Clink. He remained in prison more than four years, without indictment or examination. F. J. Powicke's " Lists of the Early Separatists " included a Harry Sparowe and a Robert Sparrow for the period 1569—1571.

9 Edmond Nicolson, or Nicholson, is found on the February and April, 1590, lists.

Separatist Prisoners

Mr. Jackson	Xpofer Raper[10]	
Mr. Dunscombe	Xpofer Browne[11]	in the Clynke
	Quintan Smyth[12]	
Mr. Smyth	Androwe Smyth[13]	in the Clynke
	William Blakborowe[14]	
Mr. Phyllips	Thomas Lemar[15]	in the Clynke
	Thomas Michell[16]	
Doctor White	Anthonye Clakston[17]	in Newgate
	William Forester[18]	
Mr. Sparke	William Denford[19]	in Newgate
	Roger Waterer[20]	
Mr. Erlye	Edeth Burrowghe[21]	in Newgate
	William Burt[22]	

[10] Christopher Roper was committed close prisoner to the Counter Poultry prior to May, 1589, and appears on the April, 1590, list.

[11] Christopher Browne is found on the February and April, 1590, lists.

[12] Previously identified.

[13] Andrew Smyth appears on both lists for 1590.

[14] William Blackborough, or Blakborowe, appears only on the February and April, 1590, lists.

[15] Thomas Lemar, or LeMare, appears only on the February and April 1590, lists. Burrage says he reappears in the reign of James I as the inventor of " The Monster of Lemarisme " which was possessed of seven heads, a religious set of beliefs somewhat eclectic and synthetic (*Early English Dissenters*, I, 200).

[16] Thomas Michell, or Mitchell, was a turner, about twenty-seven years old, who was influenced to accept the views of the Separatists by one [James] Forrester. Michell is on both prisoners' lists for 1590 and was arrested at a conventicle on February 18, 1592/3. He was a member of a second assembly of Separatists in 1592, as mentioned by William Collins, and became associated with the Separatists in the Netherlands (Burrage, *Early English Dissenters*, I, 145, 222-5 ; Bancroft, *A Survay of the Pretended Holy Discipline*, p. 429 [249]).

[17] Anthony Clakston, or Claxton, is on both prisoners' lists for 1590.

[18] William Forester is on both prisoners' lists for 1590. He may have been a brother of James Forester.

[19] Previously identified.

[20] Attended a conventicle about December, 1589, in a garden house near Bedlem [Bethlem Hospital], where James Forester expounded the Bible. Waterer was arrested about the same time and imprisoned in Newgate for more than three years. Barrow mentions him as the boy fifteen years old, kept in a dungeon in irons, for a whole year, probably for his refusal to attend Anglican religious services in prison. He was a haberdasher, twenty-two years old in 1593. Therefore Barrow may be in error in saying he was only fifteen in 1589 or 1590.

[21] Previously identified.

[22] He is on both prisoners' lists for 1590.

Mr. Turnball	George Smels[23]	in the Counter Wood-
	Xpofer Bowman[24]	street
Mr. Edmonds	Robert Jackson[25]	in Counter Woodstreet
Mr. Haughton	Nycolas Lee[26]	
Mr. Gylpenne	Robert Andrewes[27]	in Counter Woodstreet
Mr. Coper	William Hutton[28]	
Mr. Archpoole	John Buser[29]	in Counter Woodstreet
Doctor Hanmer	John Fissher[30]	
[B i *recto*]		
Doctor Crooke	William Clarke[31]	in Counter Woodstreet
Mr. Trypp	Richard Maltusse[32]	
Mr. Morrison	William Fouller[33]	in Counter Woodstreet

[23] Previously identified. He is on all four lists of prisoners, and was again arrested April 8 or 15, 1593. He must have been released in 1590—2, because he attended the organizational meeting of the Separatist church in September, 1592.

[24] Bowman was imprisoned by the Privy Council for presenting " A Lamentable Petition " to the queen in March, 1588/9. He was in prison for more than three years, but is free by September, 1592, when he was present at the organization of the Separatist church, and when he was elected a deacon. He was imprisoned about March 4, 1592/3, and after his release he went to the Netherlands, and served as a deacon with the congregation in Amsterdam, Campen, and Naarden.

[25] Previously identified.

[26] Nicholas Lee, or Leye, or Ley, in the Counter Woodstreet in February, 1589/90, but in April, 1590, is in the Bridewell. After his release, he was an active Separatist, read and possessed some of Barrow's books, opened his house in Cow Lane near West Smithfield and Snow Hill for Separatist church services, was elected deacon in September, 1592, and escaped arrest in 1593. In the reign of James I, Lee seems to have been the leader and possibly pastor of the Barrowist remnant in London.

[27] Robert Andrewes, or Androes, is named in both of the prisoner lists for 1590. Nothing more is heard of him.

[28] William Hutton or Howton or Hawton, appears on both prisoner lists for 1590. In 1591 he persuaded Robert Aweburne (or Aburne or Abraham) to join with the Separatists. About 1592 Hutton died in prison.

[29] John Buser, or Bucer, named in both prisoner lists for 1590.

[30] John Fissher, or Fisher, named in both prisoner lists for 1590. Barrow wrote his letter of December, 1590, to a Mr. Fisher, who may be the same person.

[31] William Clarke was " a worker of capps," about thirty-seven years old, of the parish of St. Botolph without Bishopsgate. He was first influenced towards Separatist views in 1587—8 by John Greenwood in the Clink and Nicholas Crane in Newgate. About March or April, 1589, he protested the arrest of Thomas Legate without a warrant, and as a consequence was imprisoned himself for his protest by the constable. He was kept in the Woodstreet Counter for about a year, but was released before April, 1590. He was arrested again about March 4, 1592/3, and examined twice.

[32] Richard Maltusse appears on both prisoners' lists for 1590.

[33] William Fouller, or Fowler, appears on both prisoners' lists for 1590.

Separatist Prisoners

Mr. Crowe	Richard Skarlet[34]	
Mr. Browne	Roger Rippine[35]	in Counter Woodstreet
Mr. Hall	John Clarke[36]	
Mr. Moslee	Rowland	
	Skipworth[37]	in the Counter Poultrye
Preacher at Bridewell	George Knifton[38]	
Mr. Anderson	Richard Hayward[39]	in Counter Poultrye
Mr. Gardiner	John Lankaster[40]	
Mr. Cotton	Thomas Endford[41]	in Counter Poultrye
Mr. Cheyne		
Mr. Mollins	Henry Barrowe[42]	in the Fleete
Mr. Androwes	John Greenwood[43]	
Mr. Hutchinson		

[34] Richard Skarlet appears on both prisoners' lists for 1590.

[35] Roger Rippine, or Rippon, or Ryppon, appears on both prisoners' lists for 1590. In 1592 some of the meetings of the Separatist church were held in his home at Southwark. About the end of September he participated in the formal organization of the church, but in December disaster overtook the infant church with the arrest of its pastor, Francis Johnson, and some of its members, including Rippon. On February 16, 1592/3, he died. His corpse was carried in a coffin from Newgate to Cheapside. Affixed to the coffin were libels announcing the death of Rippon, as well as that of fifteen or sixteen others who had died for their beliefs, and denouncing the Archbishop of Canterbury, the ecclesiastical commissioners, and justice of the peace Richard Young, as murderers of the saints and the queen's faithful subjects. The destination of the coffin was the door of Richard Young's house.

[36] John Clarke, husbandman, about forty-seven years old, came from Walsoken, Norfolk. He was seized in a conventicle about December, 1589, in an assembly of Brownists [not Barrowes, as Burrage says, *Early English Dissenters*, I, 130, 132; II, 38], January, 1589/90, and remained in Newgate more than three years. In April, 1593, because of his refusal to attend a parish church or hear divine service, the ecclesiastical commissioners decided to send him to Bridewell, to grind in the Mill.

[37] Roland [Rowland, Rowlett] Skipworth appears on both prisoners' lists for 1590.

[38] George Knifton, Kniffton, Kniveton, Knyviton, was twenty-one years old, an apothecary, of Newgate Market. He appears on both prisoners' lists for 1590. In 1592 he was elected an elder of the Separatist church. In his testimony of 1593 he admitted that he had conferred with Barrow, Greenwood, Penry, and [Robert ?] Browne. In 1595 he was an elder in the church at Naarden, in the Netherlands.

[39] Richard Hayward appears on both prisoners' lists for 1590.

[40] John Lankaster, or Lancaster, appears on both prisoners' lists for 1590.

[41] Thomas Endford is listed as a prisoner in the Counter Poultry in February, 1589/90. In the April, 1590, list, he is listed as Thomas Eynesworth, in the same prison. We hear no more about him, or them.

[42] Barrow appears on all lists except that of October 8, 1587. His arrest came on November 19, 1587.

[43] Greenwood appears on all four lists of prisoners.

John Greenwood

Doctor Saravea	Daniell Studley[44]	in the Fleete
Mr. Gravet	Walter Lane[45]	
Mr. Fissher	Edmond Tomson[46]	in the Gatehouse
Mr. Judson	John Nicolas[47]	
Mr. Temple	William Dodson[48]	in the Gatehouse
Mr. Allison	John Barrens[49]	
Doctor Blague	John Cranford[50]	in the Gatehowse
Mr. Herd	Richard Wheeler[51]	
Mr. Harvye	Thomas Canadine[52]	in the Gatehowse

[44] Daniel Studley appears on both prisoners' lists for 1590. He aided Barrow in publishing his books, was elected an elder in September, 1592, and was arrested about December 24 or 31, 1592. With Barrow and Greenwood, he was indicted for publishing and dispersing seditious writings, found guilty, kept in prison, liberated in 1597, went to New-foundland with Francis Johnson in the " Hopewell," returned to England, and fled to the Netherlands, where he continued as a Separatist elder.

[45] Walter Lane appears in the two prisoners' lists for 1590, in the Fleet. He died in prison, very likely in 1591 or 1592, since he is not examined in 1593.

[46] Edmund Thompson, or Tomson, is listed as a prisoner for October, 1587, February, 1589/90, and April, 1590. His absence from the list of May—June, 1589, indicates that his first imprisonment was shorter than that of Henry Thompson. He attended the meeting of the formal organization of the Separatist church in September, 1592. There is no record of an arrest or examination thereafter.

[47] John Nicholas, or Nicolas, of Smithfield, a glover, age thirty-three, is listed as a prisoner in the Gatehouse, both in February and April, 1590. He was imprisoned by the Privy Council in March, 1588/9, together with Christopher Bowman and John Sparrow, for presenting " A Lamentable Petition " to the queen. He was bailed or released about the summer of 1592, was present at the organization of the Separatist church in September, 1592, was arrested February 18, 1592/3, and examined on March 8 and April 2, 1593.

[48] William Dodson, or Dodshoe, appears on both prisoners' lists for February and April, 1590, in the Gatehouse.

[49] John Barrens, or Barnes, age twenty-three, a tailor, of Duck Lane, east of West Smithfield, appears on both prisoners' lists for 1590. His house, near St. Bartholomew, was used for meetings of the Separatist church, and communion was administered there. He was present at the organization of the Separatist church in September, 1592, and was a part of a second group which hoped to organize formally and elect officers and minister. He was arrested on March 4, 1592/3, examined March 8 and April 3, 1593. Sometime before 1596, " beeing sic unto death was caryed forth and departed this life shortly after."

[50] John Cranford, or Craneford, appears on both lists of prisoners for 1590.

[51] Richard Wheeler is on the list for February, 1589/90, but is not on the April, 1590, list.

[52] Thomas Canadine, or Canadyne, is on both lists of prisoners for 1590. We hear no more about him in England, but in the reign of James I he is associated with the congregation of Francis Johnson, John Smyth, and the Waterlanders.

10.

THE NAMES OF YOUR HONOR'S POORE SUPPLIANTS, PRISONERS

[APRIL, 1590]

This list is taken from the petition to Lord Burghley about April, 1590. It is found in Lansdowne MSS. 109, folio 42, number 15. The petition is a request for a free and christian conference, for the right of obtaining bail, or at least for the privilege of having the Separatist prisoners brought together in one prison, the Bridewell, or any other convenient place. Between February and April, 1590, fifteen prisoners had been transferred to the Bridewell, five from Newgate and ten from the Counter Woodstreet. Two new prisoners, Luke Hayes and Richard Umberfield, and William Broomall, who is on the May, 1589, list, are also in the Bridewell. Those who were transferred from Newgate to the Bridewell were: William Burt, Anthony Claxton, James Forester, William Forester, and John Fraunces. Those who were transferred from the Counter Woodstreet to the Bridewell were: Robert Androes, John Bucer, John Clarke, John Fisher, William Fowler, William Hutton, Nicholas Lee, Richard Maltusse, Rodger Rippon, and Richard Skarlett.

Of the fifty-two prisoners in the February list, forty-eight are on the April list. The four persons who have been bailed or liberated are William Clarke, Thomas Endford, Thomas Settel, and Richard Wheeler, but if Thomas Endford and Thomas Eynesworth are the same person, then only three persons from the February list are missing in the April list. There are eleven new names on the April list: Mr. Auger, William Broomall, Mr. Cooke, Thomas Eynesworth, John Gualter, Luke Hayes, Anthonie Johnes, Thomas Legatt,

Edward Marshe, Thomas Reave, and Richard Umberfield. Of these eleven persons, eight appear for the first time, or nine if Thomas Endford and Thomas Eynesworth are different persons. William Broomall and Thomas Legatt, who are missing from the February list, reappear from the May list.

* * * * * * *

[April, 1590]

In the Gatehouse: [10]
John Gualter
John Nicholas
John Barnes
John Craneford
Thomas Canadyne
Thomas Reave
William Dodshoe
Father Debnam
Edmond Thomson
Thomas Freeman

In the Fleet: [5]
Henry Barrowe
John Grenewoode
Danyell Studley
Robert Badkyne
Walter Lane

In Newgate: [3]

William Dentforde
Widdowe Boroughe
Rodger Waterer

In Bridewell: [18]
William Broomall
James Forester
Anthony Claxton
Nicholas Lee
John Fraunces
William Forester
John Clarcke
John Fisher
John Bucer
  [Buser ?]
Rodger Rippon
Robert Androes
Richard Skarlett
Luke Hayes
Richard Maltusse
Richard Umberfield
William Fowler
William Burt
William Hutton

In the Counter [3]
Wood Street
George Smells
  [Snells ?]
Christopher
  Boweman
Robert Jackson

In the Clinck: [10]
George Collier
John Sparrowe
Edmonde Nicholson
Christopher Browne
Thomas Michell
Andrew Smith
William
  Blackborough
Thomas Le Mare
Christopher Roper
Quintan Smithe

In the White Lion: [5]
Thomas Legatt
Edward Marshe
Anthonie Johnes
Cooke
Auger [Awger ?
  Anger ?]

In the Counter Powltry:

[5]
Rowlett Skipworth
  [Skipw[i]th ?]
George Kniffton
Thomas Eynesworth
Richard Hayward
John Lancaster

Prisoners Deceased: [10]
John Chaundler — out of the Counter Powltry
Georg Brightie — out of the Counter Woodstreet
Richard Jackson — out of Newgate

John Greenwood

Widdow Maynard — out of Newgate
Widdow Roe — out of Newgate
Nicholas Crane — out of Newgate
Thomas Stephens — out of Newgate
Henry Thomson — out of the Clinck
Jerome Studley — out of the Clinck   [Total in prison — 59]
John Purdy — out of Bridewell   [Total deceased — 10]

11.

ALPHABETICAL LISTS OF PRISONERS

[1587 - 1590]

These alphabetical lists of prisoners enable the reader to see which prisoners remain in jail, which ones are liberated, and which ones are added from time to time. There are twenty-two names on the October list, but Gamble was excused for some reason — perhaps for his willingness to testify freely. Of the remaining twenty-one, six are women and fifteen are men. Eleven names are continued on the May list. Of the remaining ten, eight do not reappear again, but two names, Thomas Freeman and Edmond Thompson, although absent from the May list, reappear on the February and April lists.

The May list contains twenty-six names. Actually, this list contains twenty names of prisoners, inasmuch as six have died. Of the six deceased persons, four are on the October list (John Chaundler, Nicholas Crane, Margaret Maynard, and Alice Roe). Two were subsequently arrested and died before May, 1589 — George Bryghte and Richard Jackson. Of the twenty prisoners still living in May, 1589, six persons, who are found on the October list, have been in prison for a year and a half. These six are Boyce, Burry, Collier, Greenwood, Smells, and Henry Thompson. Robert Griffin has been bailed, " being very sicke." Of the fifteen new names, eleven are prisoners, two have been bailed (Badkinge and Alyce Chaundler) and two have died (Bryghte and Richard Jackson). There are five persons who are on the May list only. Alice Chaundler, mother of eight children, was bailed, probably because of the death of her husband, John Chaundler, in the Counter Poultry. George Bryghte, Richard Jackson, John Purdye, and Jerome Studley are found on this May list, but

327

Bryghte and Jackson are already dead, and by February, 1589/90, Purdye and Studley have died.

In summary, we may say that of the twenty-six names, six are dead and twenty are living. Of these twenty, three have been bailed. Of the remaining seventeen persons, six have been in prison since October 8, 1587, and eleven appear on the May, 1589, list for the first time.

When we come to the list of fifty-two prisoners in February, 1589/90, we find thirty-eight new names, six old names from the October 8, 1587, list, and eight new names from the May, 1589, list. Of the six old names, Edithe Burry, George Collier, John Greenwood, and George Smells have been on every list. Thomas Freeman and Edmond Thompson are on the October 8, 1587, list, are not on the May, 1589, list, but reappear on the February, 1589/90, list. The eight persons who continue from the May, 1589, list, excluding the four who appear on every list, are: Badkinge, Barrow, W. Clarke, Denford, Frances, Robert Jackson, Roper, and Quintin Smythe. Of the six who do not continue, John Purdye, Jerome Studley, and Henry Thompson have died in prison. Evidently Edward Boyce, William Bromell, and Thomas Legate have been bailed, but the latter two reappear on the April, 1590, list.

The April, 1590, list is the longest, with fifty-nine prisoners, plus ten deceased (see Appendix C 10, 12). Of the fifty-nine, nine are new names counting Eynesworth. Forty-eight are also found on the February, 1589/90, list. The other two are William Broomall and Thomas Legatt, who are missing from the February list, but who are both on the May, 1589, list. Four persons from the February list are missing from the April list: William Clarke, Thomas Endforth (who may be identical with Thomas Eynesworth), Thomas Settel, and Richard Wheeler.

On all four lists are Edith Burry, George Collier, John Greenwood, and George Smells. On the last three lists are seven persons — Badkinge, Barrow, Denford, Frances, Robert

Jackson, Roper, and Quintin Smythe. On the first, third, and fourth lists are Thomas Freeman and Edmond Thompson.

Thomas Stephens is not on any list of prisoners, but is listed with those who had died by 1590. I have included, but not counted, three persons who should be on the May, 1589, list, but are not listed: [Christopher Bowman, John Nicholas, John Sparrow].

*　　*　　*　　*　　*　　*　　*

October 8, 1587	*May* 1589	*February* 1589/90	*April* 1590
Allen, Peter			
		Andrewes, Robert	Androes, Robert
			Auger [Awger ?]
	Badkinge, Robert	Batkine, Robert	Badkyne, Robert
	(bailed)	Barrens, John	Barnes, John
	Barrow, Henry	Barrowe, Henry	Barrowe, Henry
		Blakborowe,	Blackborough,
		William	William
	[Bowman,	Bowman, Xpofer	Boweman,
	Christopher]		Christopher
Boyce, Edward	Boyes, Edward		
	Bromell, William		Broomall, William
		Browne, Xpofer	Browne,
	Bryghte, George		Christopher
	(dead)		
Burry, Edithe	Barrowe, (widow)	Burrowghe, Edeth	Borough,
			(widdowe)
		Burt, William	Burt, William
		Buser, John	Bucer, John
		Canadine, Thomas	Canadyne, Thomas
	Chaundler, Alyce		
	(bailed)		
Chaundler, John	Chaundler, John		
	(dead)	Clakston,	Claxton, Anthony
		Anthonye	
		Clarke, John	Clarke, John
	Clarke, [William]	Clarke, William	
Collier, George	Collier, George	Collier, George	Collier, George
			Cooke, [?]
Crane, [Nicholas]	Crane, Nicholas		
	(dead)	Cranford, John	Craneford, John
		Debenham, John	Debnam, Father
	Denford, William	Denford, William	Dentforde, William
		Dodson, William	Dodshoe, William
		Endford, Thomas	
			Eynesworth,
			Thomas
		Fissher, John	Fisher, John
		Forester, James	Forester, James
		Forester, William	Forester, William
		Fouler, William	Fowler, William
	Frances, John	Francys, John	Fraunces, John
Freeman, Thomas		Freeman, Thomas	Freeman, Thomas
Gamble, Clement (*vacat*)			
Grenwood, John	Greenwood, John	Greenwood, John	Grenewoode, John
Griffith, Roberte	Gryffin, Robert (bailed)		
			Gualter, John
			Hayes, Luke
		Hayward, Richard	Hayward, Richard
		Hutton, William	Hutton, William

Jackson, Anne			
	Jackson, Roger [Richard] (dead)		
	Jackson, Roger [Robert]	Jackson, Robert	Jackson, Robert
			Johnes, Anthonie
		Knifton, George	Kniffton, George
Lacy, Roberte			
		Lane, Walter	Lane, Walter
		Lankaster, John	Lancaster, John
		Lee, Nycolas	Lee, Nicholas
	Legate, Thomas		Legatt, Thomas
		Lemar, Thomas	LeMare, Thomas
		Maltusse, Richard	Maltusse, Richard
			Marshe, Edward
Martin, Henry			
Maynerd, Margaret	Meynard, [widdow] (dead) [Nicholas, John]	Michell, Thomas	Michell, Thomas
		Nicolas, John	Nicholas, John
		Nicolson, Edmond	Nicholson, Edmonde
Owin, Katherin [Onyen, Unyen ?]	Purdye, John		
			Reave, Thomas
Redborne, Robert			
		Rippine, Roger	Rippon, Rodger
Roe, Alice	Roo, [widdow] (dead)		
	Roper, Christopher	Raper, Xpofer	Roper, Christopher
Russell, Thomas			
		Settel, Thomas	
		Skarlet, Richard	Skarlett, Richard
		Skipworth, Rowland	Skipw[or]th, Rowlett
Smells, George	Smalles, George	Smels, George	Smells, George
		Smyth, Androwe	Smith, Andrew
	Smythe, Quyntin [Sparrow, John]	Smyth, Quintan	Smithe, Quintan
		Sparowe, John	Sparrowe, John
		Studley, Daniell	Studley, Danyell
	Studley, Jerome		
Thompson, Edmond		Tomson, Edmond	Thomson, Edmond
Thompson, Henry	Tomson, Henry		
			Umberfield, Richard
		Waterer, Roger	Waterer, Rodger
		Wheeler, Richard	
Wyman, Agnes			

[Thomas Stephens is not on any list of living prisoners, but he is listed as one of the deceased prisoners from Newgate in the April, 1590, list. His name also appears in a 1596 list of twenty-five persons who had died in prison.

I have included three prisoners in the list for May, 1589, although they are not found on the original list. These men are: Christopher Bowman, John Nicholas, and John Sparrow,

John Greenwood

and their names are enclosed within square brackets. They
were put in prison about March 17, 1588/9, on the order of
the Privy Council, because they had presented " A Lamentable
Petition " to the queen on March 13. I have not counted
these three names in the statistics.]

12

PRISONERS DECEASED

[1587 - 1590]

PRISONERS WHO HAD DIED BEFORE APRIL, 1590[1]

Brightie, Georg — out of the Counter Woodstreet
(died 1588 or 1589)
Chaundler, John — out of the Counter Powltry
(died 1588 or 1589)
Crane, Nicholas — out of Newgate (died 1588)
Jackson, Richard — out of Newgate (died 1588 or 1589)
Maynard, Widdow — out of Newgate (died 1588 or 1589)
Purdy, John — out of Bridewell (died 1589 or 1590)
Roe, Widdow — out of Newgate (died 1588 or 1589)
Stephens, Thomas — out of Newgate (died before April, 1590)
Studley, Jerome — out of the Clinck (died 1589 or 1590)
Thomson, Henry — out of the Clinck (died 1589 or 1590)

PRISONERS WHO DIED, 1590-1596[2]

Aweburne or Aburne or Abraham, Robert
Barnes, John
Bellot, Scipio
Bowle, Robert
Debnham, Father
Denford, William

---

[1] This list is taken from the Petition to Lord Burghley, April, 1590, in Lansdowne MSS. 109, no. 15, f. 42. See the Appendix, C 10.
[2] This list is taken from [Henry Ainsworth ?], *A True Confession of the Faith* ([Amsterdam ?], 1596), sig. A iii *recto*, margin. Henry M. Dexter has John Swaltee, but the correct marginal reading, which is poorly printed, is John Gwalter. See Dexter, *The Congregationalism of the Last Three Hundred Years*, p. 207 n.

Drewet, Thomas
Farret or Farrer or Farrot, Margaret
Gwalter, John
Hawton or Hutton or Howton, William
Hewet, Thomas
Lane, Walter
Myller, Myllet, Mylier, Myliet, Judith
Ryppon, Roger
Tailour, Anna

D. A CHRONOLOGICAL SUMMARY

[1585 - 1590]

1585

September ? — Greenwood resigns his benefice in Norfolk

October 7 — Robert Browne makes his recantation to Archbishop Whitgift

Robert Harrison probably died this year

1586

April — Robert Browne presented to the Bishop of Peterborough

October 29 — Session of Parliament began, after two prorogations, and continued to March 23, 1586/7.

November — Robert Browne appointed master of St. Olave's School, Southwark.

1587

Summer ? — John Bridges, *A Defence of the Government Established*, published.

October 8 — Arrest of twenty-two Separatists at a conventicle, including Greenwood.

October ? — Greenwood's son, Abel, born.

November 19 — Arrest of Barrow while visiting Greenwood in the Clink.

November 19 — Barrow's first examination at Lambeth Palace.

November 27 — Barrow's second examination at Lambeth Palace, before the Court of High Commission.

December ? — *A Breefe Sum of Our Profession* sent to Gifford.

John Greenwood

1588

March	John Feilde (or Field) dies.
April ?	Gifford replies to the articles of the Separatists.
May ?	Barrow and Greenwood indicted upon the statute of 23 Elizabeth, *Caput* I.
May 6	Dr. Some's *A Godly Treatise* entered in the *Stationers' Register*.
June ?	Barrow writes his marginal replies to Dr. Some's *A Godly Treatise*.
July 20	Spanish Armada sighted off the Lizard.
August ?	Barrow writes his reply to Dr. Some's *A Godly Treatise* in an interleaved copy.
September	Enlarged edition of Dr. Some's *A Godly Treatise* issued.
October	Martin Marprelate controversy begins with publication of *The Epistle*.
November	Martin Marprelate's *The Epitome* published.

1589

January 1	Barrow's third examination, in the Fleet (first conference).
January	Thomas Cooper's *An Admonition to the People of England* published.
February 4	Parliament summoned for November 12, 1588, but prorogued until Tuesday, February 4, 1588/9. Dissolved March 29, 1589.
February ?	Barrow's second conference with Dr. Some and Sir Henry Goodere.
February 9	Richard Bancroft's sermon at Paul's Cross.
March 13	" A Lamentable Petition " presented to the queen.
March 17	Christopher Bowman, John Nicholas, and John Sparrow imprisoned for presenting " A Lamentable Petition."
March 18	Barrow's fourth examination before the Privy Council.

A Chronological Summary

March 24	Barrow's fifth examination before a Special Commission.
March 24	Greenwood's examination before a Special Commission.
May	Dr. Robert Some, *A Godlie Treatise wherein Are Examined* published.
May 11	Dr. Some appointed Master of Peterhouse, Cambridge University.
August 14	The Martin Marprelate press seized near Manchester.
December ?	*A True Description out of the Worde of God, of the Visible Church* published.

1590

February 25	Letter of Bishop Aylmer commissioning the clergy to confer with the Separatists in prison.
March 9	Conference between William Hutchinson and John Greenwood.
March 14	Conference between Thomas Sperin and Henry Barrow.
March 17	Conference between William Hutchinson and John Greenwood.
March 18	Conference of William Hutchinson and Lancelot Andrewes with Henry Barrow.
March 20	Conference of John Egerton and Thomas Sperin with Henry Barrow and John Greenwood.
March	Christopher Bowman's petition to Lord Burghley.
April	Separatists' petition to Lord Burghley.
April 3	Conference of Mr. Cooper and Thomas Sperin with Henry Barrow and John Greenwood.
April 13	Conference of William Hutchinson and Lancelot Andrewes with Henry Barrow and John Greenwood.

John Greenwood

April	Petition from fifty-nine prisoners to Lord Burghley.
May ?	Gifford's *A Short Treatise against the Donatists of England* published.
May ?	*A Collection of Certaine Sclaunderous Articles* published.
July ?	*A Collection of Certain Letters and Conferences* published.
August ?	Greenwood's *An Answere to George Gifford's Pretended Defence of Read Praiers* published.
August 27	Petition of fifty (or sixty) prisoners to the Privy Council.
September	Richard Alison, *A Playne Confutation* published.
September 13	Letter from Barrow and Greenwood to Lord Burghley.
September 13	*The First Part of the Platforme* sent to Lord Burghley, with a letter.
September 18	Letter from Barrow and Greenwood to Lord Burghley.
October 30	Thomas Cartwright imprisoned.
December	Barrow's letter to Mr. Fisher.
December ?	Barrow completes *A Brief Discoverie of the False Church.*

INDEX

Index